ADVANCES IN PRESERVATION AND ACCESS

Volume 2

ADVANCES IN PRESERVATION AND ACCESS

Volume 2

Edited by
Barbra Buckner Higginbotham

Learned Information, Inc.
Medford, NJ
1995

Manufactured in the United States of America.

Published by: Learned Information, Inc.
143 Old Marlton Pike
Medford, NJ 08055-8750

Composition: M. Heide Dengler
Crystal R. Davenport

Cover Design: Jennifer Johansen

Price: $49.50

ISBN: 0-938734-88-1

For my mother
Mozelle Myra Wilson Buckner

Contents

Introduction xi
    Barbra Buckner Higginbotham

Part 1: Preservation's Future-Present.. 1

Preservation as Vanishing Act (and Art?): Print-Era
    Organizations in the Electronic Age 3
    Dan C. Hazen

Don't Swat the Skunk: The Preservation Imperative.................... 24
    David B. Gracy II

Toward Developing a North American Preservation Program:
    The Chicago Preservation Planning Conference............................ 37
    Gerald J. Munoff

Part 2: Science and Technology Assisting Preservation 53

Library Air Pollution: Sampling and Mitigation......................... 55
    Randy H. Silverman, Constance K. Lundberg,
    and Delbert J. Eatough

Mass Deacidification of Archives and Manuscript Collections.................. 77
    Kristi L. R. Kiesling and James Grant Stroud

Inventing the Future of Preservation Microfilming 101
    C. Lee Jones

Optical Disk Applications in the Federal Government:
    Sharing and Preserving Unique Collections 118
    Alan Fusonie and Richard F. Myers

Part 3: Technology as a Tool for Managing the Work of the
    Preservation/Conservation Unit... 131

The Role of the Computer in the Preservation Operation 133
    John Michael Bruer

Comprehensive Production Software (That Works!) for Preservation 146
    Errol Somay and Marc Reeves

Application Development for the Conservation Laboratory..................... 156
    Walter Henry

The House that Jack Built: The Preservation Management
    Information System, A Primer for Design 180
    Erich J. Kesse

**Part 4: Preservation Planning, Condition
    Surveys, and Needs Assessment** 191

Managing Collection Information for Preservation Planning 193
    John F. Dean

A Collection Condition Survey Model for Public Libraries 210
    Nancy Carlson Schrock

Regional Preservation Needs Assessment: The Central New York
    Preservation Needs Assessment Project 234
    Martha Hanson and Jeannette Smithee

Computer-Assisted Preservation Surveys 254
    Stuart A. Kohler

Part 5: Preserving Special Formats 267

Observations on the Effect of Freezing and Thawing Microfilm 268
    Sharon Gavitt

The Challenge of Film Preservation in the 1990s 280
    Anthony Slide

Here Today, Gone Tomorrow? Why We Should
    Preserve Electronic Documents 293
    Jan Michaels

Part 6: Preserving Special Collections 309

Preserving Music Materials: Past and Future 310
    Kathleen Haefliger and L. Suzanne Kellerman

Documenting Dance and Preserving the Collections 329
    Leslie Hansen Kopp

Experience and Examples in the Preservation of
    Scrapbooks and Albums 339
    Sherelyn Ogden

**Part 7: Education and Training for Librarians,
    Archivists, and Readers** 353

Educating Preservation Librarians: Perspectives on
    Curricular Issues and Answers 355
    Sheila S. Intner

Archival Preservation Education: An Overview of
    the Society of American Archivists' Programs
    and New Directions for the Future 376
    Evelyn Frangakis and Christine Ward

Access Services: The Human Factor 391
    Ann Paietta

Disasters for Directors: The Role of the Library or Archive
    Director in Disaster Preparedness and Recovery 400
    Barbra Buckner Higginbotham and Miriam B. Kahn

Index 413

Introduction

PRESERVATION IN THE MID-1990s: WHAT ARE THE ISSUES?

The purpose of each new volume of *Advances in Preservation and Access* is to explore a group of contemporary preservation and conservation-related topics in which librarians and archivists have expressed considerable interest. With each issue of *APA* the editor endeavors to take the measure of current preservation concerns, identify a group of qualified and knowledgeable authors, and produce a new edition that examines some of the issues of particular interest to librarians and archivists.

This second volume of *Advances* is a large one, 25 papers organized into seven sections. The essays in Part 1, "Preservation's Future-Present," provide both a "state of the union," as well as a vision of what the future may hold. Part 2, "Science and Technology Assisting Preservation," examines several methods of stabilizing and preserving information resources, whether by extending their lives or transferring the information they contain to more stable or accessible media. In Part 3, "Technology as a Tool for Managing the Work of the Preservation/Conservation Unit," the theme of science and automation as preservation's partners continues: technology can be used not only to accomplish the work of preservation, but also as an instrument to manage the preservation department or conservation laboratory.

We cannot preserve everything; for this reason, tools that help determine which materials to save and what priorities to assign to them are very valuable. The papers in Part 4, "Preservation Planning, Condition Surveys, and Needs Assessment," explore a variety of approaches to collecting preservation-related management information; computer support and analysis is important in all of them. Part 5, "Preserving Special Formats," and Part 6, "Preserving Special Collections," acknowledge that today's collections include many different formats and material types, with correspondingly different preservation needs; often the difficulties associated with special collections derive from the fact that each contains a multitude of different formats. The papers in Part 7, "Education and Training for Librarians, Archivists, and Readers," make the point that, if our collections are to be properly cared for, it is essential for librarians, archivists, and readers to be well trained in the principles and applications of preservation.

CONTEMPORARY THEMES AND CONCEPTS

As interesting as the papers themselves are the interrelationships and recurring themes they share; these represent another goal of *Advances in*

Preservation and Access. In addition to assembling a compact collection of papers on preservation topics of current interest, *APA* aims to present these essays in a way that permits librarians and archivists to sort through and think about shared concepts and ideas, identifying some of the more important themes in contemporary preservation thinking and research. Three major themes (each with its own subtopics) run through volume two of *APA*. The first of these one might call "reconceptualizing preservation," the second "the new information paradigm," and the third "understanding our collections."

Reconceptualizing Preservation

The philosophy of preservation is changing; under the rubric of "reconceptualizing preservation" fall several ideas that are rapidly gaining ground among librarians and archivists. A number of authors (Hazen, Gracy, Haefliger and Kellerman, Kopp) comment on the shift from an item approach to a collection approach; perhaps this stems in part from what Hazen calls respect for collection integrity. This growing interest in approaches that address entire collections, coupled with an emphasis on the preventative (versus the curative) aspects of preservation (Gracy, Frangakis and Ward), is reflected by the importance assigned to sound environmental controls (Silverman et al., Gracy), staff and reader education (Intner, Paietta, Gracy), and emergency planning and recovery (Higginbotham and Kahn, Gavitt, Gracy).

In the beginning, preservation was a word associated with books and other paper-based materials. Today our concerns are much broader, further evidence that we are reconceptualizing the field. A number of papers (Slide, Kopp, Ogden, Haefliger and Kellerman, Gavitt) examine the special needs of non-print, non-paper formats. Additionally, there is more emphasis on access to preserved items (Fusonie and Myers, Slide, Haefliger and Kellerman, Hazen). Slide observes that preservation without access is meaningless, while Fusonie and Myers see technology as a potential solution to the long-standing conflict between preservation and access.

One of the reasons preservation has always seemed so daunting is that the universe of materials is so great, and the available resources are (comparatively speaking) so small. This has sometimes led to a sort of paralysis—we can't possibly do it all, so we'll do nothing—or fostered the idea that only large, well-funded research libraries are capable of establishing preservation programs. Hazen and Gracy promote the newer idea (one closely akin to Patricia Battin's "80 percent solution") that preservation is not a "one-time, knock-out blow" (Gracy) but rather a series of many manageable steps. Similarly, Hazen observes that we now understand permanence differently from before: not every preservation approach has to save the items to which it is applied forever, or even for 500 years. Some intermediate period of safe-keeping employing media that require "refreshing" activity is now acceptable.

Another example of our new way of viewing preservation is what Hazen calls the "tiered" (versus the "single solution") approach to saving our collections. Gracy and Kiesling/Stroud also suggest that every library or archive will need to employ a variety of preservation techniques, owing to the differing needs of various collections and materials. Among these methods are binding (Dean, Haefliger and Kellerman), microfilming (Hazen, Jones, Haefliger and Kellerman), mass deacidification (Kiesling and Stroud, Haefliger and Kellerman, Hazen), and digitization (Fusonie and Myers, Hazen, Jones, Haefliger and Kellerman). Dean and Frangakis/Ward emphasize the importance of viewing preservation as an integrated part of the library or archives organization, rather than a more or less independent enterprise; this approach is critical when seeking either local or external funding and support.

The New Information Paradigm

The idea of the electronic age and its new information delivery models pervades much of *APA Volume 2*. Hazen suggests that the emerging "new information paradigm"—strong reliance on machine-mediated access to electronic information—will challenge our present understanding of preservation, potentially stimulating, transforming, or diminishing the field. How best to preserve electronic information resources is a recurring theme (Michaels, Hazen, Gracy); associated with this issue are questions of hardware and software obsolescence and the relatively short shelf-life of many electronic products. The issue of preservation responsibility is also of considerable concern—who will preserve electronic media, and what will tomorrow's preservationists need to know in order to accomplish their work? (Hazen, Frangakis and Ward, Intner)

Understanding Our Collections

Almost every author acknowledges that we cannot save everything. In such an environment, understanding library materials—the purposes for which they exist within our collections—is critical, if we are to establish appropriate preservation priorities (Gracy, Dean, Schrock, Hanson and Smithee, Kohler). Munoff and Dean emphasize the importance of planning for preservation; according to Dean, it is systematically gathered management information based on analysis of the collections and the preservation operation itself that should drive the process of selecting for preservation. Several authors (Henry, Dean, Schrock, Hanson and Smithee, Kohler) describe a variety of survey types (needs assessment, condition, action) useful in generating this type of data.

Each of these surveys employs computers to gather and/or analyze data. There are also many other ways in which automation can be a valuable management tool, increasing productivity, enhancing capabilities, and expanding access to preservation and conservation information. Bruer, Somay and Reeves, Henry, Kesse, and Kohler examine a variety of hardware, software, and design issues related to using computers to manage the preservation department or conservation lab. Laptop computers play an important role in many of these applications; networking permits the preservation unit to share information with other departments in the library, and the use of data interchange formats (generalized or descriptive markup language) allows locally developed programs to be shared with other institutions.

FUTURE DIRECTIONS IN PRESERVATION AND ACCESS

Volume 2 of *Advances in Preservation and Access* raises almost as many questions as it answers; chief among these is the impact new information delivery systems will have on preservation, and the permanence of newer preservation approaches like mass deacidification and optical technologies. It is clear that there will be ample future fodder for *APA*. The editor welcomes all comments and suggestions.

PART 1:
PRESERVATION'S FUTURE-PRESENT

Taken together, these three papers offer a solid and consistent preservation "state of the union," as well as a vision of what the future may hold. Dan Hazen assesses the current state of preservation from the standpoints of technique (microfilming, mass deacidification), approach (reformatting versus saving the artifact), and scope (collections versus individual items). He explores the rather pressing issue of preserving electronic information, as well as the more basic questions of who will own this material and where the preservation function will be located (in libraries? in computer centers? in publishing houses?). At the same time, he examines the political realities of preservation, showing why certain disciplines, institutions, and countries are better advantaged than others in the present environment.

Hazen suggests that the emerging "new information paradigm"—strong reliance on machine-mediated access to electronic information—will challenge our present understanding of preservation, potentially stimulating, transforming, or diminishing the field. He believes that the future will call for a tiered approach to preservation, where mass deacidification is used to stabilize large print collections, microfilming will save embrittled materials, and electronic reformatting provides access to high-demand fragile materials.

David Gracy agrees that preservation is changing rapidly and, in his words, "is not what it used to be." He proposes that the preservation issues for the 1990s are format, cost, and scope: in what formats, he asks, should we maintain information? And, how do we preserve the most material that is deemed worth saving, at the least cost? To make appropriate preservation choices, Gracy suggests that librarians and archivists need a thorough understanding of the purpose for which materials exist in their library collection or archives; then they will be able to decide what to save, and whether to extend the lives of the items themselves (books, for example) or transfer information from one medium to another (paper to film, perhaps) in order to prevent its loss. Like Hazen, Gracy is concerned about electronic media and the many preservation issues they provoke. He concludes his essay with nine suggestions for developing a preservation program. Readers will find it reassuring that most of these activities are not large, costly projects, but rather things they can do today, in their own institutions, that will make a real difference. Gracy encourages us not to approach preservation as "a one-time, knock-out blow," but rather as many steps taken over time, permitting us to see and enjoy the benefits of our work as we progress.

In his paper about the Preservation Planning Conference held in 1992 at the University of Chicago, Gerald Munoff presents the thinking of research librarians about the best way to develop a comprehensive North American preservation program. The goals of this invitational conference were to provide a forum to advance the planning for such a program, to identify the needs the program should address, and to develop a strategy for meeting these needs. Munoff explains the underlying concerns that prompted the conference—the perception that institutional, national, and international programs' efforts are not being adequately coordinated and managed, and that preservation programs are often shaped more by funding agencies and their priorities than in any systematic fashion by research institutions.

Munoff examines the vision statement for a North American program developed by conference attendees, as well as the range of organizational structures they considered. While the conference did not provide any immediate solutions for the preservation problems research libraries face, Munoff describes its success in establishing an agenda for further action.

Preservation as Vanishing Act (and Art?): Print-Era Organizations in the Electronic Age

Dan C. Hazen

Librarian for Latin America, Spain, and Portugal
Harvard College Library

INTRODUCTION

Preservation has come of age. Its entrenched institutional infrastructure includes well-publicized models for individual libraries and highly visible national organizations.[1] As the field has matured, the preservation imperative has joined ever more closely the issues of cooperative access and resource sharing to considerations of local staffing, procedures, and techniques. Increasingly refined conceptual frameworks and operational structures have allowed us to gain ground in the battle to save brittle books.

Efforts to structure national and international preservation strategies have also advanced. Many governments and a number of foundations now support preservation assessment and reformatting programs throughout the world.[2] Similarly, resources for preservation have expanded. Significant gaps remain, but the prospects are increasingly bright.

Thus, many aspects of the preservation endeavor seem under control, and at least we understand some of the issues that are not yet resolved. Accelerated innovation characterizes several other areas. New preservation technologies are rapidly evolving.[3] Full-scale mass deacidification is at last underway. Color microfilming seems on the verge of practical applicability. Digital scanning equipment and protocols have been employed in several experimental settings. And non-print materials are receiving more and more attention.

However, the preservation field also faces some fundamental uncertainties. A major source of doubt lies in the anticipated (though yet unconsummated) transition to a "new information paradigm." The model-to-come will embrace machine-mediated access to remotely held electronic information, to complement or even replace local ownership of books and journals. Such a transformation has the potential to dwarf emerging initiatives specifically relevant to preservation. As the "new paradigm" challenges the very nature of libraries, it will necessarily challenge our understanding of preservation as well.

This essay reviews and reassesses the concepts and strategies of an enterprise in rapid evolution. It also considers preservation's place in an even more swiftly evolving information world. Upon what foundations has preservation achieved its current vitality? How should it respond, in the face of new possibilities and demands? Will emerging information needs and technologies invigorate, transform, or marginalize the field?

CONTINUING QUESTIONS OF THE (QUITE RECENT) PAST

Winners and Losers: Preservation Funds and Preservation Politics

As recently as the late 1980s, mainstream preservationists sought, above all, to extend the field's impressive momentum. Proven technologies and procedures, most notably microform reformatting, were widely accessible. The dominant philosophy held that local piece-by-piece reformatting to a permanent medium (in conjunction with appropriate bibliographic control to minimize duplication) could save our written heritage. The paramount questions were where to find and how to allocate the massive financial resources required to rescue our deteriorating collections.

Certain trends, however, indicated that the deployment of microfilming dollars would not be "discipline-neutral." Some scholarly endeavors seemed likely to benefit, others to become increasingly at risk. The trade-offs were complex and reflected discipline-specific research strategies and agendas, the relationship between strong collections and institutions prepared for large-scale preservation, and the realities of fund-raising. Questions of transnational equity and access in an increasingly international environment were perhaps even more urgent, given the world's division between "have" and "have not" societies.[4]

All these issues persist. Disciplines like history or literary criticism, whose scholarly fodder remains overwhelmingly documentary, enjoy only limited financial resources: they are directly impoverished as brittle materials crumble to dust. External funds, particularly from government agencies and foundations, have enabled us to address only a fraction of the need. Some scientific and professional fields, by contrast, combine a limited role for historical materials with greater affluence. They can anticipate a more stable documentary base.[5]

The issue grows still more complicated as the focus becomes international. The United States, Japan, and many nations in Western Europe enjoy sufficient resources to at least begin preserving their written heritage. Many Third World countries scrape along at the brink of starvation and chaos: preservation initiatives comparable to those of the developed world cannot even be imagined. But efforts to preserve their documentary heritage would reinforce (or even create) a sense of national identity, and also augment our collective record of human achievement. These materials are often available only in the countries of origin. Deploying external funds to preserve them remains a matter of debate.

Bandwagons, Entrepreneurs, and Control

Microform reformatting is today's preservation treatment of choice. Some major repositories have established in-house filming units. Others sustain microfilming partnerships with commercial firms. As the availability of preservation microfilming grants has intensified competition, the ability to join the reformatting bandwagon has become one measure of preservation respectability.

By now it is common wisdom that all libraries have preservation needs: deteriorating collections are not an exclusive concern of a few elite "repositories of record." However, different kinds of libraries and collections require different preservation strategies. Libraries with sparse holdings of unique materials may be ill-advised to establish a microfilm reformatting program, even if many of their holdings are not yet on film. Consortial structures to manage archival storage and the distribution of copies may be more enduring and efficient than efforts that graft these functions onto local library staff with other core responsibilities. Similarly, multi-institutional filming centers can simplify the process of completing incomplete sets or broken serial runs. And excessive dispersion of film masters and print negatives can complicate rather than enhance our collective access.

Suggesting that most preservation microfilming be deliberately limited to only a few major players, whether single libraries or consortia, is nonetheless controversial. The prospect will be particularly distasteful to institutions that might then be frozen out of the funds and fame associated with major microfilm projects. The politics of participation may mandate preservation microfilming programs, and dollars, for all. Should a pattern of widely scattered film masters prevail, we will need to consider more closely how we locate and use both information about films and the films themselves.[6]

Political realities will inevitably shape national and international preservation strategies. We also need to balance the mandate for overall efficiency with support for innovation and entrepreneurship. Some of our more successful preservation ventures have been founded in individual initiative and voluntary participation, and remained well outside any bureaucratic mainstream. To cite just one example, over several years the "Intensive Cuban Collecting Group," an ad hoc committee of bibliographers from collections with strong Cuban holdings, has identified important periodicals from the island and either verified that preservation microfilm is available or arranged within the group to assemble and film full runs. The films themselves remain dispersed among the participants. Any large-scale preservation plan or structure must allow room for similar efforts.

Added Values, Program Costs, and Preservation Finances

Heavy infusions of outside funds are essential even for today's less-than-comprehensive preservation effort. Microforms are currently sold in accord with two principal pricing philosophies. Commercial prices reflect full production and marketing costs (too often, exclusive of appropriate bibliographic control), profit margins, and start-up capital for new endeavors. Commercial filmers necessarily perceive their operations as continuous and expanding. They also focus on projects for which demand—and sales—are expected to be high. The impetus to film lies in the market.

In contrast, most libraries film in response to their own preservation priorities, which may be fairly broad when external funds are at stake. Film produced by libraries is often priced to reflect only out-of-pocket expenses. Sometimes there is no choice: preservation grants routinely require film copies to be available at cost. In other instances, libraries may simply assume an ethical mandate that precludes preservation "profits." One effect is a self-imposed limitation on preservation revenues, available reformatting funds, and how much we can film.

Alternative price structures could be devised. One approach would reflect the value added during the processes of preservation reformatting and the creation of appropriate bibliographic records. Preservation microforms with full online catalog records are qualitatively superior to deteriorated single copies; their prices might so reflect. Libraries might also mimic commercial filmers in aggressively marketing films that have been priced above cost, in order to sustain their own reformatting programs. Several Latin American collections have built substantial in-house filming programs by pricing films to recover costs after five to seven outside sales. Revenues from additional sales are plowed back into new efforts. Partnerships between libraries and commercial filmers can provide similar financial advantages, while also relieving the libraries of marketing distractions.

Charges for access to out-of-print materials, whether by supplying photocopies or microfilm of scarce originals, or through interlibrary loan, could likewise be recalculated in accord with the holding institution's real costs of acquiring, cataloging, housing, and preserving an item, in some cases as further adjusted for copyright. In all these scenarios, the goal would be to address our continuing need for preservation funds by explicitly recognizing all the associated costs and benefits.

The ensuing price structure might well be complex. Subsidized microfilm would remain relatively cheap. Items reformatted with an eye to stimulating or satisfying market demand would exhibit variable though generally higher prices reflecting costs, anticipated sales, and competition. These prices would obtain regardless of whether the filmer were a commercial firm, a library, or a partnership. Finally, low-demand materials filmed or loaned on the basis of isolated external requests might be relatively expensive.

Were this sort of structure to emerge, we would need to consider more carefully the types of materials appropriate for each approach to filming. A multi-tiered price structure based primarily on market dynamics might further distort the allocation of preservation dollars among disciplines and world areas. It could also limit scholarly horizons at institutions without strong libraries. Any benefit would lie in the potential for strengthening preservation finances.

"Micro" and "Macro" Treatments: A Shifting Balance

Preservation is an enterprise encompassing several distinct emphases. One stream concentrates on overall library environments through "macro" measures that affect many or all holdings. Decisions to install climate controls or provide filtered lighting, for instance, will extend the lives of entire collections. A related "macro" approach focuses on such preemptive preservation practices as increasing the initial durability and strength of library materials. Perhaps the outstanding success story here is the expanding utilization of acid-free paper among developed-world publishers. Improving the quality of incoming materials reduces the subsequent need for far more expensive item-level care or reformatting.

A second preservation emphasis focuses on "micro," or piece-level, treatments to conserve and restore individual documents. Reformatting operations similarly function at the piece level, and most often involve the transfer of page images (or intellectual content) from impermanent to permanent paper, or from paper to microfilm.

Two other areas of long-standing concern are only now emerging as full-fledged components of library preservation programs. The first involves the preservation needs of many non-print media and the specialized measures to address them. Sound recordings, video materials, and photographs have been fairly fully explored. The corresponding "macro" measures include efforts to promote durable base products and storage standards, while "micro" techniques are used to stabilize or reformat specific items. Particularly for audio media, preservation commonly entails reformatting (for example, from vinyl disks to magnetic tape), followed by periodic "refreshing" of this impermanent storage medium. These processes raise ongoing questions for organizational arrangements and funding, but also offer important precedents as we look toward electronic resources.

A second shift involves mass preservation. Mass deacidification, the most promising approach, was until recently both experimental and highly controversial. While some controversy remains, a number of libraries have begun large-scale treatment programs. This new "macro" approach may have a substantial impact on both local and cooperative preservation strategies.

The Strategic Implications of Mass Deacidification

Preservation options have long emphasized piece-level treatments. Our energies have necessarily focused on how to address an enormous collective problem through coordinated local action, with very limited resources. The continuing consensus is that one-time reformatting to a permanent medium (normally silver halide microfilm) will effectively save individual items and, eventually, entire literatures. Within this context, librarians have been challenged to secure adequate financial and institutional resources, maximize efficiency by eliminating duplication, and devise strategies by which we can choose between what we save and what crumbles into dust.

The conservation or restoration of physical artifacts—single volumes—has typically been considered the responsibility of individual libraries. Single restored copies primarily benefit a local clientele, in contrast to the readily reproducible products that are the result of microfilm reformatting. One corollary is that records for restoration work need only meet the holding library's immediate needs. Decisions concerning appropriate treatments for particular items are likewise local.

The progress of mass deacidification from a disaster-prone laboratory exercise to a viable and cost-effective commercial technology has changed our basis for action.[7] Both demand and treatment capacity are still developing, and some problems remain. Nonetheless, libraries can now stabilize large numbers of acidic materials at a unit cost far below that of item-level reformatting: Harvard foresees eventual deacidification costs of $6-10 per volume, compared to $90 for preservation microfilming (including the associated bibliographic control).[8] Experiments to strengthen paper are also underway. If successful, these measures will enable us to rejuvenate deteriorated collections, rather than merely stopping further embrittlement.

We have thus gained the capacity to neutralize unprecedented numbers of acidic books, and to conserve collections as well as single volumes. The change in scale means that mass deacidification can become a preservation process complementary to item-level reformatting or restoration. For instance, little-used collections might be deacidified and sent to environmentally sound storage facilities. When a volume was subsequently requested for local use or interlibrary loan, but still considered too fragile for handling, it might then be reformatted. Mass deacidification would buy time for large numbers of books and thereby complement the more expensive microfilm reformatting that definitively rescues selected and fewer items.

Mass deacidification may also enable us to combine cost-effective preservation with respect for collection integrity. In theory, the reproducibility of microfilmed materials means that libraries can simply replace their deteriorating volumes with microfilm copies. Not only will the replacements be permanent, but the collection will remain intact. In practice, microforms are more difficult to use than traditional books and journals. Moreover, libraries seldom interfile their books and microfilms (a practice which would itself raise preservation concerns). Microfilm replacements thus lose their physical place within our classification-based shelving systems.

Equally important, relatively few selectors (or preservation administrators) have either the funds or the inclination to replace large numbers of deteriorated titles. Most libraries deliberately focus their energies and resources on current publications. Incomplete retrospective holdings are routinely excused on the grounds that microfilmed materials can be purchased upon demand.[9] Yet we know that our collections, as mutually supportive arrays of interrelated books and journals, provide physical, bibliographic, and information contexts superior to those afforded by scattered resources. A piecemeal approach to replacements thus bodes ill for collection integrity. Mass deacidification could slow the volume-by-volume attrition associated with microfilm replacements and conscious collection gaps.[10]

Integrating mass deacidification into our preservation structure requires more than treatment facilities, processing procedures, and a sense of when this approach is appropriate. While far cheaper than any kind of reformatting, mass deacidification is still expensive, and money remains scarce. Once we articulate a strategic place for this technique, in local collections as well as for larger contexts, we must find the funds to follow. The best prospects may result from adjusting our preservation funding priorities to reflect mass deacidification's potential role.

Preservation units document reformatting activity in great detail, in order to minimize unnecessary duplication. Queue dates and other codes, for instance, identify materials in the microfilm reformatting stream on both RLIN (Research Libraries Information Network) and OCLC (Online Computer Library Center). Deacidification, however, has been identified with the manual conservation processes relevant only to local collections. Any bibliographic conventions to identify treated materials therefore remain local and idiosyncratic.

As mass deacidification emerges as one element in a multifaceted strategy for preservation, the information that one library has deacidified an item may affect another institution's reformatting decision. As the retrospective conversion of North American collections becomes more and more inclusive, the costs of bibliographic annotation will decline. Recording deacidification treatments may thus become both feasible and desirable.

The library community remains hesitant in accepting mass deacidification, despite the initiatives of a handful of institutions. Some of the resistance may reflect unreasonably high expectations. Does mass deacidification really require permanence and perfection? Or is it rather a way for us to buy time? The commonest drawbacks associated with mass deacidification include minor variations in smell and appearance.[11] Even these flaws are not universal, and the alternative may be permanent losses to our overall stock of books and journals. As a cheap, simple, and effective process, mass deacidification affords possibilities—and deserves a place—that we have not fully acknowledged.

THE ELECTRONIC REVOLUTION:
THE "NEW PARADIGM" AND PRESERVATION

Information Age Libraries: Electronic Switching
Points or Museums of the Book?

Libraries have traditionally been based in physical objects. Thus they have been concerned with the archival functions of preserving and maintaining their holdings, as well as with organizing information and extending it to their users. New electronic information formats seem inherently less susceptible to library ownership than traditional books and serials. The role of local archival functions may eventually diminish.

Few informed speculations on our information future expect any near-term, wholesale reformatting of existing library holdings into digital files.[12] Electronic publishing, while noticeable, remains minimal next to the continuing stream of hard copy materials. In other parts of the world, electronic information—or even access to computers—remains beyond the reach of all but a tiny minority. Books and journals will remain with us for a long time to come.

Nonetheless, change is on the way. One scenario for the future anticipates a bifurcation between the electronic information that will either be directly accessible to users or mediated through specialized service institutions, and the hard copy resources held by libraries. Libraries will be defined first and foremost in terms of their archival mandate to preserve the tangible objects that they have acquired and continue to add. In this scenario, preservation might come to virtually define the organization. An alternative vision sees libraries aggressively brokering access to information in all formats, with necessarily increasing attention to digital data. While both of these visions may be somewhat premature, each portends major change for preservation.

Although the future remains murky, we can already discern at least three aspects of electronic information technology that especially affect the field of preservation. The first involves the creation of electronic products, based on hard copy sources, in order to facilitate specific educational or scholarly endeavors. A second anticipates the somewhat broader issue of capturing and then preserving information prepared only in electronic formats. And the third looks to the role of electronic technologies in expanding our traditional preservation options.

Digital Enhancement of Traditional Resources

Originally, computers were used almost exclusively to record and manipulate current information. The scope has broadened as new constituencies confront electronic technologies. While electronic publications have been slow to emerge, there is considerable academic interest in developing such applications as educational software, hypertext guides, and special databases. A few of these initiatives have applied computer capabilities to traditional scholarly resources.

Large and already rather long-lived electronic databases based on hard copy sources include the American and French Research on the Treasury of the French Language (ARTFL) and the Thesaurus Linguae Graecae (TLG).[13] In these and similar products, large numbers of texts have been keyed into machine-readable databases. Sophisticated software enables retrieval and analysis both within and across the individual sources. These databases thus facilitate research that requires large-scale assessments of, for instance, word usage or word associations. They particularly support philological, literary, and historical scholarship.

Commercial as well as academic entrepreneurs have recognized the scholarly "added value" associated with digitized files. The Patrologia Latina Database, recently released as a commercial CD-ROM, thus affords new possibilities to analyze this (literally) canonical literature.[14] A host of other electronic products similarly anticipates new academic uses and demands. While reformatting massive amounts of text to digital files entails a wealth of preservation possibilities and concerns, preservation has been at best incidental to these initiatives.

Digital Preservation Where There Is No Hard Copy

Archivists and scholars alike are concerned about the increasing volume of electronic information that no one even attempts to capture.[15] Messages, memoranda, and discussions from electronic networks or bulletin boards are routinely deleted by both senders and recipients. Novels, articles, and reports are typically compiled on word processors: early drafts and obsolete versions simply disappear. As the source materials vanish, insights into both institutional decision-making and the individual creative process become virtually impossible. Can we find a way to preserve these evanescent materials?

Electronic publications raise similar questions, though in some cases they are created with a premise of continued access to some sort of archival file. The rapid obsolescence of reading machinery can render these files useless; editorial and corporate transitions also undermine the organizational stability implicit in permanent access. Technical issues abound concerning such matters as document encoding, storage standards, retrieval software, and access protocols.

Finally, the digital text databases being prepared to support current research, while often based in hard copy originals, are increasingly the stuff of scholarship. These files are created to satisfy research needs rather than preservation concerns. However, they are also new scholarly resources that go beyond the texts from which they draw, and are therefore independent parts of the scholarly record. Preserving them is an emerging issue.

Cybernetic Preservation

Preservation is at best a tangential concern when traditional documents are converted to digital files to meet educational or scholarly goals. Other information is created and destroyed electronically in ongoing processes of research or decision-making, and some scholarship and data are disseminated via electronic means only. Preservation and permanence are open questions. However, several recent experiments have been specifically designed to explore the viability of electronic media as preservation formats.

Two initiatives have attracted particular attention.[16] A project at Cornell University has employed scanning technology to create electronic page images. In addition to exploring and refining the capabilities of scanning equipment, this project has studied workstation retrieval and display options. Deteriorated texts have been replaced by permanent, superior hard copies based on the scanned image files. Among other things, Cornell is now exploring means for long-distance transmission of these images.[17] Yale University is at an earlier stage in a venture to scan microfilm in order to create digital image files. Microfilm, while a permanent and reproducible archival medium, is clumsy to use. Electronic files are ephemeral but highly adaptable. The Yale project thus explores whether these media can be successfully combined to support both preservation and scholarship.[18]

The Cornell and Yale projects are instructive as research and development projects sited at libraries, supported by a broad spectrum of preservation organizations, and implemented by teams combining private industry, scholars, and librarians. Mutually-beneficial partnerships appear both possible and necessary in these early moments of electronic preservation.

Electronic reformatting with preservation as the goal focuses on such aspects as accurate transcriptions, textual integrity, and high-quality reproduction of images and text. Requirements for accuracy and integrity are reflected in an emphasis on digitized page images. Mechanisms to store and display the image files, and to provide hard copy upon demand, are under development. The relative benefits of creating digital files from microfilm or hard copy, and of using electronic image files as a basis for generating preservation microfilm, are all in question. These preservation efforts are also largely limited to materials in the public domain: numerous obstacles face those who would create readily reproducible electronic files for materials protected by copyright. The field remains volatile, and also very exciting.

Digital Reformatting and Preservation:
Transforming Our Libraries One Byte at a Time

The initiatives described above suggest some of the hurdles, as well as attractions, associated with digital-age preservation. As we systematically explore alternatives and solve problems, we will come closer to workable solutions. A number of broader issues remain.

Preservation has always assumed durability as its guiding principle. Acid-free paper, archival microfilm, and proper storage environments are defined in terms of "permanence" measured in hundreds of years. Yet digital resources are inherently ephemeral. Electronic storage media—tapes, disks, and the like—are impermanent. Equally troublesome, the machinery and software with which these files can be read have a brief life span: the dizzying evolution of computer systems and products means that any electronic storage medium will become unusable fairly quickly. Even reformatting from brittle paper to an electronic format means moving to a medium with a shorter, rather than longer, life expectancy. This paradoxical feature raises some fundamental questions about how we perceive preservation.

Many authorities have suggested that we must reconceptualize preservation as an operation to sustain messages rather than containers.[19] As we look to the very transient life cycles of our new information platforms and storage media, the lessons of non-print preservation—particularly for audio materials—can guide our thoughts. Here, part of the established routine is to clean and recopy magnetic tape transcriptions of original sound recordings. Analogous electronic treatments will become increasingly pervasive, though where this function should be sited—in libraries, in computer centers, in central service agencies—remains unclear.

We also do not know how to ensure the integrity of electronic information, since it is virtually impossible to prevent unauthorized alterations. This problem has two aspects: identifying and maintaining a "master file" of electronic documents, and ensuring the accuracy of newly digitized texts. Both manual rekeying and optical character recognition produce errors; flawless electronic versions of hard copy originals remain prohibitively expensive.[20] The creation of tainted texts in reformatted versions is essentially antithetical to preservation. Another challenge concerns the different kinds of added value associated with digital files. Hard copy documents can be electronically reformatted through several distinct processes. Scanning technologies that produce electronic images of the original document can guarantee textual integrity. The original's appearance can even be electronically enhanced to restore lost clarity. However, any text contained within these digital images cannot be electronically manipulated. Storing high-resolution images, particularly if gray-scale illustrations are included, requires large amounts of computer memory; transmitting them can likewise strain network capacities.

Conversely, electronic reformatting accomplished through rekeying or by optical character recognition produces versatile text files that the computer can manipulate. The results support research that may be prohibitively cumbersome when based on either hard copy originals or image files. Any illustrations must be separately stored as images. Completely accurate transcriptions of original materials are still extremely expensive. Moreover, the utility of these files is highly dependent on the associated searching software, which remains bewilderingly diverse.

Electronic preservation raises a host of issues concerning how we provide intellectual access to individual documents, to collections of texts, and to our growing array of digital data. The processes to convert documents to electronic formats, or to produce electronic originals, are still in their infancy. Standards are only gradually taking shape for numerous technical requirements including search and retrieval software, appropriate scanning resolutions, image compression formats, and so on.

Common procedures to index both whole documents and portions thereof are likewise necessary. "Markup languages" (for instance, the Standard Generalized Markup Language, or SGML) are designed to facilitate searching and retrieval by ensuring that electronic text files consist of more than undifferentiated masses of words. Encoding texts, however, is now both slow and expensive. Providing an ongoing bibliographic grounding in the specific works under examination at any one time, particularly as search software unobtrusively shuffles users among the separate documents of large databases, is similarly daunting. Even recording the existence of electronic files in bibliographic databases presents problems not yet completely resolved.

Measures to move electronic files from place to place are under development. One issue involves transfer protocols, as data hurtle about the Internet and are captured by users with different configurations of equipment and software. Less immediate concerns center on the network itself. Internet costs are transparent to most academic users in the United States. Access has never been free to most outside of this country. It is probable that costs will become both higher and more visible over time; expectations of freely flowing data may diminish correspondingly.

We remain only dimly aware of the problems and the promise of very large electronic databases comprised of digitally reformatted texts. The field as a whole is one of rapid innovation. While standards and control are necessary, they will best evolve in an environment and at a pace that encourages continued experimentation. They should likewise reflect reality: most electronic research and development is based outside the academic community, and standards created in isolation are unlikely to prevail.

Many complex questions associated with file-level control, transfer, and access are thus upon us. Existing Internet resources, despite their potentially high rewards, are already difficult to track.[21] Electronically preserved materials are likely to attract readers less eager for cybernetic adventure than do resources created as digital files. As we become more competent in digitizing hard copy resources, we must thus find new ways to manage these electronic files. The prospect of billions upon billions of pages of text jostling one another in cyberspace can be nightmare or utopia; the means of access and retrieval will make much of the difference.

FROM PIECES TO PATTERNS: A BIGGER PICTURE AND A BRIEF AGENDA

Are Electronic Texts Compatible with Library Preservation?

This discussion has underscored the dynamism of preservation. It also suggests that the field's immediate agenda remains quite full. Longer-term prospects are more difficult to discern. If electronic technologies for producing and reformatting information become as ubiquitous as some analysts suggest, preservation as we know it may disappear. So may the artifacts to which we direct our present preservation energies: digital reformatting can quite literally mean "vanishing books."[22]

Some electronic visionaries begin with the premise that books and journals are not themselves texts, but rather representations of texts. Electronic files are simply different representations of the same texts. The vastly enhanced utility of properly encoded electronic texts renders a preservationist's preoccupation with the original codices both superfluous and somewhat benighted. The future belongs to digital data, not to hard copy collections.

The preservationist's response, at least in the short term, focuses on our continuing inability to produce accurate electronic transcriptions. Electronic files based on either optical character recognition or human keying contain errors, and are therefore unacceptable as preservation masters. Digital images, at this point, represent the limits of electronic possibility. Improved technology for optical character recognition may shift the balance.

More fundamental issues are also at hand. Even fully encoded text files cannot now be displayed in a manner faithful to the original document. In many cases, the loss is inconsequential. But appearance can be an integral element in a work's substantive message. In these cases, capturing only text will sacrifice significant meaning. Will improved technologies allow us to create dual, interconnected text and image files as a matter of course? Under what circumstances does our tinkering with preservation platforms (book to microfilm to electronic file, fluid digital database to static paper printout) and appearances (color to black-and-white; or altered page sizes, formats, or typefaces) so alter an original that our archival intentions are belied?

If, and as, electronic reformatting becomes the preservation approach of choice—assuming better technologies and levels of funding sufficient to support this process and its substantial added value—the mechanics of preservation may no longer belong to a single library unit. Digitizing particularly fragile or unusual materials may require special expertise. Mainstream preservation might revert to its past, as an enclave for labor-intensive restorations of particularly valuable artifacts. The bulk of activities to convert hard copy texts to digital files, and to organize and maintain our electronic resources, might then fall to new units defined in terms of computer technologies.

Several analysts suggest that the acquisitions function will face similar changes as we move toward a digital environment.[23] As hard copy resources become peripheral, and as access overrides ownership, traditional orders and receipts will atrophy. Our libraries of the future will instead package, transmit, receive, and process electronic documents and information. Their acquisitions departments will best survive (if indeed their survival is in our general interest) by serving as the point units for electronic interchange. The shift will be profound.

For the foreseeable future, however, traditional books and journals will continue to predominate in many fields' scholarly resources. Contemplating the impact of our digital revolution may help us both to accommodate and influence change. But preservation, and other functions based on the book, are nowhere near extinction. The electronic millennium is not yet at hand.

Preservation Options, Head-to-Head

Electronic reformatting is but one of the preservation possibilities now available. The full array of techniques also includes individual repair or restoration, microfilming, and mass deacidification. Each approach has its own characteristics and benefits.

Individual repair or restoration returns isolated deteriorated items to local collections. Almost any item can be treated, though the benefits are normally limited to the holding library. Costs and the need for specialized expertise or equipment can be fairly low for such routine procedures as rebinding and minor repairs to ordinary circulating materials. Elaborate restorations can be expensive and require special materials and skills. In either case, costs are almost always borne by the holding library. Materials are preserved as artifacts, with little added value. Record keeping, if any, reflects the library's internal needs. The expected lifespan of treated materials may be quite long. However, the combination of high costs and local benefit means that item-level restoration alone will not solve our aggregate preservation problem.

Preservation microfilming enables libraries to reformat hard copy materials to a permanent, reproducible medium. Illustrated volumes and colors present special problems that have not been fully resolved. Archival filming requires expensive equipment and trained technicians. Unit costs are fairly high, and shared bibliographic records are considered essential in order to minimize unnecessary duplication. While preservation microfilming enjoys substantial foundation and governmental support, available funds fall considerably short of the need. As a reproducible medium, preservation microfilm provides substantial added value over deteriorated hard copy originals—even though films are clumsy to use and seldom welcomed by scholars. Microform replacements for deteriorated hard copy materials may also undermine a collection's physical integrity, in libraries where this remains a factor.

Mass deacidification, while still controversial, is a relatively inexpensive process whose unit costs should continue to decline. The technique neutralizes acidic paper and thereby halts additional deterioration; at this point, we cannot strengthen embrittled materials. This emerging technology remains inappropriate for coated papers, water-soluble inks, and certain other substances. In conjunction with appropriate storage environments, mass deacidification can prolong the life of large quantities of library materials. The treated materials cannot necessarily be reproduced, and there is no consensus to share information about what has been stabilized. The development of mass deacidification processes has involved the de facto collaboration of the federal government, local institutions, and industry. For the present, ongoing treatment programs must be sustained by local libraries.

The preservation possibilities of electronic reformatting have captured the imagination of the preservation community, just as electronic media preoccupy the profession as a whole. The field is evolving rapidly, with technological refinements and new procedures for producing and exchanging data announced almost daily. Digital reformatting is an item-by-item process whose costs are even now competitive with preservation microfilming. Organizing and managing electronic files, however, are continuing challenges. Electronic storage and playback equipment, as well as operating systems and software programs, are short-lived; digital files require regular recopying. Protocols for access and retrieval will become increasingly necessary as electronic text files increase in number and extent. Questions of copyright mean that, in practical terms, electronic reformatting must focus on materials in the public domain.[24] Current reformatting processes cannot ensure the integrity of digital text files, so electronic preservation is, for the time being, limited to digitized images of pages.

PRESERVATION: A VALE OF TIERS

These four principal preservation technologies are very different in terms of processes, costs, and implications. None does all that we might like, and each continues to evolve. Carefully combining these approaches might permit a more cost-effective preservation strategy than the less inclusive panorama that now prevails. A vision of how these approaches might complement one another could also encourage continued efforts to address the drawbacks associated with each.

Some proponents of electronic reformatting already envision a tiered sequence of digital and microfilm preservation, with each level associated with specific thresholds of costs, benefits, and demand. Preservation microfilm, still our longest-lived archival medium, would satisfy demand for the bulk of deteriorating materials that generate little use. Retrieval is slow, but the consequences are slight. Items generating higher demand would be scanned, with the digital image files electronically stored at a remote location from whence they could be transmitted as required. Finally, heavily used materials would be maintained in local digital files ready for immediate use. The application of optical character recognition and full encoding to appropriate high-use files might be the next step in adding value. The costs would jump, but so would the benefits.

A more inclusive strategy would also consider stable hard copy collections. These resources, whether chemically stable books and journals, deacidified publications, or volumes that had been individually repaired or restored, might be considered out of immediate danger. Large-scale programs for mass deacidification would rapidly increase the number of these "safe" materials. When used for chemically unstable materials enjoying copyright protection, mass deacidification would also sidestep the legal complexities associated with reformatting. Different sorts of preservation reformatting could then be applied to the scarce, embrittled, or high-use materials that remain at risk.

A large mass of stable, hard copy materials would thus comprise the core of preserved library resources. As particular items were requested for use, these could be microfilmed to ensure both reproducibility and permanence. Files of electronic page images could enable faster access to materials in heavy demand. And digital text files, amenable to computer manipulations, could be created as warranted by funding and user demand.

Microfilm reformatting, in this tiered scheme, would provide permanent copies of endangered materials. Until we are better able to manage archival electronic files, preservation microfilm will be necessary even when electronic reformatting is also conducted. Archival microfilm will also remain appropriate for materials needing rescue but unlikely to generate enough demand to warrant digital conversion.

AN EMERGING STRATEGY AND SOME INITIAL IMPLICATIONS

This tiered strategy looks to stabilized hard copy collections as our basic preservation option and goal, at least until cost-benefit ratios become substantially different. Microform reformatting will save embrittled materials and categories of books not now amenable to mass deacidification, as well as enhance access to some particularly scarce publications. Electronic reformatting, at present through digital images, merits support for research and development.[25] These efforts should focus on appropriate procedures to capture, store, maintain, transmit, and receive electronic data and, perhaps even more important, on the need to manage immense image and text databases in an online environment.

This strategy recognizes that preservation is no longer forever—or, perhaps more accurately, that we now understand permanence differently from before. Some time ago we accepted the need periodically to "refresh" sound recordings reformatted to tape and hard copy texts reformatted as digital files. Mass deacidification is similar in that it allows us to prolong the lives of hard copy materials for a while. Archival microfilming has encouraged a perception of preservation as all or nothing: treated items are permanently saved, and untreated items will disappear. Our new options let us also think in terms of longer and shorter.

Our preservation context remains one of scarce dollars, with costs a central constraint. The relatively low expense of mass deacidification may nonetheless enable us to wiggle past the most acute dilemmas of preservation equity. By cheaply stabilizing the bulk of our own collections, we could free up funds to intensify preservation microfilming for other materials in our own country, and for filming in countries where mass deacidification remains impractical. Reallocating preservation resources or, better yet, adding to the pot, will move us toward a better protected worldwide written heritage.

A tiered preservation strategy also acknowledges the different levels of added value associated with each treatment option. Mass deacidification (or individual restoration or repair) curtails the loss of value associated with embrittlement and eventual crumbling. Preservation microfilming generates durable and reproducible copies of single documents. Electronic reformatting produces accessible and portable materials. And means to produce accurate digital text files promise new capacities for the machine manipulation of texts.

At the present time, the highest added values are associated with substantial expense. Until further development drives down the costs, electronic efforts may most appropriately be supported by external grants, exploratory consortia, and commercial pioneers. Bread-and-butter preservation should focus on more pedestrian approaches, with their lower added values. The tiered cost structure proposed above for preservation microfilming could further refine this model.

Implementing this strategy will require institutional involvement and support. Several needs are particularly obvious. Mass deacidification should be recognized as an essential element in our common preservation strategy, and therefore become eligible for federal and foundation grants.

Digital preservation requires additional support for research and development from individual institutions, library-business partnerships, and consortial bodies. Organizations like the Commission on Preservation and Access (CPA), the Association of Research Libraries (ARL), the Research Libraries Group (RLG), and OCLC have particularly important roles to play in guiding the flow of effort and funds.

As mass deacidification and electronic reformatting gain momentum within the overall preservation strategy, microfilming stands to lose some ground. Preservation microfilming might thus focus on carefully designed projects to capture materials that are not appropriate for mass deacidification. Publications on newsprint are fragile, and the large pages and columnar format of newspapers complicate electronic reformatting. Here, microfilm remains our most satisfactory preservation medium. Materials on coated papers, which are particularly prevalent in architecture and fine arts collections, would likewise require special measures. Most libraries in the Third World cannot now implement programs of mass deacidification or electronic reformatting: microfilming is their primary preservation option. Embracing a tiered approach will shift preservation emphases within the United States, and also redirect some energy and resources abroad.

It is still too early to say whether preservation will vanish as a function when (and if) libraries and their books disappear into cyberspace. Emerging electronic technologies are forcing us to rethink our preservation operations and assumptions. Mass deacidification, along with any mass paper strengthening techniques that may emerge, will do the same. While the speculative process is useful, it is perhaps more important to focus on the shorter term. Inadequate resources, immense need, and both proven and experimental processes define our current possibilities. This context encourages us to rethink our preservation strategy in terms of a coordinated and tiered effort.

NOTES

1. See, for instance, Association of Research Libraries, *Preservation Organization and Staffing*, SPEC Kit no. 16 (Washington, D.C.: Association of Research Libraries, 1990). Workshops for preservation administrators, many aimed at institutions where this assignment is combined with other responsibilities, have become commonplace. The Washington-based Commission on Preservation and Access plays a central role in preservation. Its many publications both document its activities and afford continuing coverage of developments and debates affecting preservation programs and technologies worldwide.
2. See Hans Rütimann, *The International Project 1992 Update, Including "Microfilming Projects Abroad"* (Washington, D.C.: Commission on Preservation and Access, January 1993). The International Federation of Library Associations and Institutions, IFLA, has designated selected libraries as "Preservation and Conservation Centers." Each PAC is charged with stimulating preservation in a particular geographic area.

3. The *Newsletter* and other publications of the Commission on Preservation and Access are particularly useful.
4. Some of these issues are explored in Dan C. Hazen, "Preservation in Poverty and Plenty: Policy Issues for the 1990s," *Journal of Academic Librarianship* 15 (January 1990): 344-51. Available preservation technologies also skewed efforts: in the absence of effective techniques to microfilm color illustrations, for instance, sources for art history were often left aside.
5. The sciences and professional fields are by no means exempt from cost pressures. Possible distortions resulting from our emphasis on "big science" are particularly contentious. Constance C. Gould and Karla Pearce, *Information Needs in the Sciences: An Assessment* (Mountain View, Calif.: Research Libraries Group, 1991) demonstrate that historical materials receive heavy use in some scientific fields.
6. The "access" model for libraries assumes a network of fully portable resources distributed across the country, and beyond. This image does not square fully with cuts that are almost universal in acquisitions funds and receipts: the "new paradigm" is too easily invoked to excuse local cutbacks enacted with no sense of shared acquisitions responsibility. Dispersed microfilm masters could enable some libraries to project an illusion of providing the rest of us with "their share" of unique materials.
7. The Library of Congress' widely publicized rejection of several bids for commercial mass deacidification has been more than balanced by various research library contracts to begin large-scale treatment. See Peter G. Sparks, ed., *A Roundtable on Mass Deacidification: Report on a Meeting Held September 12-13, 1991 in Andover, Massachusetts* (Washington, D.C.: Association of Research Libraries, 1992). Other announcements include "LC Responds to Deacidification Bids from Industry: All Offers are Turned Down," *LC Information Bulletin* 50 (23 September 1991): 347, and Judy Quinn and Michael Rogers, "News: LC Turns Down All Deacidification Preservation Bids," *Library Journal* 116 (1 October 1991): 14. The libraries of Harvard, Johns Hopkins, and Northwestern Universities are among those currently engaged in mass deacidification.
8. Harvard's costs in the first year of a pilot project for mass deacidification, during which about 3,500 volumes were treated, were about $12.40 per volume (including transportation between Massachusetts and Texas). Costs are expected to drop; even now they are roughly comparable to expenses for binding. See *Mass Deacidification in the Harvard University Library: A Report on the 1991/92 Pilot Operational Program* (Cambridge: Harvard University Library Preservation Office, January 1993). The preservation microfilming costs cited include three generations of film plus bibliographic control; about half the $90 reflects actual filming costs, and the other half additional staff time. Deacidification costs include no provision for bibliographic upgrades or annotation.
9. Some libraries are weighing proposals to provide local catalog records for microform masters held at other institutions when local hard copy volumes are withdrawn but not replaced.
10. Space limitations make it common practice to split collections between active segments housed in a central repository and less-consulted materials shipped to remote storage facilities. Physical dispersal of a collection can compromise cohesiveness and integrity far more radically than less-than-comprehensive replacement policies. More sophisticated systems of electronic description and control may eventually restore some of the coherence now being sacrificed through dispersal.
11. Other more serious problems cluster in certain types of materials—items with coated paper, water-soluble inks, leather bindings, and the like. Work to improve

treatment technology may allow these items to be deacidified in the future. (Of course, microfilm reformatting is itself problematic for some categories of materials.) In mass deacidification projects, particularly troublesome categories can simply be bypassed.

12. See, for example, William M. Bulkeley, "Information Age: Libraries Shift from Books to Computers," *Wall Street Journal*, 8 February 1993, B4; or David C. Churbuck, "Good-bye, Dewey Decimals," *Forbes* 151 (15 February 1993): 204-205.

13. Other electronic databases are listed, in an already-dated appendix to the Research Libraries Group's *Information Needs in the Humanities: An Assessment* (Stanford, Calif.: Research Libraries Group, 1988). The Center for Electronic Texts in the Humanities at Rutgers University is a source for this kind of information; the Text Encoding Initiative seeks to include many digital endeavors, using guidelines that enable some degree of standardization and thus facilitate exchange. New products or initiatives seem to be announced almost daily.

14. See the account of Eric Calaluca's presentation on the PLD in James Daly, ed., *Workshop on Electronic Texts: Proceedings* (Washington, D.C.: Library of Congress, 1992), 22-24. The document describes a host of electronic initiatives, ranging from boutique databases to very substantial efforts.

15. See, for example, Page P. Miller, "Point of View: Insuring the Preservation of Electronic Records," *Chronicle of Higher Education*, 3 February 1993, A44.

16. Other efforts are planned or underway at the Columbia University Law School, the Chicago-Kent School of Law at the Illinois Institute of Technology, Pennsylvania State University, and the University of Tennessee (the latter in conjunction with the so-called "LaGuardia Eight" group, whose activities enjoy strong support from the Commission on Preservation and Access). Spain's Archivo General de Indias has digitized massive numbers of historical documents in conjunction with the Columbian Quincentenary; it is now exploring long-distance transmission of these image files. Last but not least, Duke University has advertised for a "Preservation Access Officer" whose responsibilities would include "to develop and manage a digital preservation laboratory that provides an affordable way to save the intellectual content of library materials" ("Bulletin Board" section, *Chronicle of Higher Education*, 10 February, 1993, B37). This ambitious reading of our current situation suggests that digital reformatting has become our newest preservation bandwagon.

17. The Cornell Project is described in a number of sources, including the Library of Congress *Proceedings* mentioned in note 14 above. Also see Anne R. Kenney and Lynne K. Personius, *Joint Study in Digital Preservation, Phase 1: A Report to the Commission on Preservation and Access* (Washington, D.C.: Commission on Preservation and Access, September 1992).

18. Yale's "Project Open Book" is also described in various sources, including Donald J. Waters and Shari Weaver, *The Organizational Phase of Project Open Book: A Report to the Commission on Preservation and Access* (Washington, D.C.: Commission on Preservation and Access, September 1992).

19. See Patricia Battin's presentation, Daly, 59-61. Some visionaries imagine eventual "smart" digital storage media, programmed to restore themselves once they have deteriorated to a certain point. These are not realistic current options.

20. Carl Fleischhauer, as reported in Daly, 25, notes a rekeying industry standard of 99.95% accuracy; to eliminate all error, costs would reportedly double. Stuart Weibel (Ibid., 67) reports that OCLC, in experiments to merge inputs from multiple optical character recognition systems, has reduced errors "from an unacceptable rate of 5 characters out of every 1,000 to an unacceptable rate of 2 characters

out of every 1,000." A subsequent personal communication adds, "Even after the correction procedures, one is still left with an unacceptably high error rate that would not pass muster in any serious production system."

21. The continuing struggle to master the Internet may be instructive: the insider's jargon of "surfing" and "zen" reflects the system's many unpredictable aspects (as well as the 1960s or retro-'60s inclinations of many electronic pioneers). "Browsing" suggests some of the same serendipity as it emerges in traditional stack arrangements.

22. Scanning is most efficient with continuously fed single sheets, meaning books must be disbound.

23. See, for instance, Ross Atkinson, "The Acquisitions Librarian as Change Agent in the Transition to the Electronic Library," *Library Resources & Technical Services* 36 (January 1992): 7-21; also Peter S. Graham, "Electronic Information and Research Library Technical Services," *College & Research Libraries* 51 (May 1990): 241-50.

24. Anthony M. Cummings, et al., *University Libraries and Scholarly Communication: A Study Prepared for the Andrew W. Mellon Foundation* (Washington, D.C.: Association of Research Libraries for the Andrew W. Mellon Foundation, 1992), especially 153-60, offers a cogent synopsis of copyright issues in an electronic environment.

25. Research and development might also target materials not fully served by existing preservation techniques, for instance, illustrated volumes on coated paper.

Don't Swat the Skunk:
The Preservation Imperative

David B. Gracy II

*Governor Bill Daniel Professor in Archival Enterprise and
Associate Dean, Graduate School of Library and Information Science
The University of Texas at Austin*

The Northeast Document Conservation Center (NEDCC), the fine conservation facility in Andover, Massachusetts, receives many unusual calls, but none more so than one from a librarian who, upon opening her library one morning, found a skunk inside. Her first reaction was to throw open the front door as wide as it would go and begin talking to the skunk, trying to reason with it about why its departure would be in the best interest of both of them. The skunk only turned and headed farther into the library. The librarian next opened all of the doors and requested, then begged, the skunk to leave by any exit it wished. The skunk did not budge.

Finding oral persuasion unsuccessful, the librarian left to get a broom. When she returned, the skunk was still right where it had been. She cautiously eased the broom toward the animal with the intent of gently pressuring it into moving, so she could guide it, like a four-legged hockey puck, toward a door. Her nudging got the skunk moving all right, but it headed in a contrary direction.

Frustrated and panicked by the fear that she was losing, the librarian decided that her next move should be to deliver a swift, well-aimed blow to knock the skunk out the nearest door, or so close to the door that the animal would accept the advantage of its momentum and scurry away. The librarian swung back the broom with all her might to deliver the blow. Unfortunately, she and the skunk were so positioned that instead of hitting the animal on the forward stroke, she swatted it on her wind-up, and sent it flying backwards. In horror, she watched it disappear from sight over the threshold of the stairs on its way to the basement. You know the rest: when it landed, the startled skunk sprayed all the books within range. That was when the librarian called NEDCC for help.

THE DEFINITION OF PRESERVATION

"Preservation" isn't what it used to be. So says Ann Russell, Director of the NEDCC, from whom I heard this story. Almost anyone conscious of preservation in libraries and archives (that is, preservation of book and paper-based materials) would agree. Fumigation and removal of skunk scent and stain are, at a minimum, out of the ordinary, yet they were essential to saving the affected volumes for use, which is the basic goal of preservation!

My Webster's *Third International Dictionary* defines preservation in words common to all such volumes I have seen: "deliberate, planned, or thoughtful preserving, guarding, or protecting: a keeping in a safe or entire state." Though "protecting in a safe state" and "deliberate guarding" would seem to encompass dissuading an angry skunk, basically and more commonly they suggest fighting off the ravages of time and use. By this definition, preservation is:

1) Putting a university's priceless Gutenberg Bible (whose condition has deteriorated imperceptibly in the more than 500 years since it was printed and bound) on display in an environmentally self-contained case and regularly turning the pages so that the binding of the open book does not become warped.

2) Washing burned fragments of Faulkner poetry in baths of distilled water, ammonium hydroxide, and magnesium bicarbonate to neutralize destructive acid that is breaking hydrogen bonds (thus weakening the matrix of the fibers constituting the paper), then strengthening the remaining fibers by coating them with hydroxypropyl cellulose.

3) Chemically and physically stabilizing the single most famous document in Texas history (the "Victory or Death" letter that William Barrett Travis, commander of the Alamo, sent out of the besieged fortress on February 24, 1836, the day after the Mexican Army arrived and besieged the garrison, appealing in stirring, brave, and heroic terms for reinforcements), then housing it in its own case for both display and safekeeping, protected from air, moisture, abrasion, and ultraviolet light.

4) Applying polyvinyl acetate (PVA) glue with a knitting needle behind the end papers and inside of the cover of a book to strengthen a shaken hinge.

This treatment of individual items, particularly to stall the decline or correct the injuries of damaged or deteriorating books and documents so that they can function again, is called "conservation" by practitioners when they mean skilled work done to maintain the artifactual value of the item, and "repair" when they mean treatment designed simply to correct a visible mechanical defect. Repair sacrifices intrinsic value in the original book or document for speed and cost savings in the treatment. Rather than a lesser choice, in many cases (for example, keeping a volume in circulation in a public library) repair is the only appropriate option.

Remedial treatment of one kind or another is what many people, inside and outside of libraries and archives, conjure up when they think of preservation. In fact, however, the treatment of individual items is only one part of preservation as it is defined for archival and library material in the 1990s. It may be the more sentimentally compelling, but it is really not the most significant. Maintaining access to recorded knowledge as far into the future as possible is the other, and perhaps more important, aspect of preservation. Not every book, or even every Bible, is a Gutenberg. Not every volume needs to be kept on the shelves forever; most are there simply to circulate. These will wear out, and so be it.

Similarly, not every letter is a Travis letter that, once housed in an archives, needs to be maintained in its original form. This is true even of some rather unusual items, such as those found among the papers of one genealogist. One day while searching microfilm, she came upon information for which she had been searching a very long time. When she prepared to take down the data, she found herself without paper. Abruptly she faced a choice: she could get up from the reader and find some paper, or make other arrangements. Knowing that gremlins live inside microfilm readers and wait for opportunities like this (when people momentarily absent themselves from a machine) to jiggle the film, so that the frame that was on the screen when you left is gone when you return—knowing this, she determined not to leave the machine.

The lady opened her purse and rummaged for something—anything—on which she could write. And there they were. She loved popsicles and had in her purse a fine supply of popsicle sticks which she fished out and used to copy the precious information. After she died, her papers, along with the valued popsicle sticks, passed to the Thomas County Historical Society in southern Georgia, where they remain. But no one recognizes popsicle sticks as an information-bearing medium. Consequently, the staff of the archives carefully positioned the wooden pieces on the glass of a photocopy machine and reduced the information to traditional, comfortable, 8.5 x 11-inch paper form. Maintaining access is not always synonymous with preserving original format.

For many, many documents and books, a microfilm copy is quite adequate. Preservation in these cases means extending the life of the information when the original, because of the poor quality of the paper on which it exists, will not survive or is not worth the cost to conserve it. Particularly is this so with data recorded on preprinted forms, such as the information gathered by census takers. The National Archives has disposed of quantities of huge, original census documents. But any researcher can still easily find the entry in the 1850 census of Alamance County, North Carolina, for William Lasten. (Apparently he was a man with a remarkable perspective on honesty, as he listed his occupation as "thief"! For whatever reason, his name is missing from the 1860 census of Alamance County.)

Yes, preservation is not what it used to be. The issues in the 1990s are:
1) In what form do we best maintain information?
2) How do we accomplish, at the least cost, preservation of
the largest amount of material worth preserving?
Considering the two aspects of preservation, then, the definition that I use
has both physical and intellectual properties. For me, preservation of library
and archival material in the 1990s is:

Extending the life of material *for the purpose for which the
material exists in the library collection or archives* (which
may be permanently, or well may not be), and maintaining access to recorded knowledge as far into the future as possible.

By this definition, preservation consists of either or both:
1) A systematic program on a repository- or collection-
level basis for extending the life of the carriers of information (books and paper in particular) to serve the purpose for which the carriers and the information they
contain were acquired.
2) A program of systematic and timely transfer of information from one carrier or medium to another, so that access is not lost simply on technical grounds.

PRESERVATION MEANS ACCESS AND USE FOR OUR TIME

When one thinks about it, maintaining access as far into the future as possible actually is very immediate. In certain respects, we are living in our own
future. The 1960 census (produced only one generation ago) was compiled
and manipulated on a magnetic tape technology long obsolete in the 1990s.
At last count, only two machines remain in the world that can read the tape—
one in Japan, the other disassembled in the Smithsonian Institution.

Closer to home, the personnel records of one state agency in Texas were
microfilmed during the early 1960s, and two copies produced. The agency
placed one copy in the State Archives for preservation, and kept the other
for use. Eventually the agency copy became so scratched that staff no
longer could read it. At that point, the agency called the State Archives: did
we still have the other copy, the caller asked. Of course! Well, the caller
continued, the job of the agency was to use the information on the film,
which it no longer could do. And, was it not the job of the Archives to preserve things? You could say that, I replied. Well, the caller concluded in tri-
umph, you send us your copy to be used and we'll send you ours that you
can keep just as long as you want to! Clearly the agency understood the important concept of a use copy and a preservation copy, but had not grasped
the idea of a preservation master.

We live in our own future, because we cannot say with certainty what information will be needed at what juncture. Only a year or two ago, the state of Oklahoma was paying $18,000 per year in royalties to use the title song from the musical *Oklahoma* in its advertising. Then someone found a letter in the Oklahoma State Archives in which Oscar Hammerstein gave the state the right to play the song "long and loud and often." The state now pays only $1.00 per year in royalties. Preservation in that case was worth $17,999.00 per year, in the present and future.

The point is that preservation of archival and library materials is not something we do only for an audience in an unspecified and indefinite future. It is work we perform for ourselves, which has the happy and satisfying benefit of contributing to generations that will follow us.

THE CHALLENGE OF PRESERVATION

The Newer the Medium, the More Fragile

The generations that preceded us have left a terrible and challenging paradox with which we must wrestle—the paradox of technology. Each new medium developed for recording information has been and is more fragile and vulnerable than its predecessor. Each, consequently, to survive (that is, for us to have access to its data) requires more human involvement than its forerunner.

The clay tablet was practically indestructible, and became only more stable as a result of fire. I know of librarians and archivists who argue that one of the worst missteps taken by humanity was abandoning use of the clay tablet. Paper burns—slowly when compressed in files and boxes, rapidly in single sheets. Otherwise, it can last hundreds of years if made with materials that do not produce in it the acidic seed of its own destruction, and if it is housed under favorable conditions. The useful life of paper that is not well manufactured and maintained is measured in months (years, at best); newsprint is a prime example. Audiotape produced on an acetate substrate that was common not that many years ago is now dimensionally unstable. While polyester substrate solved that problem, it has no effect on the loss of signal caused by eventual failure of the binder that holds the iron oxide magnetic particles to the tape. Flame need not touch it: only heat (and low heat at that) is needed to cause distortion sufficient to lose the content.

Videotape has a shorter useful life than audiotape. I feel sorry for people who are recording their family's happy occasions on videotape, expecting to replay those memories into the indefinite future. But, at the same time, I feel sorry for myself, because the 8mm movie film I have clung to is now virtually impossible to find. Our best choice at this moment seems to be recording on perishable videotape, followed by conversion to movie film. Even then, maintaining the movie projector becomes a greater challenge every year, making this only a temporary solution.

The Electronic Record

The sum of the matter is that, while we used to consider the medium for holding information (books) sturdy and durable because it lasted longer than a human lifetime, such stability can no longer be assumed for information-bearing media. And, as with the 1960 census tape, the ability to access the information in newer media requires a machine to pull up the content: no longer is having the original information-bearing object the same thing as having the information. Without the equipment to access the medium, the information on the tape or the disk might as well not exist. For information on tape and disk, we have reached the point that a generation is no longer computed in terms of a human lifetime, but rather by successive improvements in software and hardware that make their predecessors obsolete.

To this point, the items we have been considering are all tangible. At least we have the security of something we can see and hold. As we move into the electronic age, however, we are losing that certainty. Records created and maintained in electronic form, as electronic mail and databases manipulated in the hypermedia environment, have no physical existence except as specific joinings of data are printed out to serve given needs. Otherwise, the physical aspect of the document (that is, the medium on which the information is recorded) is separated from the logical aspect (that is, the grouping and organization of data into a record). Information about the creation of the document—by whom and when it came into existence—its provenance—is separated from its content.

We see this every day in working with data in computers, where we have to go to the directory screen to learn the last occasion on which we worked with a document. Otherwise, we call up and work on the document, unconscious of its provenance. The significance of this type of information became an issue of national importance when a federal judge in the case of Armstrong vs. The Executive Office of the President (the PROFS case) ruled that the content of an electronic mail document alone is an insufficient record. Preserving the text by itself is not enough. In fact, the provenance data are essential for the record to have its full meaning, for its authenticity to be determinable.

The growing challenge to preserve records in electronic form comes into focus when we hear the prediction that by the year 2000, some 75 percent of federal government information will be created in electronic form. Certainly academic institutions and commercial enterprises, if not all segments of society, will not be far behind in exploiting the electronic environment. Of all the media for generating, manipulating, and carrying information, then, the electronic (the most modern) is consistent with technology's paradox: it is the most fragile and vulnerable. As a result, the greatest challenge of preservation is still ahead.

This is true because the solution to the looming problem is unlikely to be found in the place we commonly prefer to look, namely in a machine. Even when machines have been developed to accomplish preservation ends, they often have been misused by well-meaning but misinformed persons, or they have simply been incapable of meeting the full need they were supposed to address. The laminator, for example, was developed by William J. Barrow to speed and improve a process of strengthening paper weakened by acid attack. Some persons assumed that if lamination was a good process for documents in need of attention, it must be wonderful for those still in good condition. In one archives, wax seals were cut out of diplomatic documents on paper more than a century old and in fine condition, so that the document could be laminated without having the wax melt and ruin the machine. As another example, the microfilm of the 1885 census of Dodge City, Kansas, simply does not convey the aesthetic quality of the original in which the census taker identified ladies of the evening by recording their names in red ink.

The Importance of a Sound Environment

Recognizing the importance of preservation is recognizing that the building housing the archives or library is an essential part of any preservation plan. As such, the most important consideration in designing a structure must be the contents it will hold, not the architectural statement it might make. Just because archives are records that no longer are being used for the purpose for which they were created does not mean that any old building originally constructed for another purpose can serve well for archival preservation. A "warehouse" is not an "archives," and "dead storage" is not a synonym for "preservation." Specifically, glass is a poor insulator, and a building in which most of the walls are glass is a building which is challenging to the preservation administrator. Sometimes the greatest difficulty is the site itself, especially when, as happened at one university, the facility constructed to house a substantial portion of the library was built over a spring, requiring a sump pump on the bottom floor and inevitably resulting (despite the pump) in some destructive floods.

Becoming attentive to preservation is recognizing that the action of humidity and light is harmful if not controlled. When working on a book on the early 1960s governor of a tropical American territory, I needed to use records that, considered to be of little importance after the administration concluded, were stored in a locked and leaky facility, creating stale air and high humidity. The result was that silverfish found the masses of files perfect for their habitation and gustation. In various folders of papers I found true canyons left by the silverfish, which severely compromised the documents for my use. Moreover, the excrement of the creatures was so abundant that I had to tie a handkerchief over my nose to keep from breathing it into my lungs. Even if the environment had not attracted silverfish, it would have been detrimental to the paper, as high humidity (and especially the daily and seasonal changes in humidity) speeds acid attack.

When I came to the Texas State Archives, I found the famous Travis letter on permanent display. It had been in the same case under fluorescent light almost every day since the building opened some 16 years prior to my arrival, so that every school child could see it at any time. This laudable goal (from the perspective of any one visitor) has had tragic consequences for the document. On one side the paper is a healthy, slightly yellowish color; on the other it is an irreversibly washed-out white. Barely legible any longer is a poignant note written in pencil on the back. Scrawled by the messenger who carried the letter out of the besieged fortress, the note reports heavy cannon fire and urges that supplies of ammunition and reinforcements be sent to the Alamo as quickly as possible. Even one of Travis' biographers missed seeing the note.

THE NATURE OF A PROGRAM OF PRESERVATION

Preservation of library and archival material begins in earnest when the leadership and staff of an institution adopt a mission of stewardship toward the holdings and collections, and accept as their principal responsibility extending the life of the material to serve most fully the purposes for which the books and papers were acquired. Stewardship is a way of thinking about library collections and archival holdings, and prioritizing actions in a world in which resources are painfully finite. In developing a preservation program, there are nine functions that custodians of library and archival material must combine and prioritize. The more of these that are employed in a program, the stronger the program will be. With the exception of the first function, the nine are presented in no order of importance.

1. Maintaining an optimum environment

All things considered, the most important single element in a preservation program is controlling the environment—specifically, controlling humidity and temperature. Fluctuation in these two conditions is the prime cause of the movement of acid through paper, leading to the paper's internal chemical destruction. The greater and more frequent the fluctuations, the more severe the damage. Though temperature and humidity can never be prevented from wavering at least a few degrees or percentage points, different optimum temperature and humidity levels are recommended for different materials. The advice of experts varies, but to achieve an environment acceptable for virtually all forms of records and books most authorities call for a temperature at or slightly cooler than that comfortable for humans, namely 68-72 degrees, and a humidity at about the mid-point of the scale, that is, 55 percent with a variation of a couple of percentage points on either side.

The importance of providing consistent and proper humidity and temperature can easily be seen when one considers the situation of one library that moved its collection out of the building during a renovation. The books were packed neatly into three trailers that were closed during the still, humid night and opened during the day. In the Gulf Coast city, humidity and temperature fluctuated widely; in a short period the books became a museum of mold and bugs, damaging the collection more severely than anyone had ever imagined when the idea of trailers was hit upon to solve the temporary storage problem. Turning off all air-handling equipment at night and on weekends leads to a similar result; it just takes longer for the problem to reach severe proportions.

2. Making the building as preservationally sound as possible

Among the many matters to consider when constructing or renovating a building, preservation must be central for the library or archive to function well for the purpose for which it was intended, that is, holding a capital asset of books and papers whose value far exceeds that of the structure. The air-flow characteristics of the facility are one of the most important considerations, since humidity increases in stale, stagnant air.

I know of one library whose air supply first passes through the campus gymnasium. The librarians always know when an event with a large attendance is about to occur, because the temperature in the library plummets as the gym is cooled in anticipation of the crowd. And after the event, some say the library smells strangely like a locker room. Another library I know of failed to check every element of the architect's design and ended up with all the fire alarms concentrated along one wall, rather than positioned around the entire perimeter of the stack area.

3. Preparing for disaster and planning for recovery

Preparing for disaster offers one of the best ways of initiating a preservation program, because gathering information needed to survive an event that is unexpected when it happens, yet has serious consequences for the material and the institution affected, requires a review of both physical matters concerning the building and current practices of the institution and staff. The outcome of the exercise is a plan that will significantly mitigate the affects of fire, water, or other emergency.

An important lesson learned from dealing with disasters is *never* to leave materials on the floor. One small-town librarian learned the hard way. She had put the overflow books from the library in an old house on the outskirts of town, and stacked many of the volumes on the floor. After the city built out to the house, water and sewer hookups followed, but no one thought to tell her. The plumbing in the house had been designed to handle the low pressure of a self-contained, gravity water system. When the crew opened the valve sending city water to the house, the sudden and greatly increased pressure literally blew the toilet off the floor, and of course soaked books throughout the house.

Fire detection and suppression systems, once shunned in archival and library settings on the grounds that water ruins paper and books, now are appreciated. First, materials reduced to ashes cannot be recovered, but those that are water-soaked can. Second, these systems have been improved so that only sprinkler heads in the area of the fire engage, rather than all the heads throughout the system. The National Fire Protection Association reports that three-quarters of all fires in sprinkler-equipped buildings are extinguished by four or fewer heads.

Naturally, for sprinkler systems as well as for traditional plumbing, it is essential for the librarian, archivist, and preservation administrator to know the location of the cut-off valve for the water main. Many disasters, from Stanford University to the Chicago Historical Society, have been greater than they needed to be because, when the broken pipe was discovered, precious time was lost trying to find the master valve to shut off the flow of water. An unanticipated consequence of the successful salvage of the water-soaked books at Stanford was that, though the university was able to save all but some 30-odd books out of more than 30,000 affected, returning the water-damaged books to the shelves required 12 percent more shelf space, as the swollen paper and bindings did not shrink to their original size.

4. Improving the care with which material is handled

Encouraging clean hands when handling archival material, requiring cotton gloves when working with photographs, and prohibiting eating and drinking in the library all are obvious improvements. The most overlooked improvement for libraries is redesigning, if not eliminating, the book drop. The physical abuse books sustain in falling through book drops is much greater than it need be. One student of mine who recently returned from a job interview in a brand-spanking-new library described all of the right preservation considerations that had been incorporated into the facility, until he got to the book drop. After negotiating the chute, books fell three feet to a tile floor, where they crashed one upon another, their spines twisting, boards bending, pages being creased and crumpled with sickening regularity.

5. Conducting a program of holdings maintenance for archives, or stack maintenance for libraries

With slightly different meanings because of their different environments, these two activities relate to materials' immediate environment. In libraries, the emphasis is on keeping dust levels in the stacks (where the books spend the majority of their time) at a minimum. Dust is abrasive and attracts vermin. Holdings maintenance in archives is based on the proposition that good housing of the material (particularly flat paper) in folders and purpose-designed boxes is worth the investment, because it provides a more stable environment and reduces damage from handling.

6. Reformatting deteriorating materials

Sometimes transferring content from a deteriorating medium (book papers brittle from acid attack) to a stable and easily reproducible medium (such as microfilm) is the most positive preservation solution available. To prevent the waste of money resulting from many institutions' reformatting the same title, a national register of microform masters exists; repositories can use it to locate already-reformatted copies of volumes they desire. At this juncture and in this country, reformatting represents the most visible expenditure of moneys designated specifically for preservation functions. This work is common to research libraries.

7. Conserving and repairing damaged items

Clearly, item treatment is an essential function of preservation. For archival material, conservation typically consists of deacidifying paper, then giving it strength and protection by sealing it between two sheets of inert polyester in a process called encapsulation. For books, repair usually means mending damaged pages and strengthening or replacing damaged cases (covers); conservation may range from treating these same conditions to saving hand-painted illustrations and unique bindings.

The challenge is determining when to reformat and when to conserve or repair an item. Various models have been developed to guide selection for reformatting, each with its strengths and weaknesses. As useful as the models are, every decision made in the context of one of them must also be vetted by the custodian's best judgment. That is one of the reasons why preservation is such important and challenging work. It requires the best human intelligence we can devote to it, in order to accomplish the most preservation for the most material at the least cost.

8. Educating consumers

Ours is an ambivalent society with regard to preservation. On the one hand, ours is a throw-away generation; we want to rid ourselves easily of that which we no longer need. Disposable diapers and disposable packaging (styrofoam burger containers; plastic shopping bags) head the list. Yet this is also the age of environmental conservation, and the preservation of archival and library materials has a close relationship to that movement. Convincing the public, as well as the library or archival staff, that stewardship is the responsibility of each and every one of us is an essential part of any program of preservation, if we are to hope for any real success in ensuring the information we and our successors need is accessible when it is needed.

9. Administering a preservation program

While each of the first eight functions of preservation can be accomplished by any organization, having a person on staff to prioritize, coordinate, and focus attention on them is essential if preservation is to be much more than a tangential activity. Clearly, a program of preservation in some form is essential to the mission of every library and archives. Like any other undertaking, it does not happen just because it is a good idea. And certainly it will not happen if it is only treated as work added to already full job descriptions.

PRESERVATION IS STEWARDSHIP WITH A VISION

If stewardship is the responsibility to manage well the information resources for which we archivists and librarians are responsible, then we should acknowledge the value of the asset for which we are accountable. Some years ago one expert valued the holdings of the Texas State Archives at $150 million. Today, that is a conservative figure. We have in our nation's research libraries probably 450 million volumes, whose replacement would cost approximately $100 each, for a total value of $45 billion. Above that figure, we have the capital asset of the building, and the continuing costs of maintaining the environment and providing the personnel to administer and protect—nay, to extend—the life of those assets. The public has little notion of the value of the library and archival asset, or the cost of maintaining it. As part of our program of education, we in preservation must drive home the point that the public's investment in the holdings and collections of archives and libraries is large enough to be worth protecting, and then some. Libraries and archives are big business.

Rather than stewardship simply in the sense of protecting what *is*, preservation of archival and library materials in our time is an opportunity to shape the future of information handling. Even if we wanted it so, the work of preservation cannot be just restoring information materials to their former condition and maintaining information only in technologies of earlier times. The advent of electronic communication is as much a reason for this circumstance as is the cost of trying to restore massive quantities of materials. To be good stewards, we should use preservation as a tool to shape the libraries and archives of the future. We must explore what the nature of libraries and archives should be in the electronic future. Among the questions we need to answer are:

> 1) How do the virtual library and virtual archives articulate with the physical library and physical archives with which we are familiar?

2) In what form should we strive to preserve what
   material?

Clearly, preservation is not just a responsibility, not just a striving to maintain the status quo. It is, in fact, one of the most exciting opportunities ever to come to the archival and library communities!

CONCLUSION

Preservation represents as important a job, challenge, obligation, and opportunity as we have in the information-handling world, both in the present and for the foreseeable future. Information-bearing material is becoming more varied, more fragile, and requires more preplanning and handling than ever, just to ensure access to its content. What we are gaining in speed and facility of access, as well as in holding capacity, we are losing by the impermanence of the medium in which the information is stored. But our need to have access over time to quantities—multiplying quantities—of information has not diminished. Moreover, preservation is a technical and multifaceted business. It is coping with deterioration of materials in traditional formats, and it is developing strategies for maintaining access to recorded knowledge in all its forms, as far into the future as possible—a future measured in both short machine-generations and longer human ones.

While there is much we need to do, there is much that we can accomplish in fairly short order, so that we can see and enjoy the benefits of our work. We can take immediate steps, for example, to improve temperature and, especially, humidity. We can prepare our institutions to minimize the effect of the disaster that sooner or later must be expected to happen. We can extend the life of material by simply handling it more responsibly.

The challenge and need are great. The imperative is to understand the scope of the problem and to take action. But whatever one's present emotion about preservation—eager or grudging, enthusiastic, uncertain, or inspired—what we can see is that action must be taken. Moreover, it is obvious that preservation is essential to the mission of any and every information institution, and that it is a long-term commitment. Whatever you do, I urge you not to undertake preservation as a here-today-gone-tomorrow priority, or to try to achieve a one-time, knock-out blow. Whatever you do, please don't swat the skunk!

Toward Developing a North American Preservation Program: The Chicago Preservation Planning Conference

Gerald J. Munoff

Deputy Director
University of Chicago Library

INTRODUCTION

The University of Chicago Library, with the cosponsorship of the Association of Research Libraries (ARL), convened an invitational Preservation Planning Conference in May 1992 in Chicago. Attending were the directors, preservation officers, and heads of collection development from sixteen ARL members with well-established preservation programs, and representatives of other organizations with a demonstrated interest in the preservation activities of research libraries.

The goal of the conference was to provide a forum that would significantly advance the planning for a North American preservation program for research libraries. The objectives were to identify the needs that must be addressed in a comprehensive cooperative program, and to develop a strategy for addressing those needs. While it was understood that such a program must ultimately include all types of libraries, participants' first responsibility was to define and articulate the needs of research collections.

This paper describes the issues and problems that gave rise to the idea for such a meeting, as well as the thinking and planning that led to the conference. It also provides a brief summary of conference deliberations and outcomes, and outlines the work that remains to be done if we are to realize the original goals.

INVENTING THE CONFERENCE

The idea for the conference was born out of my personal concern, beginning in 1990: while a number of key preservation issues were being discussed in a variety of forums by several groups of interested parties, little progress was being made on these points. Resolutions to complex questions were being sought when basic problems and definitions had not yet been agreed upon. While preservation programs continued to develop in response to specific local needs, there were insufficient opportunities to consider fundamental issues important to research libraries.

Despite the absence of a clear conceptual foundation, preservation operations in North American libraries have continued to grow. In 1990-91 ARL reported statistics on preservation activities of 117 of their members.[1] Of these, 55 ARL libraries had a full-time preservation administrator, and there were 1,744 full-time equivalent staff doing preservation work. Nearly $71 million was spent that year on preservation, only about $7 million of this sum from "external sources." Approximately 1 million conservation treatments were performed and 123,233 volumes were filmed.

This level of activity and expenditure indicates a need for more interlibrary coordination and collaboration. Many if not all of the components for a comprehensive North American preservation program already exist, and some have been developed to various degrees. The brittle books program is well-established and successful. With the leadership of the Commission on Preservation and Access and ARL, and funding from the National Endowment for the Humanities (NEH), much progress has been made in reformatting endangered materials. ARL and the Northeast Document Conservation Center (NEDCC) cosponsored a meeting that was critically important to the continued development of mass deacidification, and more attention is being given to physical treatment.

However, as these programs develop at the institutional, national, and international levels, it is increasingly clear that the relationships among them are not being adequately coordinated and managed. It is also clear that there is no uniform view of what a North American program should be. Thus, while these individual components continue to develop, the research library community must also systematically and comprehensively articulate and reach general agreement on the elements of a North American program, and how the relationships among these various activities will be managed.

A basic concept underlying all of these discussions is the need to distinguish between a genuine program and a group of federally-funded projects. A comprehensive preservation program for research libraries must consider all the defined needs of research collections throughout North America, regardless of the source of funds used to address these needs. There may be components of such a program for which federal funds are inappropriate, or elements in which communication and coordination are more important than funding. Research libraries' needs must be defined based on programmatic merit, so that questions about the source of funds or the appropriate use of federal money can be addressed subsequently, as an implementation issue. Only then can a true North American program be realized.

Contributing to the overall problem was the absence of an arena in which people with different organizational perspectives could discuss these issues and deal with fundamental questions. Hence, the solution proposed was a conference to bring together directors, heads of collection development, and preservation officers from research libraries that had developed large preservation programs, as well as representatives from other institutions concerned about preservation issues in research libraries. From discussions in many meetings and with a number of people, it seemed clear that it was time to take this next step.

PLANNING AND ORGANIZING THE CONFERENCE

I first discussed the idea of the conference with Martin Runkle, Director of the University of Chicago Library, who supported my idea and efforts to develop the conference. In order to ensure that finances were not an impediment, we agreed that the University of Chicago Library would shoulder all expenses, including meeting rooms, meals, facilitators, and materials, as well as lodging for participants. Subsequently, contributions to help defray the costs of the conference were given by several institutions (Johns Hopkins University, Stanford University, the University of Michigan, the New York Public Library, the University of California at Berkeley, and the University of Texas at Austin).

Next the idea for a conference was discussed with a number of people. Early supporters were Duane Webster, Executive Director of ARL; Patricia Battin, President of the Commission on Preservation and Access; George F. Farr, Jr., Director of NEH's Division of Preservation and Access; and a number of ARL directors, preservation officers, and collection development officers. At the October 1991 ARL meeting, I explained our plans to hold the conference to the Committee on Preservation of Research Materials and asked for their endorsement of ARL's cosponsorship. The committee enthusiastically supported the proposal, and the ARL Board approved it.

Assisting in planning the conference were Duane Webster and Jutta Reed-Scott, ARL Senior Program Officer for Preservation and Collections Services, together with two University of Chicago Library staff members, Sherry Byrne, Preservation Librarian, and William Garrity, Assistant to the Director. Susan Jurow, Director of the ARL Office of Management Services, agreed to facilitate the conference and contributed much to its organization and structure.

To keep the group to a productive size, the invitation list was developed using criteria based on ARL preservation statistics. Invitations were issued and we received an overwhelmingly positive response, confirming our assessment of the timeliness of the conference. It was announced that, in addition to those who received an invitation, any ARL director who wished to attend would be welcome. A number of faculty members were also invited, but none was able to attend.

Next, an Advisory Committee to help define the objectives of the conference, make recommendations about its structure, and serve as a leadership group during the meeting was appointed. I chaired the committee and its members included Millicent Abell (Yale), Scott Bennett (Johns Hopkins),

Margaret Child (preservation consultant), David Farrell (Berkeley), Anthony Ferguson (Columbia), Carolyn Clark Morrow (Harvard), Jutta Reed-Scott (ARL), William Studer (Ohio State), and Sherry Byrne (Chicago).

The libraries that were represented at the conference were:
> University of California, Berkeley
> University of Chicago
> Columbia University
> Cornell University
> Harvard University
> Johns Hopkins University
> Library of Congress
> University of Michigan
> National Library of Medicine
> New York Public Library
> Northwestern University
> Ohio State University
> Stanford University
> University of Texas at Austin
> University of Toronto
> Yale University

Interested organizations that sent a representative were:
> American Association of Law Libraries (AALL)
> Association of Research Libraries (ARL)
> Center for Research Libraries (CRL)
> Commission on Preservation and Access
> Council on Library Resources (CLR)
> Harry Ransom Humanities Research Center, University
> of Texas at Austin
> Research Libraries Group (RLG)
> School of Library Service, Columbia University

This was an unprecedented gathering to discuss preservation. The mix of attendees (including a high level of participation by directors) ensured that we were well-positioned to make progress toward an enduring and comprehensive cooperative preservation program that would integrate well with local efforts. It would be important that cooperative national preservation activities become an integral part of our libraries' ongoing activities, rather than a periodic special effort.

We needed to take full advantage of the conference and focus our attention on those items that were not only of the highest priority, but also those which would have the broadest impact and enable further activities to be developed. Obviously, there was much more work that needed to be done than we could possibly accomplish in the time allotted. Many important items were placed outside the scope of this planning conference. It was necessary for the agenda to be selective, while also remaining flexible and responsive.

THE PRECONFERENCE QUESTIONNAIRE

The conference was intended to articulate what a North American program should be, develop consensus, identify areas that needed more attention, and formulate plans for implementation. In order to build a focused agenda, we developed a preconference questionnaire which was mailed to each participant. The circular solicited their views of a potential mission and goals for the program, identified key issues and components and their relative priority, explored which elements required management and coordination, and asked for anticipated conference outcomes.

The questionnaire generated a good response. Everyone answered either individually or in a consolidated reply with colleagues. Many commented on how informative and valuable it had been for their institutional team to sit down together and complete the questionnaire. The circular was successful in provoking thought and discussion, and elicited a wide variety of ideas. The participants held many common views on which we planned to build, as a basis for forging cooperative approaches and striving to achieve a high degree of consensus. A summary of the questionnaire responses, giving both the full range and emphasis of the comments, was sent to the participants before the conference so that everyone was fully informed and could consider all the issues raised.

Based on the responses to the questionnaire, we formulated these three agenda items that were fundamental to other considerations, and proposed that participants take the time necessary to reach consensus on each item before proceeding.

1. Develop and articulate a clear vision of what research libraries hope to accomplish collectively in preservation. Produce a statement that is explicit and sufficiently detailed to provide a framework and context for the many and varied activities that must follow from it.
2. Agree on a coordination strategy that articulates what research libraries hope to accomplish and how we intend to go about it. Consideration may also be given to a specific mechanism, if there is time.
3. Agree on the major components of a cooperative plan and determine the items that are most critical or of the highest priority.

With this as our basic agenda we had a starting point to begin our difficult task. It was up to the conferees how far we would progress, but the group was well designed to deliberate these issues. If we could reach consensus and commit ourselves to accomplishing these things, the necessary groundwork would be laid to allow continued systematic progress.

Susan Jurow facilitated our discussions and the Conference Advisory Committee continued to help shepherd progress throughout the conference. However, the purpose of the conference remained to provide a forum for those individuals and institutions who have a substantial commitment to preservation to decide for themselves what the future direction of our preservation efforts should be. The conference brought together 54 experienced people with a variety of perspectives. The following is a brief account of the conference proceedings; it is based on a summary of the conference written by William Garrity.[2] A reading of the complete summary is necessary for an understanding of the full breadth and depth of the deliberations.

THE STRUCTURE OF THE CONFERENCE

The aim of the conference was to document our agreements and differences, as well as the further work that was required to achieve a comprehensive preservation program for North American research libraries. The conference was structured to facilitate this goal, yet was flexible enough to allow shifts and changes as the meeting progressed. Participants were assigned to small groups to work on specific items, and each small group reported to the larger body of all participants.

To achieve the goals of the conference, we progressed from *vision statement*, to *key issues*, to *operational components*, to *action planning*. The objective for the meeting's first day was to develop a vision statement on which participants could agree, raising all associated issues that required discussion. Later, after developing this statement, participants considered key issues and identified program components. We did not focus on the components of the general preservation environment, but rather on the particular parts that involve shared, coordinated activities. Finally, after the group identified these program components, it discussed options for their coordination and management.

GENERATING A VISION STATEMENT

The conference began with participants immediately gathering in small groups to write vision statements for a North American cooperative preservation program for research libraries. Groups were asked to develop and articulate what they thought research libraries should hope to accomplish collectively in preservation in the next five to 10 years. Participants were encouraged to begin fresh, set aside biases, track their disagreements, think broadly, and consider the points of view of all interested groups (readers, collection builders, preservation administrators, etc.).

The large group of all conference participants then discussed each small group's vision statement, as well as the commonalities and differences among them. Finally, several members of the Advisory Committee drafted a conference vision statement and presented it to participants for approval. After two subsequent iterations and discussion, we arrived at the following:

Vision Statement for a North American Preservation Program for Research Libraries

Preserving our intellectual heritage for current and future generations of users is a collective and constant responsibility of North American research libraries. The scope of the preservation problem is such that the most effective effort is a coordinated preservation program that responds both to local and shared needs. The program must make information available in the most appropriate way, which may vary from discipline to discipline. A North American preservation program would coordinate the stewardship activities of individual libraries and encourage the integration of preservation with other library activities. The program would be international in scope, and responsive to activities where economies of scale, standardization, and other benefits of cooperative action may be realized. The program would encourage research and development, and application of technology to preservation. It would advance partnerships among research libraries, users, resource allocators, and others to identify problems and implement solutions.

More specifically, the program would:
- Create a set of widely shared understandings about key issues in preservation.
- Require a set of operational components.
- Have outcomes that satisfy the needs which mandated the program.
- Depend on coordinated leadership.

It was clear to conference participants that there are problems an individual institution cannot solve with the resources available to it, so there is reason to discuss a coordinated North American program and how it might respond to those needs.

DEVELOPING THE KEY ISSUES

In the next stage of the conference, participants addressed key issues, focusing on the potential conflicts between local activity and what is happening (or can happen) at national levels in the United States and Canada. In our discussion we cited tensions over individual institution's responsibilities in a North American program, as well as those between institutional and group needs, preventive and remedial measures, and preservation of and access to information.

Participants identified a number of major issues. One was internal resource allocation in libraries: the way in which an institution allocates its resources reflects the priority of preservation for that institution. Another issue was selection of materials for preservation: since not all research library materials can be saved, what are the criteria for selection and funding for preservation? Participants also discussed the related issues of preservation of electronic media, digitization as a preservation technology, and paper as an archival medium.

Other issues covered by participants included the need for support from the public (and whether or not it is a matter of public policy—a public good—to preserve research library collections) and the limited number and focus of funding sources. The full list of key issues included:

- Internal resource allocation (the tension between developing collections and preserving collections)
- Selection for preservation (priorities, how to select, options for preservation action)
- Balance (local versus broader, North American needs)
- Participants in a North American program (who are they, and what are their responsibilities?)
- Paper and its viability as an archival medium
- Electronic formats as archival media and the viability of digital preservation
- Technology
- Balance between remedial and preventive measures
- Preservation versus access
- Time as an imperative
- Cost models (one way of understanding choices about preservation)
- Access models
- International concerns

DETERMINING THE OPERATIONAL COMPONENTS

Conference participants next progressed to discussing the operational components that should exist in a comprehensive North American preservation program, focusing on the critical need for each element and on the nature of the coordination, leadership, and management it required. Through small and large group discussions we identified these as important components:

- Training and education
- Research and its interpretation
- Standards
- Management information needs
- Bibliographic access (knowing what has been preserved and how it has been treated)
- Coordination
- User involvement
- Infrastructure
- Collaboration with others involved in preservation (commercial firms, international efforts, other interested agencies)
- Effective public policy and advocacy (building North American consensus; effecting public policy for preservation)
- Fund raising
- Selection (including reader involvement)

HOW SHOULD A NORTH AMERICAN PRESERVATION PROGRAM BE MANAGED?

"Coordinated leadership" and "management" were initially omitted from the list of operational components, since they were to be addressed after the other elements had been discussed and it was determined how they needed to be administered. Then, conference participants were asked to consider the list of potential activities and to determine what kinds of coordination, leadership, and management they required. Options for management or coordination ranged from the status quo (defining the aggregate of present activities as the operational component of the North American program), to establishing a body that would coordinate individual activities, to forming an organization whose responsibility it was to carry out the operational component. Particular attention was given to what already exists: there might already be adequate resources, or perhaps existing resources could be strengthened, to accomplish what needs to be done.

The large group discussion began with an appeal from one participant that the group discuss how its goals and objectives related to the Commission on Preservation and Access (CPA). If the group were looking to the Commission to take the leadership role in a North American program, was the Commission properly conceived and constituted to do this? If the group instead foresaw more of a partnership, this would raise other important implications for how it should plan to implement the work of the conference. On the other hand, if the group saw no role for the Commission, then that should also be discussed.

A number of the small groups discussed a coordinating body based on the Coalition for Networked Information (CNI) model. However, if an existing organization like the Commission were to transform itself to fit that model, problems could ensue: for example, the Commission might sacrifice the speed with which it is able to address issues if it had members to whom it was accountable. Then a question arose concerning the value and promise of increased coordination, sharing, and cooperation. Did conference participants really believe that much more could be done by way of collaboration, and that a new mechanism must be found to accomplish this? Responses to this fundamental question included the following:

- Collective thinking educates, legitimizes, and stimulates growth and development.
- Conference participants know that progress has been made in preserving materials, yet they continue to develop lists of things that need to be done. The call for greater coordination of effort indicates that participants are not satisfied with current progress, and that something different should be tried.
- If there is consensus, the community will have a stronger political voice, which leads to better use of existing funds and helps to secure additional funds from other sources. It will be difficult to achieve consensus without working together.
- If a North American preservation program is the aggregate of the roles of the players, then a better organized, coordinated, and cooperative effort with greater visibility will attract additional players (the "band wagon effect").

Some of the discussion focused on lessons that might be learned from RLG. Does RLG successfully facilitate close coordination and collaboration for the common good of its members? If not, why not? Conferees were encouraged not to underestimate how difficult it can be to achieve consensus: as organizations such as RLG have grown larger, they have found it more difficult to arrive at consensus.

Other points of discussion in the large group concerning operational components included:

- The community needs to plan how to preserve the information and knowledge carried by multimedia technologies.
- It is essential to build public awareness and to secure better funding; this undergirds everything else. There is a need to build the rationale that preservation of research library resources is a public good and is worthy of increased public funding.
- It is important to avoid redundancy in what is preserved, both for the sake of credibility with funding agencies and

in order to obtain maximum results from limited resources.
- What is an adequate level of funding, if what is now available is not enough? There are no ready answers other than "a lot more than what is now available."
- Discussions need to include the entire community taking part in the preservation effort, remembering the players that did not attend the conference.
- A goal for a comprehensive North American preservation program should be significant progress in rescuing endangered materials. If, over time, progress is not made, if the preservation problem continues to grow, as seems to be the case, then not enough is being done.

ACTION PLANNING

We concluded the conference by considering the organizational options for providing an ongoing forum to discuss preservation. Three proposals were discussed: maintain the status quo; work within a structure that already exists (ARL, CPA, and RLG were the chief possibilities); or establish a new organization, perhaps a coalition for preservation similar to the Coalition for Networked Information.

Establish A New Organization

Participants cited the following characteristics desirable in a new entity, if one were to be established:
- Broad-based, representing a wide range of interests
- Accountable, by being membership-based
- Inclusive, involving people with a variety of roles (preservation librarian, collection development librarian, scholar)
- Encouraging various levels of participation
- Providing a sense of community (homogeneous organizations may be able to accomplish more)
- Encouraging collective decision making and priority setting

Participants expressed concerns about establishing yet another association. Organizations have substantial costs, both direct and indirect (the latter including the time working librarians devote to collaborative efforts). The community must be certain that another group will produce valuable outcomes, rather than serving as just another administrative apparatus.

The Coalition Model

A preservation coalition would be a membership organization with broad representation; as a coalition, it would enable institutions to buy into the North American program, yet avoid creating a large organization to run it (the association would have a secretariat or other small central staff). The coalition would be a collaborating group of libraries, institutions, and organizations, private and public sector, international and national, whose members would drive activities.

The group learned how CNI, a potential model, was established: the three member organizations (ARL, CAUSE, and EDUCOM) felt that there was more work to be done in computer networking than any of them could do individually. The notion of a coalition grew out of informal discussions among leaders from the three groups, and ARL was able to provide the legal and organizational framework, as well as key staff.

Participants wondered if library directors would extend the resources to support a coalition for preservation. (Unlike with CNI, whose dues are generally divided between an institution's library and its computer center, support for a preservation coalition would likely come exclusively from the library.)

Work Within a Structure that Already Exists

Another option was to bring the North American preservation program to an existing organization, asking it to set new goals. Some of the potential plans were thought to be well-suited to organizations that are presently active. One option was to have the Conference Advisory Committee approach existing entities to inquire with which items these agencies could help.

The organizations that were identified included:
American Institute for Conservation of Historic and
    Artistic Works (AIC)
American Library Association (ALA)
Association of Research Libraries (ARL)
Commission on Preservation and Access (CPA)
Center for Research Libraries (CRL)
Library of Congress (LC)
National Archives and Records Administration (NARA)
National Endowment for the Humanities (NEH)
National Historical Publications and Records Commission
    (NHPRC)
National Library of Medicine (NLM)
Online Computer Library Center (OCLC)
Research Libraries Group (RLG)
Society of American Archivists (SAA)
Southeastern Library Network (SOLINET)

Although organizations like SAA and AIC would not be appropriate because of their narrower focus, all the above were cited by respondents to the preconference questionnaire as having elements of activity and structure useful to coordinating and managing a North American program. ARL and CPA were suggested as the two organizations most likely to be able to do something constructive with the conference discussions; these ideas were also put forward:

RLG as Sponsoring Organization: Make RLG the sponsoring organization; it has expertise and experience with preservation. For this model to be successful, institutions that are not members of RLG must be allowed to join the effort. (It is also possible that some RLG institutions would see a separate organization outside of RLG as competitive, and would not join it.)

Establish a Think Tank: It is true that the North American preservation program for research libraries is not yet perfectly defined, and it might be difficult for existing organizations to respond to the many ideas for action. Therefore, establish a think tank enterprise (or a series of think tanks) to discuss and clarify the issues articulated above, such as selection, paper as an archival medium, and the balance or tension between preservation and access, in order to clarify the agenda.

This idea, however, is not an action proposal that will actively move the preservation program forward; it is instead a mechanism to continue the discussion of certain issues. (White papers might also be written and presented to existing agencies.)

The Commission as Sponsoring Organization: CPA will work to further clarify issues (perhaps by convening a think tank itself), define the plan for action, and then convene another North American meeting. The Commission may or may not need to redefine itself as a membership organization to accomplish this.

ARL Creates a Group: ARL will create a new body, perhaps a group of research libraries concerned with preservation; this group will interact with the Commission and other organizations.

A TASK FORCE IS ESTABLISHED

Conference participants agreed that some ongoing forum to discuss preservation at the policy level was needed by the research library community, and that existing organizations, for various reasons, did not fully provide it. (One reason the conference was convened was that there was no such forum.) Conferees were uncertain whether or not a new organization might be necessary, but they felt some opportunity for continuing discussion must be created. Participants did not thoroughly discuss what the new platform should be, since they did not yet have a full view of what was to be accomplished. While the need for coherent and forceful action on a variety of issues was accepted, it was decided that the appropriate organizational structure could only be determined after the issues were further defined and developed.

Thus, we decided that a task force would be formed to develop options and present them at a later date to the conference participants. This smaller group was asked to consider process (how decisions can best be made), rather than to determine the content of the program; it was also to develop options for each of the issues articulated during the conference, and recommend how priorities might be set.

The conference participants gave the following general charge to the task force, but agreed to leave the formulation of the final charge to the group itself:

- Review the conference documentation to identify key issues that are now inadequately served.
- Review existing activities to ensure inclusion of all activities relevant to the agenda.
- Define the scope of the community for a comprehensive preservation program.
- Set in motion a mechanism to develop a strategic plan.
- Define alternatives for forums to discuss priorities for research library preservation activity decision-making.
- Formulate a draft agenda for the forum.
- Define alternative mechanisms for acting on priorities.
- Make an interim report at or through the October 1992 ARL Preservation Committee meeting.

The task force is accountable to the conference participants and will submit its report to them, perhaps in a second conference, relying on the deliberations of the conference and the needs and issues that were identified therein. It is to develop these issues further, and design specific proposals that sort through the various options. The nature of the task force's discussions and deliberations will suggest the next steps.

After considerable discussion of how to ensure the task force was adequately supported so that it could accomplish its work, the conference participants delegated to the members of the ARL Committee on Preservation of Research Materials who were present at the conference the determination of the membership of the task force. It was agreed that the role of the ARL preservation committee is to provide organizational support; it is not a mechanism through which the task force reports, nor an oversight organization.

POST-CONFERENCE ACTIVITY

The conference concluded with a great deal of enthusiasm and optimism about the potential for continued progress in building a North American preservation program. The members of the ARL preservation committee who were present met immediately after the conference adjourned and developed a list of task force members. Appointed to the task force were Ross Atkinson (Cornell), Patricia Battin (Commission on Preservation and Access), Kenneth Harris (Library of Congress), Jan Merrill-Oldham

(University of Connecticut), Carole Moore (Toronto), Carolyn Clark Morrow (Harvard), Barclay Odgen (Berkeley), Eugene Wiemers (Northwestern), and Martin Runkle (Chicago), chair.

Documentation needed by the task force in order to begin its work was produced and a summary of the conference was written, reviewed in draft form by the task force members, and distributed to each conference participant and others who requested copies. The task force met in August 1992 and reported on its progress at the ARL meeting the following October. Robert Street (Stanford University) became chair of the task force in June 1993. A draft report was written and submitted to the ARL Board in May 1994.

A report to the conference participants is very important. As was discussed at the conference, it may be desirable for the conference participants to reconvene to discuss the report and act upon its recommendations.

CONCLUSION

The conference was successful as an unprecedented effort to bring together a core group of people, all responsible for the preservation of collections in large research libraries to discuss the collective preservation needs of North American materials. Issues were identified and a structure was established to pursue available options, strategies, and a decision-making model.

It was never anticipated that the conference would provide immediate solutions for any of the preservation problems that research libraries face. The conference was intended as a point of departure and a catalyst. Preservation issues affect a wide range of institutions and people, and there are important roles for many groups in identifying solutions. However, it was important for those primarily responsible for preservation in the research library community to come together in a way that has not occurred before, to think differently about the issues, to develop new perspectives, and to initiate a new process that will subsequently involve many others. The preservation of North America's important research materials is an enormous responsibility that can only be accomplished by a strong cooperative effort.

NOTES

1. Jutta Reed-Scott and Nicola Daval, *ARL Preservation Statistics 1990-91* (Washington, D.C.: Association of Research Libraries, 1992).
2. William F. Garrity, *Preservation Planning Conference Summary* (Chicago: University of Chicago Library, 1992).
3. Reed-Scott and Daval, 13.

PART 2:
SCIENCE AND TECHNOLOGY
ASSISTING PRESERVATION

The proper care, handling, and repair of library and archival materials are essential to their survival; however, modern science has given us many new tools with which to stabilize and preserve the information resources in our custody. In some cases, technology can be used to extend the lives of books, manuscripts, and other materials; in others, we use it to transfer the information these items contain to more stable or accessible media.

Providing a sound physical environment is the most basic preservation technique librarians and archivists can employ. In their paper about the mitigation of indoor air pollution, Randy Silverman, Constance Lundberg, and Delbert Eatough make the point that improvements in heating, ventilation, and air handling systems represent an excellent investment for any institution, because these affect the entire collection, reducing the risk of deterioration caused by air pollution. The authors review the literature of indoor air quality in libraries, describe a relatively inexpensive air sampling study conducted at two academic libraries during 1992, and examine the effectiveness of two different pollution filtration systems.

Mass deacidification represents another way in which new technologies can be used to address the preservation needs of entire collections in their original formats. Kristi Kiesling and James Stroud examine the logistics and technical issues associated with a two-year study of mass deacidification of archives and manuscript collections, including transportation, security, costs and cost centers, and the post-treatment review process. They identify the issues that must still be addressed before librarians and archivists can employ mass deacidification with complete confidence and analyze the arguments against mass deacidification. Because not all material types are suitable for mass deacidification, Kiesling and Stroud also explore selection philosophies and rationales.

Lee Jones describes his vision of the future of preservation microfilming, a technology he sees as both an end in itself, as well as a means to a different and equally important end. We are all familiar with the concept of microfilming as a way to preserve the information content of deteriorated or fragile paper-based materials; in his paper Jones describes the role of The MicrogrAphic Preservation Service (MAPS) in accomplishing and improving the quality of this work. He also examines the constraints, equipment, film, standards, and economics of preservation microfilming, describing contemporary advances in the technology and its materials. Jones goes beyond the traditional role of microfilming to suggest its added importance as an intermediate platform, significant for launching a variety of alternative formats, including paper and digital; he explores the ways in which high-quality preservation microfilms will be integrated into the new digital world.

Alan Fusonie and Richard Myers demonstrate that what some may think of as the electronic future is indeed the electronic present. In their paper they profile five optical disk projects (both digital and analog) designed to improve the long-term survival of valuable documentary resources; these projects incorporate both print and image collections, including photographs, slides, art works, posters, videotape, and motion picture film. Fusonie and Myers suggest that these applications may represent an effective solution to the longstanding conflict between access and preservation. In the future, image networking and high-capacity digital communication structures will extend the capacity for access even further.

Library Air Pollution: Sampling and Mitigation

Randy H. Silverman

Preservation Librarian
Marriott Library, University of Utah

Constance K. Lundberg

Associate Dean and Law Librarian
Brigham Young University

Delbert J. Eatough

Professor of Chemistry
Brigham Young University

INTRODUCTION

The deleterious effects of gaseous and particulate pollutants on museum[1, 2] and library[3, 4, 5, 6] collections are well documented, yet to date few libraries have begun to address the issue. To help increase awareness of current air quality detection and mitigation practices, this essay describes the experience of two libraries that identified and acted to moderate indoor gaseous pollutants.

Determining whether a library's gaseous or particulate pollutant levels are elevated is the essential first step if corrective measures are to be undertaken. At a minimum, knowledge of the local air quality can alert one to potentially serious pollution-related preservation problems.

Outdoor pollution levels have a direct effect on indoor pollution, although there is no simple one-to-one correlation. For example, Druzik et al. demonstrated that ozone concentrations in 11 museums, art galleries, historical houses, and a museum library in Los Angeles were dramatically higher in well-ventilated buildings without air-conditioning systems than in air-conditioned buildings.[7] Additionally, some indoor building surfaces (such as wallpaper[8]) absorb gaseous pollutants while others (including new concrete,[9] fresh carpeting and oil-base paint,[10] plywood,[11] and urea-formaldehyde foam insulation[12]) release them.

Techniques for mitigating indoor gaseous pollutants vary in expense and complexity. These include:

1. Limiting the rate of makeup (or outside) air during periods of heavy pollution (i.e., in Los Angeles, limiting air-exchange between 8:00 a.m. and 5:00 p.m. when pollution levels are highest, and maximizing air-exchange in the evenings).[13]

2. Controlling indoor sources that generate gaseous pollutants (through the choice of raw materials used in new
furnishings and construction, the application of sealants
to prevent excessive off-gassing in existing materials,
and the improvement of existing ventilation systems).
3. Installing gaseous and particulate filtration equipment in
restricted areas such as display cases, storage rooms or
collection areas.
4. Installing gaseous and particulate filtration equipment in
the library's heating, ventilating, and cooling (HVAC)
system to address the problem building-wide.[14]

It should be noted that even the most costly of these mitigation options—building-wide pollution filtration—is not exorbitantly expensive
when compared with normal installation and maintenance costs of an
HVAC system operated for human comfort.

A BRIEF HISTORY OF POLLUTION DETECTION

Current awareness of air pollution and acid rain make these problems appear to be linked to the industrialization of the 19th and 20th centuries.
However, historical evidence suggests the problem is much older, with the
first investigation into air quality conducted in 1284 by a Royal Commission
in London.[15] Little is known of the outcome of this early work, and further
evidence of pollution studies does not appear in the literature for over three
centuries. Interest was revived in the second half of the 17th century in
England, however, because of increasing urban smoke problems resulting
from the widespread shift from wood and charcoal consumption to the use of
coal.[16] John Evelyn, in his *Fumifugium* of 1661, describes early industrial
smog as "drawing a sable curtain over Heaven"[17] that "spreads a Yellowness
upon our choycest Pictures and hangings."[18] Coal use in London increased
2.5 times from 1680 to 1780, spurring the invention of the first antipollution
device by a member of the Royal Society of London in 1686,[19] followed by
the first air pollution regulation in the United Kingdom in 1814.[20]

By the end of the 19th century, librarians began noting problems relating
to the role of acidic gasses such as sulfur dioxide (SO_2) in the breakdown of
library materials. Printer and scholar William Blades[21] wrote in 1880 in his
Enemies of Books that the deleterious effect of his "triple gasalier" (gas
light) on the leather valance hanging above his window, "was, of course,
due to the sulfur in the gas fumes, which attacks [the leather known as] rus-
sia quickest, while calf and morocco suffer not quite so much."[22] Blades
went on to say, however, that "the paper of the volumes is uninjured,"[23]
leaving us to speculate that his well-meaning conclusions were, of necessity, limited to superficial observations.

Blades' opinion about the influence of gases on library collections was probably based on the research conducted by Michael Faraday and his associates earlier in the 19th century. Originally trained as a bookbinder, throughout his lifetime Faraday maintained a sufficient interest in the arts to participate in a number of studies pertaining to the deterioration of paintings caused by "coal gas" lighting in museums. Following his initial report to the House of Commons in 1850,[24] Faraday's Commission set up a second experiment comparing color shifts in a number of pigment and varnish samples exposed to 16 museum environments for a period of two years. In 1859 the Commission was overly optimistic, observing "no indications respecting the action of coal gas," but noted that seven of the samples did "show signs of chemical change in the fugitive white lead, due to either a town atmosphere, or want of ventilation." However, exercising great foresight, Faraday's Commission concluded that "this type of experiment. . .should be continued for a longer period, and indeed be carried out on a more extensive scale."[25]

In reaction to the rapid and widespread deterioration of leather bookbindings (commonly termed "red rot") at the beginning of the 20th century, the Society of Arts in London organized a subcommittee to investigate the problem. Composed of bookbinding luminaries such as T. J. Cobden-Sanderson, Douglas Cockerell, and Sarah Prideaux, this subcommittee tested various leather samples by subjecting them to aggressive levels of gas fumes, heat, and light to isolate the effects of different catalysts on the breakdown of leather.[26] Their conclusion—that sulfur was present as an impurity in natural gas, and that libraries with unventilated gas lighting were subjecting their collections to a steady source of sulfur dioxide (SO_2)—is consistent with the modern view that SO_2 is easily oxidized into SO_3 (sulfur trioxide), which can in turn combine with atmospheric moisture to form sulfuric acid (H_2SO_4).[27] Underscoring their concern for a problem that lacked a technical solution until the introduction of electric lighting, the subcommittee found "that of the deleterious influences to which books are subjected, the fumes of burnt gas are the most fatal."[28]

Although advances in lighting technology over the next 30 years brought cleaner environments to libraries, Kimberly and Emley of the United States National Bureau of Standards (NBS) still suspected that air quality remained a key to achieving collection permanence. Their testing in 1933 revealed that book papers stored in urban, heavily polluted environments were more deteriorated than books stored in clean rural environments.[29] Concurrently, they investigated pragmatic methods for removing SO_2 from the library environment, settling on the use of an alkaline-wash system.[30] Air washing with misted water was designed as a component to be added to the building-wide air conditioners invented by Willis Carrier in 1902.[31] Air conditioners gained increased popularity and application during the 1930s because of improved cooling efficiency resulting from the use of Freon™.[32]

The Folger Shakespeare Library in Washington, D.C. installed the first alkaline-wash system in the 1930s, but discontinued its use soon after because of mechanical problems.[33] Taking advantage of advances in this technology, the National Gallery of Art installed an alkaline scrubbing system in 1941[34] that operated until its replacement by more sophisticated equipment in 1983.[35] To date, however, very few libraries in the United States have installed gaseous filtration equipment. These include the Newberry Library, the Library of Congress Madison Building, the New York Public Library's Bryant Park expansion, the south stack area of Green Library at Stanford University, and the Special Collections of Teacher's College in New York.[36] This limited use of gaseous pollution filtration equipment in libraries seems to stem from three factors: a lack of familiarity with the technology, an assumption that the detection and mitigation of gaseous pollutants is prohibitively expensive, and a general lack of awareness that indoor air pollutants cause the deterioration of library materials.

EFFECTS OF GASEOUS POLLUTANTS ON LIBRARY MATERIALS

A large part of what is known about the effects of air pollution on collection permanence has been learned recently, within the past 30 years. The research has focused almost exclusively on museum objects, explaining to some extent the current lack of awareness many librarians profess concerning the issue. However, many similarities exist between museum and library collections including like raw materials, the damage that occurs as a result of indoor air pollution, and the mitigation options available.

The gaseous pollutants considered the greatest threat to library materials today (as they were for museum objects when ranked by Garry Thomson in 1965 [37]) are sulfur dioxide (SO_2), nitrogen oxides (NO_x), and ozone (O_3). Recent research includes formaldehyde[38] in the list which might easily be expanded to include formic acid, acetic acid, hydrochloric acid, and hydrogen sulfide,[39] although these last four pollutants are outside the scope of this essay. Additionally, libraries and museums have long experienced housekeeping problems related to dust and airborne particles that are now considered conservation[40] as well as health concerns.[41]

Sulfur Dioxide

Sulfur dioxide (SO_2) is a common outdoor pollutant originating from five primary sources:
1. Fossil fuel combustion for the production of heat or electricity
2. Processing sulfide ores of nonferrous metals
3. Ferrous metal production including coke production and use

4. Oil refining and treatment of oil products

5. Sulfuric acid production from native sulphur[42]

SO_2 is pervasive throughout the industrialized world, notorious as one of the most studied and controlled pollutants.[43, 44] It is presently monitored on a continual basis in every metropolitan area of the United States.[45]

The deleterious effects of SO_2 on materials commonly found in libraries are well documented. Zeronian found that fabrics made from cellulose degraded in the presence of SO_2 in a reaction that resembled exposure to dilute sulfuric acid.[46] Brysson et al. calculated an increased rate of deterioration proportional to the amount of SO_2 to which samples of cotton duck were exposed.[47] Zeronian et al. also determined that the degradation of nylon fiber could be caused by SO_2 without first being converted into sulfuric acid.[48]

Surprisingly small quantities of SO_2 and its byproducts are capable of destroying the connective bonds in paper's cellulose chains, causing paper to become discolored and brittle.[49] This form of breakdown may be one of the reasons the exposed outer edges of the textblock deteriorate faster than the center of the book, as suggested by Parker,[50] Hudson and Edwards,[51] Hudson,[52] and Smith.[53]

Spedding et al. reported that a variety of commercial leather samples exposed to SO_2 in conditions of high relative humidity absorbed the pollutant evenly across the leather's surface regardless of the location in the hide from which the sample was removed. This rate of absorption decreased if the leather's surface contained a finish or a dye.[54]

Nitrogen Oxides

Cotton textiles exposed to nitrogen oxides (NO_x) in sunlight have been shown to become weaker.[55] Consequently, researchers infer that NO_x may cause a similar deleterious effect to the cellulose in paper, although this chemical's effect on library material is presently not well understood. NO_2 is known to play a role in collection damage as a precursor of ozone and other photochemical oxidants.[56]

In the early 1970s Zeronian et al. found evidence that NO_2 had a deleterious effect on acrylic, nylon, and polyester fabrics.[57] Salvin et al. demonstrated that NO_2 causes fading of dyes in cellulose acetate fabrics.[58] Further, Whitmore and Cass observed measurable color changes in 10 of 12 organic and inorganic pigments on paper and silk exposed to NO_2, including a dramatic color shift in iron gall ink,[59] the most common manuscript ink prior to the 20th century.

Ozone

Ozone (O_3) is routinely associated with urban photochemical smog and has been linked to fading and color changes in textile dyes and the cracking of rubber.[60] Zeronian et al. reported in 1971 that O_3 damaged acrylic and nylon.[61] Bogaty et al. noted cellulose was damaged by exposure to O_3 in concentrations equal to those found in the earth's atmosphere, especially in conditions of high relative humidity.[62] Ozone is also known to participate in the formation of oxidants that convert sulfur dioxide (SO_2) to sulfuric acid (H_2SO_4), and nitrogen dioxide (NO_2) to nitric acid (HNO_3).

Examining the effects of ozone in concentrations equal to those found in photochemical smog, Shaver et al. reported in 1983 that watercolor pigments exposed to O_3 faded in the absence of light.[63] Salvin found that ozone caused fading in a wide range of dyes tested on various fabric substrata, a condition exacerbated by the presence of moisture.[64] Whitmore et al.[65] and Cass et al.[66] documented fading in a variety of Western and Japanese organic colorants on papers exposed to ozone.

Ozone (as well as peroxides and oxidizing gasses) has also been found to contribute to the formation of microspots (or microblemishes) on microfilm.[67, 68] Librarians in the Los Angeles basin where ozone levels are high, for example, have reported the formation of microspots that completely destroyed microfilm images in less than 10 years.[69]

Formaldehyde

Formaldehyde has been shown to cause deterioration in museum objects including lead coins and calcareous materials such as sea shells,[70] usually resulting from storage in formaldehyde-producing display cases or storage areas with limited air exchange. The effect of formaldehyde on components making up library materials—calcium and metallic ions in paper, for example—have yet to be evaluated. Its negative effects on health are well documented,[71, 72] however, as formaldehyde has been linked to "sick building syndrome."[73]

Gaseous Pollution and Deacidified Paper

In related work, Daniel et al. at the Centre de Recherches sur la Conservation des Documents Graphiques in Paris, examined papers deacidified by aqueous and nonaqueous means after exposure to gaseous pollutants to determine if the alkaline salts in deacidified paper caused increased absorption of acidic pollutants. Their finding caused considerable concern, because, according to Daniel, certain deacidified papers might "suffer. . .greater deterioration. . .if deacidified than if not."[74]

Grosjean and Associates, under contract to the Getty Conservation Institute (GCI), independently corroborated this work in 1990,[75, 76] but interpreted the results differently. Summarizing Grosjean's research, Peter G. Sparks hypothesized that the increased concentrations of SO_2 and NO_2 in deacidified papers might indicate that pollutants were bonding with the alkaline salts deposited in the paper as a result of deacidification, leaving minimal amounts of free gas available to attack cellulose. In other words, the buffering achieved by deacidification was protecting the paper from external sources of acidity as it was designed to do.[77]

Particles

Dust and particles inside libraries have long been known to produce an overall "dinginess."[78] If the source of the particulate matter is coal- or oil-based, permanent dark staining can result.[79] Attempts to characterize the deposition of particles within buildings are extremely recent[80] and to date are exclusively museum-oriented. Through modeling, Nazaroff and Cass demonstrated the variety of forces at work allowing particles to be deposited on walls (including hanging works of art) and ceilings.[81] Besides the problem of exposed surfaces becoming darkened (such as Michelangelo's frescoes on the Sistine Chapel ceiling), dust containing microbial contamination can cause surface abrasion to the inner leaves of books as it filters from the outer edges into the textblock as a result of use.

Mitigation

In a simulated museum environment, Gibbons et al. successfully modeled the removal of SO_2 using carbon filters.[82] In 1984, Hackney reported installing activated carbon filters in the Tate Gallery in London that virtually eliminated SO_2 from the air-conditioned sections of the building.[83] Cass et al. also "found that activated carbon air purification systems can effectively eliminate more than 90% of the ozone from the indoor air under actual museum operating conditions."[84] Williams and Grosjean tested two types of activated carbon and three types of permanganate-impregnated alumina (PIA) in a laboratory setting, finding carbon out-performed PIA for a broad range of pollutants.[85]

Sparks noted in 1991 that when using an HVAC system, "oxides of nitrogen $[NO_x]$ are far more difficult to chemically filter out than sulfur dioxide $[SO_2]$."[86] For example, in 1990 Salmon et al. found that in two Los Angeles museums—one filtered with activated carbon, the other lacking any gaseous pollution filtration capability—concentrations of nitric acid (HNO_3, an oxidation product of NO_2) were equally deposited onto the interior surfaces of both buildings (i.e., ventilation system, ceiling tiles, and collection) rather than effectively removed by the filtration system.[87]

Dust in the building may be related to problems with HVAC maintenance practices. Upgrading the rated efficiency of existing bag filters and manually installing filtration media in the air diffusers (air vents) at the individual room level can help eliminate the problem of excess dust. Further, while it is true that particle filters operate more effectively when they are dirty (because the collected dirt helps restrict the passage of additional dirt), changing extra-dirty filters can result in large amounts of dust being shed directly back into the HVAC system—and the collection—emphasizing the need for a regular maintenance schedule.

CURRENT NATIONAL RECOMMENDATIONS FOR ARCHIVAL STORAGE

Indoor air quality standards for the archival storage of library materials are currently limited to the American National Standards Institute (ANSI) standards for storage of processed safety film,[88] processed photographic plates,[89] and black-and-white photographic paper prints.[90]

In the absence of standards that address overall air quality requirements for the storage of library and archival collections, the Committee on Preservation of Historical Records[91] and the National Bureau of Standards[92] have each published recommended guidelines. These recommendations prescribe indoor pollution levels that are considerably more stringent than the current National Ambient Air Quality Standards designed to safeguard human health.[93] NISO draft standards for environmental storage of paper-based records in libraries and archives have been proposed,[94] but as of this writing these proposed standards have not yet been ratified. However, the cumulative data listed above are quite useful when attempting to specify library indoor air quality requirements for materials preservation. [TABLE 1]

AIR SAMPLING AT TWO UNIVERSITY LIBRARIES IN PROVO, UTAH

Brigham Young University's two research libraries, the Harold B. Lee Library and the J. Reuben Clark Law Library, engaged in planning for major building additions in 1992-93 with the expectation of breaking ground within a five-year period. In establishing the priorities for the project, building planners were forced to determine how important the control of gaseous pollutants and airborne particles were to the goals of the libraries. The answer to this question (which originated with the Preservation Department) was unravelled by addressing four additional questions:

1. What level of air quality is required for optimal preservation of library material?
2. If air pollutants are undermining the permanence of the collection, which are being brought in from the outside and which are generated within the building itself?
3. How effective are the various configurations of gaseous pollution filtration systems and the different types of filtration media?
4. What level of financial commitment—both initial and ongoing—is the institution willing to expend to protect its collections from gaseous and particulate pollutants?

SOURCE OF RECOMMENDATION	GASEOUS POLLUTANT LIMITS			PARTICULATE REMOVAL	
	SO_2	NO_2	O_3		
	Primary	Primary & Secondary	Primary & Secondary	Primary	Secondary
Environmental Protection Agency	80 µg/m^3 (30.6 ppb) ann. avg. 365 µg/m^3 (139.4 ppb) max. 24 hrs. Secondary 1300 µg/m^3 (496.6 ppb) 3 hr. cncentrtn.	100 µg/m^3 (53 ppb) ann. avg.	235 µg/m^3 (120 ppb) hourly avg.	150 µg/m^3 24 hour average	50 µg/m^3 annual average
National Bureau of Standards	1 µg/m^3 (0.4 ppb)	5 µg/m^3 (2.5 ppb)	25 µg/m^3 (13 ppb)	75 µg/m^3 TSP (HiVol)	

Table 1 - Recommended Indoor Pollutant Levels for Libraries and Archives

ASHRAE Weight Arrestance Effeciency

SOURCE OF RECOMMENDATION	SO_2 Primary	NO_2 Primary & Secondary	O_3 Primary & Secondary	Prefilter[a]	Intermediate filter[b]	Fine filter[b]
American National Standards Institute-Draft Standard Proposal	≤1 µg/m^3 (0.4 ppb)	No standard	≤ 2 µg/m^3 (1 ppb)	≥ 80%	≥ 95%	No standard
National Research Council	≤ 1 µg/m^3 (0.4 ppb)	Best available technology	≤ 2 µg/m^3 (1 ppb)	≥ 80%	≥ 95%	No standard

Key: ASHRAE- American Society of Heating, Refrigeration, and Air Conditioning Engineers
TSP-Total Suspended Particulates
[a]For outside or makeup air.
[b]For supply (both outside and recirculated) air.

Source: Data courtesy: Cf. 40 C.F.R. §50.4, 50.5, 50.6, 50.9, 50.11; Norbert S. Baer and Paul N. Banks, "Indoor Air Pollution: Effects on Cultural and Historic Materials," The International Journal of Museum Management and Curatorship 4 (1985), 17; and National Research Council, Preservation of Historical Records (Washington, DC: National Academy Press, 1986), 26-27.

Table 1

Unfortunately, the first question is impossible to answer precisely with what is currently known about the effects of pollutants on library material. Established guidelines (such as those listed in Table 1) are based upon "qualitative or even anecdotal" data according to Baer and Banks,[95] revealing a significant body of research still needing to be conducted before precise "quantitative relationships between pollutant concentration levels and damage"[96] can be defined.

Identifying pollutants in the ambient air, on the other hand, is a relatively simple matter. All states are required to measure ambient levels of the "criteria" pollutants—sulfur dioxide (SO_2), nitrogen oxides (NO_x), ozone (O_3), carbon monoxide (CO), lead, and particulate matter measuring 10 microns or less in diameter (PM-10).[97] The State of Utah Department of Health,

Bureau of Air Quality, for example, provided the University with complete copies of its annual air-pollution monitoring reports for the previous five years. These data revealed all the pollutants listed above (other than lead) in the Provo area exceeded recommended limits for library preservation.[98] Mathematical models for predicting indoor pollution concentrations based on outdoor monitoring exist and can provide more precise information,[99] but the initial evidence alone was convincing; the collections were indeed threatened. [TABLE 2]

A more accurate method of measuring the concentrations of indoor pollutants—active air sampling—requires drawing samples from the immediate vicinity outside the building and comparing them with samples taken from various locations within the library itself. The authors designed and conducted such a program for the Lee and the Law libraries in the winter of 1992. Brigham Young University's (BYU) Department of Chemistry contributed the equipment and analysis, requiring the libraries to pay only the out-of-pocket staff costs for the tests. Consequently, the total expense for the work was much less than its fair market value.

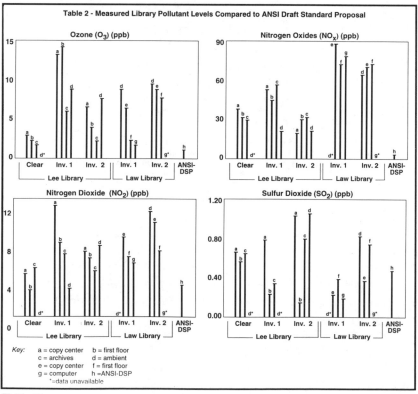

Table 2

The monitoring concentrated on pollutants identified in the national guidelines as creating significant preservation problems: sulfur dioxide (SO_2), oxides of nitrogen (NO_x), and ozone (O_3), although measurements for nitrogen dioxide, gas phase nitric acid, particulate nitrate, particulate sulfate, particulate acidity, and gas phase ammonia were taken as well. Monitoring within the libraries was done in low traffic areas of the stacks, as well as densely populated public service areas, student computer centers, and copy centers. Samples were taken during periods of winter inversion when ambient pollution levels were high and, by contrast, immediately after the passing of a weather front when ambient pollution levels were low. Samples were obtained throughout the day to account for differences in traffic patterns and other human activity. Test results were subsequently reported in *Proceedings of the International Conference on Measurements of Toxic and Related Air Pollutants of the Air and Waste Management Association.*[100]

In conjunction with the active air sampling tests, ChemSense passive dosimeters (manufactured by Advanced Optochemical Research, Inc., and supplied by the Getty Conservation Institute, or GCI) were used to field-test the hypothesis that these devices, usually used to detect pollutants in the workplace that pose potential human health risks, might be effective in detecting pollutants within a library environment.[101] Interest in testing the effectiveness of commercially available dosimeters was connected with GCI's interest in identifying inexpensive yet accurate methods for sampling indoor air quality to prevent conservators from having to resort to more expensive active air sampling procedures. Three of the types of dosimeters tested were calibrated against the active air sampling results for sulfur dioxide (SO_2), oxides of nitrogen (NO_x), and ozone (O_3). A fourth was used independently to test for formaldehyde, as the active air sampling protocol did not include formaldehyde. Unfortunately, test results revealed that the tolerance levels of the ChemSense passive dosimeters were not sufficiently precise to correlate accurately with the results from the active air sampling.

Data from the active air sampling verified that both libraries' HVAC systems were pulling gaseous pollutants into the buildings at concentrations significantly higher than nationally recommended guidelines. Of the two, the Law Library had the more serious problem because of the unfortunate location of an HVAC makeup air duct adjacent to the building's loading zone.

Of even greater concern, the test data demonstrated that both ozone and oxides of nitrogen were being generated inside the buildings. Ozone concentrations at the copy center in the Lee Library significantly exceeded outdoor concentrations. Ozone concentrations at the copy center in the Law Library were significantly higher than concentrations elsewhere in that library. Nitrogen oxides (NO_x) in both libraries exceeded ambient concentrations.

Not surprisingly, the study confirmed that the quality of Provo's ambient air, which regularly exceeds National Ambient Air Quality Standards for carbon monoxide (CO) and fine suspended particles of less than 10 microns in diameter (PM-10) during periods of winter inversions, was not significantly improved by being drawn into the libraries through their unfiltered HVAC systems. It also revealed that both libraries' copy centers generated significant amounts of ozone (O_3) and nitrogen oxides (NO_x), while the computer centers generated high levels of nitrogen oxides (NO_x). Consequently, the study suggested that both libraries required the installation of gaseous filtration systems for both makeup and recirculated air to address their air quality problems.

The estimated cost to retrofit gaseous filtration equipment into the existing HVAC systems of both libraries, as well as to include it in the new additions, forced the University's planning department to seek out alternative approaches to address the problem. Their inquiry led them to commission a consulting engineer specializing in conservation environments to evaluate the data from the study, review the two libraries' existing HVAC systems, and offer recommendations. Marx Ayres (Ayres & Ezer Associates, Los Angeles, California) was chosen for the task because of his demonstrated depth of experience in the field of engineering and his familiarity with the problem of achieving conservation environments that meet museum specifications.

THE CONSULTANT'S RECOMMENDATIONS

To meet the primary objective of the planning study, that is, improving the permanence of BYU's library collections through the control of indoor air quality, the University's planning department had to determine if the benefits of installing gaseous filtration as a preventive measure would justify the cost. While the addition of gaseous filtration can be viewed as a luxury component in the design of an HVAC system, the consultant was quick to point out the relative insignificance of this expense when compared with the proposed multi-million-dollar HVAC system designed strictly for human comfort.

Building planners assigned the highest priority for protection to the University's most valuable collections. Since the Law Library owned relatively few rare materials, gaseous filtration came to be viewed as less critical for that collection than achieving stringent relative humidity and temperature controls. On the other hand, the Lee Library's significant special collections and archival holdings were scheduled to be moved into its new addition, so that design parameters for that addition's HVAC system became the primary focus of the study. Were funding available to retrofit the existing building as well, the consultant prioritized the need to reroute the copy center's return air ducts directly outdoors to eliminate the reintroduction of high levels of ozone into the collection.

The Lee Library's new addition, projected to occupy approximately 300,000 square feet on two floors below grade, was designed to be serviced by a single HVAC system. University engineers suggested a significant ongoing cost savings could be realized by filtering only the makeup air as it was brought into the building, thereby minimizing energy use and filtration media replacement costs resulting from continuous filtration of both makeup and recirculated air. While this approach was economically advantageous, the consultant identified a serious drawback to this design as it did nothing to remove gaseous pollutants generated within the building. He did note, however, in the design's favor, that makeup air for the entire 300,000 square foot addition could be filtered for approximately the same cost as filtering both makeup and recirculated air for the special collections and archives alone— approximately 20 percent of the building.

The University's engineers asked the consultant to compare the cost and effectiveness of the two primary types of filtration media—permanganate-impregnated alumina (PIA) and activated carbon—in order to clarify the level of ongoing financial commitment required to maintain a gaseous filtration system. In order to provide this information, the consultant compared BYU's air quality test data with a 1990 study conducted by Grosjean and Associates at the Gene Autry Museum in Los Angeles.[102] In that study, Grosjean measured the effectiveness of using PIA and carbon mounted in series (as recommended by Purafil, a manufacturer of PIA), as opposed to a

Table 3 - Average Indoor and Outdoor Pollutant Levels

LOCATION	DATE	FILTRATION SYSTEM	AVERAGE POLLUTANT LEVEL (ppb)					
			Ozone			NO$_2$		
			Outdoor	Indoor	Ratio	Outdoor	Indoor	Ratio
Gene Autry Museum[a]	5/7/90	PIA+Carbon[c]	10.7	4.3	0.40	44.6	23.7	0.53
	5/8/90	Carbon only[d]	18.2	3.6	0.20	39.1	11.5	0.29
BYU Lee Library (Archives)[b]	2/11/92 (clear day)	None	9	5	0.56	2	6	3.00
	2/28/92 (inversion day)	None	8	2	0.25	7	4	0.57

Notes: [a]Daniel Grosjean, Edwin L. Williams II, and Mohamed W. M. Hisham, Removal of Air Pollutants by Carbon and Permanganate-Alumina Filtration Systems in Museums: A Case Study, Final Report to the Getty Conservation Institute, September, 1990.
[b]Delbert J. Eatough, Nathan Williams, Laura Lewis, Edwin A. Lewis, Constance K Lundberg, and Randy H. Silverman, "Gas and Particulate Phase Acids and Oxidants in Two Universities Libraries," Measurement of Toxic and Related Air Pollutants, Proceedings of the 1992 U.S. EPA/A&WMA International Symposium, (Pittsburgh: Air & Waste Management Association, 1992).
[c]Two units with 12 activated carbon panels + 12 Permanganate-Impregnated Alumina (PIA) panels.
[d]One unit with 12 activated carbon panels.

Source: Data courtesy J. Carlos Haiad, Ayres & Ezer Associates, Consulting Engineers.

Table 3

single-pass carbon filtration system to remove gaseous pollutants from the indoor environment. The Gene Autry study demonstrated that carbon alone was a more effective filtration medium than PIA plus carbon. [TABLE 3] Inconsistencies in Grosjean's test methodology, however, were identified by Purafil, calling into question his conclusion that there were performance (and consequently economic) advantages to relying on activated carbon filtration media alone.[103]

Despite the lack of research corroborating either position, the consultant designed a simple chart that allowed University engineers to weigh the relative cost effectiveness of the two types of filtration media. The chart estimated the costs and preservation benefits attainable with activated carbon compared with PIA plus carbon to filter makeup air alone versus both makeup and recirculated air. As Table 4 illustrates, the permanence of the library's collections can be significantly improved with the introduction of even minimal gaseous pollution filtration. Based on this information, the University's planning department opted to include an activated carbon gaseous filtration system in the makeup air of the Lee Library's addition, the least expensive of the four filtration alternatives available.

Given the relative novelty of including gaseous filtration equipment in a medium-sized research library's HVAC system and the unprecedented improvement the upgrade would provide, the University's cost-cutting measures were viewed as a satisfactory compromise for the preservation of the collection.

Table 4 - Cost Benefits Analysis of Gaseous Filtration Media

MEDIA	FILTRATION	RELATIVE COST	BENEFITS
Carbon	OSA[b]	1	10
Carbon	OSA & RA[c]	8	15
PIA[a]+Carbon	OSA	2	12
PIA+Carbon	OSA & RA	16	18

Key: [a]Permanganate-Impregnated Alumina
[b]Outside air
[c]Return air

Source: Data courtesy J. Carlos Haiad, Ayres & Ezer Associates, Consulting Engineers.

Table 4

OBSERVATIONS BASED ON BYU'S EXPERIENCE

The BYU study verified that air quality in libraries is a preservation issue even in relatively isolated geographic areas like Provo, Utah. As a result, library planners should routinely evaluate ambient gaseous pollution information—readily available from state monitoring agencies—when designing HVAC systems for research libraries where long-term preservation is a priority.

Since interior building materials such as concrete, paint, carpeting, and wood products give off gaseous and particulate pollutants as they age,[104] concern about the off-gassing characteristics of raw materials used in new furnishings and construction projects should become a significant factor in the planning process. Additionally, a "curing period" to allow new building materials time to "breathe" is necessary, though this will delay the occupancy of a new or renovated library. This tactic will minimize (though not eliminate) damage to the collection resulting from absorption of high levels of gaseous pollutants still actively generated from two to four months after construction.

Library planners should exercise care when deciding on the location of technical and public service areas such as computer and copy centers. Their position at the beginning or the end of an HVAC zone may determine how easily gaseous pollutants generated within the building can be ducted away from the collection. Ideally, these areas should be vented directly outdoors to avoid spreading gaseous pollutants (such as ozone and NO_x) throughout the collection. Care should be taken in determining the location of air intake vents so that they are not adjacent to parking lots or loading docks where excessive amounts of exhaust fumes will be ducted directly into the building. It also should be noted that the cost of filtering gaseous pollutants can be dramatically reduced if building planners strictly segregate stack space from public service areas.

Active air sampling remains an expensive test procedure and our failure to isolate an inexpensive but accurate passive monitor was disappointing. Nevertheless, our experience demonstrated that the cost of air sampling is justifiable. It effectively identified an existing problem for building planners that ultimately led to retaining a consultant and reaching university-level agreement to improve the library's indoor air quality. As the sampling and analysis took more than one year to fund and carry out, we learned that early involvement in the construction project is critical. In a university setting, a collaborative effort with a chemistry or engineering department already engaged in air quality studies may provide a relatively inexpensive way to accomplish the testing. The test's design should include input from a preservation librarian, an environmental scientist, and an HVAC engineer to ensure that accurate data about the collection, the building's air quality and the operational status of the HVAC system during the test period are all known factors.

The use of a consulting engineer familiar with achieving conservation environments in libraries can be invaluable to the planning process. Because this type of professional is familiar with the requirements for achieving a specific desired outcome and can communicate these requirements to local facility planners and engineers, his or her expertise lends credibility to the library's bid for environmental improvements. For this reason we have included in the endnotes the names and addresses of a number of conservation consultants specializing in this type of work.[105]

Data on ambient air quality are readily available from a state's bureau of air quality or an equivalent agency. This information is germane to identifying local pollution problems and is free for the asking. Additionally, we found that passive dosimeters for detecting radon gas were available free through the state, and though radon is not a preservation concern, the library administration found the information useful ("as long as we were conducting air quality tests anyway") in addressing its own concerns regarding employee health and safety.

We discovered during the planning process that, should the installation of gaseous filtration equipment be eliminated from the current project because of cost, at a minimum the HVAC system can be designed to accommodate the future addition of gaseous filtration equipment. This bit of foresight ensures the option of retrofitting the system should the issue of gaseous filtration become more critical over time. Further, installing gaseous filtration equipment is no guarantee that it will function correctly. Provision *must* be made, as a regular part of the building's maintenance, to change the filtration media when they are exhausted, and further air quality testing should be conducted periodically to verify the system is functioning as designed.

CONCLUSION

Air pollution problems are age-old and are only likely to become more critical with time. As such, the inclusion of appropriate gaseous and particle filtration systems in libraries should become the norm rather than the exception. Much research remains to be done in the area of pollution detection and mitigation. Narrowly defining the effects of gaseous pollutants on library materials and the types of filtration media most appropriate for their removal from the indoor environment are key. Published studies from other libraries are needed to inform building planners about HVAC designs that successfully achieve conservation environments.

Finally, librarians need persistence and cunning if they hope to influence the decision-making process that will ultimately determine the quality of the library's indoor environment. The opportunities for improvement are rare, coming on average once every 15 to 20 years. Many designs that successfully weather the planning stages are eliminated because of value engineering before ground-breaking or because of a last-minute attempt to bring a project in at budget. Remaining an integral player in the planning and construction phases of the project requires current and ongoing information available only through the support of the library's top administration. One does not have to be an HVAC engineer to successfully improve the existing HVAC system, but rather know when to call in a conservation consultant and how to cultivate the support of the engineer designing the new system. The collection needs an effective advocate if building-wide environmental upgrades are to be realized in preference to improvements in the building's decorative facade.

The payoff, however, can be dramatic. Even incremental improvements related to eliminating pollutants from the building's environment will affect the permanence of the entire collection simultaneously and on an ongoing basis—so long as someone remembers to change the filters!

NOTES

1. Garry Thomson, "Air Pollution—A Review for Conservation Chemists," *Studies in Conservation* 10 (1965): 147–68.
2. Garry Thomson, *The Museum Environment* (London: Butterworths, 1978).
3. National Research Council, *Preservation of Historical Records* (Washington, D.C.: National Academy Press, 1986), 15.
4. National Bureau of Standards, *Air Quality Criteria for Storage of Paper-Based Archival Records*, NBSIR 83–2795 (Washington, D.C.: National Bureau of Standards, 1983).
5. American National Standards Institute, *American National Standards for Photography (Film)—Storage of Processed Safety Film*, ANSI PH1.43–1985 (New York: American National Standards Institute, 1985).
6. Norbert S. Baer and Paul N. Banks, "Indoor Air Pollution: Effects on Cultural and Historic Materials," *International Journal of Museum Management and Curatorship* 4 (1985): 9–20.
7. James R. Druzik, et al., "The Measurement and Model Predictions of Indoor Ozone Concentrations in Museums," *Atmospheric Environment* 24A (1990): 1813–23.
8. D. J. Spedding and R. P. Rowlands, "Sorption of Sulphur Dioxide by Indoor Surfaces: I. Wallpaper," *Journal of Applied Chemistry* 20 (May 1970): 143–46.
9. K. Toshi and T. Kenjo, "Some Aspects of Conservation of Works of Art in Buildings of New Concrete," *Studies in Conservation* 20 (1975): 118–22.
10. Steven Weintraub, "Creating and Maintaining the Right Environment," in *Caring for Your Collections*, ed. Harriet Whelchel (New York: Abrams, 1992), 28.
11. Baer and Banks, 10.
12. Ibid.
13. Fredrick H. Shair and Kenneth L. Heitner, "Theoretical Model for Relating Indoor Pollutant Concentrations to Those Outside," *Environmental Science & Technology* 8 (May 1974): 444–51.
14. William P. Lull and Paul N. Banks, "Conservation Environment Guidelines for Libraries and Archives in New York State." Unpublished paper, 8–9.
15. Peter Brimblecombe, "Interest in Air Pollution Among Early Fellows of the Royal Society," *Notes and Records of the Royal Society of London* 32 (March 1978): 123.

16. Ibid., 124.
17. Cited in Peter Brimblecombe, "Air Pollution in Industrialized England," *Journal of the Air Pollution Control Association* 28 (February 1978): 117.
18. Cited in Brimblecombe, "Interest in Air Pollution Among Early Fellows of the Royal Society," 124.
19. Ibid., 128.
20. Brimblecombe, "Air Pollution in Industrialized England," 115.
21. James Moran, "William Blades," *The Library*, 5th ser., 16 (December 1961): 251-66.
22. William Blades, *The Enemies of Books* (London: Stock, 1880), 30.
23. Ibid., 31.
24. C. T. Eastlake, Michael Faraday, and W. Russell, "Report on the Protection by Glass of the Pictures in the National Gallery," 24 May 1850, Parliamentary Debates, (Commons) in *British Parliamentary Papers: Reports from Selected Committees and Commissioners on Fine Arts and on the National Gallery with Minutes of Evidence Appendices and Indices 1847-63. Education - Fine Arts*, vol. 3 (reprinted, Shannon, Ireland: Irish University Press).
25. Michael Faraday, et al., *Report of the Commission Appointed to Consider the Subject of Lighting Picture Galleries by Gas*, Cmnd. 106, 2d sess., 22 July 1859 (reprinted, Shannon, Ireland: Irish University Press, 1971), 391–92.
26. Royal Society of Arts, Committee on Leather for Bookbinding, *Report of the Committee on Leather for Bookbinding*, ed. Viscount Cobham and Sir Henry T. Wood (London: Bell & Sons, 1905), 13.
27. Chandru J. Shahani and William K. Wilson, "Preservation of Libraries and Archives," *American Scientist* 75 (May–June 1987): 243.
28. Royal Society of Arts, 13.
29. A. E. Kimberly and A. L. Emley, *A Study of the Deterioration of Book Papers in Libraries*, NBS Miscellaneous Publication no. 140 (Washington, D.C.: U.S. Department of Commerce, Standards Bureau, 1933).
30. A. E. Kimberly and A. L. Emley, *Study of the Removal of Sulphur Dioxide from Library Air*, NBS Miscellaneous Publication no. 142 (Washington, D.C.: U.S. Department of Commerce, Standards Bureau, 1933).
31. Edna Yost, *Modern Americans in Science and Invention* (New York: Stokes, 1941), 173–90.
32. Isaac Asimov, *Asimov's Chronology of Science and Discovery* (New York: Harper & Row, 1989), 509.
33. Baer and Banks, 9.
34. Ibid.
35. Joe Barnes, general foreman for operations, National Gallery of Art, Washington, D.C., telephone conversation with author, 17 May 1993.
36. William P. Lull, Principal, Garrison/Lull, Princeton Junction, N.J., telephone conversation with author, 17 May 1993.
37. Thomson, 159.
38. Cecily M. G. Druzik and Dusan C. Stulik, "Formaldehyde: Detection and Mitigation," *WAAC Newsletter* 13 (May 1991): 13–16.
39. Peter Brimblecombe, *Air Composition and Chemistry* (Cambridge: Cambridge University Press, 1986), 157.
40. Baer and Banks, 16.
41. Miloslav V. Jokl, *Microenvironment* (Springfield, Ill.: Charles C. Thomas, 1989), 165–70.
42. Peter Brimblecombe and Alla Yu Lein, eds., *Evolution of the Global Biogeochemical*

Sulphur Cycle, Scope 39 (Chichester, England: Wiley & Sons, 1989), 83.
43. Environmental Protection Agency, "Primary and Secondary Air Quality Standards," *Federal Register* 36 (1971): 22,388–92.
44. Environmental Protection Agency, "Revisions to the National Ambient Air Quality Standard for Photo-Chemical Oxidants," *Federal Register* 44 (1979): 8,201–233.
45. Cf. 40 *Code of Federal Regulations*, pt. 52 (1992).
46. S. H. Zeronian, "Reactions of Cellulose Fabrics to Air Contaminated with Sulfur Dioxide," *Textile Research Journal* 40:8 (1970): 695–98.
47. Ralph J. Brysson, et al., "Effects of Air Pollution on Exposed Cotton Fabrics," *Journal of the Air Pollution Control Association* 17 (1967): 294–98.
48. S. H. Zeronian, K. W. Alger, and S. T. Omaye, "Reaction of Fabrics Made from Synthetic Fibers to Air Contaminated with Nitrogen Dioxide, Ozone, or Sulfur Dioxide," in *Proceedings of the Second International Clean Air Congress* (New York: Academic Press, 1971): 468–76.
49. Brimblecombe, *Air Composition and Chemistry*, 158.
50. A. Parker, "The Destructive Effects of Air Pollution on Materials," in *Proceedings of the 22nd Annual Conference, National Smoke Abatement Society, Bournemouth, England, September 28, 1955* (Brighton: National Smoke Abatement Society).
51. F. L. Hudson and C. J. Edwards, "Some Direct Observations on the Aging of Paper," *Paper Technology* 7 (1966): 27–31.
52. F. L. Hudson, "Acidity of 17th and 18th Century Books in Two Libraries," *Paper Technology* 8 (1967): 189–90.
53. Richard D. Smith, "A Comparison of Paper in Identical Copies of Books from the Lawrence University, the Newberry, and the New York Public Libraries," *Restaurator* supp. no. 2 (1972).
54. D. J. Spedding, R. P. Rowlands, and J. E. Taylor, "Sorption of Sulphur Dioxide by Indoor Surfaces: III. Leather," *Journal of Applied Chemistry and Biotechnology* 21 (March 1971): 68–70.
55. National Research Council, 15.
56. Ibid.
57. Zeronian, Alger, and Omaye, 468–76.
58. Victor S. Salvin, W. D. Paist, and W. J. Myles, "Advances in Theoretical and Practical Studies of Gas Fading," *American Dyestuff Reporter* (12 May 1952): 297–302.
59. Paul M. Whitmore and Glen R. Cass, "The Fading of Artists' Colorants by Exposure to Atmospheric Nitrogen Dioxide," *Studies in Conservation* 34 (1989): 85–97.
60. Shahani, *supra* note 7, at 243.
61. Zeronian, Alger, and Omaye, 468–76.
62. Herman Bogaty, Kenneth S. Campbell, and William D. Appel, "The Oxidation of Cellulose by Ozone in Small Concentration," *Textile Research Journal* (February 1952): 81–83.
63. Cynthia L. Shaver, Glen R. Cass, and James R. Druzik, "Ozone and the Deterioration of Works of Art," *Environmental Science & Technology* 17 (1983): 748–52.
64. Victor S. Salvin, "Ozone Fading of Dyes," *Textile Chemist and Colorist* 1 (May 1969): 245–51.
65. Paul M. Whitmore, Glen R. Cass, and James R. Druzik, "The Ozone Fading of Traditional Natural Organic Colorants on Paper," *Journal of the American Institute for Conservation* 26 (1987): 45–58.

66. Glen R. Cass, et al., "Protection of Works of Art from Atmospheric Ozone: Appendix. Mathematical Modeling of Chemically Reactive Pollutants in Indoor Air." Getty Conservation Institute Scientific Program Report, June 1988.
67. National Research Council, *Preservation of Historical Records, supra* note 56, at 59.
68. R. W. Henn, D. G. Wiest, and B. D. Mack, "Microscopic Spots in Processed Microfilm: The Effect of Iodide," *Photographic Science and Engineering* 9 (May–June 1965): 167–73.
69. Nancy Martin, Deputy Law Librarian, Pepperdine Law School, interview with author, June 1991.
70. Druzik and Stulik, 13–16.
71. W. J. Fisk, et al., *Indoor Air Quality Control Techniques* (Park Ridge, N.J.: Noyes Data Corporation, 1987), 10–11.
72. Thad Godish, *Indoor Air Pollution Control* (Chelsea, Mich.: Lewis Publishers, 1989), 41–42.
73. Shirley J. Hansen, *Managing Indoor Air Quality* (Lilburn, Ga.: Fairmont Press, 1991), 55.
74. Floréal Daniel, Françoise Flieder, and Françoise Leclerc, "The Effects of Pollution on Deacidified Paper," *Restaurator* 11:3 (1990): 179–207.
75. "Exposure of Deacidified Paper to Sulphur Dioxide and Nitrogen Dioxide," *Getty Conservation Institute Newsletter* 5:2 (Spring 1990): 6.
76. Edwin L. Williams II and Daniel Grosjean, "Exposure of Deacidified Paper to Ambient Levels of SO_2 and NO_2." Getty Conservation Institute Scientific Program Report, July 1990.
77. Peter G. Sparks, "Exposure of Deacidified Paper to Sulfur Dioxide and Nitrogen Dioxide," *Commission on Preservation and Access Newsletter* 31 (February 1991): 3.
78. F. Carey, "Atmospheric Deposits in Britain, A Study of Dinginess," *International Journal of Air Pollution* 2 (1959): 1–26.
79. National Research Council, *Preservation of Historical Records, supra* note 8, at 15.
80. Mary P. Ligocki, Harvey I. H. Liu, and Glen R. Cass, "Measurements of Particle Deposition Rates Inside Southern California Museums," *Aerosol Science Technology* 13:85 (1990): 85–101.
81. William W. Nazaroff and Glen R. Cass, "Mass-Transport Aspects of Pollutant Removal at Indoor Surfaces," *Environment International* 15 (1989): 567–84.
82. H. R. Gibbons, D. Pope, and R. L. Moss, "Removal of Sulfur Dioxide from a Simulated Museum Atmosphere Using Carbon Filters." Unpublished paper, Warren Springs Laboratory, Stevenage, England, on file with NTIS, cited in Baer and Banks, 12.
83. Stephen Hackney, "The Distribution of Gaseous Air Pollution within Museums," *Studies in Conservation* 29 (1984): 105–16.
84. Cass, et al., 9.
85. Edwin L. Williams II and Daniel Grosjean, "Removal of Air Pollutants by Sorbents Used in Museum HVAC Filtration Equipment." Final Report prepared for the Getty Conservation Institute, July 1991.
86. Sparks, 3.
87. Lynn G. Salmon, et al., "Nitric Acid Concentrations in Southern California Museums," *Environmental Science & Technology* 24 (1990): 1004–13.
88. American National Standards Institute, *American National Standards for Photography (Film) Processed Safety Film—Storage*, ANSI IT.11–1991 (New York: American National Standards Institute, 1981).
89. American National Standards Institute, *Practice for Storage of Processed*

Photographic Plates, ANSI PH 1.45–1981 (New York: American National Standards Institute, 1981, reaffirmed 1989).

90. American National Standards Institute, *Practice for Storage of Black and White Photographic Paper Prints*, ANSI PH 1.48–1982 (New York: American National Standards Institute, 1981, reaffirmed 1987).

91. National Research Council, *Preservation of Historical Records*, 27.

92. National Bureau of Standards, *Air Quality Criteria for Storage of Paper-Based Archival Records*, NBSIR 83–2795 (Washington, D.C.: National Bureau of Standards, 1983).

93. United States, Congress, *An Act to Amend the Clean Air Act to Provide for Attainment and Maintenance of Health Protective National Ambient Air Quality Standards*, P. L. 101–549 (Washington, D.C.: U.S. Government Printing Office, 1990).

94. National Information Standards Organization, "Draft Environmental Conditions for the Storage of Paper-based Records in Archives and Libraries," Z39.54-199X (March 1991).

95. Baer and Banks, 16.

96. Ibid.

97. 42 U.S.C. § 103 (1990). Measurements for PM–10 supersede earlier required measurements for total particulate, a measure of more use to libraries since it provides a total dust load.

98. Utah Department of Environmental Quality, "Annual State and Local Air Monitoring Stations Report." Unpublished documents, 1987–1990.

99. Cass, et al.

100. Delbert J. Eatough, et al., "Gas and Particulate Phase Acids and Oxidants in Two University Libraries," *Measurement of Toxic and Related Air Pollutants, Proceedings of the 1992 U. S. EPA/A&WMA International Symposium* (Pittsburgh: Air and Waste Management Association, 1992): 333–43.

101. Cecily M. Grzywacz and Dusan C. Stulik, "Passive Monitors for the Detection of Pollutants in Museum Environment." Unpublished report, Getty Conservation Institute, n.d.

102. Daniel Grosjean, Edwin L. Williams II, and Mohamed W. M. Hisham, "Removal of Air Pollutants by Carbon and Permanganate-Alumina Filtration Systems in Museums: A Case Study." Final Report prepared for the Getty Conservation Institute, September 1990.

103. Chris Muller, Manager of Gas Technology, Purafil, letter to author, 12 November 1991.

104. Lull and Banks, 8.

105. Conservation consultants familiar with library, archive, and museum environmental issues include the following:

Marx Ayres
Ayres & Ezer Associates
1180 South Beverly Drive, Suite 600
Los Angeles, CA 90035
(310) 553-5285

Murray Frost
Murray Frost Cultural Building Consulting, Inc.
15515 Columbia Avenue
White Rock, British Columbia V4B 1K5
(604) 538-9223

Wendy Jessup
Wendy Jessup and Associates, Inc.
1814 North Stafford Street
Arlington, VA 22207
(703) 532-0788

William P. Lull
Garrison/Lull
P. O. Box 337
Princeton Junction, NJ 08550
(609) 259-8050

Steven Weintraub
Art Preservation Services
223 East 85th Street
New York, NY 10028
(212) 988-3869

Mass Deacidification of Archives and Manuscript Collections

Kristi L. R. Kiesling

Head, Department of Manuscripts and Archives
Harry Ransom Humanities Research Center, The University of Texas at Austin

James Grant Stroud

Chief Conservation Officer
Harry Ransom Humanities Research Center, The University of Texas at Austin

INTRODUCTION

Mass deacidification, long anticipated by the library community as a solution to the problem of paper deterioration, has arrived. It is not neatly packaged nor is it fully ready for consumption. It has arrived at a time when alternative approaches to the preservation of collections, microformatting and digitization, are being promoted as the preferred tools for access. The polarization of viewpoints about which of the technologies is the most reasonable, in the larger perspective of the national collection, is great.

Unlike microformatting or digitization, the purpose of mass deacidification is to maintain and use the book or document in its original format. As recent tests by several institutions have shown, the process is suitable for a variety of library and archive materials, but not for *all* materials. For example, it may be less suitable for items of very high monetary or intrinsic value, or complex items that conservators should treat individually. Some materials, like leather bindings and photographs, can be damaged by the existing processes. However, mass deacidification may very well be the least expensive preservation option available in terms of per-item cost, and it will allow institutions to deal with a large quantity of material for a smaller dollar investment than reformatting would require. Nonetheless, in light of the millions of books and linear feet of archives in need of treatment, the collective cost may still be prohibitive.

Of course, the path of least resistance is for libraries and archives to adopt a "wait and see" attitude toward mass deacidification. A number of arguments that libraries have posited against the process have been summarized by Richard Frieder: 1) digitization will make it unnecessary to preserve paper, 2) the maintenance of excellent environmental conditions will produce the same result as deacidification, and 3) if we wait a few more years, the technology will be better.[1] The technology *will* be better in time, and paper strengthening may yet be incorporated, but that will only happen if institutions work with vendors now to improve existing technologies. No authoritative research has compared the long-term effects of deacidification with those of maintaining our holdings at optimum temperature and relative humidity in lignin-free and acid-free boxes and folders. And by the time digitization is an affordable, routine preservation technique for most institutions, we may already have lost valuable information. Can we afford to wait?

Results of current treatment tests indicate that mass deacidification (especially the diethyl zinc, or DEZ, process) may be even more effectively applied to archives and other non-bound materials than to books. Treatment results for archives and manuscript collections at the Harry Ransom Humanities Research Center (HRHRC) at The University of Texas at Austin have for the most part indicated very complete, even deacidification. This paper will address issues related to undertaking a mass deacidification program, discuss the initial results of the National Endowment for the Humanities (NEH)-funded HRHRC mass deacidification project, and identify issues that still need to be addressed before the library community can embrace mass deacidification without reservation.

RECENT DIALOGUE AND EXPERIMENTATION

Two key gatherings of conservators and library administrators to discuss mass deacidification have taken place in recent years. The first was A Roundtable on Mass Deacidification held in Andover, Massachusetts, September 1991, sponsored by the Association of Research Libraries (ARL) and the Northeast Document Conservation Center (NEDCC). The second was the New York State Seminar on Mass Deacidification, held in Albany, New York, October 1992, sponsored by the New York State Program for the Conservation and Preservation of Library Research Materials.

The published proceedings from these two seminars illustrate the wide diversity of opinion held by library and preservation administrators and conservators about the effects of mass deacidification. Some libraries are ready to embrace the process as the only way currently available to save decaying collections. Others are still doubtful that mass deacidification is the best alternative. Institutions that have already performed some testing of mass deacidification are largely optimistic. However, there is no question that the available processes are not perfect. Improvements need to be made and are being made, but libraries and archival repositories must step forward to have an impact on the development of the techniques.

The DEZ process has undergone extensive testing as an application for bound volumes in library collections. The Library of Congress (LC), which originally developed the process, has tested the DEZ process for nearly 20 years and remains convinced that DEZ is a highly effective and broadly applicable mass deacidification technique. LC has conducted a wide range of process efficacy tests and toxicology studies, and has been involved in the design, construction, and operation of several pilot plants.

In the last few years several institutions have furthered the Library of Congress' work on mass deacidification. These include Harvard University, Johns Hopkins University, Northwestern University, the Harry Ransom Humanities Research Center at The University of Texas at Austin, and the Committee on Institutional Cooperation (CIC), which includes Michigan State University, Northwestern, Ohio State University, Pennsylvania State University, Purdue University, and the Universities of Chicago, Illinois, Indiana, Iowa, Michigan, Minnesota, and Wisconsin. Of these various projects, only the HRHRC's has focused primarily on mass deacidification for archives and manuscript collections. While there have been some comparative studies utilizing several deacidification technologies, most of the projects have tested the diethyl zinc (DEZ) process for its effectiveness on a variety of library materials.[2] DEZ is emerging as the preferred method for mass deacidification, as test results have shown it to be somewhat more effective in neutralizing acids and depositing an alkaline buffer than the other available processes.[3]

The HRHRC is confident that most of the major issues related to the deacidification of paper have been resolved by the work of the Library of Congress. As the majority of this work, however, has focused on the treatment of bound books, the Center's conservators have been studying the application of the process to the manuscripts and documents in the HRHRC collections. One of the ongoing concerns of the Ransom Center has been the effects of the treatment on the writing inks and media that are represented in the collections.

BACKGROUND OF THE HRHRC DEZ PROJECT

Initial Explorations

In 1990 at the invitation of Akzo Chemicals, Inc., the Ransom Center sent a shipment containing a wide variety of non-collection materials, in order to study the effects of DEZ treatment on visual appearance and tactile quality of treated items. It was believed that any visual changes that might occur during the treatment would be related to either the deposit of zinc oxides on exposed surfaces, the pH sensitivity of treated materials, or the heating and cooling cycles which occur during the treatment process.

Of initial interest to conservators and collection staff at HRHRC was the visual comparison of treated materials with untreated samples. Though the HRHRC is relatively certain of the efficacy of DEZ in neutralizing acid in paper, it was far less confident of the effects of treatment on the range of colorants, dyes, pigments, and binders that have been used in the production of 20th-century writing and artists' media, and in modern papers, photographs, and books. Visual comparison of control samples with the wide range of materials submitted during the test run substantially increased staff knowledge of the types of material which would be adversely affected by the DEZ treatment.

A variety of results were observed in the materials subjected to treatment. These included a slight yellowing of some book papers, occasional color shifts in colored papers and printed colors, considerable darkening of thermofax and other papers with heat sensitive coatings, significant changes in certain types of artists' media, occasional blockage of heat-sensitive copying process inks, disturbances in the texture and color of pyroxylin book cloth covers and hot melt adhesives, temporary though serious dehydration of boards and textblocks, and the formation of iridescent interference colors on some photographs. In general, plastics of many varieties fared quite poorly. They stretched, yellowed, and darkened. Foams shrank and became brittle and powdery. In a tightly packed box, fusion occurred between adjacent sleeves of an unidentified type of polyester film.

Most encouraging was the effect, or lack of effect, of the treatment on writing inks and papers. Of the roughly 1,000 samples of writing and typing inks submitted, it was difficult to find a dozen which had been visually disturbed. It was this that encouraged the Ransom Center to develop its proposal to the NEH and to focus the project on the treatment of manuscripts and archive materials.

The Scope of the Project

In January 1992, HRHRC was awarded funding by the National Endowment for the Humanities for a two-year study of the logistics and technical issues of mass deacidification of archives and manuscript collections. A total of 350 linear feet of 20th-century literary archives and manuscripts from the Center's collections were targeted for deacidification during the course of the project. The deacidification treatment was provided by Akzo Chemical at their diethyl zinc mass deacidification pilot plant in Deer Park, Texas.

The 35,000 linear feet of manuscripts and archives at the HRHRC focus predominantly on literature of the 19th and 20th centuries. These centuries are noted for the accelerated growth of industrial manufacturing technologies which resulted in the increased complexity of materials used in the manufacture of ink, paper, and adhesives. One of the hallmarks of these products is their inherent instability, caused in large part by acids used either in their production or occurring naturally in their chemical make-up. These acids, along with those arising from poor storage conditions and air pollution, are the chief cause of the deterioration and embrittlement of paper. The process of paper deacidification is designed to chemically halt this deterioration.

To prevent the bulk of the HRHRC's modern collections from deteriorating beyond the point of usability, a process was sought which would effectively neutralize the acids in large groups of paper records. To be cost effective, such a process must be safe for a wide variety of materials, so that very little testing and culling of collection items is needed to ensure that individual components will not be damaged by the process. Based on its experience with the mass deacidification treatments currently available, the HRHRC believes that several factors make diethyl zinc deacidification the treatment best suited for application to its collections.

Why DEZ?

In contrast to other mass deacidification treatments, all of which use organic solvents to deliver deacidification compounds into paper being treated, diethyl zinc deacidification is a gaseous process; thus the paper never associates with liquid solvents during the treatment. This characteristic is important for collections of manuscripts and archives, as the gaseous process prevents inks which are soluble in water or organic solvents from softening, dissolving, or spreading on the paper. The process takes place in a vacuum chamber where the gaseous DEZ penetrates the paper records, neutralizing acidic components in every sheet, and leaving an alkaline reserve of zinc oxide and other alkaline zinc compounds to prevent acid-forming gases present in the environment from contaminating the material in the future.

The results of the DEZ project have been very encouraging. Experimentation with packing density has shown that the document cases must be packed relatively loosely to allow the materials to dehydrate sufficiently for the DEZ to react completely with acids in the paper. A longer dehydration phase is required for archives than for books, and at a slightly higher temperature. Chemical analysis has indicated that even very acidic paper (pH of 3.9 4.5) is completely and consistently neutralized by the process, and an alkaline buffer is deposited.

Concerned that collection materials were being unnecessarily subjected to excessive heat during rehydration, HRHRC conservation staff are encouraging the use of lower process temperatures. A longer rehydration period is now routine for both books and archives, and allows the short-chain alcohols thought to be responsible for the odor commonly associated with DEZ-treated materials to be circulated out of the system. The odor is no longer a significant issue.

SPECIALIZED TREATMENT CONTAINERS AND SHIPPING OVERPACKS

Akzo designed and provided two types of specialized containers for the transport and treatment of the Ransom Center collections: a document treatment container and a shipping overpack. The document container is a cage, slightly larger than a standard Hollinger document case, made of steel wire coated with nylon. It takes 72 cages to fill the DEZ treatment chamber. The shipping overpack is made of heavy-duty corrugated cardboard. The base and lid of the overpack are constructed of rigid polymer, and a sheet of plywood placed in the bottom of the base supports and distributes the weight of the loaded treatment cages. A full overpack can weigh over 600 lbs. The dimensions of the overpack accommodate 42 cages and a surrounding layer of Ethafoam to cushion the materials during transport. The overpack is designed to be moved with a forklift or hydraulic hand truck.

TRANSPORTATION AND COLLECTION SECURITY

Depending on the transportation vendor a library chooses, the logistics of getting the materials back and forth from the treatment plant can be problematic, although none of the repositories involved in testing mass deacidification processes reported any specific difficulties at the Andover and Albany conferences. Considerations as basic as the design of the loading dock and its compatibility with transportation equipment or the absence of a pallet jack can have some unexpected results. Making space for a staging area to prepare the materials for treatment and to examine them upon return can also be difficult, given the space constraints in most libraries and archives. Careful planning should eliminate any problems in this area.

For the HRHRC project, Akzo has provided transportation for the collection materials to be treated. The Akzo trucks are temperature-controlled and fitted with air-cushioned suspension. The schedule for pick-up and delivery has been tailored to the availability of the DEZ chamber so that the collection materials are absent from the HRHRC for only as much time as is necessary for treatment.

Ty-wraps™, or plastic self-locking plastic strips, were initially used to keep the document containers or cages containing the collection materials closed during handling and transport, and as an indicator of any tampering with the contents of the cages. Because the Ty-wraps™ are commercially available and can be removed and replaced with new ones, and because they are somewhat embrittled by DEZ treatment, the Ransom Center is investigating alternative security devices, such as pendant seals or locks, for the treatment cages.

Tracking collection materials during shipment and treatment is not currently an issue, given that treatment facilities are small enough that only one institution's materials are typically present on-site at any given time. However, security of materials could become a concern if collections from several different repositories were being treated simultaneously in a full-production facility. The Ransom Center staff is interested in the use of barcodes to track shipments. They do not seem necessary at the present stage of the project because of the ease of counting the treatment cages.

Nonetheless, as Akzo begins to scale up its operation, it is believed that a barcode system, which could communicate through telephone lines or the Internet, would prove advantageous.

RECORD KEEPING, INVENTORYING, AND MONITORING COLLECTIONS

The type of record keeping needed to document the treatment of collection materials will depend on the situation at each repository. Considerations to keep in mind for record keeping include the purpose of the records. Will they be public? Is it necessary to track specific materials to ensure that a volume or box of manuscripts is not treated twice? Will reports need to be generated? With an online system, it is a simple task to add information to the bibliographic record that a specific item or portion of an archive has been deacidified. To track treatment information for uncataloged archival collections, a database can be designed to fit institutional needs.

For example, at HRHRC a database has been created to track each treatment cage by the number of the call slip used when the material is removed from the stacks. A copy of the call slip is kept with the materials throughout the treatment process. Information such as the collection name, box number, summary of condition, and types of materials in the document case is also included. Post-treatment examination notes are added if there are unusual treatment results. For materials that are deselected before treatment, the standard separation sheet used by the Department of Manuscripts and Archives is placed in the folder from which the item was removed. When the item is replaced after treatment, the separation sheet is retained in place to indicate that specific items were withdrawn before treatment. Boxes are also marked to indicate that the contents have been deacidified.

While it would be impossible to mark each item in an archive to indicate that it had been deacidified, marking treated books would be less problematic. Seminar discussions have centered around whether it is enough to tag the bibliographic record or if the item itself also needs to be marked in some manner. Again, this is an area of institutional discretion.

A REVIEW OF THE DEZ TREATMENT PROCESS

Originally, the diethyl zinc mass deacidification process required three basic treatment steps: *dehydration*, *permeation*, and *rehydration*. After sealing the materials to be treated in a vacuum chamber, a vacuum is created and the temperature is raised to remove moisture from the paper. This *dehydration phase* is done in a nitrogen environment in order to flush air from the chamber. During dehydration a vacuum of 0.1 torr is pulled in the chamber and this level is held until the temperature ceases to change, indicating that no more moisture can be removed at that pressure. The temperature can reach 135 degrees F and this phase may take up to 35 hours.

Following dehydration, the diethyl zinc gas is introduced into the chamber. This begins the *permeation phase*, in which the DEZ reacts with acids in the paper to form zinc salts, and with residual moisture in the paper to form the zinc oxide buffer. The process liberates ethane, and takes approximately 12 hours. This is followed by approximately 20 purges of the chamber with dry nitrogen gas to flush the diethyl zinc and the ethane from the chamber. This process takes about five hours.

The final, or *rehydration,* phase involves the circulation of humidified nitrogen through the system to rehydrate the paper. This phase requires anywhere from four to 12 hours. Since the beginning of the Ransom Center project, a *post-treatment phase* has been incorporated into the procedure. The purpose of the post-treatment phase is to flush the odors from the treated paper and to continue the rehydration process. This phase originally consisted of a 72-hour wash with humidified nitrogen. Because the nitrogen wash must occur in vacuum, it was done in the treatment chamber follow ing completion of the previous three treatment phases.

The post-treatment phase has been successful in the elimination of the odor traditionally associated with DEZ- treated materials. The products which cause the odor, which are thought to be straight chain alcohols, only react with moisture. Once these compounds are liberated by the humidified nitrogen, they are flushed out of the system by the circulating wash. Were it not for the desire to eliminate the odor, the rehydration could take place in the library or archive environment. Akzo has now replaced the nitrogen wash with a humidified air wash. Because an air wash does not require a vacuum chamber, the treated materials are removed from the chamber for post-treatment processing in an auxiliary unit, thus freeing the chamber for other treatments. This has implications for cost savings by allowing greater throughput of shipments in the vacuum chamber.

The auxiliary unit used for the post-treatment is a temperature-controlled trailer which is divided into a storage and control area and a treatment area where the actual humidification takes place. Outside air is drawn into the treatment section and moved by blower over a heater. The heated air is directed through a spray humidification system which is controlled by a sensor that maintains the humidity of the forced air stream at 25-30 percent. Because the paper is quite dry after the basic treatment, it is thought prudent to begin the re-humidification at a relatively low level and to allow the moisture content in the paper to increase gradually. The process takes 72 hours, at which time the relative humidity in the room is thought to reach approximately 40-50 percent. Akzo installed a recording hygrothermograph in this area to ascertain actual variations in the relative humidity.

POST-TREATMENT TEMPERATURES
AND THE ISSUE OF ODOR

HRHRC conservators have expressed concern about the elevated temperatures used during the post-treatment phase. In the first run, the temperature during the three-day post-treatment nitrogen wash was a constant 140 degrees F. Project staff were concerned that this temperature was too high. Akzo felt that this temperature was necessary for optimal removal of the moisture-activated compounds which are responsible for the DEZ odor. It was thought, however, that a lower temperature might also be reasonably effective toward this end, and project staff requested Akzo to lower it to 100 degrees F during the second run. While Akzo continued to use the 140 degree temperature in its post-treatment of collections from other institutions, it processed all subsequent runs for the HRHRC at 100 degrees F. As far as HRHRC staff are concerned, the odor problem has become relatively insignificant, partly because of the effectiveness of the extended post-treatment wash and partly because of the highly purified diethyl zinc which Akzo had used for all of its runs during the past year and a half.

SELECTION PHILOSOPHIES

Karen Turko refers to "process-driven" and "collection-driven" selection criteria.[4] "Process-driven" selection simply means that certain kinds of mass deacidification processes are not suitable for all the materials a repository might wish to treat. For example, current research has shown that DEZ reacts negatively with pyroxylin, causes some adhesives to detach, and is not particularly effective on coated papers. The FMC process has even more pronounced effects on book bindings and adhesives, and has been known to cause inks to feather.

Thus, the library will select a vendor based on the materials to be treated. Ideally a mass deacidification process will treat most library and archives materials without deselection, but at the present time, none of the processes is at that stage. "Collection-driven" selection can involve a variety of parameters—identifying the most heavily used items from a collection or the most valuable, selecting items that are slated for permanent retention, identifying specific formats of materials or subject collecting areas, or working in cooperation with other libraries to select a large volume of materials to reduce per-volume costs.

Institutions that have performed mass deacidification on collection materials have used a number of selection criteria. Selection rationales discussed at the Andover and Albany conferences included materials for which the institution has special collecting responsibility in a cooperative collection development environment, material that it is desirable to maintain in its original format, materials that are becoming brittle or are at risk of becoming brittle,

materials for which there is high user demand (as judged by circulation statistics), unique materials, and materials that do not have high artifactual
value. Still other selection criteria involve choosing materials to be deacidified from existing work, such as sending all newly acquired materials for immediate treatment, sending materials before they are rebound, etc.[5]

In an archives setting, process-driven selection will most likely come into
play. That was certainly the case in the HRHRC project, as it was determined
that the gas-phase DEZ process was more appropriate for archival collections
than a liquid-phase process. However, since it was known that DEZ has an
adverse effect on a number of types of materials frequently found in archival
collections, such as prints from some photographic processes, cellulose acetate sleeves, and thermofaxes, these types of items were culled from the materials to be treated; the few stray items that were overlooked were returned
with predictable results. Treated cellulose acetate sleeves were so embrittled
that they literally crumbled when handled, and had to be replaced.
Thermofaxes darkened significantly and became illegible. Overall, however,
DEZ had very little noticeable effect on various papers and inks, areas of primary concern for archival collections.

Deselection criteria are just as important as selection criteria. Obviously
materials that are already embrittled should not be deacidified, as the process
will not strengthen them. Newly acquired library materials that are printed on
acid-free paper should not be sent for treatment, nor should materials that
would likely be damaged by the process. Library materials that are not expected to be permanently retained because they are frequently updated
should also not be treated.

Ultimately each institution will need to develop its own selection criteria,
depending on its needs, but there now exists a solid base of experience on
which the repository can base selection criteria. Peter G. Sparks' suggestion
that it is reasonable to expect that a certain amount of preselection or pretest-
ing will be required for any mass deacidification process still holds true.[6]
Institutions must also be cognizant that a certain amount of risk is involved.
Especially with archives and manuscript collections, there is a high potential
that a few items unsuited for deacidification will be overlooked during the
preselection process and will return damaged in some way. While the object
of a mass treatment program is to avoid as much preselection as possible, institutions must balance the potential risk to a small number of items against
the greater benefits of deacidification to an entire collection.

PRESELECTION AND RESULTS OF
THE FIRST HRHRC TREATMENT RUN

Prior to the first treatment run, the collections originally designated in the
project proposal as candidates for deacidification were reviewed. The collec-

tion chosen for the first run included general correspondence files, accounting and legal records containing a wide assortment of papers and marking media (including groundwood second sheets), mimeographed finding lists and appraisals, typed and handwritten correspondence, preprinted forms, and receipts. Nearly two-thirds of the paper in this collection could be classified as terminally brittle. This collection was chosen because the materials cover a broad time span reflecting the range of dates (1920-1950) and types of materials found in the Center's manuscript holdings.

The inclusion of brittle paper in mass deacidification treatments is a subject of serious debate. While there is no reason to believe non-aqueous deacidification will protect these papers when they are subsequently handled, the HRHRC believes that the neutralization of their acids will slow down their chemical deterioration. More importantly, it is believed that better quality papers, inevitably housed within brittle collections, will be better able to withstand contact with the highly acidic papers with which they are stored.

When they were noted, photographs, thermofax photocopies, and bound materials were set aside during the transfer of materials to the treatment cages. Other items were flagged if they were considered to be unsuitable candidates for treatment based on the HRHRC's previous experience during its trial run. These flagged items were reviewed by Conservation Department staff and, with the approval of the Project Curator, a sampling of these materials was included in the run to ascertain the effects of the DEZ treatment. Other than this, there was no reorganization or "leaf by leaf search" of the records to cull treatment-sensitive items.

EXPERIMENTAL FOCUS FOR THE FIRST SHIPMENT AND EVALUATION OF THE TREATMENT EFFECTS

The objectives of the first shipment to Akzo were primarily non-technical. The Center needed to establish selection procedures consistent with the concept of a mass treatment process. Project staff wanted to develop packing standards which would ensure the safety of the treated materials during transit and handling, but would not impede effective treatment. The first run was intended to develop a general awareness among project staff about the overall process. The evaluation process was to focus on visual assessment of the treated materials.

Much of the paper in the collection chosen for the first shipment was so brittle that any movement or lack of support would cause breakage of the individual sheets. Use of document cases inside the wire treatment cages provided additional protection and support for the documents and eliminated their contact with the metal rods of the cages. While tight packing would curtail movement of the materials in the document cases, questions concerning the ability of the DEZ to penetrate through thick groupings of tightly packed materials resulted in the use of a variety of experimental packing styles to determine whether packing density was a factor in treatment and collection safety.

The majority of the cages were packed in the following manner: A document case with the lid cut away was placed in the treatment cage; documents in their original folders were placed in the box; support cards were placed inside the front, back, and sides of the document case to restrain movement of the documents. Though our intention was to evaluate the relationship of packing techniques to security during travel by packing some of the boxes very loosely and some quite tightly, the majority were packed to a medium density in order to facilitate effective penetration of the diethyl zinc gas during treatment.

Results of the treatment were mixed. There was very little apparent structural damage to materials that were loosely packed, because of movement during transportation. There were, however, excessive deposits of zinc oxide on the majority of materials. These deposits manifest themselves in several consistent forms: deposits around the perimeter of smaller items stacked next to larger items, rings formed in areas of high density or pressure in tightly packed records, deposits in areas of planar distortion in the paper, surface sheen, iridescent patches. In the worst cases these were visible under both ultraviolet light and visible light. Often, they were only visible as an orange fluorescence under ultraviolet light. Although not a quantitative evaluation, the use of ultraviolet illumination is valuable in determining the presence and distribution of zinc oxide in treated paper. Though optical brighteners and other additives in paper can interfere with this evaluation, the characteristic bright orange fluorescence of zinc oxide, when exposed to ultraviolet light, provides a useful tool to assess the uniformity of the treatment and the ability of the gas to penetrate enclosed areas such as phase boxes and partially sealed polyester sleeves.

The problems occurring during the first treatment run appear to have been caused as a result of the packing density and the incomplete (or uneven) dehydration of the paper during treatment. It is believed these factors resulted in erratic or incomplete removal of moisture from the sheets during the dehydration phase of the treatment, or the incomplete penetration of the DEZ into the stacks of paper. During dehydration, it appears that moisture can be trapped in the stacks of paper in areas under tight pressure and in closed spaces, creating incompletely dried sites that react preferentially with the DEZ to form the zinc oxide surface deposits.

THE SECOND HRHRC TREATMENT RUN

The second treatment run contained materials from the same collection, comparable to those used in the first. This allowed the project staff to compare similar groups of materials from both treatment runs and capitalize on the previous experience as a form of quality control. Several document cases from another archive were also included in this run to serve as a pretest for evaluation of color change in the variously colored "second sheets" which are predominant in the collection. The objective of the second treatment run was to eliminate the excessive deposits of DEZ reaction compounds. All boxes were packed with a medium-to-loose packing density. The criterion for packing the document cases was that the packer could easily insert his or her hand so that the fingertips touched the bottom of the box. Akzo and HRHRC personnel determined that a lengthened dehydration phase during the treatment, coupled with less dense packing, would significantly reduce excessive and erratic zinc oxide deposits.

The second treatment run was very successful in terms of our objectives. There was no physical damage to the loosely packed materials caused by transport. The looser packing allowed more even dehydration and eliminated the problems caused by pockets of excess moisture being retained in the stacks of paper. Post-treatment evaluation showed only very minor visible deposits of zinc oxide on the surface of a few of the materials. When viewed under ultraviolet light the distribution of zinc oxide appeared to be even.

Upon initial inspection of the returned materials, however, project staff noted a gritty particulate had accumulated at the bottom of the folders and the open document cases. Closer investigation revealed that the same grit was present on and between the treated leaves. Low power microscopic examination of a bulk sample of the particulate debris revealed the grit to be composed largely (more than 95 percent) of gray-white irregular chunks which were presumed to be zinc oxide. The remainder of the material appeared to be a variety of silicates and aluminates of widely varying colors and textures. Three potential explanations were proposed by Akzo.

One suggested that a freshly sandblasted "knock down pot" in the system may have had residual sand; another postulated a leak in one of a pair of double block valves that may have allowed a local accumulation of zinc oxide at the leak (where the DEZ would react with steam and other process gases). A third explanation implicated poorly purged sandblasted pipes used in the plant's original construction, but this historical problem had not recurred and was considered an unlikely explanation at the time. A sample of the debris analyzed by a firm retained by Akzo showed the particulate to be 100 percent zinc oxide, thus supporting the idea that the particulate formed at the block valve. Akzo established procedures to monitor this potential problem and believes that the likelihood of its recurrence is extremely low. Project staff easily removed this particulate debris by gently brushing the affected materials. It was a simple though time-consuming procedure.

THE THIRD HRHRC TREATMENT RUN

The third treatment run contained a full load of documents from the archive that had been pretested in the second run. Initial inspection showed that the treatment of the paper in this collection was as effective as that of the second run. The records exhibited remarkable consistency, uniformity, and unobtrusiveness of treatment, exhibiting no significant shifts in color or texture of the inks and papers. All papers in the run fluoresced evenly under ultraviolet light. There was no grit such as was discovered in the second treatment run. It could have been described as a perfectly treated collection.

There were, however, some problems. The third run was the first to process groups of records containing significant amounts of polyester sleeves, a number of which fused together during the treatment. The Center had experienced fused sleeves in its initial test run, but staff attributed this to tight packing and to the possibility that the sleeves were not a standard polyester film. Though wary of the sleeves in the third shipment, they believed the looser packing style would eliminate the risk.

Additionally, the collection contained cellulose acetate sleeves. The treatment caused embrittlement of these sleeves by apparently driving the plasticizers from the plastic. Finally, we noted some minor water damage to two boxes of documents and evidence that high humidity had caused moderate distortion of folders and documents in several other boxes.

In an effort to understand the problem of moisture in the third run, a scenario was proposed which is now believed to be an accurate description of the problem's cause. The post-treatment phase occurred in an auxiliary unit, requiring that the treatment cages be removed from the treatment chamber and placed in the post-treatment trailer where they would be subjected to a three day sweep of humidified air. On opening the treatment chamber after the rehydration phase to remove the contents to the auxiliary post-treatment unit, Akzo personnel noted that standing water was present in the bottom of the chamber. It was surmised that this water was the result of condensation caused by the contact of the humidified nitrogen with the cool walls of the chamber. Because the rehydration phase occurs in vacuum, it was also thought that the breaking of the vacuum to fill the chamber with air prior to its opening might have caused a turbulence in the chamber which forced the condensed water to splash onto the document boxes. The affected document cases were those at the bottom and outside perimeters of the metal bed in the chamber on which the treatment cages were stacked.

HRHRC and Akzo personnel were seriously concerned with the presence of the condensation water in the chamber. There have been long-standing concerns at the Library of Congress that water might collect in the chamber and, on several occasions, splash barriers have been installed along its walls to prevent this water from contacting treated materials. Generally, however, the presence of water in the chamber has not been thought to be a serious problem. Prior to the use of the auxiliary post-treatment trailer, the post-treatment phase of the previous runs occurred in the treatment chamber; any water which might have condensed in the chamber would have evaporated by the end of the three day post-treatment phase.

Akzo staff determined that the source of the moisture was condensation from the humidified nitrogen used in the rehydration phase. Akzo has since established a system for monitoring the amount of moisture going into the chamber in the nitrogen stream, and has reduced its moisture content to a level which appears to have eliminated the formation of condensation.

With greater clarity about the problem of water in the chamber, it was hypothesized that the problem of fusion between adjacent polyester sleeves in the treated materials might be related to the higher levels of humidity in the bottom of the chamber. All of the sleeves that were affected were in the lowest level of the stacked treatment cages and thus in closest proximity to the moisture in the chamber. Experiments to replicate this phenomenon have been unsuccessful. The problem with the embrittlement of cellulose acetate sleeves is less of a concern. Cellulose acetate can be expected to become brittle and its removal prior to treatment must become part of the screening process.

THE FOURTH HRHRC TREATMENT RUN

The returned shipment was virtually flawless in terms of process mechanics and the treatment of the records. The treated papers were unaffected visually and their treatment was even, so that they fluoresced uniformly under ultraviolet light. Analysis of the pH of cold water extracts of treated and untreated test samples demonstrated that the treatment had achieved desired pH levels. Isolated occurrences of materials such as cellophane and thermofax papers which escaped the culling process produced predictable results: the cellophane was terminally embrittled and the thermofaxes were rendered nearly unreadable by the process. These effects are expected to occur. Part of the selection process is to balance the efforts required to completely remove such materials from a collection prior to treatment, with the potential loss of information. There were no identifiable problems with excessive humidity in the treatment, and polyester sleeves included in the collection were not affected. If anything untoward could be attributed to the treatment it was a slight increase of perceptible odor. This suggests that the use of higher temperatures in the post-treatment phase might indeed be appropriate. While the odor was more noticeable than in the second and third shipments, it was of low significance and not at all offensive.

THE FIFTH AND SIXTH HRHRC TREATMENT RUNS

The collections processed during the fifth run contained a wider variation of formats of materials than the previous runs, including paper-bound manuscripts, hardcover scrapbooks, and proofs. Additionally there was a considerable amount of material in polyester sleeves. A substantially larger number of bound manuscripts were originally scheduled for this treatment, but the department had received a DEZ-treated bound book which displayed a scorched appearance along the edges of its textblock. Concerns about this phenomenon encouraged the project staff to delay shipment of a large group of bound manuscripts until the nature and cause of this problem could be determined. Test samples of photographs and examples of early document and architectural plan copying processes were included in the treatment.

If there were any remaining questions about the effect of packing density on completeness of treatment, the fifth shipment definitely answered them. Confident in the process, the Center elected to send cataloged collections for treatment. In packing the treatment cages, a one-to-one box transfer took place—one full document case of fully processed materials was placed in the cage. This, in effect, made for a tighter packing density than was used in the second, third, and fourth runs, resulting in the same type of incomplete dehydration and penetration observed in the first treatment, though not to the same extent. Symptoms included pressure rings and visible surface deposits of zinc oxide. Additionally (though sporadically), polyester sleeves used for housings in the collection appeared to have complicated the issue of the dehydration of the paper. When viewed under ultraviolet light, these sleeves manifested patches of a fluorescent compound on the plastic film around the perimeter of the documents housed within them. There was no fusion between the polyester sleeves.

Alerted again to the need of careful attention to packing density, the sixth shipment was packed according to more conservative protocols. The results, as expected, were excellent.

TIME REQUIREMENTS FOR PRE- AND POST-TREATMENT PROCESSING

Thus far in the HRHRC project six full shipments of collection materials, totaling 432 document cases or approximately 180 linear feet of documents, have been mass deacidified by the DEZ process. While a breakdown and cost analysis of the specific activities associated with collection processing for mass deacidification is still being developed, pretreatment processing time (selection and packing) currently averages 38 hours and post-treatment processing (inspection and rehousing) has averaged 70 hours per shipment. Because of the problems encountered with various treatment runs, these statistics represent a fairly broad variation. The most expeditious processing times were encountered in the pretreatment processing of the third run at eight hours (these materials were already organized in document cases), and

24 hours for post-treatment processing of the fourth run (where there were virtually no discernable problems). The most extensive processing times were 72 hours for preprocessing the first shipment and 152 hours for post-processing the second shipment.

While these hours do not reflect all activities associated with the project, they offer a general indication of the time normal processing could entail. It is believed, however, that processing time will be substantially reduced as experience with collection treatment is increased.

COSTS

Some library administrators feel that the costs for mass deacidification are still too high and that their institutions cannot afford to take on this new technology in times of great budgetary constraints. The per-volume costs, however, are the lowest of any preservation treatment currently available, and promise to go down when vendors are able to scale up production. Certainly, library budgets as they now stand are not adequate to address the entire problem, but a portion of each institution's preservation budget could be diverted to deacidification. Outside funding from national grant programs and private foundations will be needed, and it is reasonable to assume that a significant level of funding will be available.

Harvard's pilot project (3,700 books, 4,688 maps) resulted in treatment costs of $12.40 per volume and $4.35 per map, including shipping costs but not including staff time spent preparing the shipments or examining the materials upon return.[7] The CIC project estimated a cost of $15 per volume treated.[8] Compared with estimates of $65-90 per volume for microfilming, the relative cost of deacidification is quite low. In addition, the benefit of having the material preserved in its original format, a format preferred by library patrons and librarians alike, is compelling. However, some books may require rebinding after treatment to make them useable, so those figures should also be factored into the total cost for deacidification. The HRHRC project cost estimates run approximately $70 per document case of material, or $167 per linear foot, exclusive of staff time for preselection and shipping. Depending on the type of materials in the boxes, the estimate is 7-14 cents per sheet.

Mass deacidification process vendors estimate that current costs will be halved when they are able to treat materials at production level. While there is no way to assure these estimates at this time, this would certainly be a welcome development. Peter G. Sparks estimated in 1990 that the total national cost for mass deacidification would be in excess of $100 million.[9]

REMAINING ISSUES RELATING TO MASS DEACIDIFICATION

Now that a significant amount of testing of current mass deacidification processes has taken place, and the body of knowledge about the effects of treatment is growing, will the library community need to repeat the process when vendors scale up to full production capacity to determine if treatment is as effective and complete as it was during the pilot phase? It is hoped that the testing will not need to be as extensive, but the effectiveness of treatment will need to be monitored.

There is still some concern that the long-term effects of mass deacidification are not known, and that there could possibly be some unforeseen toxicity problems. The Request for Proposals issued in September 1990 by the Library of Congress required extensive toxicity and environmental testing (in fact, it was one of the four major criteria in the solicitation[10]) and the results of studies to date indicate that toxicity is not an issue. Studies by the Battelle Memorial Institute indicate that toxic effects from zinc oxide occur only after exposure several orders of magnitude greater than would be expected to exist in library stacks or while handling treated materials.[11] Therefore, library staff and patrons should suffer no ill effects from prolonged exposure to treated materials. Accelerated aging tests have shown that deacidification with DEZ will extend the life expectancy of paper three to five times.[12] Why then do institutions balk at applying mass deacidification to their collections?

There are still a number of unknowns. For some institutions, *any* risk to collection materials is too much. Other institutions want the process to be perfect, with no deleterious effects to any of the wide variety of papers, bindings, inks, dyes, or adhesives found in collection materials. Undoubtedly, however, it is the cost associated with treatment that inhibits many repositories. Serious consideration needs to be given to the long-term effects of storage under optimum conditions. It is estimated that "a volume transferred to the Harvard Depository's environment of 50-60 F and low humidity will have its useful life extended some tenfold."[13]

Joseph Rosenthal writes, "Even though the costs that had been projected for preservation as a whole, and for mass deacidification as a part of a preservation program, seem very large, they are relatively small when compared with the value of the collections that are addressed."[14] In William Studer's opinion, "Mass deacidification is indeed nothing short of an investment in ensuring access for future generations of scholars, and equating failure to act with dereliction of responsibility is not too strong an evocation."[15] And Scott Bennett has indicated, "Action may require conviction, but conviction does not require that all of one's uncertainties about mass deacidification be fully resolved."[16] These are compelling arguments from directors of major research libraries. Clearly there is strong support in the library community to continue the investigation of mass deacidification.

The HRHRC project has answered initial questions about the applicability of mass deacidification to archives and manuscripts, but other issues have emerged. In the remaining treatment runs, project staff will concentrate more directly on the effects of the treatment on the pH and color of paper and media, its effects on photographs and other materials not normally considered appropriate for deacidification, and the comparison of traditional and experimental quality control techniques.

Given the encouraging results of the Ransom Center's project, it is now incumbent upon archival repositories, in addition to traditional libraries, to get involved in the improvement of existing mass deacidification technologies, for now their collections stand an even better chance of benefitting from treatment.

ADDENDUM

On December 14, 1993, the Ransom Center received a letter from Akzo Chemicals, Inc., stating its intention to "terminate its involvement" with the DEZ process, and citing as its rationale what it saw as limited prospects for the adoption of the process in the near future by the library community in general. Fortunately, the Ransom Center was able to complete the 10 treatment runs for the NEH project before the pilot plant closed in April 1994.

While the future of the diethyl zinc process is uncertain, the results of the Ransom Center's project indicate that the process is quite effective in deacidifying archival materials with a minimum of deselection needed and little, if any, damage to the materials. While more research and refinement of the process may be required for the treatment of bound collections, we feel that this turn of events is a great loss to the library community, and hope that it is only temporary.

QUALITY CONTROL AND RESEARCH: AN APPENDIX

Ransom Center staff are investigating quality control procedures to determine the effectiveness of the treatment on the collections. As of this writing, the quality control research effort has achieved four of its major goals:

1. The standard protocol for cold-extract pH (TAPPI T 509 om-88)[17] has been modified by blender pulping, electrode monitoring, and purging rather than boiling to meet the needs of DEZ-treated samples, and certain major experimental interferences have been characterized.

2. A large body of cold-extract pH data has been accumulated, the results presenting a picture that is unsurprising in light of the thermodynamics of zinc oxide-water interactions.

3. The standard protocol for determination of alkaline reserve (ASTM D 4988 - 89)[18] has been modified by blender pulping, electrode monitoring, and purging rather than boiling to meet the needs of DEZ-treated papers, and significant experimental interferences have been identified.

4. Significant experimental work to characterize the morphology of the deposited alkaline reserve has been performed in concert with faculty members of the Chemistry and Electrical Engineering Departments of The University of Texas.

Extensive investigation pinpointed several significant experimental interferences and problems in the cold-extract protocol promulgated by TAPPI. These fall into two classes. Several are broadly relevant to all users of T 509 (and TAPPI T 435 om-88),[19] and are accordingly being brought to the attention of the appropriate committee. The others are the result of the application of this protocol to aged papers and to DEZ-treated papers. Stated very briefly, the most important of these interferences and problems are:

1. The cold-extract protocol method explicitly excludes unbuffered papers from its scope (section 1.2), presumably because of the difficulty of measuring the pH of a low ionic-strength solution. This problem, as with several of the others, was overcome by switching to a double-junction, platinum-wired electrode[20] capable of measuring solutions having ionic strengths as low as that of distilled water.

2. Section 10.4 of TAPPI's protocol dictates: "Before recording the pH, leave the electrodes in the solution until there is no measurable drift in 30 s[econds]." With a pH meter having three-decimal-place digital display, this drift of $\Delta pH<0.001$ units per 30 seconds is rarely reached within 24 hours,

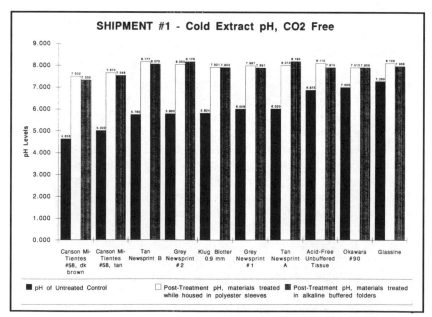

Figure 1

even with a double-junction electrode whose drift is less than 0.002 pH units per day. Among the sources of such drift are the first-order kinetics of the irreversible conversion of the weak base $CaCO_3$ into the strong base CaO, which becomes the strong soluble base $Ca(OH)_2$, in the presence of water, that occurs when a stream of CO_2-free purging gas is used to occlude and remove CO_2 from the solution, and the irreversible first-order kinetics of the hydrolysis of alum and related salts in alum-rosin size.

3. Another problem is that pH decrease caused by uptake of CO_2 is substantially greater than $\Delta pH < 0.001$ units per 30 seconds, which is the reason that section 10.3 specifies that research tests shall be conducted under a CO_2-free atmosphere with bubbling. If one complies with this requirement, the pH increase due to CO_2 removal also occurs at a greater rate than $\Delta pH < 0.001$ units per 30 seconds at least until the sample is purged of free CO_2, usually about 60-180 minutes if the original cold extraction is performed with CO_2-free water. The end of the period of CO_2 purging is the endpoint chosen for reporting the final pH. In order to facilitate the determination of this endpoint, a chart recorder is attached to the pH meter's output terminals. With a 100 millivolt scale and a 1 mm/min chart speed, this point of free-CO_2 depletion is readily recognized by a change in the slope of the drifting millivoltage. This complies with the spirit, if not the letter, of section 10.4, which doubtless does not anticipate the use of meters with three-decimal-place accuracy.

For manuscript materials, we find that most materials having a starting pH in the moderately acidic to neutral range (pH of 5 to 8) return with an ending pH of 7.95 ± 0.25, and that strongly acidic materials (those with a starting pH less than 5.0) return from treatment with an ending pH that approaches this threshold, (i.e., between pH 7.3 and 7.8). Materials with an alkaline starting pH actually show a slight decrease in pH. A typical set of results is shown in Figure 1. The underlying chemical processes are understood at least to the level of a good first approximation. This picture of cold-extract pH as a measure of effectiveness and evenness of mass deacidification will, if confirmed by other investigators, require a reconsideration of the appropriateness of cold-extract pH as a quality control technique. This is because the cold-extract pH indicates primarily that the material has been treated, without giving any indication of the extent or evenness of treatment. This is unsurprising, given that a standard 75 ml extraction volume is zinc hydroxide-saturated by 0.0001 grams of zinc oxide,[21] an amount roughly two orders of magnitude smaller than is present in a typically treated one gram sample, and given that a saturated solution of zinc oxide/hydroxide alone has a pH of 7.985 ± 0.005.

Four protocols[22] appear to be in common use for "alkaline reserve"; all have problems. Without discussing their relative merits in detail, one can note that they vary substantively with respect to controls on moisture in paper, control over or compensation for water quality, titration endpoint, filtration of the sample, ability to deal with aged, colored, or alum-rosin sized samples, and whether they attempt to assay only zinc oxide, as well as on less substantive issues such as the sample mass and reaction volume. At the HRHRC, alkaline reserves are determined by a method that:

1. Uses the dry basis weight of the sample for maximum inter-laboratory reproducibility
2. Does not involve a filtration step, because, as explained above, only about 1/100th of the zinc oxide present in a typical treated sample is actually dissolved while the remainder is either suspended in the solution or is physically bound to a paper fiber
3. Uses a double-junction pH electrode rather than indicators to determine pH at the endpoint in order to better deal with colored samples and to permit the choice of pH 7.0 as the endpoint
4. Uses blender pulping
5. Uses CO_2-free extraction water and a CO_2-free purging gas rather than boiling to remove CO_2 interferences without hydrolyzing alum-rosin size

Analysis of alkaline reserve in treated papers indicates that between 0.65 percent and 1.80 percent zinc oxide buffer (expressed as calcium carbonate weight percent equivalent) is deposited in treated papers.

A quantity of experimental evidence, particularly that generated by X-ray photoelectron spectroscopy and UV-fluorescence microscopy, has been accumulated with the generous help of research groups in the departments of Chemistry and Electrical Engineering at The University of Texas. These results will be presented in a more appropriate venue, but strongly confirm the intuitively obvious model of zinc oxide deposition in treated paper. The morphology of the zinc oxide deposition is a sheath-like layer on the individual paper fibers, having a protective thickness that appears to be too deep to be penetrated by even the most reactive of acid and acid anhydride pollutants.

Most directly related to the development of reliable quality control protocols is the collaboration with a research group in the Electrical Engineering (EE) Department. This group specializes in the development of fiber-optic instruments for the spectroscopic analysis of fluorescent materials, and is particularly well known for its work on a spectrofluorometric detector for certain diseases of the eye. Since the deposited zinc oxide fluoresces under ultraviolet light, it was logical to propose that the effectiveness and evenness of DEZ treatment could be quantified using spectrofluorometry. An instrument design for a single-purpose fluorometer was developed by project staff, and the EE group agreed to pursue preliminary studies of the fluorescent behavior of DEZ-treated papers.

To date, three-dimensional studies of various treated and untreated papers have been completed. The resulting emission-excitation matrices (EEMs) provided the preliminary information necessary to build an inexpensive fiber-optic fluorometer (perhaps less than $2,000) capable of a nondestructive determination of the zinc oxide alkaline reserve. In order to better understand the placement of the alkaline reserve within the lignocellulosic structure of the paper, the group has also pursued fluorescence microscopy. The layers of zinc oxide deposited are so thin that optical methods are inadequate to study the problem. This necessitated their procurement of a high-resolution charge coupled detector (CCD) camera, along with the requisite installation and fine-tuning of a high vacuum system. All available evidence from this collaboration and others indicate that this morphology is a uniform sheath-like coating on individual paper fibers.

NOTES

1. Richard Frieder, "CIC Cooperative Project—Logistics and Management Issues," in *Proceedings of the New York State Seminar on Mass Deacidification* (New York: Columbia University Libraries, 1993), 58.
2. Ed Rosenfeld and Robert J. Milevski, "Experiences with Trial Treatments," in *A Roundtable on Mass Deacidification: Report on a Meeting Held September 12-13, 1991 in Andover, Massachusetts*, ed. Peter G. Sparks (Washington, D.C.: Association of Research Libraries, 1992), 98-103.
3. Donald K. Sebera, "Results of Independent Laboratory Testing of Deacidified Books," in *A Roundtable on Mass Deacidification: Report on a Meeting Held September 12-13, 1991 in Andover, Massachusetts*, ed. Peter G. Sparks (Washington, D.C.: Association of Research Libraries, 1992), 76-78.
4. Karen Turko, *Mass Deacidification Systems: Planning and Managerial Decision Making* (Washington, D.C.: Association of Research Libraries, 1990), 10.
5. Eugene Wiemers, "Selection for Mass Deacidification: The Collection Development View," in *A Roundtable on Mass Deacidification: Report on a Meeting Held September 12-13, 1991 in Andover, Massachusetts*, ed. Peter G. Sparks (Washington, D.C.: Association of Research Libraries, 1992), 28-30.
6. Peter G. Sparks, *Technical Considerations in Choosing Mass Deacidification Processes* (Washington, D.C.: Commission on Preservation and Access, 1990), 13.
7. *Mass Deacidification in the Harvard University Library: A Report on the 1991/92 Pilot Operational Program* (Cambridge: Harvard University Library Preservation Office, 1992), 15.
8. Frieder, 54.
9. Sparks, 6.
10. Gerald Garvey, "Recent Developments at the Library of Congress," in *A Roundtable on Mass Deacidification: Report on a Meeting Held September 12-13, 1991 in Andover, Massachusetts*, ed. Peter G. Sparks (Washington, D.C.: Association of Research Libraries, 1992), 19.
11. Michael Placke, "Toxicological Issues and Testing Related to Treatment Processes," in *A Roundtable on Mass Deacidification: Report on a Meeting Held September 12-13, 1991 in Andover, Massachusetts*, ed. Peter G. Sparks (Washington, D.C.: Association of Research Libraries, 1992), 64.

12. Sparks, 3.
13. Richard De Gennaro, "The Institutional Context for Mass Deacidification," in *A Roundtable on Mass Deacidification: Report on a Meeting Held September 12-13, 1991 in Andover, Massachusetts*, ed. Peter G. Sparks (Washington, D.C.: Association of Research Libraries, 1992), 13.
14. Joseph A. Rosenthal, "Funding Strategies," in *A Roundtable on Mass Deacidification: Report on a Meeting Held September 12-13, 1991 in Andover, Massachusetts*, ed. Peter G. Sparks (Washington, D.C.: Association of Research Libraries, 1992), 50.
15. William J. Studer, "Funding Strategies and Public Relations," in *A Roundtable on Mass Deacidification: Report on a Meeting Held September 12-13, 1991 in Andover, Massachusetts*, ed. Peter G. Sparks (Washington, D.C.: Association of Research Libraries, 1992), 43.
16. Scott Bennett, "Management Issues: The Director's Perspective," in *A Roundtable on Mass Deacidification: Report on a Meeting Held September 12-13, 1991 in Andover, Massachusetts*, ed. Peter G. Sparks (Washington, D.C.: Association of Research Libraries, 1992), 17.
17. "Hydrogen Ion Concentration (pH) of Paper Extracts (Cold Extraction Method), T 509 om-88," reprinted in *TAPPI Test Methods*, 1991 (Atlanta: TAPPI Press, 1990).
18. *Standard Test Method for Determination of Calcium Carbonate Content (Designation D 4988-89)* (Philadelphia: American Society for Testing and Materials, 1989).
19. "Hydrogen Ion Concentration (pH) of Paper Extracts (Hot Extraction Method), T 435 om-88," reprinted in *TAPPI Test Methods*, 1991 (Atlanta: TAPPI Press, 1990).
20. Specifically, we use a Ross® electrode manufactured by Orion. We find that the ease of use of the combination-style electrode in no way compromises the quality of the results.
21. "Physical Constants of Inorganic Compounds," in *CRC Handbook of Chemistry and Physics*, 52d ed., ed. R. C. Weast (Cleveland: Chemical Rubber Co., 1971), B-154.
22. *Standard Test Method for Determination of Calcium Carbonate Content (Designation D 4988-89)*; *ANSI Standard PH1.53-1978* (New York: American National Standards Institute), section 6.2; *Texas Alkyls JA-806* (Deer Park, Texas: Akzo Chemicals); and *Texas Alkyls JA-805* (Deer Park, Texas: Akzo Chemicals).

Inventing the Future of
Preservation Microfilming

C. Lee Jones

President
Linda Hall Library

*[When he wrote this paper, Mr. Jones was President of
MAPS, The MicrogrAphic Preservation Service, Inc.]*

INTRODUCTION

The future is only as bright as it is envisioned to be. That vision must change as expectations are realized and new opportunities present themselves. Those whose original vision led to MAPS, The MicrogrAphic Preservation Service, were attempting to reach one of society's most important goals, the preservation of the record of human achievement so that our past becomes the foundation for future progress. The MAPS view of the future of preservation microfilming is not intended as prescriptive, but indicative of what that future may hold for the preservation community.

CONTEXTUAL ROOTS

The Council on Library Resources (CLR) secured funding for and operated a set of initiatives in the late 1970s and early 1980s that were designed to stimulate the development and refinement of bibliographic structures in the United States.[1, 2] The intent was to create a spirit of shared leadership among the principal bibliographic database services. While it is arguable whether the programs were successful in terms of establishing a cooperative spirit, there is little question that the Council's Bibliographic Service Development Program (BSDP) influenced and stimulated the development of authority control systems, highlighted the research needed to improve online public access catalogs, and assisted in the evaluation of alternative approaches to sharing bibliographic information.

The BSDP was never seen as a program that would continue beyond the stimulus stage; in 1984 it completed its mission. As the BSDP came to a close, it was widely expected that the Council's next major program would focus on problems of access to information. If one could now expect to find the location of required information, the question became how to obtain that which has been found. Initial studies of the issue, however, indicated quite a different set of problems than those that were anticipated. More often than not (timeliness aside) the limitation to access was not institutional policy, but the poor condition of the material requested. Frequently the item sought was too fragile to lend and, just as often, too fragile to photocopy. Faced with these facts, the Council altered its earlier intention and decided to seek support for a program aimed at *preservation* and access.

During the course of its evaluation of the access issue, CLR forged a relationship with the Exxon Education Foundation; Exxon quickly understood the importance of preservation in the context of assuring access to information for future generations. As a consequence, Exxon made available a grant of $1.2 million for a three-part project:

1. A public awareness initiative that led to *Slow Fires: On the Preservation of the Human Record*, a film that has been shown many times on public television
2. A planning initiative that (directly or indirectly) led to the formation of the Commission on Preservation and Access (CPA), an organization charged with providing leadership in planning for a coordinated approach to preservation
3. A reformatting demonstration project that led to the creation of the Mid-Atlantic States Cooperative Preservation Service, charged with creating a high-productivity, high-quality reformatting service[3]

This latter organization later became the Mid-Atlantic Preservation Service, known as MAPS, and finally, as MAPS, The MicrogrAphic Preservation Service.

While specific documentation is not available concerning Exxon's expectations for the reformatting project, it is generally conceded that they believed that the medium to be employed would be some form of scanning. However, CLR's first action after the receipt of the grant was to evaluate the available reformatting options and their long-term preservation promise. Optical and digital scanning systems were considered and compared with microfilm. The conclusion was that the only enduring reformatting medium was preservation-quality microfilm. Eight years later, despite explorations of a variety of alternative techniques, this judgment continues to be valid. Thus when MAPS came into existence late in 1986, it was as a preservation microfilming laboratory devoted to developing and testing strategies for producing high-quality microfilm in a high-production environment.

The Council passed the leadership baton to five research libraries: Columbia, Cornell, and Princeton Universities, The New York Public Library, and the New York State Library. Donald W. Koepp, Princeton's librarian, was the first and only chair of the new organization's board; there was some thought of locating the service in Princeton, New Jersey. However, Peter Likens, President of Lehigh University, had just concluded the acquisition of the Bethlehem Steel Research Campus on South Mountain in Bethlehem, Pennsylvania. He invited the MAPS board to locate the service on the expanded Lehigh campus. With a strong employee pool and modest living costs in the area, this attractive offer was accepted.

In order to broaden the perspective of the group, the five founding MAPS members added other institutions. Representatives from the University of Delaware, the University of Maryland, Syracuse University, and the Pennsylvania State Library also joined the board. Shortly after the physical facility at Lehigh was established, a representative from that university was added. During the early months of 1986 the board was heavily occupied with getting the service going; it eventually recruited a consultant to develop the basic organization and begin initial operation. The consulting assignment included identifying possible leaders for the fledgling organization; however, at the conclusion of the contract, the consultant was engaged to continue as the operating head of MAPS.

In October 1990 MAPS made the important decision to ally itself with OCLC. State-of-the-art cameras were required to move to the next level of service and performance, and the OCLC link provided a guaranteed $1.5 million for capital expenditures and operating support. The stability brought by OCLC's backing not only permitted the upgrading of the camera studio, but gave MAPS the confidence to explore a variety of new systems and products. Without this alliance, MAPS would probably have become just one more preservation filmer, struggling to produce marginal products while yearning to produce better ones.

THE MISSION

The mission of the fledgling organization was threefold and daunting. First, it wanted to become a leader in preservation microfilming. Second, it wanted to help improve access to preserved materials. Third, it wanted to monitor technological developments to determine if and when an alternate reformatting technology could become a viable alternative to microfilm.

There were at least two reasons for the founding institutions to be interested in establishing a pilot reformatting facility, even though all five operated some form of micrographics laboratory. That some of these local laboratories were large and costly operations had some influence. If preservation were to become a more demanding priority, managers wondered whether their own laboratories could gear up for the increased load and compete successfully with external vendors in terms of cost. The poor quality and uneven performance of some external microfilming vendors also played a role in stimulating the creation of MAPS.

At the very least, it was expected that MAPS could deliver preservation microfilm services for less than could be done by in-house facilities. At the very most, sufficient information might be developed to turn some of the in-house labs into high-quality services themselves. (Over time, one founding member closed its micrographics laboratory except for very special projects that could not be sent outside the institution. Other founding members decided against expanded in-house filming services. One upgraded its laboratory, with the stimulus of substantial external funding.)

From the point of view of the founding five, MAPS would be a success if it were able to deliver lower-cost preservation microfilm of higher quality than that currently produced in local filming laboratories or by external vendors. The charter of the organization specified that it would be a nonprofit service devoted to the preservation and access needs of the library community. The definition of "library community" is interpreted broadly to include archives, museums, historical societies, and government agencies, especially those with library or archival concerns.

Providing Leadership in Micrographics

Just as with any new organization, MAPS had to walk before it could run or lead; as one interested party put it, MAPS had to learn to "do chicken right." The last months of 1986 and most of 1987 were spent learning how best to make preservation microfilm consistent with preservation standards. The Research Libraries Group (RLG) guidelines for preservation microfilming, considered to be the strictest existing procedures, were used to define the operating parameters that would become the MAPS' modus operandi.[4] The obligation to produce the highest quality film possible required these early decisions; to date, they have served the organization well.

With both the Exxon resources and subsequent support from the Andrew W. Mellon Foundation, MAPS was in a position (and perhaps had the obligation) to explore new patterns of operation in a micrographics laboratory. A variety of operating patterns were examined, many focusing on how much filming an operator can do before loss of quality and productivity result. Ergonomic issues were investigated in order to create the most stress-free working environment possible, consistent with the requirements of a repetitive series of operating steps. The team concept was tested, with two operators splitting time between camera and quality assurance (QA) work; then a third person was added to the team and the group was assigned to function over two shifts, with each operator filming six hours a day.

In 1993, operators worked six hours at the camera and two hours in quality assurance or other assignments; there will certainly be further changes ahead. When more filming power is required, rather than adding high-cost cameras, an overlapping shift is arranged, so that operators work only eight hours, but overlap one another in such a way that each films for six hours and does quality assurance work for two. The camera is in operation for 12 hours but no operator works more than two hours at the camera without a break either for rest, lunch, or QA.

Providing Access to Filmed Materials

To meet that part of the mission related to access, MAPS began a print master storage service that assured prompt access from the stored collection. Clients retain ownership of the stored film, which is duplicated and sent to requesters only upon authorization of the owning institution. The next step will be to broaden the duplicating services associated with material stored in the MAPS vault: when a holdings note attached to a microform's bibliographic record indicates availability through MAPS, ILL requests can be forwarded to MAPS (rather than to the owning institution). The item will be supplied within a day or so and sent to the requester with an invoice. When MAPS receives payment from the customer, it will forward a predetermined fee to the owning library. (Facilitating access to preserved materials can also take quite different forms, as we shall see below.)

Monitoring Technological Developments in Micrographics

The final requirement of the MAPS mission is to monitor technological developments that may have promise for replacing or complementing microfilm as a preservation reformatting medium. While there is no requirement to do research into possible alternative formats, MAPS has done some basic exploration.

One of the first initiatives was to examine the development of a digital camera, but it became apparent that, for now, there are at least two problems with this approach to preservation reformatting. First, there is no known way to capture a digital image at resolutions that rival those of film, which has a theoretical limit determined by the size (actually, the mix of sizes) of the silver grains in the emulsion. The digital camera could not record at a preservation-quality resolution level but, more importantly, because of its relatively poor resolution the film that was produced could not subsequently be rescanned easily into a digital format.

Two technology projects focusing on preservation caught MAPS' attention, and they have been monitored for progress and indications that might have an impact on microfilm as the preservation format of choice. The Cornell/Xerox/Commission on Preservation and Access project uses scanning techniques to capture printed material in digital format for preservation purposes, for producing paper copies, and to test production of film from the digital data.[5] Yale's Project Open Book approached the problem differently—first by filming, and then by scanning the film to produce a variety of digital products and access systems.[6, 7]

The Cornell/Xerox/CPA project represents one of the most admirable efforts to explore technologies other than microfilm as the initial reformatting medium. The sponsors reported that, despite scanning at 600 dots per inch, it was not possible to meet the preservation standards for film resolution when the digital data were used to produce a microfilm copy. Part of the problem stems from the "Rule of 25.4," a generalization based on the number of millimeters in an inch (25.4), and the way resolution is expressed in scanning environments (dots per inch, dpi) and in film environments (lines per millimeter, lpm): if the Cornell/Xerox project scans data at 600 dpi, it is collecting data at 23.6 lines per millimeter (600 dpi divided by 25.4 mm per inch). When attempting to create a microfilm image from this data, even with some algorithmic manipulation, one cannot achieve the current minimum resolution required for preservation microfilm (120 lpm). Despite suggestions to the contrary, the solution is not to reduce the resolution standard for preservation microfilm. As we shall see, there is mounting evidence that increasing the minimum resolution may better serve future generations.

In a report on the Cornell/Xerox/CPA project, there are suggestions that scanning costs will come down consistently each year for the next 10. That may prove to be true. However, in a comparison of scanning costs with those of microfilming, there was no allowance for declining micrographic costs: instead, microfilming costs of the present are assumed to be the model for the next 10 years. Not only can it be demonstrated that unit costs for microfilming of a given quality have come down (and will probably continue to do so), but at the same time microfilm quality, at least at MAPS, has risen substantially.

Project Open Book at Yale capitalizes upon the "Rule of 25.4." By scanning preservation microfilm in order to accumulate the digital database from which access and production systems are generated, Yale begins from a position of considerable strength in terms of resolution. In fact, project staff do not capture all of the resolution extant in their film when creating digital copies. But, as digital scanning systems improve (and they will), previously scanned film can deliver even more information under improved scanning systems than it does under current ones. (Here we define "more information" as both increased line sharpness and increased steps on the gray scale.) The minimum acceptable resolution for preservation film is 120 lpm or, when converted to the measure used to evaluate scanning systems, 3,048 dpi. It will be some time before film scanners are able to capture detail at this resolution.

As will be noted below, there are now some cameras that produce resolutions that exceed our routine ability to measure. What is the ultimate resolving power of film? How fine is the detail that can be captured? Theoretically, film can capture detail no smaller than the grains of silver in the emulsion. Silver grains are not all the same size: those used in low-contrast film have a more even mix of large and small grains than those in high-contrast film and will capture more detail. The theoretical resolution of Kodak's preservation-quality microfilm (Imagelink HQ) is 800 lpm or 20,300+ dpi. The Kodak direct duplicating film, 2470, has a theoretical resolution of 1,000 lpm or 25,400 dpi.

While the limit of a film's resolution is theoretically at the grain level, practically it is limited by the quality of camera optics and processing control. Even with high-quality cameras, there is much room for improvement in resolution. In fact, there is room for improvement in a number of areas important to preservation micrographics.

CONSTRAINTS ON PROGRESS IN PRESERVATION MICROGRAPHICS

For an activity dedicated to the preservation of our intellectual heritage for future generations, preservation micrographics is disconcertingly constrained by its equipment, supplies and image recording medium, preservation standards themselves, and important economic considerations.

Equipment Constraints

The most widely used preservation camera in the world today is the Kodak MRD series. This is a camera that was designed in 1935, released to the public in 1936, and not fundamentally changed since. As advances in optics, electronics, and computing were made, the MRD remained substantially unchanged. Finally, in 1989 Kodak announced that it would no longer manufacture the MRD, but that components would continue to be available for at least another 10 years. Within a year of that decision, the distribution and manufacturing rights to the MRD were sold to Connecticut Micrographics— Kodak would no longer be responsible for any part of the MRD. Preservation micrographic labs the world over are now faced with acquiring parts to keep their MRDs in operation. Two manufacturers of the finder light for the MRD have either walked away from the market or announced that they soon will. Every preservation micrographics lab depending on the MRD is facing serious maintenance, modification, and replacement issues.

Supplies and Image Recording Medium Constraints

Supply constraints have received a great deal of attention in the last few years. There are now many reliable sources of preservation-quality microfilm enclosures and reels; however, there is still only one manufacturer of button and string ties that meet preservation standards, and this should cause some concern about future supply.

But the most important constraint is the image recording medium itself, the film. The camera film used for preservation microfilm is high contrast, appropriate for high-contrast materials—dark ink printed on white paper. As the relative contrast between ink and paper narrows, it becomes more difficult to produce a high-quality image. When manuscript collections are filmed, often rife with low-contrast materials like letterpress books, it takes expert skill to use the high-contrast medium to capture the data. Further, when it comes to capturing both a halftone illustration and text in a single frame, one is guaranteed that two separate frames will have to be shot, one for the text and one for the illustration.

There are low- and medium-contrast films available, but they are intended as duplicating films rather than camera films. It is certainly possible to develop preservation-quality camera films for a variety of contrast situations, but this has not yet been done and is not likely to be done, probably because of the very small part of the overall micrographic market (far less than one percent) represented by preservation micrographics. Indeed, preservation is so small a part of the market that there is just a single United States manufacturer of 35mm microfilm cameras. Unfortunately, it is attempting to update the 1936 MRD with solid state electronics and computing, without taking a fundamental look at requirements for preservation microfilming.

Constraints of Standards

How can standards represent a constraint on progress? They have always been considered constraints by those who try to push the frontier of an area subject to standards. In preservation microfilming, many of the camera-specific standards are a function of the operating limits of the MRD camera. The classic example is in the area of resolution. The design specifications for the MRD indicate that the range of acceptable resolution is from 75 lpm to 120 lpm. The preservation standard is 120 lpm. Normal engineering caution would preclude requiring as a standard a resolution that represents the best the camera can be expected to do. Some labs have altered their MRDs in order to achieve better resolution, but the vast majority spend a significant amount of time tuning them to achieve and then maintain 120-lpm images.

Yet another preservation standard which can probably be traced to the operating limits of the MRD is the density variation standard, which is not supposed to vary more than .20 density points (a rather wide range) within a reel of film. The MRD exposure controls are designed to provide gross control only. So, when a small adjustment is made on an MRD volt scale, the result is often a large adjustment in illumination, and thus a large change in resulting densities. With the operating constraints of the MRD, it is clear why such a wide density range is permitted.

While unrelated to standards, it will be useful to highlight yet another area in which the MRD has been the model for the preservation microfilming community. It is not unusual for a filmer to receive a Request for Proposal (RFP) that requires, at least theoretically, that the successful vendor follow all RFP requirements. One common instruction is to deal with a particular filming situation by "adjusting illumination," an instruction that is MRD-specific. In fact, illumination may not be the proper camera adjustment in order to achieve satisfactory results. One may find it more useful to correct shutter speed, an adjustment not available on an MRD.

Given the fact that the MRD has been the preservation camera workhorse, it is easy to see how the current standards came to be established. The standards must also contain some expression of hope that something better or improved can happen with the MRD, since so many of the specified parameters represent the maximum performance of the current camera. With the advent of a wide variety of alternative preservation cameras, and the understanding that the film we are producing will also serve as a platform for generating digital formats, it is time to evaluate existing standards not in terms of what one camera can do, but rather what is required to support the information and access needs of future generations of scholars and researchers.

Economic Constraints

There is a very large in-place investment in MRD cameras for preservation purposes, a significant investment in the creation of current preservation standards and guidelines, and very little power within the preservation field to motivate film manufacturers to develop new micrographics products.

The very small size of the preservation portion of the micrographics market is likely to preclude the development of preservation-specific films. Instead, the preservation market will be required (as it always has been) to adopt those films which are available. Nowhere is this a more important principle than in the availability of Ilfochrome (the former Cibachrome), the only color microfilm with acceptable longevity characteristics.[8] The market for Ilfochrome is not strong, though there are some signs of increasing use for preservation. If the manufacturer decided to trim low-volume products, Ilfochrome would certainly be a candidate. Should Ilfochrome be dropped, there would no longer be a color microfilm option for the preservation community.

The in-place investment in preservation standards is significant, though there are periodic reviews of every standard on the books. Significantly, the principal influence in establishing standards used by the preservation community has often been service bureau personnel, though a new AIIM (Association for Information and Image Management) committee for the representation of library interests provides a mechanism to assure that the library and preservation sides of an issue will be heard. It is imperative that those who set standards understand that preservation film is not just for next year, or five years from now, or 10, but that it is intended as a medium of information transfer capable of supporting digital and analog access systems for the next five centuries.

Finally, the most significant economic constraint is the enormous amount of capital invested in MRD cameras. Replacement cameras which are able to support the next evolution of preservation filming cost a minimum of $35,000, a far cry from the $14,000 to $15,000 cost of a new MRD in 1986. The price range of state-of-the-art preservation microfilm cameras is from $60,000 to $125,000, depending on the film format, optic quality, and degree of operating sophistication. A micrographics lab of 10 MRDs is faced with a camera replacement capital investment requirement of between $350,000 and nearly $1,000,000. With 15-year amortization schedules, how much preservation work will it take to offset these capital expenditures? Only the most confident preservation filmers will make the investment.

ALTERNATIVE PRESERVATION CAMERAS

The MAPS experience in upgrading from a completely MRD micrographics lab to much higher quality equipment can be considered indicative of what others will face. MAPS recognized the need to replace its inventory of MRD cameras in 1987, two years before Kodak abandoned the MRD. Fortuitously, MAPS discovered Herrmann & Kraemer (H&K), a high-quality micrographics firm in Garmisch-Partenkirchen, Germany. Frustrated by their inability to find micrographic equipment that met their demanding internal standards, H&K began building their own cameras, processors, duplicators, etc. They agreed to build and sell to MAPS one of their 16/35mm microfilm cameras.

When the first H&K arrived and completed its shakedown period, MAPS realized that the nature of its participation in preservation microfilming had changed. Nonetheless, the first H&K camera acquired by MAPS was not perfect for preservation; in fact, it had some serious limitations. In discussions with H&K, the company agreed to modify its basic camera to meet MAPS' needs. Among the MAPS-specific modifications were an automatically adjustable mask system, the capability to turn the head under power to any desired filming position, and finer control over exposure parameters, shutter speed, and illumination.

The camera was already a computer-controlled unit supplied with some of the best optics available. Even without precise adjustment, resolutions in excess of 160 lpm were routine. For the first time, MAPS staff began to be able to distinguish the 18 pattern on test targets filmed on some of the H&Ks. (The 18 pattern is the smallest pattern on the standard test targets used in preservation microfilming.) Clearly, this camera was going to meet all preservation standards for resolution and, in some cases, beat those standards by more than 60 percent.

Finally, after significant camera design changes by H&K and following the alliance with OCLC, MAPS placed an order for 12 of the customized H&K 16/35mm cameras. This order took up the entire camera production capacity of H&K for just under two years. In the meantime, MAPS staff were developing an exposing system for capitalizing on the unique characteristics of the H&K camera.

It should be noted that the Herrmann & Kraemer is not the only new 35mm preservation-capable camera available. MAPS has also acquired a Gratek Congress camera, designed according to a set of specifications prepared by and for the Library of Congress. Unfortunately, these specifications were not reviewed by others in the preservation microfilming community, and the Congress camera has some limitations. The most serious limitation from MAPS' point of view is that, while it uses microprocessors to control various camera functions, it uses analog switches and dials to initiate changes and does not use a display screen or keyboard. Further, a set of fixed mask templates is used to change mask size; thus, mask changes are discrete increments and not infinitely variable.

Gratek, based in England, makes an interesting argument for staying with one mask size on each reel of film. It declares that the resulting film will be far easier to scan, if all frames are of the exact same size. This does not address reduction ratio changes, but that is another matter with which scanning technology must contend.

Despite these limitations, Gratek has produced a quite serviceable camera with an excellent pneumatically controlled and adjustable book cradle. It is the most adjustable book cradle MAPS has tried, in terms of the amount of pressure that is applied to each item during filming. The book cradle itself justifies the presence of this one Gratek among 13 H&Ks, cameras with which it cannot compete in terms of resolution.

Other cameras available to the preservation laboratory (but with which MAPS has had no operational experience and so can offer no judgment) include those manufactured by Zeutschel, though it advertises its illumination system as a fluorescent based system; Gottschalk, a German company; Connecticut Micrographics, with its computerized MRD; IKM, a Dutch family of cameras; and Elke, another British camera maker. There are undoubtedly others with which I am not familiar, but these appear to be the principal manufacturers of preservation cameras at this time. (My apologies in advance to those manufacturers whose product is not known to this author.)

THE BIRTH OF EXPOSURE™

When the first H&K was installed at MAPS, it was brand new, it was computer controlled, and technicians did not like it. It was nothing like an MRD. It was silky smooth and a little intimidating to those unfamiliar with computer-controlled equipment. Consequently, a series of operators tried their hands at the H&K, as MAPS sought an operator who could be comfortable with the camera and its computer interface.

Finally, an inventive camera technician was assigned to the H&K and

managed to establish an operating rapport with the computerized "new kid
on the block." However, he noticed that despite finer controls, smoother operation, and incredible resolution, the H&K, like the MRD, still had some
trouble achieving the evenness of density required by the RLG guidelines, a
spread of no more than .20 density points on any given reel.

A variety of exposing systems had been tried at MAPS, with mixed results. Some operators could use the crutch offered by a particular exposure
determination strategy better than others. The H&K technician began to think
about the various exposing systems in use, and he discovered a reflectance
densitometer from a long-ago failed effort to develop yet another exposing
system. With very little encouragement from management and using his own
home computer, Mike Riley created a completely new exposing system.
Once completed and dubbed ExpoSure™, it was evaluated for uniqueness
and granted a patent in the summer of 1992. Its incorporation into the MAPS
filming system propelled MAPS' film quality to a new level highlighted by
extraordinarily narrow density ranges on every reel produced.

Not only did the exposing system work for the H&K, but it was discovered that it could be applied to the MRD with equal ease, though with a
slightly wider range of results. Retakes for out-of-range densities became a
thing of the past. It is not uncommon for the maximum density variation over
an entire reel to be .05 density points or less. The only requirement is that an
operator take reflectance densitometer readings at appropriate intervals as the
background color of the material being filmed changes. It did not take long
to realize that ExpoSure™ could be built into the computer that controlled
H&K camera operation. H&K was skeptical, but built an interface and was
as surprised as MAPS was pleased to find that ExpoSure™ worked very well
when integrated into the H&K computing system.

Once the patent was awarded for ExpoSure™, MAPS began to make the
system available through licensing. The first institution to take advantage of
ExpoSure™ was the National Library of Germany. Any college or university micrographics laboratory is eligible for a license. The only requirements are reflectance densitometers at each camera station using the
system, and precise daily control over film processing. Film processing
must remain stable from day to day for the exposing system to function
properly. Those who alter processing according to the camera that generated the film will not be able to use ExpoSure™.

PRESERVATION MICROFILM:
A MULTIMEDIA PLATFORM

It is unfortunate that microfilm has achieved a stodgy reputation; it offers
no glitz or sparkle to the increasingly technologically oriented managers of
academic, research, and government institutions. But the truth is quite the

opposite: while it may not seem exciting when compared to certain emerging technologies, microfilm is one of the most capable platforms ever devised for launching a variety of alternative formats.

The most obvious format launched from 35mm preservation microfilm is other types of film. For years UMI has had conversion cameras capable of transforming 35mm film to fiche format for service copies. So important is the service copy to the law library community that almost all preservation filming for law has been in fiche format to begin with. Fiche has some wonderful access qualities. It can be easily and cheaply duplicated and so given away to someone who needs a fiche or two. Unfortunately, we do not yet have fiche-specific preservation standards and hence must attempt to apply 35mm standards to its production. MAPS' camera supplier, H&K, is in the process of debugging a camera which will convert 35mm preservation film to fiche for service copies. The modest added cost seems to be worth it for those interested in providing fiche as the end-user format for their constituents.

There are also systems available for the reconversion of film or fiche to paper. The old Copyflow machines are no longer manufactured by Xerox, but units can be purchased from a small firm that makes a business of building and rebuilding Copyflow units and keeping others in good repair. A number of other film-to-paper units are available, the newer ones having laser-quality output. So far these units are rated at 300 dpi quality, but it cannot be long before a 600 dpi film-to-paper unit is available. The chief constraints on these units are their cost and the uneven demand for paper copies from preservation film.

But the most exciting formats into which preservation film can be converted are digital formats. Mekel, one of the leaders in scanning microfilm, offers units capable of scanning 16mm, 35mm, and 105mm fiche. In fact, the scanning element of Yale's Project Open Book is a Mekel scanner repackaged by Amitech and married to a huge hard drive and OCR-capable software. Mekel is just one of several film scanning units available. Scanners are often relatively low-cost parts of more complex systems, as is the case of the system being used at Yale.

Actually, any film can be subjected to scanning. The key is that higher resolution film with even densities and consistent mask sizes tends to be the easiest to scan (that is, it causes the fewest work stoppages while operators seek external decisions because of film variations). MAPS has had film scanned into a CD-ROM product with support from the Commission on Preservation and Access, but the most disappointing aspect of the project was the search engine supplied on the disks. Most CD-ROM search software is specially designed for the content of the disk. In order to convert preservation film to CD-ROM in a useful format, a search engine that is generalizable over a variety of subjects and formats must be developed. Clearly, no matter how powerful the software, it will do little good without quality indexes to the scanned film. Part of the answer seems to be to use OCR techniques on certain portions of the scanned data, to capture index information before the CD-ROM is created. No doubt there will be even more effective alternatives to indexing this medium.

While it is extraordinarily important to search for reformatting techniques that offer longer, more assured information preservation, it is not yet time to discard microfilm. Consistent with the search for new technologies is the continuing exploration of how best to use the currently accepted preservation medium, preservation-quality microfilm. The view that preservation microfilming represents a commitment to a dead technology is incompatible with the results of recent efforts to convert film to a variety of digital formats. Film has a 500-year life when properly prepared, stored, and managed. When this is combined with its capability of being read by the human eye and its basis in an exceptionally stable technology (that of optics), film is clearly the continuing preservation medium of choice. Further, film expands the number of output and use options available to the research and academic communities. We have barely begun to scratch the surface of the format and output capabilities that can be created from preservation microfilm. Every new digital access system is likely to be supportable by film, in one of its scanned forms.

PRESERVATION OF GRAPHIC IMAGES: CTF

We have already seen that the film used for preservation microfilming is a high-contrast film that is inappropriate for graphic images. Even when great care is taken to achieve as much detail as possible, seldom is this film capable of capturing more than eight steps on the 20-step gray scale.

During negotiations with Herrmann & Kraemer for MAPS' first H&K camera, it was discovered that the company had a proprietary continuous-tone filming (CTF) system for capturing graphic images, prints, photographs, slides, halftones, etc. An agreement was reached which would have licensed MAPS to use H&K's proprietary CTF system in a non-competitive market; but for a number of reasons the licensing could not be concluded. H&K, however, began to provide MAPS staff with suggestions about how to achieve CTF images. Tests went on over a period of three years with H&K providing additional assistance as they understood how serious MAPS was about developing and offering a CTF service to the U.S. preservation community. The MAPS developmental constraint was that whatever process evolved, it had to meet preservation standards. Finally, late in 1992, with a very important suggestion from the Image Permanence Institute, MAPS completed development of its own CTF technique. The results were shared with H&K personnel who were stunned with the quality of the images and admitted that using their own technique, they could not match MAPS' image quality.

MAPS employs a Kodak duplicating film used routinely in preservation duplication as its camera film for CTF and processes it completely normally. The result, using MAPS' H&K cameras, is film exhibiting a resolution of 196 lpm or higher, while capturing from 15 to 19 steps on the gray scale. From an aesthetic point of view, most clients specifying CTF filming prefer the 15-step images. The more steps above 15 that are captured in a CTF image, the more detail is lost at the light end of the scale. MAPS has never achieved images exhibiting all 20 steps on the gray scale, though it can dependably produce film in which 19 steps can be distinguished.

While the camera master images exhibit very high quality, the duplicates continue to do the same. Theoretically, we know that we must experience some loss of resolution during duplication, but often that loss cannot be measured using the standard technical targets. In the Cornell/Xerox/CPA report on costs, scanned material is preferred because there is no loss of resolution from generation to generation. Further, it is suggested that microfilm experiences a 10 percent loss of resolution from one generation to another. Clearly, the degree of loss is a function of how well the duplication process is executed and the kind of film used in duplication from generation to generation.

As with normal preservation microfilm, CTF images have the capability to support a wide array of digital access systems, but one is of particular interest today. As CTF began to be offered to MAPS' clients, a relationship was established with Digix, a company providing high-quality Kodak Photo CD images. Initial and subsequent tests in which CTF film was scanned into the proprietary Kodak image encoding scheme indicated that the Photo CD could function as a powerful entrée for CTF images into the digital world. The fact that images can be copied from the Photo CD into any receptive computing environment (MAPS uses the Macintosh platform) indicated that a new panoply of access and communication options was available for use with preservation graphic images.

There are also inexpensive pieces of software that can be used to display, catalog, and access collections of graphic images. The announcement by WLN (Western Library Network) of a service to catalog individual graphic images, including a digital image of the item being cataloged, indicates that we have just begun to see how broadly the digital world and the graphic world will interact. And, the source of the graphic images may well be preservation-quality CTF images.

FOUNDATIONS FOR THE FUTURE

Our future will be defined by our expectations and our experience. Therefore we may glimpse what the long-term future for preservation reformatting will be by reviewing current progress in a number of areas.

1. The Mekel and similar film scanners have already been linked to OCR software systems. While they may only be used for creating indexes at the

moment, can we be far from completely OCR-ed preservation film available in CD-ROM format or some other very large data base?

2. The Kodak Photo CD system, when used to capture and store high-quality graphic images like preservation-quality CTF images, creates a fixed format capable of supporting the creation of a wide variety of access and communication systems. The Photo CD is so new that access and distribution systems not yet imagined are waiting to be developed from this base.

3. Minolta has announced a relatively large piece of equipment which is capable of scanning 16mm, 35mm, and fiche; storing the scanned image and providing for its manipulation by a microcomputer; and allowing the altered image to be printed, faxed, or output to a floppy disk. So far, the company has not seen much demand for these services in libraries, but the system is indicative of what a library might offer to users of its microfilm collections. As usual, copyright issues will have to be addressed and resolved.

4. It will not be long before a relatively modest-sized film reader, supporting both 35mm and fiche, will be available either in the library microfilm area or at a scholar's work station. The unit will be linked to a microcomputer. Once the appropriate information is found on the film, it will be scanned, possibly even OCR-ed, and output to a floppy disk or hard disk for further manipulation or use. The film remains in its original format, but its contents have now been copied and can be used in the scholar's digital world.

5. The move to create a nationwide information highway with high bandwidth cannot help but expand the way any information format will be used, including preservation microfilm, whether scanned as images or text. Will we see collections of film used to respond digitally to information requests? We suspect that this is true, though we have no feeling for the time frame. However, it will probably happen sooner than we suspect.

6. The RLG microfilming guidelines (1992) have just recently been updated and revised. We have a standards system that requires validation of each standard every five years. If the object of preservation reformatting is to serve the information needs of future generations, and we believe that the information future of the coming age will be more digital than less, we must examine the standards used to produce preservation film. Those standards should be pushing us toward higher and higher quality film. They should not be focused on the most capable cameras, whatever those might be; rather they should be aimed at the anticipated needs of coming generations. If that means digital information systems, and that seems a reasonable assumption, then we need to capture all of the resolution of which we are capable at this time. We also need to recognize that the film we are using can capture more information than the optics we currently use can resolve, even the superb optics of the H&Ks.

The future is for all of us to define. MAPS, in concert with a number of organizations including the Commission on Preservation and Access, the Council on Library Resources, OCLC, Herrmann & Kraemer, the Image

Permanence Institute, the Research Libraries Group, and many others, has taken steps to influence that future. We know that there are cameras that are far better than the preservation workhorse of the 1930s, the Kodak MRD and MRG series. We know that there are techniques to control the range of densities on a given reel of film, techniques like MAPS' ExpoSure™. We now know how to produce continuous-tone film with extraordinary resolution substantially retained during duplication, and blessed with a minimum of 15 of the 20 steps on the gray scale. Best of all, we know how to integrate the product of this equipment and these techniques—high-quality, preservation microfilm—into the digital world.

We are at an early stage in defining how digital information, whether originally resident in paper or microfilm, will be used by current and future generations of scholars and researchers. It is clear that we have an obligation to continue defining how best to serve the digital future and how to improve the products and services available to and from the preservation community. These are obligations readily accepted by The MicrogrAphic Preservation Service and its colleagues.

NOTES

1. C. Lee Jones and Nancy E. Gwinn, "Bibliographic Service Development," *Journal of Library Automation* 12 (June 1974): 116-24.
2. Warren J. Haas, Nancy E. Gwinn, and C. Lee Jones, "Managing the Information Revolution: CLR's Bibliographic Service Development Program," *Library Journal* 104 (15 September 1979): 1867-70.
3. Princeton University, "The Mid-Atlantic States Cooperative Preservation Service." Press Release, 22 July 1985.
4. Nancy E. Elkington, ed., *RLG Preservation Microfilming Handbook* (Mountain View, Calif.: Research Libraries Group, March 1992).
5. Anne R. Kenney and Lynne K. Personius, *Joint Study in Digital Preservation, Phase 1: A Report to the Commission on Preservation and Access* (Washington, D.C.: Commission on Preservation and Access, September 1992).
6. Donald J. Waters, *From Microfilm to Digital Imagery* (Washington, D.C.: Commission on Preservation and Access, June 1991).
7. Donald J. Waters and Shari Weaver, *The Organizational Phase of Project Open Book: A Report to the Commission on Preservation and Access* (Washington, D.C.: Commission on Preservation and Access, September 1992).
8. James M. Reilly, "A Summary of Recent Research at the Image Permanence Institute." Report to the Board of the Image Permanence Institute, Rochester, N.Y., Fall, 1992.

Optical Disk Applications in the Federal Government: Sharing and Preserving Unique Collections

Alan Fusonie

Historian and Head of Special Collections
National Agricultural Library

Richard F. Myers

Senior Appraisal Archivist
National Archives and Records Administration

INTRODUCTION

There is a good deal of excitement in Washington today—and this excitement is not connected with the numerous congressional debates in the nation's capital. Rather, it stems from the growing number of optical disk applications being used by offices of federal agencies to improve the long-term survival of valuable documentary resources, as well as access to these collections.

Access and preservation, preservation and access—these twin goals in the world of libraries, archives, and museums are all too often at odds with one another. Today's optical disk technology offers an effective solution to the longstanding conflict between access and preservation, as well as a host of other potential benefits. This is demonstrated in the projects and systems that are operating in the federal agencies discussed in this paper, and many others not included here. These agencies and their staffs have seized the day and harnessed the exciting technological tools available to them to improve service to their customers, both government and public, today and tomorrow.

The excitement associated with these projects stems in part from the nature of the technology itself, which represents breathtaking, accelerated change. It has truly revolutionized the way we manipulate, store, and display information. However, the enthusiasm of professionals who provide access to and preserve documentary materials arises from something more profound: this technology offers them a means to meet their responsibilities at a level of sophistication and effectiveness of which they had once only dreamed. Seeing dreams become reality is definitely exciting.

The projects discussed here include both analog and digital systems, reflecting the evolution of imaging technologies over the last 15 years. Initially, analog systems utilizing the National Television System Committee (NTSC) standard television format provided a relatively inexpensive approach to the production of optical laser disks containing documentary images. Such disks offered the possibility of distributing large numbers of images (50,000 or more) in a form in which the images could not be altered. Furthermore, the user could display the analog images using a relatively inexpensive player and a standard television.

More recent developments in digital imaging systems make it possible to scan original images at reasonably high resolutions and record them on optical media. While digital systems are more expensive, they offer a significant benefit in that the images may be transmitted to users over existing communications networks. Digital images may be altered once the file resides in a user's environment, but work is progressing on verification coding techniques that will indicate any alterations that may have been made.

Two of the agencies profiled here (the Smithsonian Institution and the National Gallery of Art) began with analog systems and have added digital capabilities; two other agencies (the National Library of Medicine and the National Agricultural Library) continue to use analog systems. The Library of Congress project employed both analog and digital technologies from its inception. Decisions on using analog or digital systems (or integrating both technologies) involve a host of considerations including agency mission and project goal, costs and available resources, the nature of original material, collection size, and intended audience.

The innovative projects discussed here are presented in broadly descriptive profiles that are not technically detailed. Each of the individuals interviewed will be pleased to provide additional information on a specific project or system; their names, addresses, and telephone numbers follow this paper's endnotes. Federal agencies hope that optical disk technologies will help to democratize knowledge and better ensure its long-term survival. While the lifespans of these new information and image technologies are uncertain, the enhanced access they provide to collections is stunning; at the same time, they help to ensure the survival of original documents, by significantly reducing researchers' need to handle or reproduce them. The focus of two of the projects described here, the *American Art from the National Gallery of Art* videodisk and the American Memory project, is placed more squarely on education and access than preservation; they are included here because of the promise their technical approaches show for other library, archival, or museum environments where protection of original documents is of key importance.

NATIONAL INSTITUTES OF HEALTH: THE NATIONAL LIBRARY OF MEDICINE

On the campus-like setting of the National Institutes of Health (NIH) in Bethesda, Maryland, just north of the District of Columbia, the National

Library of Medicine (NLM) occupies a prominent position overlooking the NIH complex. NLM, one of the three national libraries in the United States, maintains one of the world's foremost collections of research materials on medical science. Within its History of Medicine Division, the National Library of Medicine Prints and Photographs Collection houses a unique collection of medical imagery. Begun in 1879 within the Army Surgeon General's Medical Library, this collection now includes more than 59,000 fine prints, photographs, albums, ephemera, and posters illustrative of the history and development of medicine. As an important primary resource on the history of medicine, the collection is used extensively by scholars, authors, publishers, and the media.

Concern about the preservation of the collection because of its increasing use, the growing staff resources needed to service the materials and produce copies requested by readers, and the collection's availability (limited to those who can come to the Library) led to a 1981 proposal to place images from the collection on a laser videodisk, creating an "electronic picture catalog." This pilot project resulted in the *Video Picture List*, 1,000 images plus an accompanying three-ring notebook that includes related caption and catalog information. The Library distributed 100 copies of the disk and notebook to its most frequent users and to other medical libraries. The reception to this pilot package was very positive, and an accompanying survey determined that dissemination of the collection on videodisk would be a "giant step forward" for researchers.

In 1988 NLM embarked on the History of Medicine Archive/Retrieval Project to place the entire History of Medicine picture collection on a laser videodisk. An accompanying CD-ROM contains catalog information and a control program that enables the viewer to retrieve the images stored on the disk either by keyword search for specific pictures, or search by catalog number. An important element in this contractor-supported project was the decision to produce 35mm film images of each item in the collection before placing the item on disk. This decision led to two significant outcomes: the 35mm film copies make it possible to eliminate handling the original images for any subsequent duplication requests. With the collection preserved on high-quality film, it is also possible to reproduce the images for high-definition television videodisk or generate digital copies, without rephotographing the materials. Thus this project not only produced an archival copy—a 35mm intermediate—but also insured that the originals need not be handled and that access to the collection (through the videodisk and the automated database) would be significantly improved.

The PC-based retrieval system that accompanies the videodisk was developed at NLM using dBase III and Clipper. The system is user-friendly, taking the viewer's natural language keyword input and comparing it to all words and phrases in the database's keyword file. Each input request seeks one or more subjects associated with one or more images. When matches are found, the descriptive information for the images is retrieved and displayed. As the viewer selects an entry from the PC screen, the corresponding image is displayed on the video monitor. Forms for ordering photographic reproductions of the images on the disk are included in the retrieval program, allowing viewers with modems to place orders from their PCs.

Beta testing of the disk (appropriately named "PicQuick") and software will be concluded shortly, and it is likely that NLM will offer the system for sale in the near future. Summarizing his experiences in coordinating this project, Bill Leonard, Audiovisual Production Officer at NLM's National Center for Biomedical Communications, observed that the laser disk project had achieved its goals of providing easier access to this valuable collection and realizing the significant benefits associated with image preservation.[1]

SMITHSONIAN INSTITUTION: THE PRINTING AND PHOTOGRAPHIC SERVICES DIVISION

The Smithsonian Institution's Printing and Photographic Services Division (PPS) has traditionally provided photographers, a photographic studio, and photographic laboratory services to meet the needs of all Smithsonian components. More recently, under the direction of Jim Wallace the Division has begun to utilize evolving optical disk and electronic imaging technologies to realize its program responsibilities and the Institution's goals in a better, faster, cheaper fashion.

Interestingly enough, the key factor in PPS's pursuit of greater efficiency was the decision to establish a cold storage facility for the Institution's still photography collections, which include in excess of two million images. While cold storage represents an important preservation step, if it is effective, it also largely eliminates patron access to the collection. To overcome this conflict between preservation and access, the Division turned to laser videodisk technology and produced *Photographs from the Smithsonian Institution* which includes a selection of images.

The Division carefully monitored new imaging technologies as they became available. As time passed, some of its photographers were equipped with still video cameras, and the basic elements of an "electronic darkroom" (including computer capabilities and a Nikon scanner) were acquired. Critical to these developments was the desire to provide users with a quality copy of the original image stored by the Division. Many requesters are from the print and publication media, and digital imaging offers an effective means of satisfying requests using a format that can be transferred over standard communication links and is readily usable by the client. An important by-product was that, once the image was scanned, storage of the scanned data eliminated any need to remove the original from storage—in effect, providing *access* to an image meant that the original could be *preserved*.

The ability to prepare a digitized file of images from the collection led to another significant development. As online services such as CompuServe, GEnie, Prodigy, and America Online grew in popularity, PPS pursued a proposal to make Smithsonian images available electronically, through these companies. The impact of this capability is best measured in the number of actual "downloads" of images that have occurred—in excess of 50,000 over a little more than two years. More recently the Division has embarked upon exploratory projects involving the Kodak Photo CD. This product offers greater resolution and appears to have a lower production cost when large quantities of images are involved. Experiences with this technology were very positive during the Clinton inauguration; PPS photographers covered the activities, and Photo CDs were produced on-site at the Smithsonian. One of these CDs has been included in the "Information Age" exhibit in the Museum of American History.

The work of PPS underscores the importance of imaging technology as a collection of tools to accomplish the basic mission of the Smithsonian Institution. The Division has been guided by a keen appreciation of the need for flexibility and a willingness to experiment. No single technology answers every question or solves every problem. While today's imaging technology is in a state of transition, the programs of PPS demonstrate how much can be accomplished in terms of preservation and access when imaging technologies are effectively implemented and harnessed in a mission-oriented context.[2]

THE NATIONAL AGRICULTURAL LIBRARY

As part of a major productivity improvement initiative, the National Agricultural Library (NAL) developed two analog laser disks containing images of the most-requested agricultural and forestry photos and slides held by the United States Department of Agriculture (USDA). These disks addressed NAL's need to increase awareness and access, improve non-print reference services, and reduce the handling of original resources.

In 1986 the U.S. Forest Service provided a research and development grant to the National Agricultural Library and the University of Maryland; the resulting laser disk tool was to be duplicated and distributed. The Forest Service's historical photo file of 60,000 of its most-requested black-and-white photos, along with an extensive collection of color slides, had recently been transferred to the National Agricultural Library's Special Collections Unit. This collection provides a unique visual record of forestry, man, animals, and the changing environment in the 20th century. From a pictorial documentation of the westward movement, to the special focus on foresters, miners, cowboys, wildlife, and Native Americans, the browsing file was a rich but largely untapped visual vein. With the application of laser disk technology, the opportunity for reaching an expanded audience was both exciting and real.

The project staff at NAL included one full-time leader and four part-time college students. The image-capturing process was complemented by the development of a computer database of information about each image, accessible by subject, location, name of photographer, date, accession number, and so forth. In cooperation with Image Concepts of West Boylston, Massachusetts, a beta test C-Quest photo database management system was linked to the laser disk to provide keyword searching. Photos and slides were filmed on 35mm motion picture film and transferred to a broadcast-quality videotape. A quality-control check disk was then generated, and later mastered to a 12-inch analog commercial disk. [FIGURE 1]

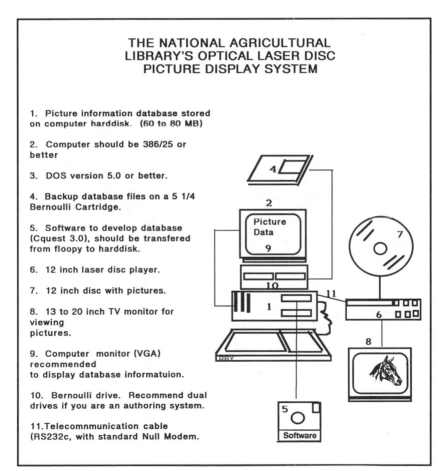

THE NATIONAL AGRICULTURAL LIBRARY'S OPTICAL LASER DISC PICTURE DISPLAY SYSTEM

1. Picture information database stored on computer harddisk. (60 to 80 MB)

2. Computer should be 386/25 or better

3. DOS version 5.0 or better.

4. Backup database files on a 5 1/4 Bernoulli Cartridge.

5. Software to develop database (Cquest 3.0), should be transfered from floopy to harddisk.

6. 12 inch laser disc player.

7. 12 inch disc with pictures.

8. 13 to 20 inch TV monitor for viewing pictures.

9. Computer monitor (VGA) recommended to display database informatuion.

10. Bernoulli drive. Recommend dual drives if you are an authoring system.

11. Telecomnmunication cable (RS232c, with standard Null Modem.

Figure 1

The completed NAL/Forest Service Photo Collections Disk contains an introduction about the project by Alan Fusonie, Historian and Head of Special Collections, along with more than 34,000 black-and-white photos in 69 general subject chapters, 500 color slides, 55 color botanical illustrations, 175 maps, and an award-winning 60-second Smokey the Bear public service announcement. Recorded on magnetic media, the database occupies over 20 megabytes.

In September of 1987, NAL began another laser disk project with the Photographic Section of the USDA Office of Governmental Affairs using student aids from both Catholic University and the University of Maryland. This photo library covered the broad area of agriculture, food, nutrition, insects, plants, and livestock. For this project, botanical illustrations from *Plantae et Papiliones Rariores . . .* (1748-57) by Georg Dionysius Ehret (1708-1770) and a selection of original fruit art from the Pomological Watercolor Art Collection of the USDA were also incorporated. This time an

Photo by J. Swab

Ron Young (seated, left), the Visual Specialist of the Special Collections staff, demonstrates to Secretary of Agriculture Mike Espy (seated, right) the optical laser videodisk and computer database developed by NAL to provide instant access to Forest Service photographs. The men standing and observing the demonstration are, left to right, Joseph Howard, NAL Director; Lavelle Green, Office of Operations; Alan Fusonie, Head of NAL's Special Collections; and Brian Norris, Public Affairs Office.

upgraded high-resolution video camera recorded full-screen images directly onto an analog 8-inch WORM (Write Once, Read Many Times) disk that is immediately usable. Within USDA, duplicates were made for use and review purposes. The culmination of the project was the production of the commercial 12-inch disk for distribution and use.

Together, these two laser disks not only offer greater access to a larger number of photos and slides than was previously possible, but also stimulate more interest among scientists, authors, editors, publishers, newspaper reporters, television producers, and education media specialists in using USDA photo collections. A digital approach with interactive multimedia CD-ROMs containing text and photo images is also being aggressively pursued. For example, NAL (in cooperation with the University of Florida's Institute for Food and Agricultural Sciences and Michigan State University's Cooperative Extension Service) has just completed a very exciting do-it-yourself horticultural landscaping CD-ROM called *Plant It! CD*. The disk contains 1,000 full-color full-screen images with information about plants and the climate zones of the United States where they grow best. NAL and the University of Pittsburgh School of Library and Information Science have begun a project involving the digitization of images from the collection of hand-colored plant illustrations that appeared in the *Curtis Botanical Magazine*, published between 1787 and 1905. NAL also has a selection of slides on wildlife, Mount Saint Helens, and historic nursery and seed trade illustrations available online in Section 16, NAL Collection of Graphics Forums (Go Gallery) of CompuServe. It is important to USDA and to the National Agricultural Library to be current with the new and improved image information technologies; USDA agencies seek to position themselves to benefit long-term from changing image information technologies.[3]

LIBRARY OF CONGRESS: THE AMERICAN MEMORY PROJECT

The Library of Congress' (LC) five-year pilot project known as the American Memory traces its origins to Librarian of Congress James Billington, who began his tenure in 1987 with a strong commitment to providing computerized access to the Library's collections. Billington named the project to emphasize that LC's holdings contain a significant portion of our nation's history. American Memory is the next step in the Library's automation process that began in the 1960s with MARC and continued in the 1980s with the Optical Disc Pilot Project, which experimented with local access to print materials, still photographs, motion pictures, and sound recordings.

In contrast to its predecessors, American Memory places its greatest emphases on content and service to remote locations. As the name implies, the project is intended to provide access to selected Library of Congress collections of Americana. By the end of the pilot, American Memory will have prepared about one dozen collections for computerized access. Some had been previously defined by the Library's archivists, like the Mathew Brady Civil War Photographs (1861-1865), the Federal Writers' Project Life History Manuscripts (1936-1940), and the Daniel Murray Collection of African-American Pamphlets (1820-1910), for example. Other collections, such as the American Variety Stage and the Evolution of the Conservation Movement, were specially organized for American Memory.

The conversion of content to electronic form required a family of approaches and an array of specialist contractors. Still photographs, for example, were rephotographed on motion picture film, then digitized or converted to analog video. In one instance, a set of historical documents was microfilmed; the film was scanned to produce the digital images. In other cases, the original paper copies themselves were scanned. Books, pamphlets, and other bound materials were scanned using special, non-damaging book-edge equipment. The project's staff reports that the best value and greatest accuracy were provided by rekeying contractors when texts were converted into machine-readable form; attempts to use optical character recognition (OCR) devices were generally less successful. American Memory machine-readable texts are encoded with Standard Generalized Markup Language (SGML). The various reproductions of content are accompanied by cataloging (sets of bibliographic records in the United States Machine-Readable Cataloging, or USMARC, format).

American Memory is intended to reach a variety of scholars. A two-year end-user evaluation has been carried out to identify the types of researchers who are best able to use American Memory collections, as well as to refine the overall software design. The evaluation reached a total of 44 library sites throughout the United States: one-third K-12, one-third college and university, and the remainder a mix of other libraries. The sites received American Memory prototypes on CD-ROM and videodisks. The greatest number of collections were configured for the Apple Macintosh platform. Four collections were produced on CD-ROM disks for IBM-compatible equipment.

As this paper was written, the end-user evaluation neared completion. The American Memory staff reports that preliminary results show surprisingly high interest at the K-12 level, where many schools had experience with educational products on CD-ROM and videodisk. Noteworthy among the test site experiences are a college student's documentary video on William McKinley that incorporated original film footage and stills found in the American Memory database with the student's own narration. At another site images from the Brady Collection were used to illustrate Stephen Crane's *Red Badge of Courage*.

The American Memory pilot will conclude at the end of 1994; during its final year the staff will focus on two major issues. First, the Library will determine how to distribute the collections. This exploration will compare options for fee-based dissemination by the Library itself with cooperative publishing partnerships with private-sector firms. Second, the project will experiment with the transfer of its disk-based programs to an online mode. This effort will receive a special boost from the University of Nebraska at Lincoln, where an Internet prototype is to be constructed.[4]

THE NATIONAL GALLERY OF ART

The National Gallery of Art is another pioneer in improving image access to art collections through the application of laser disk technology. In 1979, Videodisc Publishing Company approached the Gallery about a cooperative laser project which would transform the 700-page reference book *National Gallery of Art* into a new form; supplemented by an additional 500 paintings and new accessions, the volume was recreated as a useful and beautiful videodisk. From the Gallery's management perspective, this image technology provided the first and best step forward in the creation of a comprehensive visual catalog for research, education, reference, and documentation. More than three years were required to organize sequences of works, review and proof images and captions for accuracy (including color corrections), and transfer everything to the video master. The goal was to develop a complete resource catalog—a "visual archive."

The *National Gallery of Art* videodisk can be used on a videodisk player with interactive and random-search capabilities. Each side of the disk contains a 25-minute presentation by J. Carter Brown, then Director of the National Gallery, providing an informative history and tour of the collections. The major portion of side two is a still-frame catalog of 1,645 works of art—paintings, sculpture, drawings, and prints—each with caption information.

In March 1991, Education Resources staff at the National Gallery of Art began a second laser videodisk project. This was a more ambitious undertaking involving the latest digital imaging technology and including more images. It required the cooperation of many museum curators in assembling transparencies of several sizes and coordinating the accompanying catalog information for each individual work of art. Existing records were re-examined and corrections and enhancements to both images and information were implemented. Because of the size of the project, the digital imagebase is stored in 60 cartridges, each containing 600 megabytes. Between the time required for design and production, demonstration, color correction, and re-scanning, this project required two full-time and six part-time staff over a two-year period. The digital imaging not only minimized the linear jitter of video, but also provided the best possible image quality. In the future, these images may be used to generate CD-ROM products.

The completed laser videodisk *American Art from the National Gallery of*

Art contains over 2,600 full-frame images of works by American artists ranging from Gilbert Stuart (1755-1828) to Winslow Homer (1836-1910) to Jackson Pollock (1912-1956). Through this disk students and teachers of American art and history can explore such things as the changes an artist made to a painting, and view the documentary inscription and other details not readily visible to the viewer; they can investigate both place and culture over two centuries. For example, one can journey with George Catlin (1796-1872), American painter and traveler, who in the 1830s spent years among the Indian tribes of the Plains and the Northwest. Teachers of American history and writers concerned with Native American culture will find over 350 of Catlin's Indian paintings on this disk, to complement their textual research.

Whatever the setting, the disk provides high-quality museum art images to the viewer, removing physical or geographic restrictions. The National Gallery's main purpose for creating this newest laser videodisk is to foster education about art by bringing images of original art works to a national and international audience. Because of the random-access capability of videodisk technology, the images used can be tailored to many different educational needs; they can be shown in any sequence and related to the themes and subjects the viewer chooses. The Gallery's Education Resources department offers free-loan of laser disks (and other educational extension programs) to a variety of educational institutions. The *American Art* laserdisk is the most recent use of new technologies to broaden public awareness and access to American art and to stimulate excitement and appreciation for the nation's art collections.[5]

CONCLUSION

The image management revolution of the 1990s is significantly changing the way archivists, curators, and librarians within the federal government handle non-print images, including photographs, slides, art works, posters, videotape, and motion picture film. Federal archives and libraries should develop future-oriented practical information policies for the years ahead. In particular, critical decisions about partnerships between federal agencies and the private sector, aimed at improving access and preservation, must be made, taking into account the needs of future generations. In entering partnerships with vendors and manufacturers, agencies should insist on compliance with federal policies and procedures governing the care of public records of long-term value. The imaging industry's interest in doing business with federal archives and libraries must move beyond mere profitability and user satisfaction, to sharing in federal archives' and libraries' time-honored fundamental preservation responsibilities. At the same time, the federal government can encourage worthwhile partnerships by streamlining the administrative processes through which they become productive realities.

As federal archive and library staffs examine the benefits associated with image networking, high-capacity digital communication structures, fiber optic transmission, and the shift from analog to digital processes, they must not lose sight of the institutional need for standards, program continuity, and their fundamental responsibility to preserve the valuable materials in their custody. Each federal archive and library has its own resource problems, unique circumstances, and program priorities. The "keeping up with technology" and "me too" syndromes so prevalent in our rapidly evolving information environment should not be allowed to obscure the fact that a particular technology may be economically or programmatically unfeasible in a given organization. A cautious flexibility and attention to the institution's core mission must carry the day. The organizations and projects discussed in this article demonstrate the value of an institutional affirmation of these tenets.[6]

NOTES

1. William R. Leonard, Audiovisual Production Officer, National Library of Medicine, interview with Richard Myers, 16 June 1993; William R. Leonard and John Stokes, "The Portable Picture Collection: The National Library of Medicine Archival/Retrieval Picture Project." Unpublished paper.
2. James Wallace, Director, Printing and Photographic Service Division, Smithsonian Institution, interview with Alan Fusonic and Richard Myers, 16 March 1993.
3. See Alan Fusonie and Richard Myers, "Our Agricultural Landscape: Improving Image Preservation and End-User Image Access Through Laser Disc Technology," *Journal of Imaging Science and Technology* 36 (January-February 1992): 60-62; see also the technology section of *National Agricultural Library Annual Report, 1992,* comp. & ed. Brian Norris (Beltsville, Md.: National Agricultural Library, 1993). For a discussion of new digital imaging equipment at the USDA Photography Division see Larry Rana, "Digitizing Photos Pixel," *Government Communications* (January-February, 1993): 10-11.
4. Carl Fleischhauer, Project Director, American Memory Project, Library of Congress, interview with Richard Myers, 30 March 1993.
5. Ruth R. Perlin, Head, Education Resources, National Gallery of Art, interview with Alan Fusonie and Richard Myers, 15 April 1993.
6. The opinions expressed are the authors' and do not necessarily reflect those of the National Agricultural Library or the National Archives and Records Administration.

APPENDIX

The following individuals will be pleased to provide additional information on the systems and projects profiled in this article:

Ruth R. Perlin
Head, Education Resources
National Gallery of Art
Washington, DC 20565
(202) 842-6273

William R. Leonard
Audiovisual Production Officer
Lister Hill National Center for Biomedical Communications
National Library of Medicine
Bethesda, MD 20894
(301) 496-5721

James Wallace
Director, Printing and Photographic Services Division
Smithsonian Institution
Washington, DC 20560
(202) 357-1487

Alan Fusonie
Head, Special Collections
National Agricultural Library
Beltsville, MD 20705
(301) 504-5876

Carl Fleischhauer
Project Director
American Memory
Library of Congress
Washington, DC 20540
(202) 707-6233

PART 3:
TECHNOLOGY AS A TOOL FOR MANAGING THE WORK OF THE PRESERVATION/CONSERVATION UNIT

Technology can be used not only to accomplish the work of preservation (as described in part two of this book) but also as a tool to manage the preservation department or conservation laboratory. From the viewpoint of senior library management Michael Bruer describes the value of computers in simplifying and facilitating tasks typical in any preservation operation. He observes that, while the implementation of technology in conservation is more recent than in other areas of library activity, the same principles and rationales that apply to circulation, cataloging, and other functions also pertain to preservation. Bruer reviews some of the instances in which computerization may not be the best solution and identifies costly mistakes, such as permitting available hardware to dictate application, and extensive customization. He recommends several important indicators useful in planning computer applications for preservation.

Errol Somay and Marc Reeves bring a different perspective to the use of computers in preservation: they are actually using automated systems to accomplish the work of the units they manage. Somay and Reeves describe a plan for a comprehensive preservation processing system that was jointly developed by systems and conservation staff; the objective was to justify the expense of automation by building a highly efficient system for preservation selection, specification, and processing. The authors explain the system's components and structure, and demonstrate its benefits in terms of increased productivity and cost-effectiveness; they include several examples of "before and after" preservation activity to underscore the system's efficiency.

Automation is also a valuable tool in the conservation laboratory. Walter Henry examines some of the issues surrounding software design for conservation, including those that enable systems to be shared among institutions. Among the applications he discusses are survey sampling, recording survey observations, treatment record systems, and clinical applications such as leaf casting, solvent blending, and matting. Henry also explores a number of important database issues, including time-stamping or digital signatures, data refreshing, and the pivotal question of whether the record system will be used as a record system or an authoring tool. He makes the point that the information contained in local conservation laboratory systems can be of considerable interest to staff in other institutions; for this reason, the use of data interchange formats that transcend the local institution's platform is critical. He suggests generalized or descriptive markup language as one promising avenue.

In a paper that demands quite a bit of the reader but rewards the determined, Erich Kesse discusses the prerequisites for the design of an automated, relational, fully integrated preservation management information system (MIS). Rather than addressing technical issues such as operating systems, programming, or record length and structure, Kesse examines the nature of the system's architecture, including its shape and function. Like Henry, he sees the value in cooperative development, making systems transferable from one institution to another. The preservation system, he suggests, should be part of a much larger library MIS, demonstrating interconnectivity with other library modules such as those supporting acquisitions, cataloging, circulation, and collection management.

The Role of the Computer in the Preservation Operation

John Michael Bruer

Associate Director and Chief of Preparation Services and Systems
The New York Public Library—The Research Libraries

INTRODUCTION

The New York Public Library, known more familiarly as NYPL, is one of the world's great cultural institutions. It boasts a strong tradition of service to the public and support of scholarship dating from its founding in 1895. It is composed of two major departments: The Research Libraries, which are the focus of this analysis, with a collection of more than 38 million items including almost 10 million books and book-like materials; and The Branch Libraries, whose holdings of 9.6 million volumes are serviced through a network of 82 lending locations. NYPL is a quasi-national organization whose broad collecting and service responsibilities are exceeded within the United States only by the Library of Congress. It is a private institution with a public mission that includes free and unrestricted access to the collections and resources by all patrons and scholars, as well as a strong commitment to conservation consistent with its status as a library of record.

The staff of The Research Libraries, which are largely funded by gifts, grants, and endowment, consists of more than 500 positions organized into five primary service units, each of which is managed by an associate director:

1) Performing Arts Research Center
2) Schomburg Center for Research in Black Culture
3) Science, Industry, and Business Library
4) Social Sciences and Humanities Library
5) Preparation (Technical) Services Division (Acquisitions, Cataloging, Conservation, and Systems, or computer-based operations)

Within the Preparation Services Division, major operational subdivisions such as Conservation are in turn managed by an assistant director whose expertise is widely recognized in the profession.

The library makes extensive use of computers at all levels, but the broad application of microcomputer technology in the Conservation Division of The Research Libraries is particularly noteworthy. Some of the more important developments in this regard are the subject of this paper.

The New York Public Library operates one of the world's oldest and largest preservation programs. During fiscal 1991/92, the latest year for which complete figures are available, more than 1,500,000 volumes were cleaned, bound, filmed, restored, or otherwise preserved. The staff of the Conservation Division consists of approximately 80 full-time-equivalent positions, supported by an annual budget exceeding $3,000,000, and is functionally organized into six major units:

1) Preservation Administration Office
2) Collections Improvement Project
3) Preservation Reformatting Office
4) Preservation Microfilm Laboratory
5) Shelf and Binding Preparation Office
6) Conservation Laboratory

The Conservation Division serves The Research Libraries and the general public as an information resource on all aspects of the conservation and preservation of research library and archival materials. In addition, the division coordinates all preservation activities within The Research Libraries, and delivers various preservation services, or contracts for the delivery of these services, to all units. These services include binding and repair, microformatting, digitization, fumigation, physical conservation treatment (e.g., restoration and mylar encapsulation), collections cleaning, environmental monitoring, and salvage of water-damaged materials.

This division plans and coordinates fiscal and budgetary support for existing preservation programs; gathers and reports statistics of preservation activity and expenditures on an annual basis; articulates library policies; identifies and adopts appropriate standards; implements procedures that have a bearing on the preservation, protection, and security of the collections; and recommends new ones when appropriate. It represents The Research Libraries in local, state, and national forums concerned with the conservation of research and archival materials.

The Conservation Division responds to requests for information pertaining to the preservation of books and other research materials received from the general public and from other institutions by mail, telephone, or in person. In addition, it provides information on the administration of the libraries' preservation programs to professional colleagues from around the world and provides tours of the preservation facilities upon request. The Division Chief serves as selection officer in The Research Libraries for subjects relating to the preservation of research and archival materials. Additionally, a nationally recognized internship program in preservation administration is supported with funding from the Andrew W. Mellon Foundation.

UNDERSTANDING THE ROLE OF THE COMPUTER

This sketch of the Conservation Division illustrates the potential scope for the application of computer technology in preservation operations. It is true that most conservation programs in this country are not as extensive or broad-based as NYPL's, but this paper will suggest that almost any aspect of a library's conservation effort will benefit from the rational application of computerization. The Research Libraries' long experience with automation dates from the 1960s, and is today characterized by the widespread use of computers of all sizes in every aspect of library operations. Although the implementation of technology in conservation endeavors is more recent than in other areas of library activity, it turns out that the same principles and rationales apply to preservation applications as to circulation, cataloging, or any other function.

Early in the 1986/87 fiscal year the automation of preservation-related activities using microcomputers began to expand significantly in The Research Libraries of NYPL. An assessment of automation needs was initiated at that time, and application development proceeded at a rapid pace. Currently, there are more than 50 microcomputers of various configurations employed throughout the Conservation Division. The applications mentioned in this paper are just a sample of the major activities and can be given only brief expositions. A more detailed description of some of the significant developments may be found in the Somay and Reeves paper that follows.

Before discussing the proper role of computers in preservation activities, it may be useful to review some of the ways in which computerization is *not* the indicated solution or desired approach to a given situation. All too often in the author's experience, organizations have undertaken automation efforts that ended in addressing the wrong problem, or providing the wrong solution, or failing to take into account the larger systemic environment, or in a host of other misdirected or inappropriate outcomes. The consequences can range from minor inconvenience to outright fiasco, and since conservation is charged with the care of the collections, it follows that equivalent care should be exercised in the implementation of computer-based solutions. The fact that the use of computers in preservation activities is a relatively recent development, when compared to applications such as circulation, for example, adds emphasis to the need for careful planning. Some of the more common examples of the misapplication of computers may be summarized as follows.

• *The "because it's there" syndrome*

This malady may also be called computerization for the sake of computerization. We should always remember that technology is only a tool, one of many that might be used to advance a given agenda. It may well be that a computer is one way to deal with an issue, but perhaps not the best way or the cheapest way. We have only to look to the excitement being generated by advances in digitized imaging for sufficient reason to raise a cautionary flag. Clearly, there are many instances when computer-controlled digitized imaging offers the opportunity to improve access and extend preservation. One of the projects at NYPL that relies on digitization is the effort to capture a series of early 20th-century Russian architectural periodicals on brittle paper. But we must accept the fact that, as of this writing, not all materials are suitable for digitizing, and we should remember that preservation microfilming is not yet ready to be designated an historical curiosity.

• *Even when it has been determined that automation is the right step to take, some organizations (especially larger institutions) fall prey to the idea that their conception of a system design is the only acceptable one*

This tendency was more common in the years before the market was flooded with commercial products, but even today too many libraries embrace the idea that their way is the only way, with the result that very specialized programs have to be written by the vendor or (even worse) by the library's staff, in order to provide for every nuance that may be conceived by the institution. A good example that relates to preservation is that of binding modules for serials control systems. Very few, if any, commercial products include anything more in their serials systems than the capacity to tell when something has been sent to and returned from the bindery, which is certainly a far cry from full control of the library/bindery interface. In their zeal to have a "fully integrated" system (whatever that means), some libraries have insisted that special programs be written either by the vendor or by their own staff, in order to achieve adequate communications with their binders. A perfectly logical alternative is to purchase specialized software from another vendor, such as the ABLE (Automated Binding Library Exchange) system offered by Megatronics Inc. and recently installed in The Research Libraries, with a view toward eventually developing a reasonably seamless interface with the serials control application, perhaps through local area networking.

• *A fairly common mistake made by libraries that become interested in computerization is permitting the application to be determined by the hardware that happens to be available*

Larger research libraries, for example, often select a given software solution simply because their institution's computer center happens to own a mainframe machine from the required manufacturer. Another vendor's software may be far more appropriate or desirable, but it is passed over because it turns out to be incompatible with the existing hardware. This is a "cart before the horse" solution. The correct sequence of events in the rational implementation of automation should be to determine the nature of a problem or issue, to select the software that best meets the requirements of the situation, and to let the hardware then be determined by the demands of the software.

Admittedly, this approach is sometimes difficult or impossible to follow. The Research Libraries, for example, received a gift of several dozen IBM-compatible microcomputers during the mid-1980s. In most cases, the results achieved through program development were perfectly satisfactory, but in hindsight it is also clear that some staff, including a few in Conservation, would have been better served if the resulting applications had been developed on a Macintosh platform instead of in a PC-DOS environment.

• *One of the most difficult problems to guard against in the use of computers for library operations is the prospect that too few staff members will have adequate knowledge of a given application*

The risk of this happening is especially severe in the case of microcomputers, which have become both ubiquitous and increasingly powerful. On one hand, management does not want to stifle the innovation of enterprising staff members who develop useful applications on the machines assigned to them. On the other hand, one has to worry about what happens when a program fails and the developer is no longer on staff.

Some years ago, the Conservation Division employed an individual in the microfilming preparation unit who developed an interesting application using FoxBase, a database program for microcomputers. Unfortunately, he was the only person on the staff who had any experience with FoxBase, and in fact his was the only known use of FoxBase anywhere in The Research Libraries. After the staff member's departure, the microfilming preparation unit changed its focus in systems implementation and thus avoided any operational problems with FoxBase, but the broader issue continues to crop up in various units throughout the library; the only answer seems to be eternal vigilance.

Although these cautionary points about systems development should not be taken lightly, they are not meant to suggest that there is no legitimate role for the computer in the conservation arena. In fact, almost any activity of reasonable complexity is a potential candidate for automation. While it is true that the availability of computer applications for conservation purposes is a relatively recent development, there is substantial evidence that the same principles that apply to systems development in general also apply to potential conservation functions.

Of course the conservation community has used the computerized environment of the bibliographic utilities for microfilming queuing for many years, but the widespread use of computers in preservation units has been slowed by market factors, including the perceived lack of commercial viability for conservation systems, and by technological factors, such as the absence of reliable, accurate, and inexpensive methods of digitizing images. In recent years the picture has begun to change substantially: microcomputers have become much more powerful; off-the-shelf programs such as database management software have become more sophisticated and easier to use; library staff members who have the skill and inclination to develop applications for preservation have become more numerous; and the commercial sector has begun to take notice by offering stand-alone, often micro-based, programs, or by implementing preservation-related subsystems as part of an integrated library system.

The proper role of the computer in preservation operations can be determined by applying the same tests one would use for any prospective automation effort. If the planning process indicates that a sufficient number of certain characteristics applies in a given circumstance, there is good reason to conclude that automation will produce a successful outcome. Some of the most important indicators that should be considered in planning computer applications include these:

- Increased productivity
- Enhanced capabilities
- Expanded access
- Extended functionality

Any one of these indicators may be adequate justification for computerization, if the promised improvements are not eclipsed by the cost or effort to implement the application. Each of these characteristics is examined below, and reference to some of the experiences of The Research Libraries may be instructive in this regard.

DIVISION-WIDE PRESERVATION DATABASE

All four of the indicators mentioned above are present in the effort to develop a single database environment to serve the libraries' entire Conservation Division. In January 1993, separate bibliographic and operational databases in the Preservation Reformatting Office, the Preservation Microfilming Laboratory, and the Conservation Laboratory were combined to provide a single selection, specification, and processing environment designed to encompass the entire range of preservation options offered in The Research Libraries. The resulting integration of previously discrete operations reflects NYPL's desire to move toward collections-based preservation management in which a comprehensive range of treatment and reformatting operations is available during selection and specification. Full implementation of the new database environment was completed in the summer of 1993.

Starting with machine-readable records for the items to be treated, each office and laboratory generates all necessary documentation, work products, and tracking information for different preservation treatments. All treatment information (methods, materials, time, staff) is maintained in this database, as well as sketches of repairs, scanned photographs, and other documentary material. The multi-user relational database software used for this system is Helix Express. The Preservation Database itself, currently containing approximately 22,000 titles, resides on a Macintosh Quadra 800, and may be accessed by an additional 14 Macintosh computers on an Ethernet network throughout the three offices. Dial-in remote access for survey applications is provided to three portable PowerBook computers by a Shiva LanRover/4E port server and Apple Remote Access software. Cordless dial-in access is available through a cellular modem interface carried by the PowerBook 180s.

PRESERVATION REFORMATTING OFFICE AND MICROFILMING LABORATORY

Increased productivity is illustrated by the operations of the Preservation Reformatting Office and the Preservation Microfilming Laboratory, closely related units in that the office prepares and controls the material that the laboratory films and produces. These units have been supplied with micro-computer hardware consisting of eight machines in the Reformatting Office and two machines in the Photo Lab. The Reformatting Office also employs PageMaker software to produce eye-legible targets for each reel of film, and to create and revise a variety of processing forms.

The Office maintains a database of jobs in progress using both Double Helix and EXCEL software. Record structure incorporates not only basic bibliographic information such as author and title, but also includes process-ing instructions and special requirements. With full implementation of the Preservation Database and the acquisition of new equipment, further im-provements in methodology are anticipated during the next fiscal year.

Additional data are input later when filming is completed by the Photo Lab; this includes technical information such as reduction ratio, image orien-tation, number of feet and reels, and the time required to finish a job. Separate files are maintained for public orders, as distinct from the libraries' internal conservation filming operations. It is estimated that production costs have been reduced by 50 percent with the introduction of microcomputer support for targeting and processing. This has freed up resources for a variety of important applications including reformatting into microfiche pamphlets under 50 pages in length, and the more comprehensive implementation of certain operations such as searching and queuing of jobs, to avoid costly and unnecessary duplication. More detailed information regarding these develop-ments may be found in the essay by Somay and Reeves, which follows.

SHELF AND BINDING PREPARATION OFFICE

Another example of productivity improvement occurs in the Shelf and Binding Preparation Office, which is primarily responsible for overseeing the routine binding of NYPL's monographs and serials, most of which are shipped to outside commercial binders. A PC-compatible computer is con-nected through a black box to a pair of Quietwriter printers and a ProPrinter to support both processing and statistical analysis. All binding shipments are logged in and out, and the data recorded in this process permit the unit to track workload factors, produce statistical breakdowns by type of material and by binder, and calculate various fund balances.

On the processing side, one of the Quietwriters is configured to accept a special labeling device (Se-Lin) that simultaneously prints an accurate spine label and encloses it in plastic tape. Macros have been written so that long runs of class marks in a given shelf location can be produced with minimum effort. This technique is also used for labeling other containers, such as folders for sheets of music. The advantage to this approach is not just an increase in production, but also much greater accuracy, compared to a clerk's typing each label.

The Shelf and Binding Office has also formulated ambitious plans to integrate its internal processing with the serials control subsystem in the Acquisition Division and the automated ticketing and shipment systems implemented by the major commercial binders. In 1989 a commercially available software package called ABLE was selected for implementation on IBM-compatible microcomputers, and substantial progress has been realized in making this application available to some of the larger public service divisions, in addition to the Shelf and Binding Office itself.

COLLECTIONS IMPROVEMENT PROJECT

The potential for enhanced capabilities was realized in the Collections Improvement Project through the judicious application of computer technology. The primary objectives of the Collections Improvement Project include systematic volume-by-volume cleaning and inventorying of the libraries' collections, as well as identification, description, and recording of specific items requiring more extensive conservation treament. The latter objective constitutes the condition evaluation phase of the project, which is recorded in a local database providing support for informed decisions and future treatment programs. Bibliographic data are keyed from the shelflist under contract to an outside vendor, then input by floppy disk in standard machine-readable cataloging (MARC) format to a file controlled by Advanced Revelation software. This approach provides a side benefit unrelated to preservation: the capture of data in MARC format means that these records may be added to the libraries' online public access catalog without further processing in a retrospective conversion project.

The Advanced Revelation database includes extensive information regarding the condition of individual volumes; it is fully indexed to permit retrieval of records on the basis of a wide variety of characteristics, and to provide for reports on major categories of material for which programmatic funds and administrative authorization may be sought. Hardware architecture is complicated not only by the database design and application, but also by the use of laptop computers (Toshiba 5100s), which are used to capture condition information immediately, on-site, in the libraries' more than 100 miles of book stacks. The central computer is an IBM PS/2 Model 80-311 running at 20MHz with 10MB of RAM and a pair of 314MB fixed disks. In the future, field data (currently transferred by floppy disk) will be downloaded from the laptops via IBM token-ring adapters and local area network software. When material is selected for treatment, descriptive information from this database will be delivered to the Conservation Laboratory in machine-readable form to support the next stage of processing.

PRESERVATION ADMINISTRATION OFFICE

In addition to routine office management functions, the Preservation Administration Office also oversees a number of activities that are substantively related to the Conservation Division's mandate to conserve the libraries' collections. A particularly striking example of expanded access is the Armbruster Collection Data Base Project. The collection consists of 5,800 photographs of Long Island, from Brooklyn to Montauk, taken between the 1890s and the 1930s. The majority of the photographs are from the 1920s, when local historian Eugene L. Armbruster attempted to document the area. Armbruster published a number of pamphlets on the history of Long Island; as part of his research effort he was especially concerned with photographing some of the old homesteads, which he knew were endangered by the rapid growth of the area. A broad range of other subjects is also represented in the collection which was donated to The Research Libraries in 1934.

The collection has been put into polyethylene sleeves and housed in three-ring binders with slip cases. This provides the material with an acid-free environment and protects it from excessive handling. Annotations, which were made on the backs of the photographs in Armbruster's cryptic hand, have been "decoded" and transferred to a database using dBase III Plus software. The fields used in each record include item and volume numbers, village, township, year and month of photograph, family name of occupants as noted by Armbruster, descriptor of subject (e.g., "house," "church," "windmill," etc.), and a notes field for other information such as street location. The database is indexed on various fields and printouts can be made available as finding aids. A patron is thus able to obtain, for example, all the photographs and annotations associated with John Howard Payne's boyhood residence, about which he composed the song "Home, Sweet Home."

The dBase III program is also used to support a database for the Pamphlet Volumes Collection which totals several hundred thousand items. These pamphlets, covering virtually every subject, have been collected over a period of years and often provide information that can be found in no other way. Although they are individually cataloged in the printed book catalog of manual catalog records created through 1971, they are not represented in The Research Libraries' online catalog, and there is no easy way to identify bibliographically and then bring together all of the items on a given subject. It would also be useful to be able to include appropriate parts of the pamphlet collection in subject-oriented microfilming projects, as funding for such activity periodically becomes available.

Toward these ends, subject headings based on the libraries' Billings classification system have been identified for each bound volume of pamphlets. These subject headings, along with the associated class marks, have been recorded in a dBase III file which permits easy retrieval of all material that relates to, for example, the British Museum, or all of the pamphlets contained in the Talleyrand collection, or the single volume that includes Fourth of July orations. An example of a potential large-scale microfilming project might be the 50,000 pamphlets related to economics, transportation, and commerce that can now be identified and retrieved from this database.

CONSERVATION LABORATORY

In addition to its commercial binding operations, NYPL is fortunate to have an extensive Conservation Laboratory whose staff provides a wide range of treatment options for materials in The Research Libraries' collections. These in-house capabilities support extensive artifactual treatment and are highly diversified, including rebinding/recasing, phase boxing, encapsulating, deacidifying, matting/hinging, and drop-spine box production. Development of enhanced functionality through computer-based applications is equally extensive and is discussed in detail in the article by Somay and Reeves. Applications include a multi-access conservation treatment database; a database of equipment, supplies, and vendors; a system to support box-making calculations and labeling operations; telecommunications access to the Conservation Information Network (CIN); and various administrative processes such as spreadsheets for purchase orders, reports, and personnel, as well as software for word processing, organization and flow charts, forms generation, signage, labels, and worksheets.

Hardware architecture has recently been expanded with the addition of a Macintosh Quadra 800 computer and a large-capacity disk drive that acts as file server for the other computers in the unit. A Macintosh IIx is also being used to monitor environmental conditions in specific locations, such as Rare Books and general stacks, by receiving and storing in real time data collected by temperature and humidity devices installed in strategic locations. The conservation treatment database is implemented under Helix software and is used to track the 400-600 items which move through the treatment laboratory every month. Record structure is relational, providing logical connections among the item record, treatment record, photo documentation record, and ongoing development of the condition report/specification record. A graphics link which provides sketches of tears, losses, and other graphic information to the item record has been implemented. A wide variety of reports provide information on production statistics by type of material and individual staff member; lists of items in process and their exact location; summaries of the number of items waiting at various treatment points (used to limit the amount of material submitted by public service divisions); and other aspects of preservation activity.

The unit's box-making operation is a particularly striking example of productivity increase provided by automation. Output is considerably greater than that in other large conservation programs where little or no computerization has been introduced. In drop-spine box production, the system supports entry of the required measurements; calculates board, lining, and covering materials dimensions; allows batch cutting of components; and reduces cut-off waste. The phase box operation, on the other hand, begins with uploaded book measurement, label, and bibliographic information from the Collections Improvement Project or the public service divisions, calculates component measurements and creasing locations, automatically generates half-inch labels in accordance with NISO standards, and provides production statistics. Current production rates are in the range of 40-50 phase boxes per day per staff member, in contrast with the norm of five to 10 per day reported by other libraries.

COMMUNICATIONS AND SYSTEMS DEVELOPMENT

From this summary of some of the more important systems installed in a large research library preservation program, it should be apparent that significant progress has been achieved in a relatively short period of time. Nevertheless, the implementation of computer-based applications in the Conservation Division, or for that matter in The Research Libraries as a whole, is not without its hazards and difficulties. Two of these, if one is permitted a bit of neologistic jargon, may be described as developmental cross-talk and inter-application communication. It may be useful to touch briefly on these issues, with special attention to the symbiotic relationship between them.

Managers are well-advised to encourage imaginative thinking and initiative among staff members at all levels. In the context of the present topic, this can manifest itself in a sort of "weedy" growth in the number of microcomputers and software programs found throughout the organization. From the general manager's point of view, the goal is to strive for rational growth and maximum utilization of resources, and to minimize duplication of effort and implementation of incompatible software. The department or unit head, on the other hand, is motivated by the need to get a job done in the face of increasing demands and declining resources, and to take advantage of readily available automation in the form of microcomputers.

As a consequence, potentially related applications may be developed with incompatible architectures, or data may be encoded in ways that limit their subsequent use in another context, or methodologies that have undesirable fiscal implications may be selected. This developmental cross-talk can be exacerbated, and in some cases obscured, by a feeling on the part of staff that management has failed to provide adequate technical resources and personnel to meet their requirements. In the early days of microcomputer implementation at NYPL, the strategy was, in fact, to place PCs in various divisions and units without formal or rigid guidelines, allowing staff maximum flexibility and encouraging hands-on experience. It is now clear that development in some areas, such as the Conservation Division, has been so rapid and extensive that more rigorous oversight is indicated.

In this "big bang" phase of microsystems development, it is understandable that incompatibilities may arise which, under other circumstances, could have been avoided. Even when the administration recognizes the seriousness of the situation, as is the case at NYPL, events may outstrip the capability of the institution to deal with them in a truly effective manner. Indeed, data processing managers have grappled with this problem since the time microcomputers became commonplace in the work environment. Experience has shown that, as noted above, the best solution is eternal vigilance.

In those cases where the problem of incongruity in systems development is considered to be of minor consequence, there still remains the issue of inter-system communication. Indeed, it may be said that communication is at once the most fundamental as well as the most complex aspect of systems development. Many research libraries are dealing with the implementation of local systems, whether microcomputer-based or otherwise, as well as problems associated with the interconnection of these systems among themselves, with the various bibliographic utilities, and with other external systems: there are many examples of this phenomenon in the foregoing exposition of microcomputer application development in NYPL's Conservation Division.

Mention has been made of the Preservation Microfilm Office's need to search and queue candidate records prior to filming. Ideally, the microcomputer used to support the processing database would also be configured to access appropriate external files for searching and queuing purposes, within the context of a sophisticated communications environment. Another example is the process in the Conservation Laboratory by which public service divisions submit records to the preservation treatment database. Most of these divisions prepare their worksheet records in MS-DOS format; floppy disks are then hand-carried to an IBM machine for transmission to the Macintosh computer via modem. With an appropriate communications infrastructure in place, it would be possible to transmit the information directly from each producer, with consequent improvement in productivity.

The New York Public Library recognizes the importance of these issues and has initiated a telecommunications project, the goal of which is to meet the growing and changing communication requirements of NYPL in a flexible, economic, and timely manner. The New York Public Library Network (NYPLNET) provides wide area connectivity to support all voice and data communications throughout the institution, including seven AT&T System 75XE Private Branch Exchanges (PBXs) linked by Distributed Communication System (DCS) control software. Principal computing locations, including those with mini and mainframe computers, are connected by T-1 transmission circuits capable of passing data at 1.5 million bits per second (MBPS). The Research Libraries Local Area Network (RLLAN) is attached to NYPLNET and provides Ethernet connectivity among the units of The Research Libraries. Applications and networks at the unit level, as for example in the Conservation Laboratory, will then be accessible from microcomputers and other terminal devices throughout the facilities, made possible by RLLAN and NYPLNET.

The projected wide area and local area network environment is expected to accommodate major changes in the levels and types of library communications by increasing telecommunications capacity. It is designed to improve productivity and control the cost of library communications by adding new telecommunication features and capabilities. With respect to the applications and issues described in this paper, it seems certain that by introducing a communications standard the developing network will simplify the configuration and operation of workstations, the pooling of expensive resources, and communication between systems. In a wider context, the new network will facilitate the delivery of services and sharing of resources by interconnecting with metropolitan, state-wide, regional, and even national and international telecommunications networks. And finally, it is perhaps not too much to hope that full implementation of the network will position The Research Libraries to adopt future telecommunications technology as it becomes available.

This brief sketch of the Conservation Division's automation efforts illustrates the potential scope for the application of computer technology in preservation operations. It is true that most conservation programs in this country are not as extensive or broad-based as NYPL's, but, as this paper suggests, almost any aspect of any library's conservation effort will benefit from the rational application of computerization.

Comprehensive Production Software (That Works!) for Preservation

Errol Somay

Coordinator, Virginia Newspaper Project
Library of Virginia
[When he wrote this paper, Mr. Somay was Head, Preservation Microfilming Office
The New York Public Library—The Research Libraries]

Marc Reeves

Head, Conservation Laboratory
The New York Public Library—The Research Libraries

INTRODUCTION

Institutions managing comprehensive preservation programs respond to the problem of deteriorating library collections with an array of treatment options and strategies. Whether the approach specified for an individual item is a protective enclosure, extensive artifactual conservation, repair, binding, facsimile photocopying, or reformatting, preservation staff must help select, process, and track each item through many decision-making and production steps. There is a need to carry out this work as expeditiously as possible; in addition, the preservation officer must periodically report on the progress of the program and its related costs, often using statistical updates. Both administrative and production tasks are labor-intensive and incur significant expense for the institution.

Consider the preservation challenge at The New York Public Library (NYPL). Annually, The Research Libraries reformats over 10,000 volumes (or about 4 million pages), binds over 58,000 monograph and serial titles, treats and processes over 8,000 items in the Conservation Laboratory, creates 16,000 phase boxes and 4,000 wrappers, and processes more than 100 reference volumes for facsimile photocopying. Each year The Research Libraries' Conservation Division must meet daunting processing requirements; as in many libraries experiencing yearly belt-tightening, more must be done with fewer funds and other resources. The specter of deteriorating collections looms large, but the cold reality of the "bottom line" teaches us that only so much can be accomplished in a given fiscal year.

In the search for greater efficiencies and better use of human resources, administrators often argue for increased levels of automation. But the costs of purchase, installation, and training can result in a direct blow to almost any library budget. The preservation officer may view automation as a method for creating greater cost savings; frustration sets in when rapid developments in technology or sudden changes in administrative and budgetary priorities result in the failure to fully exploit the computer's data retrieval or processing capabilities. Computers are acquired at different times; inevitably, some become obsolete before the next generation can be purchased. Existing equipment is often cobbled together, with the hope of effecting some savings for the library budget. Systems, software, and methods multiply in different offices; each spreadsheet, production log, local database, or target-producing graphics program meets the needs of a particular selection or processing operation, but they do not work together to form a true automated system.

THE NYPL STORY

At The New York Public Library, The Research Libraries' staff in the Conservation Division, Preparation Services Division, and Systems Offices developed a plan to coordinate the purchase of necessary computer hardware with the implementation of a comprehensive preservation processing system. The Chief Librarian for Preservation provided planning support while the coauthors of this paper worked in close consultation with the Associate Director and Chief of Preparation Services and the Macintosh Systems Analyst from the Systems Office. The objective was clear: Justify additional expense for automation by creating a high-efficiency, easy-access, multi-user system for preservation selection, specification (what treatment is appropriate for this item?), and processing.

In this paper, the authors describe an automated program in operation at the New York Public Library. We hope to demonstrate the benefits gained from such a system and establish that an integrated program makes preservation work substantially more productive and cost-effective, largely through the elimination of repetitive processing activity. Equally important, this program permits administrators to address and treat whole collections—or at least significant portions of them—that include a variety of preservation needs, rather than just performing a range of discrete and frequently unrelated preservation operations on individual items. Collection-based specification also provides a basis for long-term preservation planning and grant-funded activity, perhaps increasing the likelihood that collections will receive the treatment the institution perceives to be appropriate, rather than that which outside agencies offer to fund. We will list some of our objectives for implementing an integrated automated system, describe existing hardware and software configurations, and explain the operations that are performed. We will also provide a real-world example to show that the system is more than a theoretical construct; it is one which above all else generates real products.

BACKGROUND: SYSTEMS ENGINEERING

Staff, computers, library materials, and preservation operations are the elements to be incorporated into a processing system. Virtually all preservation activities involve repetitive tasks. Human capital is expensive. Therefore, the goal at The New York Public Library was to remove repetitive aspects of preservation work and migrate remaining tasks to an automated system, letting machines perform the monotonous.

Like personnel, automation is costly. Frequently computers are under-utilized, employed as no more than advanced typewriters or expensive calculators. This may be satisfactory for certain office operations, but if there is a need to process a large body of work using similar data but generating differing products, a central database can significantly increase processing and reporting capability. NYPL's solution to the challenges of task and automation efficiency is the Preservation Database.

The Preservation Database is *comprehensive, integrated specification and processing software for preservation operations.* What does this mean? By "comprehensive" we suggest that the program handles all preservation treatment options. "Integrated" indicates that all operations, from specification to desired output, share the same processes, forms, databank, and tracking mechanisms. "Specification" (the decision-making process) is the act of determining and recording what preservation approach an item should receive. Note that this is a treatment or reformatting decision, *not* a condition survey, needs assessment survey, or data recording activity, though condition information is often gathered during specification. "Processing" implies that the program does the tedious, repetitive, mundane tasks, and never complains. The key to the Preservation Database's versatility rests in its modular structure, which provides a customized interface for each treatment option, including necessary forms and processing prompts.

GOALS AND DESIRED OUTCOMES

Our initial objectives were to:

- Implement an automated institution-wide preservation program, incorporating survey and specification of whole collections with curatorial review and approval

- Integrate all processing steps, from the survey phase through actual treatment, to the return-to-service of the item or surrogate

- Accommodate a comprehensive range of preservation options and treatments

- Achieve effective organization of workflow and item tracking (provide the appropriate work at the appropriate time to appropriate staff or contractual services)

- Reduce repetitive activity (a prime example is repeated bibliographic entry)

- Reduce errors that can occur as a result of duplicate bibliographic entry, by using barcode or other automated entry methods
- Provide information about surveyed, queued, or scheduled work to assist in planning and development activities
- Generate necessary management statistics, including inhouse and contractual costs for projects and operations, as well as productivity records for individual staff, derived as a by-product of performing the work

THE CURRENT SYSTEM

While the Preservation Database is currently a comprehensive program, encompassing all treatment options offered at NYPL, it was created over time from a number of modules automating individual operations in the Conservation Division. The first module of the Preservation Database was a protective enclosure program developed by Marc Reeves in 1987. The program's design permitted remote data entry of bibliographic information and volume dimensions directly from the stacks, using notebook computers. From this information, the program generates box dimensions, creasing patterns, and labels without further human intervention. The Phased Box Program proved to have an immediate and dramatic impact on production: Conservation Lab production increased from an average of 450 drop-spine boxes per year to over 16,000 phase boxes and 4,000 four-flap wrappers, employing the same number of staff.

The second module developed was a database for tracking items treated in the Conservation Lab. The program records the types of treatments that were done, who did them, how long each operation took, for whom the work was performed, and what materials were used. The module links the photodocumentation records (photographs of items sent to the lab to be treated) with the items themselves and exploits barcoding technology to expedite item control, reducing both the search time and the error rate during data entry. Over 8,000 items are received each year for a wide range of treatments, including different types of treatments for the same item.

Once the effectiveness of the program in several areas of preservation was established, automating other treatment options became attractive. Modules were developed for preservation facsimile, commercial rebinding, contractual protective enclosure, conservation treatment, and, finally, microfilming. The program evolved from humble origins—the need to perform tasks rapidly—rather than from a desire for a grand systems design. However, it was not until the various modules were combined into one comprehensive and integrated program that the Preservation Database could realize its full production and efficiency potential. In its latest version, the program has established that preservation treatment operations can be more efficiently performed using the integrated system, in contrast to our previous system—disparate activities performed in separate offices using separate manual or automated systems.

After working with the modules and processing a large body of work, it became clear that we were performing preservation operations on a bibliographic universe or collection, and not simply on a series of unrelated items. With an effective central processing system, decisions can be made following the premise that it is not only the item that is being treated, but also the collection that is its home. One begins thinking and planning in terms of collection care in addition to item treatment.

SYSTEM CONFIGURATION

The Preservation Database was developed using the multi-user relational database Helix Express. The database is served on a Macintosh Quadra 800 with a one-gigabyte hard drive. Sixteen Macintosh workstations of various vintages throughout the Conservation Division may work on the database simultaneously using Ethertalk connections. While much work is performed in traditional processing units such as the Preservation Reformatting Office and the Conservation Lab, the integrated program also supports remote access for survey applications at most locations in the stacks. All forms and other products, including microfilming targets and box labels, can be produced while standing at the shelf.

For this type of work, the Conservation Division may dial into the main server using PowerBook computers, Shiva LanRover/4E port, Apple Remote Access software, and a long telephone cord to the nearest phone. "Global" cordless dial-in access is available through a cellular modem interface carried by several PowerBooks, though cellular communication costs must be considered when using this feature. In the future, curatorial divisions will have access to the database for data entry and report generation, using NYPL's new wide area network. The database currently holds 32,000 bibliographic records.

It is important to note that the choice of database and operating systems is largely arbitrary: a program like the Preservation Database may be developed in either a DOS or Macintosh environment, using most full-featured relational databases. With the promised migration of the Macintosh operating system to Intel-based computers by 1995, such distinctions may soon have little meaning. Automation is a continuing saga of obsolescence and platform migration; hardware, in particular, has a limited life span. Provision must be made for the inevitable transfer of data to more advanced systems. The problem is not as complicated as it sounds, and the capability exists in most current database programs for the relatively easy transfer of data to other systems.

AN OVERVIEW OF OPERATIONS

The list below provides an overview of the activities the Preservation Database supports.

- Identification of preservation priorities by curatorial staff
- Survey and initial treatment specification by Conservation Division staff, in consultation with divisional staff
- Bibliographic searching
  Accesses RLIN, the Research Libraries Information Network
  Retrieves the FULL record
  Parses appropriate text to MARC fields in the Preservation Database
- Review and approval of specification (treatment recommendations) by curatorial staff
- Microform specification
  Generates work forms for in-house or contractual work
  Generates all targets from bibliographic data; alters these on demand
  Generates box labels for each generation of film
  Generates master negative cards
  Tracks item workflow in Preservation Reformatting Office and
      Microfilming Lab (or contractual work); provides production
      statistics for items, units, projects
  Tracks staff work and productivity for items, units, projects
  Tracks efforts at page replacement by borrowing from
      other institutions
- Preservation photocopying
  Produces work form for vendor
  Generates spine label
  Provides manifest for shipping
  Tracks progress of work, provides receipts, etc.
- Protective enclosures
  Generates orders for four-flap wrappers, phase boxes,
      and drop-spine boxes
  Generates in-house or contractual work form
  Faxes or dumps order to contractual vendor
  Dumps to in-house protective enclosure fabrication program
  Tracks workflow and generates statistics
- Commercial rebinding
  Generates binding tickets
  Generates spine label text
  Provides manifest for shipments
  Tracks progress of work, as well as shipment and return of items
  Dumps information directly to ABLE (Automated Binding Library
      Exchange) software

- In-house conservation treatment or repair
    Generates in-house repair form
    Provides labeling information
    Provides manifest for shipping
    Tracks progress of work, shipping, and return of items
    Records artifactual conservation treatment
    Completes request-for-treatment form
    Establishes the value of the item and justification for work
    Establishes labeling information
    Records exact specification (recommended treatment)
        for individual items
    Tracks performance of work
    Records time spent in treatment
(See Figure 1 for schematic rendering.)

CASE STUDY

For a better understanding of the entire process, we offer the following case study. Mark Twain said that there are few things harder to put up with than a good example; however, in a paper describing a multi-tasking, integrated automated system, a good example can be a lifesaver.

Before: Preparation for Microfilm Production with Non-Integrated Automated Systems

Anyone who has been involved in a preservation microfilming program or special project is aware of the many necessary yet labor-intensive tasks in the preparation of an item for filming. Before a volume is sent to the photo lab, a number of steps must be completed. Below is a list of the microfilming-related tasks carried out by NYPL staff *before* the installation of the filming module.

- The item is chosen and reviewed by the selection officer. A decision is made to film the title. A form is completed which notifies the preservation staff of any special instructions, whether to retain or discard after filming, an RLIN record number, etc.
- After the title is forwarded to the Preservation Reformatting Office, it is searched for microform availability using the on-line bibliographic utilities (RLIN, OCLC) and other manual sources. The technical assistant keys in the main entry when searching.
- The title is prepared for filming: staff collates the title; bibliographic data are then keyed into the local database. Eye-legible targets are generated on a desktop publishing system. Staff types a contents list for the reel, box labels for three generations of film, and a master negative card for the central in-house file. At this time, the technical assistant prepares a worksheet, adding the same data that were keyed into the online utilities.

- Once the title, targets, and other materials are assembled and reviewed, the item is ready for the photo lab.
- After filming, technical data (frames, reduction ratio, position) are keyed into a flat-file database. Supervisory staff may pull data for reports and

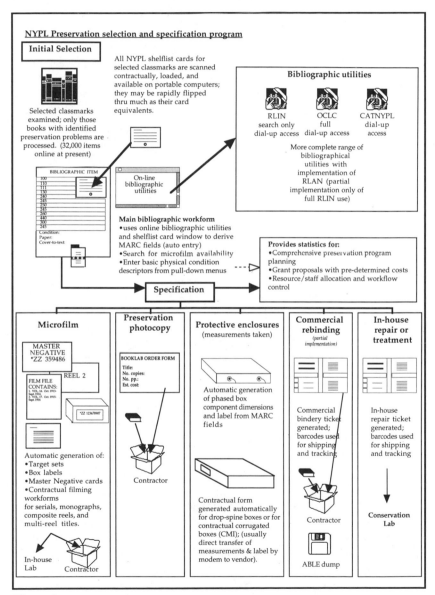

Figure 1

updates. The supervisor is also provided with statistical reports that are later added to a separate spreadsheet program.

It is important to note that preservation staff were required to key in main entry and related data seven to nine times. Automation plays a significant role in expediting office operations, but these automated tasks were not integrated. Staff used on-line utilities (necessary and unavoidable), as well as desktop publishing, database, and spreadsheet software in order to carry out the necessary tasks in the Preservation Reformatting Office. Automation created some time savings, but the prefilming scenario is quite similar to the older manual procedures of years ago. Computers had merely replaced spreadsheets, log books, calculators, and typewriters as processing tools.

After: Preparation for Microfilming with a Central Database

With the conversion to a centralized integrated program, productivity increased dramatically. Bibliographic information is entered once. The program provides a number of entry forms that are easy to understand and use. Forms with MARC-designated fields allow staff to use a familiar format; in fact, there is the capacity to download the record directly from the RLIN screen into the program. If all the required data are successfully transferred, then staff need only key into RLIN and let the Preservation Database do the rest of the work. On the other hand, if there is a reason to key directly into the program, the protocol is still straightforward. The basic steps are:

- Enter bibliographic information by keying or RLIN transfer. Titles that are keyed use MARC-designated fields. If the item is a monograph, for example, staff will enter author, title, publisher, place of publication, date, edition, and physical description. The form on the screen also has fields for other required data related to the title: search result information, project name, division name, format, requested reduction ratio and position, estimated number of frames, disposition (to cut or not to cut), service copy class mark, and other pertinent information.
- The program automatically assigns a master negative number which is then locked so that other staff accessing the main server cannot use the same number.
- A few additional mouse clicks or keystrokes automatically generate the desired product: worksheets (instruction sheets for photo lab staff), contents lists, any or all of 13 types of eye-legible targets, master negative file records, barcoded box labels (which assist in a number of inventory and access processes) for all three generations of film, and shipment manifests. Batching capabilities permit the delay of mass printing until the end of the day.
- When title and necessary printouts are assembled, the title is ready for the photo lab or shipment to a contractual vendor.

From our initial cost analysis, production of composite reels of monographs (multiple titles on one reel of film) has increased 200 percent. There are fewer keyboard-related errors, general processing has increased, and workflow has been significantly streamlined. Similarly dramatic production figures exist for the preparation of serials. In an effort to further streamline operations, staff send off-site filming vendors a disk containing relevant data for generating eye-legible targets and box labels.

CONCLUSION

For large research libraries investing substantial sums in preservation automation, every effort should be made to optimize the capabilities of available hardware and software. Because of The New York Public Library's size and the extent of its preservation challenges, it was a logical decision to design and implement a program like the Preservation Database. Libraries with smaller preservation units may find such extensive automation unnecessary.

As described in this paper, the Preservation Database creates a significantly improved selection, specification, and tasking environment. Furthermore, the Preservation Database in its day-to-day operation is elegant and easy to use. Most important, the database works! Because of its comprehensive and integrated structure, the database expands the functionality of existing automation, creating greater efficiencies; this results in measurable cost savings for the library. With library management and outside grant funding agencies closely examining unit costs for various operations, a program like the Preservation Database provides an institution with a competitive edge in the quest for scarce funds.

Application Development for the Conservation Laboratory

Walter Henry

Assistant Conservator
Stanford University Libraries

CONSERVATION SOFTWARE: DEVELOPMENT ISSUES

Computer applications for the conservation laboratory do not lend themselves to institution-wide systems planning and formal software development methodologies, because development costs cannot be amortized over a large user base. Instead, such applications tend to be developed by their end-users, a circumstance that fosters a high degree of flexibility and customization but introduces its own distinctive set of challenges. An examination of some of the issues surrounding software design for conservation, and the approaches that have been used to develop conservation applications, may suggest avenues for further investigation.

Cost-Effectiveness

It is not at all obvious that in-house programming efforts of the sort discussed here can be considered cost-effective, at least in the short term. In practice, it is not unusual for more time to be spent developing and enhancing the software than can possibly be recouped by the resultant savings over manual operations. However, we are faced with something of a paradox, since if this developmental work is not done now, we will never reach the point where the applications do, in fact, begin to earn their keep.

A recurring problem with in-house development is that programming projects are proposed with the intent of increasing the productivity of the organization, but the short-term result is that energy is shifted to implementing the new software, and so productivity decreases. About 20 years ago, I was told by a computer science student that there had never been a "profitable" computer application—that is, one that made sense in strictly economic terms. Whether or not this observation was factual, it is obvious that those experiments were necessary in order to bring about long-term improvements in efficiency and productivity, and very much the same situation obtains in our development environment.

In a sense, the kind of programming done for conservation labs has more in common with scientific programming, where software is often written by users in order to fill an immediate personal need, than it does with large-scale, team-developed software. This is programming by the end-user, for the end-user, and as such certain refinements of methodology (formal design and specification phases, rigorous documentation, formal testing or verification, and refinement of user interface) that would be fundamental to the development of, say, a cataloging module, have little relevance.

Quality Control

Despite the problems inherent in developing and maintaining end-user-programmed applications, there are some advantages that may compensate slightly for developmental shortcuts. Because the programmer is necessarily one of the users of the software, perhaps the principal user, in effect the conservation lab becomes a usability-testing lab, and program flaws tend to reveal themselves quickly. These flaws can often be remedied without working through the layer of managerial oversight that usually obtains in team-programming projects.

This is not to suggest, of course, that the quality of code produced can be compromised, but rather that program performance is the metric by which the product is judged, rather than conformance to some design document. Machines don't care much about who feeds them instructions, but they are not wont to forgive laxness, no matter the source.

"Shareability"

The simplest way to maximize the return on investment for a programming effort aimed at a small, local user-base is to distribute the product of that effort as widely as possible. To enable resource sharing of this kind, it is necessary to impose at least a minimal discipline on programming practice, by ensuring that all local or institution-specific components are strictly isolated in discrete modules. Ideally, such modules should be configurable by the end-user so that all that is necessary to install a system at a new site is to modify the configuration files. Similar discipline should be enforced in connection with hardware dependencies, especially those involving peripherals, such as printers, modems, and displays. If hardware-dependent values are isolated as configurable data, the difficulties of moving an application to a new site are significantly reduced.

Documenting Real-World Processes

One factor that restricts our ability to effect a formal and complete design process is that the real-world procedures we are attempting to model are themselves inadequately specified and, as a rule, unformed. In other words, the likelihood is great that as a program moves through its life cycle, users will realize that their actual procedures are not quite as they seemed during the design of the program. This distinguishes conservation from other functions that have been better integrated with other library operations and are more adequately understood, such as cataloging.

The ability to effect a formal program design depends largely on the extent to which we can effectively model a set of well-understood and codified conservation procedures. Once a process has developed into a relatively predictable set of routine operations, then the normal design procedures such as functional decomposition and step-wise refinement can be brought to bear on the application. In the case of conservation treatment, however, many activities are themselves in flux. Practices such as treatment documentation, for example, have not been subjected to any degree of standardization, except for a set of skeletal and discipline-specific guidelines in the AIC Code of Ethics and Standards of Practice.[1] On the other hand, the set of practices that constitute a brittle books microfilming operation has been quite well-documented, and is relatively easy to model in an application.

In general, conservation applications fall into two main categories. Ad hoc programs, that is, programs written primarily to solve a single problem or to aid in the completion of a project, account for a significant portion of the programming activity in many laboratories. A set of such programs written to aid in carrying out library surveys is discussed below. At the opposite pole, more complex and demanding applications that anchor day-to-day operations (often called "mission-critical" or "workhorse" applications) warrant a more systematic, formal development effort. Conservation treatment record or documentation systems are an important example of this type software. Another important class of programs, clinical applications (which may fall into either of the categories mentioned above), offers a promising arena for development, one that has not yet been much explored.

I. SURVEY SAMPLING

Because a library, archives, or museum collection is a massive entity and the cost of examining every item in it (a census) is prohibitive, it is common practice to survey a representative portion of the population of interest—often by random sampling—and to use observations about that sample to infer facts about the collection as a whole. Such surveys sometimes provide more accurate information about the collection than can a census, since inaccuracies of measurement and observation can result when a very large number of observations is made. Thus, surveys have become a regular and important component of the conservator's practice, and the place of computers in the recording and analysis of survey data is well-established. While the role of database management systems and statistics packages in recording and data analysis is obvious, the use of computers for sampling has not received much attention. Three examples will serve to illustrate some approaches to this type of computer-aided testing.

A. Shelf and Object Sampling

Buchanan describes a random sampling method that has become commonplace in library surveys.[2] In this "shelf and object" approach, each shelf range is numbered and a set of pseudo-random numbers (a triple) is drawn from the uniform distribution, to identify a range, shelf, and item. If it happens that there is no item at that location, or if the item has already been examined, the triple is discarded and another selected. Every item therefore has an equal probability of selection.

This is a straightforward strategy. Computer support is fairly simple and it is a trivial task to produce a set of numbers, using any number of means. However, the random number generators used in many programming languages are less than optimal and produce sequences that are not quite uniform, and/or that have short periods. Put more bluntly, "Look at the subroutine library of each computer installation in your organization, and replace the random number generators by good ones. Try to avoid being too shocked by what you find."[3] SSam (Stanford Sampler, an ad hoc program developed in-house at Stanford and refined over a period of years) provides a few advantages over casual programming.

Several algorithms exist that provide better simulation of true randomness, and SSam makes use of them to supply a consistently better approximation than can off-the-shelf generators.[4, 5, 6] While this feature would be more important in other areas of statistical work than surveying, there is no need to use inferior tools when satisfactory tools are available. SSam produces sets of random triples without replacement, so there is no risk of any item's being examined twice. In a survey of a large population, such as a library's stacks, there is little danger of this happening, but in surveys of small archival and museum collections this feature can prove quite valuable.

To ease the job of the people charged with pulling materials from the shelves, SSam offers several formatting options. For example, if two searchers are to locate 400 books between them, SSam can supply each with a list of 200 items, sorted by location. An additional list of unsorted numbers is provided to replace those that are rejected (i.e., because there is no item on the shelf at that location).

Although full-featured statistics packages such as SAS and SPSS-X have a valuable role to play in preservation surveys, for day-to-day work we often use a simple program called Stati, developed in-house for DOS machines. Stati's principal virtue is that it does not require its input to be formatted in any particular manner; it reads a group of numbers occurring in a text file in any format and calculates a useful set of descriptive statistics. For example, a volunteer might gather information from a survey site and include the raw data in an electronic mail message. With only minor editing to ensure that there are no extraneous numbers in the file, applying the finite population correction (if appropriate) Stati calculates sample size, mean, sum, skewness, kurtosis, variance, standard deviation, standard error of mean, 95 percent and 99 percent confidence intervals, minimum, maximum, range, the semi-interquartile range (q), and first, second, and third quartiles. In addition, Stati produces a stem-and-leaf graph and a histogram.

B. Pre-Search Sampling

Stanford's Archives of Recorded Sound consists of more than 200,000 recordings in a wide variety of formats. In order to develop a preservation strategy for the collection, we wanted to answer the usual questions about condition, use, housing, etc., but in addition, we wanted rather more precise estimates of the number of recordings in each format than the curators were able to provide. Because the university was undergoing severe budget and staff reductions and pressures on staff were unusually heavy, a high priority in designing the survey was to minimize both the involvement of Archives staff and the impact on the day-to-day operations of the Archives. Luckily, we had interns and volunteers who were willing to help out with the sample selection.

Portions of the collection are represented in the *Rigler & Deutsch Record Index,* and a small part is included in the libraries' catalog; however, access to materials generally requires help from the Archives staff. Because there is no shelflist, and no way to create a virtual shelflist, we were limited to some form of "shelf and object" sampling.

The easiest sampling method would have been to draw a random or systematic sample based on some form of physical measurement—for example, to measure the contents of each shelf and draw a sample such that the physical distances between the specimens are equal; this technique is similar to that commonly used with shelflist cards. However, whereas card stock of various thicknesses is randomly distributed in a shelflist file, recordings of like format and thickness (tapes or LPs or compact disks, for example) are deliberately clustered together in a collection, a factor which would have introduced a significant bias in the sample. For this reason, simple corrections such as Fussler's sampling technique (as described by Bookstein) are ineffective.[7]

During a preliminary survey, it became obvious that a simple "shelf and object" sampling strategy would dramatically increase the cost of selecting the sample, because of three factors: low hit rates arising from variability in shelving density; the unwieldiness of the objects, especially the large, heavy transcription disks; and, most important, the need for exceptional care in handling the materials. Given these constraints, we did the sample selection off-site and verified hits by employing a simple form of computer simulation.

A map of the collection was drawn and each shelf range treated as a two-dimensional matrix, having K rows and M columns of shelves. The ranges were named as well, and each shelf was assigned a set of three index keys for identification. Thus the collection as a whole was treated as a three-dimensional matrix, with a notation similar to that used for three-dimensional spreadsheets: item J,K,M identifies the shelf in the Kth row and Mth column of range J. Volunteers counted or estimated the number of items on each shelf and recorded them for entry in a database. For some large, regular areas, such as long-playing (LP) phonograph records, a mini-survey provided estimates of shelf size and these estimates were entered for each shelf in the mini-population (i.e., all LP shelves were treated as if they had the same number of recordings on them).

A dBase IV database which had one record for each shelf, indexed on a combination of range, row, and column (J,K,M), was used to record the total number of items on that shelf for each format. Using the random number generation package described above, a surfeit of random numbers J,K,M,I were generated, each representing the Ith item on shelf J,K,M. By means of a simple dBase script, the database was searched for the shelf corresponding to J,K,M. If the shelf did not exist or had fewer than I items, the item was discarded and the next quadruple selected. Otherwise, the item was selected for the sample and used to prepare survey record forms.

This simple procedure simulated the action of a human searcher but avoided the problems of physically manipulating the sound recordings. As a result, when the recordings were actually accessed for examination, there were very few "misses," those few resulting from sampling error in the areas where the shelf counts had been estimated. As an important side-benefit, the preparatory work provided us with very useful estimates of the size of the collection, broken down by format. If a similar project were to be undertaken again, we might try to facilitate data entry by bringing laptop computers into the collection and recording the shelf count data on-site, in a spreadsheet, since the generic structure of spreadsheets closely models the actual survey site.

C. Offline Sampling

In connection with the preparation of a proposal for a microfilming project, we needed to survey monographs and serials falling within a specified range of call numbers, to determine whether our collections contained sufficient material that met the funding agency's selection criteria. As is often the case, it was necessary to complete the survey as quickly as possible; however, the call number ranges included several shelving locations spread out across the campus, making a shelf and object sampling strategy very cumbersome. In this case, since the population under consideration was completely represented in our online catalog, we decided to carry out the sample selection using computer processes. In order to do this, we recreated the subset of the catalog of interest to us on a small machine, and wrote a simple program to draw a random sample from it.

Querying the OPAC by typing individual lines of text online at a terminal is tiring and often unnecessary. For projects of this type, we have occasionally typed (offline) all of the individual queries into a text file and used an off-the-shelf keyboard buffer-stuffing utility, in conjunction with a keyboard macro package, to feed the queries to the OPAC, one line at a time. Typically, a student employee uses a predefined macro that reads the query line from the text file, deletes the line and moves the next one into position, and feeds the line into the terminal's keyboard buffer (also called the typeahead buffer). The line of text is then passed to the application (in this case, the communications program that is talking to the OPAC), as if the student had typed it from the keyboard. Additional keyboard macros may be used to accept or reject the retrieved records, save them to a file, etc.

In this case, the search was such that we could formulate one very long query statement of the form "Find call=Z70* or Z799* or N38* . . ." in a text file on a Macintosh, copy it to the software clipboard, and paste it (electronically) into the keyboard buffer in a single action. The resulting dataset, consisting of several thousand records in the OPAC's brief display format, was then sent by electronic mail to a UNIX machine for further processing. This dataset represented the actual population of interest to us. In short, we had copied the complete population under consideration to a workstation where we could begin to draw a sample from it.

In this case sample selection involved, as do many of our projects, writing a simple Perl program. Perl (Practical Extraction and Reporting Language) is an interpreted language written by Larry Wall. Originally designed for the UNIX operating system, it has been ported to a number of other platforms, including DOS and Macintosh, although its functionality is somewhat reduced on these platforms. Incorporating much of the syntax and functionality of the programming languages C, Awk, and Sed, Perl is a general-purpose language commonly used for systems administration operations. However, its remarkably strong text manipulation capabilities, its expressiveness, and the flexibility of its syntax make it an ideal tool for ad hoc programming. It is not uncommon to find that a long, complex program in another language can be expressed in Perl in a very few lines. In fact, it is quite possible to write one-line Perl programs that do useful work, and to combine these "one-liners" into a text processing tool kit.

For our purposes, the key to Perl's utility is its sophisticated pattern-matching ability and its ability to work with strings of unlimited length. An entire file can be read into a data structure (such as an array or a string) in a single instruction (known in the jargon of Perl as "slurping a file"), broken into records of arbitrary and variable length based on the occurrence of some textual pattern, and processed with a rich set of text manipulation functions. For example, a program that sorts the dataset described above (with its variable-length, multi-line records) by location and call number fields embedded in a tagged display, can be written in as little as 11 lines. A program to pull a sorted random sample of records from this dataset and an unsorted set of extra records can be written in as few as 42 lines. Because of this unusual combination of terseness, expressiveness, and flexibility, it is profitable to write single-purpose programs intended to be used only once. The entire process described here, including programming, took only a few hours. That the programs can be reused is a happy bonus, but when appropriate tools are used the programming effort need not be burdensome, even for "one-shot" projects.

D. Recording Survey Observations

The Achenbach Foundation for the Graphic Arts, a component of the Fine Arts Museums of San Francisco, is a collection of nearly 100,000 prints and drawings. Until very recently, only about 14,000 of these had adequate accession numbers and registration was a completely manual system. Taking advantage of a massive renovation project at the Palace of the Legion of Honor where the Foundation is housed, the museum decided to barcode the entire collection and automate procedures for identifying and tracking objects. The numbering scheme, geared specifically to the barcoding project, provides a unique identifier not only for every print and drawing in the collection, but for each box and location throughout the museum. As items pass through the museum, their movements are recorded and a database maintains a record of both their current and permanent locations.

At about the same time, a collection condition census was undertaken at the Foundation, to determine the conservation needs of each item in the collection. The prime mover for the barcoding project, Robert Futernick, saw in these new procedures an opportunity to overcome one of the principal obstacles to efficient surveying: while the examination of the objects can be accomplished quickly, recording the observations slows the process significantly. To speed the recording process, the survey project uses a small hand-held barcode reader (a Videx Time Wand II) with a keyboard and enough memory to encode a large number of preprogrammed observations in a single session; the keyboard allows the surveyor to punch in any observations that have not been preprogrammed and associate these with the appropriate object.

The surveyor is armed with the Time Wand and a guide sheet listing 20 condition statements and four categories of treatment urgency, each represented by a barcode. Each object's individual barcode is scanned, supplying its accession number or other unique identifier. The print or drawing is examined, and one of the four priority codes appearing on the guide sheet is also scanned, indicating the urgency of conservation intervention. The surveyor then scans an appropriate condition code or codes from the guide, indicating specific defects such as foxing, discoloration, tears, etc. (in order of relative severity) and keys in an estimate of the number of hours needed for the treatment. At the completion of an examination session, the recorded transactions are loaded into a computer where they are processed and added to a database. The system is quicker, less fatiguing, and less susceptible to error than manual or keyboard data entry.

II. CLINICAL APPLICATIONS

With the exception of imaging and image processing, techniques that have been widely used in art conservation and well-documented in the literature, clinical applications have not received the attention they deserve. By clinical applications, I mean that class of programs designed to enhance the conservator's ability to make treatment decisions or to execute treatments. Such applications can be of special value when they:

- Perform a function better than a human can
- Perform a function of which a human is not capable
- Perform a function that is dangerous, tedious, or unpleasant to a human

Although to date there are relatively few examples of this type of program, a few cases may suggest areas for development.

A. Leaf Casting

Bansa describes in great detail a program designed to help the conservator calculate the quantity of pulp and water necessary to fill lacunae by leafcasting.[8] At the Folger Shakespeare Library, Frank Mowery and Charles Mazel have taken this idea further and created a system in which a video imaging system and computer program are used to replace the tedious and error-prone manual procedures for measuring lacunae and calculating the quantity of fiber necessary for filling. This calculation is critical; the pulp fill must match the fiber density and sheet thickness rather precisely in order to achieve a repair with suitable properties. Before the automated system was developed, the object was placed over a grid and the conservator attempted to estimate the area of lacunae by counting cells. This was tiring and tended to result in considerable error, because of the irregularity of the lacunae.

In the new automated system, using a low-cost video digitizer, the object is recorded against a black background and the area of loss measured by counting black pixels, a quick operation performed by a computer program custom-designed for the purpose in BASIC and machine language. The only manual input necessary is the sheet thickness, which the conservator measures with a caliper, although the system also provides a set of gray scale/contrast filters to factor out the effect of text and illustration on the calculations. The complete process takes about 15 seconds per page.[9]

What makes this application so appealing is that it not only reduces labor, but improves the quality of the treatment by reducing measurement error. Although the system used at the Folger is not unreasonably expensive, it is possible to get much the same effect by replacing the video system with a graphics tablet and manually tracing the lacunae with a light pen. Software can then integrate the area inside the marks and calculate pulp proportions in a fashion similar to that of the Folger program. This method has been used at the Achenbach Collection for several years.

B. Solvent Blending

A common conservation problem is the selection of a suitable solvent or blend of solvents to dissolve a particular substance, such as a resin, stain, accretion, etc. Sometimes a solvent is found that will dissolve the matter, but the properties of that product (e.g., toxicity or evaporation rate) are undesirable and a substitute is needed. The solubility behavior of a solvent or a substance to which it might be applied can be described by a set of three numerical parameters called fractional solubility parameters—measures of the polarity, dispersion forces, and hydrogen bonding that account for the cohesiveness (and therefore the solubility behavior) of a molecule. If a solvent or blend can be found to match the fractional solubility parameters of the targeted stain or other matter, it can be substituted for the undesirable solvent.

Teas described a graphical method for determining the fractional solubility parameters of solvent blends by plotting the components on a two-dimensional triangular graph and interpolating between the components, a method that has since come into common use in conservation labs.[10] TeasTime, a program developed at Stanford for DOS machines, automates this method by identifying all possible blends that will produce the same parameters as the target substance. The first release was written in a dialect of Prolog, a language commonly used for artificial intelligence applications.

The strength of Prolog as a language for developing an application like TeasTime lies in its deductive capabilities. Given a well-designed rule base, a Prolog program can make logically correct inferences. Thus, to develop a prototype solvent-blending system, we provided the system with a clear explanation of the rules that govern solvent blending, and asked it what solvents would match a given target at several arbitrary ratios (10:90, 20:80, etc). In addition to correctly answering this question, the prototype was able in its first execution to infer—or at least to act as if it had inferred—a chemical fact that the programmer had not thought to encode in the program: that any solvent will dissolve itself.

With the help of Erich Neuwirth of the Department of Statistics, Operations Research, and Computer Methods at the University of Vienna, the program was rewritten to determine the optimal blend ratio, rather than relying on the arbitrary ratios used in the prototype. Now that the initial version has proven its functionality, a new one is being written in a conventional programming language, to allow enhancements to performance and to incorporate more sophisticated chemical modeling. This version incorporates a database containing information on 160 resins and 300 solvents.

C. Matting

Constructing protective enclosures like mats and boxes is one of the most monotonous and repetitive procedures carried out in conservation facilities, and yet it is often one of the most valuable and cost-effective means of effecting a real improvement in the longevity and usefulness of a collection. Any significant enhancements to the methods used to measure, mark, cut, and assemble enclosures fill an obvious and real need and can have enormous impact on the productivity of the shop.

At the Achenbach Foundation, using a large graphics tablet and custom software developed in-house, a remarkably effective system has been created for measuring prints and drawings in preparation for matting. Of course these measurements have art-historical significance as well, and so are retained permanently as part of the object's registration information. Typical measurements for prints and drawings map the dimensions of several areas, usually rectangular: the image area itself, the impression formed by a printing plate (plate mark), the paper on which the image itself is printed or drawn, and any secondary supporting materials such as mats and linings. If these three sets of coordinates are known, and if mats are to be cut to a limited set of stock sizes, to be stored in boxes that are also of standard measurements, then producing a window mat becomes a simple procedure, one that can in fact be automated.

Since prints and drawings tend to be rectangular, any point on the object can be identified unambiguously by two coordinates. The Achenbach system makes use of a graphics tablet and light pen to establish a fixed coordinate system relative to the object. That is, the object is placed in a fixed position on the tablet, such that coordinates 0,0 represent the lower left corner of the object. A single touch of the light pen at the upper right corner is adequate to delimit the boundaries of the support, and a touch at the lower left and upper right corners of the plate-mark, image area etc., define those areas unambiguously. Thus, for a simple unmounted etching, five touches of the light pen are all that is needed to describe the dimensions of all the important components.

Since objects are not all alike, some additional controls are necessary. For example, some drawings consist of only a primary support and an image, in which case only three touches are necessary. A print with a more complex history might be mounted on a sheet of rag paper, which in turn is mounted on a piece of card (secondary and tertiary supports). It might have a plate-mark and perhaps a decorative border. In this case, 11 touches would be required to indicate all the important dimensions.

Identifying these various configurations requires an input technique that allows the examiner to indicate to the program what interpretation the measurement should be given. In most applications, this is handled using a keyboard or mouse, requiring that the examiner shift modes and exchange input devices—clearly, an inefficient and tiring process. In the Achenbach system, regions on the graphics tablet are mapped to codes that signal the program that a given explanation applies to the next set of inputs. For example, if the examiner touches an area between a particular set of coordinates, the next two touches are treated as the measurement of the plate-mark; if a different region is touched, the succeeding touches are interpreted as measurement of image area, and so forth. The "hot spots" are marked with paper labels which are printed with brief text ("mnemonic buttons," so to speak) and adhered to the graphics tablet.

Once a series of measurements has been recorded and imported into the appropriate database, reports that provide instructions to the mat maker are generated. In the future, a program that will accept these measurements as input and mark the matboard directly with a plotter could be developed. In principle, it should be possible to replace the plotter pens with cutting blades and cut the mats directly, but this would obviously require a considerably more robust instrument than those in common use. With some modifications, the system could be used to measure three-dimensional objects such as books, and to mark board for the construction of boxes.

III. CONSERVATION TREATMENT RECORD SYSTEMS

Conservation treatment record systems are inherently complex applications because the domains over which they function are dynamic and demanding. Such systems must be able to handle effectively the following situations, as well as many others:

- Single-component items (a single volume, manuscript, print, etc.)
- Items composed of multiple parts (a box of typescripts, a scrapbook, a photograph album, a multi-volume work)
- Groups of more or less unrelated items (batch treatments)
- Objects of a type unusual to a given collection (paintings and objects in a library collection; books in an art-on-paper collection)
- Objects on loan from another institution
- Objects that will be lent or exhibited
- Objects that have not yet been cataloged or registered, or whose catalog records are not yet complete

• Objects that will be treated, in part or whole, by
contractors outside the institution, or bound or framed by
commercial vendors

Treatments for items in any of these categories may range from simple rehousing projects with minimal documentation at the collection- or record-
group level, to sophisticated approaches involving scientific analysis,
photographic or other visual documentation, and the production of a lengthy
narrative report. The conservation record system must accommodate the need
to include in the treatment record data and images that do not exist in machine-readable form, including photographs, sketches, handwritten or typed
notes, photocopies, printouts, charts from analytic and recording instruments,
and even printed record forms, since there may be circumstances in which
the conservator chooses to use a manual documentation procedure. While it
may not be necessary that the system provide a means of importing this information (for example, by scanning), it should at least have the ability to
document the existence of such external materials. In short, system design
must accommodate the existence of information recorded or created outside
the system, without placing the integrity of the system at risk.

For institutional conservation labs, record systems may include three key
functional components:

• A logging or tracking function, for recording transactions
describing the movement of objects through the collection
• Short-term recording of treatment decisions, notes, etc.
• Permanent documentation of examination and treatment

Only the last of these is unique to the conservation record system. Logging
functions can be handled using manual methods, off-the-shelf applications, or
by incorporating conservation functions into existing systems, such as integrated library systems or museum management systems. Notes on curatorial
imperatives, treatment decisions, scheduling requests, etc., can either be incorporated into the permanent treatment documentation, or may be discarded.
Ancillary documents such as reports of production statistics may be produced
as well, but again, such reports are not "mission-critical" functions.

In a sense, however, documentation is a critical accretion, and each example of it a facet of the object's life-history that is intended to be perpetu-
ally retained; as such, it lies at the very heart of conservation praxis.
Unfortunately, the task of creating and maintaining this documentation is
often viewed as an unmanageable burden. This may be especially true in libraries and archives, where large numbers of materials of varying complexity serving widely differing functions within the collection provide a
daunting caseload for laboratories suffering from severe economic and
staffing constraints. Clearly, the principal design criterion for a conservation record system must be that it facilitates, even encourages, the creation
of the highest quality documentation; a system that places obstacles be-

tween the conservator and his or her goal will not (and ought not) be accepted by its users.

It is rather easy to be seduced by the information retrieval capabilities of database management systems, but the ability to locate and retrieve information is for most conservation facilities of little significance when compared with documentation needs. This rather bald statement may hold less true for some museum facilities, where the conservation database serves an important role as a scholarly resource. In libraries and archives, however, access to treatment records is usually infrequent enough that the need for a database management system (DBMS) as an access tool is questionable.

A. Database Issues

The central problem of recording conservation treatments in databases is that these file structures are, by their very nature, subject to change. That is, they are dynamic instruments, and it is that quality that makes them so valuable. For example, we expect that as the vocabulary of our field undergoes change (and perhaps standardization), our databases will be updated to reflect those shifts, thereby improving intellectual access to treatment records. At the same time, the treatment reports we create are documents of record; they must represent an accurate and unchanging picture, a snapshot, of the actual treatment rendered at a particular moment in time. It is therefore critical that they be protected from the sort of modifications that would be acceptable for ordinary records.

There are two possible solutions to this problem, and neither is completely satisfactory. On the one hand, we can consider the printed report to be the document of record and the database an auxiliary information source and authoring tool. This is Stanford's current approach, and anyone seeking an authoritative account of a treatment must consult the printed report. The DBMS provides information on how to access this document, as well as ancillary information which is not part of the document per se, but may be of interest. The DBMS may also contain the full text of the printed document, in a more or less altered version. Strictly speaking, this account serves as no more than a convenient, non-authoritative summary of the document of record. In practice, this summary will be perfectly adequate for nearly all uses, and the printed document may in fact be moved to remote storage without serious impact on day-to-day operations. However, because electronic records are not secure from modification they must always be considered secondary.

An alternative strategy is to try to maintain a complete and carefully controlled digital version of each treatment record. This approach has the virtue that the document of record is fully integrated into the online system and thus accessible via the DBMS's sophisticated search architecture; however, it is also troubled by the same set of problems that such electronic records present in other library and archive contexts. These difficulties are sufficiently intractable that, until they are resolved, complete dependence on electronic records must be considered inadequate. Specifically, issues of authentication—of the primary text of the treatment document and of signatures, particularly those representing curatorial authorization for treatment—are especially thorny. How can we guarantee that a given record's text has not been modified, that it represents the exact state of affairs at the time of its generation (e.g., that a condition report has not been back-dated, whether intentionally or not)?

Because problems of this nature are being addressed in other domains, especially those involving financial transactions, where matters of security are obviously critical and solutions bring with them the promise of real economic benefits, it is likely that we shall see significant developments that nullify the concerns expressed above. Work on digital signatures is proceeding on several fronts, perhaps the most important of which are NIST's (National Institite for Standards and Technology's) Digital Signature Standard (DSS) and the Internet standards for privacy in electronic mail.[11, 12, 13, 14, 15] Peter Graham has described a time-stamping system developed at Bellcore.[16] In this scheme, for each document to be time-stamped a unique numerical value is calculated based on a mathematical transformation of the document text. This transformation, called hashing, produces a single numerical code that uniquely identifies the document. Because the hashing scheme makes use of both the numerical value of the codes that represent characters (e.g., ASCII values) and the position of the character within the document, any change to the document, no matter how trivial, will lead to a different hash value. The hash value for the original or bona fide electronic document may be registered with an authoritative or "trusted" time-stamping service.

The time-stamping service maintains a permanent record of the sequence of all such hash values and employs an algorithm that ensures no modification to the sequence can occur. The service can be queried at any time to verify that a given document—that is, a text with one exact sequence of characters, and no other—either did or did not exist at a given point. Model time-stamp servers are in place now, and if the scheme finds wide enough acceptance it may well answer our need to guarantee the authenticity of conservation treatment records.[17]

The full range of issues that complicate the development of any type of electronic text archive comes into play in treatment databases. The need to provide permanent mechanisms for data refreshing (periodic recopying onto fresh media) and migration to new storage formats as old ones become obsolete is no less critical in a conservation context than elsewhere in an institution's archives, but because conservation records lack the visibility that attends the primary collections, commitment to their preservation may not be seen as an institutional priority.

Fortunately, technical and organizational strategies for handling electronic records are receiving a great deal of attention just now. Perhaps an appropriate response in the present environment might be to assert the primacy of the printed text, while laying the groundwork for eventual migration to a fully digital document management system. With this in mind, the developer of a conservation documentation system might focus his or her efforts on two diverging paths:

- Consider the DBMS primarily as an authoring tool and provide functionality aimed at enhancing the users' ability to produce printed text as efficiently as possible
- Work toward making the underlying storage formats suitable for the encoding of machine-readable textual documents by employing descriptive rather than specific or procedural markup for text[18]

B. Authoring Tools

Conservation record systems tend to emphasize either database or authoring tools, and interesting developments have occurred in both areas. In one of the earliest experiments with database management for the conservation lab, Chris Stavroudis and James Druzik, then at the Los Angeles County Museum of Art, developed but never completed a DBMS based on a hybrid hierarchical-relational model. One of the interesting features of this system was a built-in "transformer" for dates and epochs. Internally, object records contained numerical dates and country codes, but for searching, sorting, etc., the system employed a set of rules that transformed country and date values into epoch names. Thus a search for Han Dynasty objects would identify Chinese objects with dates between 202 B.C. and A.D. 220. Another interesting feature of the database presented users whose needs are different (e.g., paintings and objects conservators) with entry and search screens that, though they appeared to be similar, mapped screen fields to different sets of storage fields, much the same way that today's OPACs can map display fields to one or more MARC fields. This allowed a simple user interface to sit on top of a complex record architecture.[19]

An alternative (and, to my mind, more promising) approach is to consider the system primarily as a tool that enhances the conservator's ability to produce documents—as an authoring tool. Although such tools may also incorporate database functions, if the primary concern is text generation, the system is likely to be seen by its users as an aid to completing their work, rather than as an obstacle. This approach has served as the principle design imperative for systems developed at the Achenbach Foundation, the Oakland Museum, and the Stanford University Libraries.

At the simplest level, the system obviates the need to rekey existing text. In more sophisticated applications, it can exploit characteristics of objects and incorporate some degree of knowledge about those objects, providing efficient means of generating text about them. For example, a system might build a condition statement for a book by suggesting characteristics such as "cockling," "foxing," and "embrittlement" to the conservator, using lists; or, it could construct a description of the object's structure by offering the user the option to enter a collation formula, a sewing pattern, or an endband description. The same system, dealing with a painting, might suggest characteristics such as "planar distortion," "cupping," and "tenting," then prompt the conservator for a description of the canvas weave, stretcher/strainer construction, etc.

Library conservation laboratories share a particular problem with museum object labs, the wide variety of items subject to treatment: books, photographic prints and negatives, bound and unbound manuscripts, maps, etc. This makes documentation requirements fairly complex, compared with those for laboratories focusing on more homogeneous materials. Paintings and art-on-paper labs, for example, can capitalize on the general similarity among objects in their domains. Futernick, a pioneer in the concept of the conservation record system as an authoring tool, exploits the flatness and rectangularity of most of the items under his care by using, as part of the authoring system he has developed in Hypercard for the Achenbach lab, a graphical system to map areas of damage by means of a simple coordinate system.

The conservator can point to a generic image of a rectangular object and, by clicking in one area, generate the text "upper left corner." By clicking a graphic button indicating a type of damage and another indicating its level of severity, he or she can recast this text as, "There is severe foxing in the upper left corner." Similarly, since prints and drawings tend to exhibit a relatively limited range of defects and may therefore be fairly readily classified in a hierarchical fashion, Futernick has created a remarkably sophisticated document authoring system in which the user is able to create a basic treatment report almost entirely by selecting items from hierarchical menus.

The Achenbach's system evolved from one developed in the late 1970s for an electronic typewriter with a keyboard macro function. The typewriter allowed 100 text fragments to be stored and played back, in connection with a set of keyboard codes. During the examination session, the conservator completed a checklist which was translated by clerical staff into a minimal set of keystrokes, to produce examination reports, proposals, and treatment reports. The same fundamental method was later reimplemented on a computer with a word processor with a scripting language, and then again with a word processor using its glossary function. This system is still in use, frequently in tandem with other systems.

On the other hand, in an objects conservation lab, the heterogeneity of object-types makes such an approach difficult if not impossible. In this situation, however, we can still exploit significant similarities between one object and others by introducing the concept of reusable text. At the Oakland Museum John Burke is developing an innovative system that enables the conservator to save text fragments (e.g., a description statement, a condition report, or a treatment proposal), assign it a unique name, and thereafter include it in any document by selecting its name from a menu. The imported text can then be edited in the normal fashion. Much in the same way that contemporary software engineering encourages maximizing the return on investment in program code by designing that code to be reusable in contexts not necessarily envisioned by the designer, Burke's approach to text reusability encourages the user to get the most out of his or her text creation efforts. The on-the-fly creation of what amounts to a database of reusable textual modules helps take some of the sting out of writing a detailed or difficult conservation report, since the conservator knows that the effort also serves to ease the creation of future documents.

In what amounts to an extension of the idea of the record system as authoring tool, for several years Burke has worked with a video camera and a frame-grabber (a device that accepts analog input from a video camera and digitizes it, so that the image—a single frame of video—can be stored and processed by a computer). With these tools he creates a low-resolution image of the object, then uses this image to identify the object and indicate areas of damage, features, etc., thus saving a great deal of written description. Given the nature of object collections, with a large number of object types and a large number of similar objects within those types, images provide a shorthand identification that effectively serves as surrogate text.

Like most of its counterparts at other institutions, Stanford's LabLog is very much a work in progress; it borrows the concept of text reusability from Oakland's system. Although it is used for production work (transactions with off-site contractors, spine labels (including those for Hebrew titles), and statistics), its primary function is that of a testbed for the exploration of ideas concerning the development of conservation record systems. Moving beyond its ability to create reusable text modules, major design goals for LabLog include the minimization of keyboard input (an objective that is far from realized), reduction of opportunity for input errors, and a reasonably satisfying user interface. (Since the author is also the software's principal user, he thinks using it ought to be fun.)

C. Off-the-Shelf vs. Custom Software

Once it is determined that the record system should function primarily as an authoring tool, an important design decision presents itself: if the objective is to provide the most effective system for generating documents, that system can be constructed either by writing a single application that offers all the desired functionality in one package, or by integrating autonomous software packages into a compound system. The advantages to the latter approach are that either off-the-shelf or custom programs can be selected to provide the optimal features for each of the system's functions. A powerful word processor, spreadsheet, or drawing program can be used to perform the functions for which it is best suited. However, integrating disparate packages into a useable system may not be a trivial project. Recent developments in operating system design offer some promise in this regard, by providing mechanisms for creating dynamic links among documents created by unrelated applications. A simpler but somewhat cumbersome approach that has been used for a number of years at the Achenbach is to cut and paste text electronically between unrelated applications.

Integrating all functions (text editing, graphics, mathematical calculation, etc.) into a single application has the obvious advantage that the user need not manipulate multiple texts, and interacts with a unified user interface. This approach also provides the developer with the opportunity to customize the application in ways that would not be possible using commercial software. On the other hand, the developer may be limited in the tools available to create such an integrated system, which can in turn limit the group of features available to the user. Burke has taken this integrated approach by building on a set of application modules available for 4th Dimension, which offer access to relatively full-featured word processing, spreadsheet, and drawing programs from within the DBMS's input screens.

D. Database Use Issues

A longstanding impediment to the widespread adoption of machine-assisted authoring systems for conservation has been the tendency to locate computers in areas remote from the examination and treatment site. A system that makes it easy to generate text is only useful if the conservator has access to it while he or she is carrying out an examination or executing a treatment. Otherwise, the system merely serves as another level of encumbrance and becomes more a source of irritation than a useful tool. Few institutions can afford to provide a networked computer at each workbench, but an obvious solution is to use one or two laptops that can be moved about in the examination and treatment areas: a central computer retains the database, but a portable remote computer (a laptop) is used to create and update records.

Unfortunately, this creates what amounts to a distributed database, without the safeguards necessary to allow such a system to function properly. Since record creation, update, or deletion can occur simultaneously on more than one machine and there is no mechanism for the machines to communicate with each other, the integrity of the database is always at risk. Conventional multi-user databases handle this problem by establishing a set of real-time controls over record access, but since in the situation just described there are no links between equipment, such controls are impossible to attain. In order to preserve even a semblance of database integrity, a distributed system must maintain regular and frequent contact between nodes, so that changes in one node can be communicated throughout the system. This is clearly impossible with the configuration described here.

A relatively simple solution (one based on techniques normally used for revision control) suggests itself. Large programming projects carried out by teams of programmers are almost always subject to a form of operational discipline known as (depending on the situation and the level of complexity of the control system) revision control, source code management, configuration control, or version control. All these methods share one common feature: access to individual modules of a project (such as source code text) is strictly controlled and documented, so that changes in one module of a program that may affect other modules cannot be made except under carefully prescribed circumstances.

The key to access control is two operations: "check in" and "check out." Before a text can be changed, an author must check it out from a central database, much in the same way that a library patron checks out a book. The text is then either unavailable to other authors or, as is more often the case, is available with a set of restrictions placed on its use (for instance, it may be marked read-only). When the updated text is checked in, the system takes care of maintaining any links to documents that depend on the newly changed item. In practice, real revision control systems are more complicated than this, providing services that enable the maintenance of multiple versions, but this simplified description is adequate for our purposes.

All record creation and deletion must occur at the central database, which takes responsibility for ensuring referential integrity. When a user wishes to work with a group of records, he or she first locates them in the central database (creating them if necessary), checks them out, and transfers them to the remote computer (this requires only a single machine-to-machine connection, not a network). The central system marks the records with a stamp indicating the user (or workstation) who has checked them out and changes their status to read-only. It is important to note that this process, though similar, is not quite the same as the record and file locking employed by multi-user databases; the check in/check out control sits on top of any lower level locking scheme. The reason for this is that an item may—and often will—remain checked out for prolonged periods, perhaps weeks, during which time the underlying database system may need to unlock records to perform operations such as reindexing. The check in/check out status must survive any such locking or unlocking.

When the user has finished with the records, they are uploaded to the central database and checked in, at which time the system performs integrity checks, replaces the existing records with the updated versions, and resets the access status to make the new records available again. If desired, the earlier versions of records can be retained as a safety measure. A virtue of this scheme is that it can be applied either to a conventional database or to a more or less structured collection of autonomous text files, making it useful in organizations whose documentation systems are based on word processing programs, using off-the-shelf revision control software.

E. Information Interchange

We are accustomed to thinking of treatment reports in isolation, and there is some justice in this, as a treatment inheres in a specific object, a piece of a given collection, and those with a principal interest in its narrative are the scholars and staff who work with that collection. But from another vantage, treatment reports are of great interest to those studying objects from a pan-institutional vista. Conservators in particular will be interested in treatments that touch on particular classes of objects, materials, or techniques; for them, the treatment reports of another conservator are of no less interest than their own.

The aggregate documentation of treatments constitutes a rich, but unexploited, database. Indeed, to a great extent it is our failure to exploit this database that has hindered the development of a deep body of professional knowledge. For conservation practice to achieve the same level of authority as that enjoyed by other professional praxes, it is essential that understanding draw on the data from a very large number of cases, and our documentation is the key to this enlarged knowledge base. In order to realize this possibility, it is necessary that we begin to develop data interchange formats that transcend the platform-specific circumstances that prevail in most installations today.

Since conservation records typically consist of both text and image and may incorporate other forms of data as well, the development of multimedia standards is necessarily of considerable interest. In the sphere of graphical information, there are a number of standards either in place or under development, and each can be expected to offer at least some promise as we move toward standards-based application development. For our purposes, at the current state of evolution of conservation software, perhaps the most relevant of the existing standards are:

- *RFC 1314 A File Format for the Exchange of Images in the Internet.* This standard is based on TIFF and addresses only black-and-white images.[20]
- *Tag Image File Format Specification (TIFF).* This is a de facto standard for image interchange.[21]
- *RFC 1521 MIME (Multipurpose Internet Mail Extensions): Part One: Mechanisms for Specifying and Describing the Format of Internet Message Bodies.* Although this document focuses on electronic mail, many of the issues it addresses are important as general considerations

in the development of data interchange formats and MIME shows some signs of becoming a de facto standard for multimedia transmission even in contexts other than mail.[22]

• *Document Attribute Format Specification.* This format, which is still in early stages of development and indeed may not mature into a true standard, has an exciting and unusual focus: it concerns encoding the content of "reverse engineered" document image files, that is images of documents decomposed into their component units of meaning, such as a picture and its caption. The format provides a means of representing both "the physical and semantic information contained within a document image," information which can be used by software whose function is to understand the document, rather than merely to reproduce it.

A common application of this type is character recognition, but it has obvious implications for the development of text and image databases as well. Although DAFS may not be likely to evolve into an interchange format for conservation treatment records, the issues it addresses will need to be taken into consideration in the design of such formats.[23]

While it appears that promising formats for interchange of graphical information will be available, the situation facing ordinary text is a bit less clear. There are a number of approaches that could be taken to begin to develop interchange formats for textual material, but one promising avenue suggests itself as the core paradigm for all such development: generalized or descriptive markup. Most of the proprietary text interchange formats in use today encode information about the visual information contained in a document (fonts, spacing, etc.), but fail to encode information that describes the content of the document. Descriptive markup, as exemplified by SGML (the Standard Generalized Markup Language, ISO 8879:1986), in which the structure of the content is delimited in an unambiguous manner, lends itself to machine-mediated operations, such as maintenance of distributed textual databases, especially when heterogeneous computing environments are involved. Issues of machine dependency can be resolved neatly, because the encoding of the document represents the content of the document rather than any particular (machine-dependent) manifestation of that content.

CONCLUSION

Whether a labor of love or necessity, the systems under development today have grown largely independently and in isolation, with informal communication between the authors serving as the principal tie between the various projects. Some of the systems already in place are sufficiently mature that they can serve both as useful production tools and as prototypes for future development efforts; that the next stage in this evolution will involve development in concert seems inevitable.

NOTES

1. American Institute for Conservation of Historic and Artistic Works, "Code of Ethics and Standards of Practice," amended 1990, in *Directory, The American Institute for Conservation of Historic and Artistic Works* (Washington, D.C.: American Institute for Conservation of Historic and Artistic Works, 1993), 21-42.
2. Sally Buchanan and Sandra Coleman, "Deterioration Survey of the Stanford University Libraries Green Library Stack Collection," in *Preservation Planning Program Resource Notebook*, comp. Pamela W. Darling, rev. ed. by Wesley L. Boomgaarden (Washington, D.C.: Association of Research Libraries, Office of Management Studies, 1987), 189-221.
3. Donald E. Knuth, *The Art of Computer Programming,* vol. 2, *Semi-numerical Algorithms,* Series in Computer Science and Information Processing (Reading, Mass.: Addison-Wesley), 176.
4. Ibid., 1-177.
5. William H. Press, et al., *Numerical Recipes in Pascal: The Art of Scientific Computing* (Cambridge: Cambridge University Press, 1989), 212-53.
6. Stephen K. Park and Keith W. Miller, "Random Number Generators: Good Ones Are Hard to Find," *Communications of the ACM* 31 (October 1988): 1192-1201.
7. Abraham Bookstein, "Sampling from Card Files," *Library Quarterly* 53 (July 1983): 307-312.
8. Helmut Bansa, "Computerized Leafcasting," Restaurator 11 (1990): 69-94.
9. Charles Mazel and Frank Mowery, "Calculating the Exact Area of Loss and the Amount of Pulp Necessary to Fill Voids for Leaf Casting Operations Using a Video Digitizer System Developed for the Folger Shakespeare Library," *Book and Paper Group Annual* 5 (1986): 83-87.
10. Jean P. Teas, "Graphic Analysis of Resin Solubilities," *Journal of Paint Technology* 40:516 (January 1968): 19-25.
11. "The Digital Signature Standard Proposed by NIST," *Communications of the ACM* 35 (July 1992): 36-40.
12. John Linn, Network Working Group, Request for Comments: 1421, "Privacy Enhancement for Internet Electronic Mail: Part I: Message Encryption and Authentication Procedures," February 1993.
13. Steve Kent, Network Working Group, Request for Comments: 1422, "Privacy Enhancement for Internet Electronic Mail: Part II: Certificate-Based Key Management," February 1993.
14. David Balenson, Network Working Group, Request for Comments: 1423, "Privacy Enhancement for Internet Electronic Mail: Part III: Algorithms, Modes, and Identifiers," February 1993.
15. Burton S. Kaliski, Jr., Network Working Group, Request for Comments: 1424, "Privacy Enhancement for Internet Electronic Mail: Part IV: Key Certification and Related Services," February 1993.
16. Peter S. Graham, "Intellectual Preservation and the Electronic Environment," in *After the Electronic Revolution, Will You Be the First to Go?: Proceedings of the 1992 Association for Library Collections and Technical Services President's Program, 29 June, 1992, American Library Association Annual Conference, San Francisco, CA*, ed. Arnold Hirshon (Chicago: American Library Association, 1993), 18-38.
17. Stuart Haber and W. Scott Stornetta, "How to Time-Stamp a Digital Document," *Journal of Cryptology* 3 (1991): 99-111.

18. When we speak of markup, we are talking about extraneous signs that serve in one way or another to make machine-readable text more useful, more meaningful, or more understandable; there are different types of markup. *Presentational* markup governs how a text looks. *Procedural* markup tells the system how to achieve that look. Goldfarb describes *descriptive* markup as "markup that describes the structure and other attributes of a document in a *non-system-specific manner*, independently of any processing that may be performed on it." [Emphasis added.] (Cf. Charles F. Goldfarb, *The SGML Handbook*, ed. Yuri Rubinsky (Oxford: Clarendon Press, 1990), 137). MARC tags, for example, are a type of descriptive markup: they enable the exchange of records among machines with different operating systems. For thorough discussions of text markup issues see Goldfarb, as well as James H. Coombs, Allen H. Renear, and Steven J. Derose, "Markup Systems and the Future of Scholarly Text Processing," *Communications of the ACM* 30 (November 1987): 933-47.
19. Chris Stavroudis, telephone conversation with author, 8 May 1993.
20. Alan Katz and Danny Cohen, Network Working Group, Request for Comments: 1314, "A File Format for the Exchange of Images in the Internet," April 1992.
21. Aldus Corporation and Microsoft Corporation, "Tag Image File Format Specification 5.0." Aldus/Microsoft Technical Memorandum, August 1988.
22. Nathaniel S. Borenstein and Ned Freed (nsb@bellcore.com, ned@innosoft.com), Network Working Group, Request for comments: 1521, "MIME (Multipurpose Internet Mail Extensions): Part One: Mechanisms for Specifying and Describing the Format of Internet Message Bodies," characters 187, 424. 81 pages.
23. "Document Attribute Format Specifications (DAFS)." Draft specification, rev. 0.17, 18 May 1993, under development through DIMUND (Document IMage UNDerstanding), an Advanced Research Projects Agency (ARPA) project. Available in Conservation OnLine (CoOL); gopher to palimpsest.stanford.edu.

The House that Jack Built:
The Preservation Management
Information System, A Primer for Design

Erich J. Kesse

Chair, Preservation Department
George A. Smathers Libraries, University of Florida

INTRODUCTION

This paper discusses prerequisites for the design of an automated, relational, and fully integrated Preservation Management Information System (MIS). Although it does not address technical issues such as operating systems, programming, or record length and structure, it examines the nature of the system's architecture. Rather than providing a proposed construction, this paper discusses shape and function; its purpose is to inform design.[1]

The *Book of Knowledge*, a rambling compendium which served the children of America's 1920s as an encyclopedia, described the human body as "the house that Jack built," after Randolf Caldecott's rhyme. "These are the lungs that give the body breath. . ."; it paraphrased the verses every child knew by heart. Metaphors of building, architecture, and design could easily be used to teach any child who had ever played with blocks.

An architecture for a Preservation Management Information System might be described in similar terms. The house that Jack built was first constructed, laid out to facilitate human activity, then populated by the different types of creatures for which it was intended. Similarly, construction of the Preservation MIS requires us to identify and assemble building materials, use these in relation to defined needs, and populate the resulting structure with data that facilitates its use.

As in the building trade, an understanding of demand must precede and fashion supply. Simply put, the question must be asked, "What need is there for a preservation MIS?"[2] Much like analyses of economic indicators, one assumes that the recent proliferation of systems in support of preservation signifies a demand. Management information systems satisfy information needs (Stanford University's Conservation On-Line (CoOL) information service).[3] They document condition and treatment of collections (the National Library of Australia's conservation treatments database).[4] They assess and prioritize preservation needs within collections (the Research Libraries Group's Preservation Needs Assessment Package, PreNAPP).[5] MI systems reduce human labor and costs (the University of Florida's FILM-LOG and similar reformatting systems).[6] And, they facilitate preservation decision-making (Cornell University's brittle books processing systems).[7]

THE ANTECEDENTS OF DESIGN

The MIS must satisfy demand, and it can do so only by facilitating existing activities. This view assumes that evaluation and streamlining of current functions occur periodically, and that operations change to meet new or divergent circumstances and needs. Thus the prerequisites of design include compatibility with current activities, as well as the flexibility to assume new or different shapes characterized by standardized components.

Harking back to the building trade, the cost of construction will not be cheap. And in libraries (a small market with limited internal expertise, where preservation represents one of many concerns clamoring for automation) the Preservation MIS will be made affordable for the majority only when personnel, ideas, and other resources are pooled and shared. This assumes that preservation programs, though differentiated by local needs, are similar enough to allow cooperative systems development and that cooperative development will reduce costs and duplication of effort.

THE MODULAR APPROACH TO MIS DESIGN

Like houses, Preservation MI systems may vary to satisfy individual needs and tastes, but each will share certain basic components. Thus, component or "modular" construction must be an additional design prerequisite. Just as houses have certain rooms planned for specific purposes, preservation MI systems must have modules or subsystems designed to accommodate discrete activities, such as binding, conservation, disaster preparedness, environmental monitoring, etc. As the layout of rooms within houses relates to functions performed within them—a kitchen, for example, connects to a dining room—juxtaposition of MIS modules must be relational—a brittle books processing system, for example, can be connected to a reprographics/imaging system.

Knowing that certain activities adjoin or are dependent on others has no practical use unless one understands how operations communicate or interact. System design becomes a study of motion and workflow. It requires the assembly and study of procedures and products, in order to determine how information should move through the Preservation MIS's modules; at the same time, it makes use of the structure these provide.[8] While several sources compile preservation procedures, workflow documents, and workforms that can be used to inform the design of Preservation MIS modules,[9] there has been little analysis to suggest the uniform procedures, the consistent definition and use of data elements, required for rule-based computer processing of information. The Automation Vendors Information Advisory Committee (AVIAC) Working Group on the Communication of Binding Data Elements, for example, has analyzed documentation, standards, and thesauri for binding to suggest a standard information structure which can be used to automate the binding process.[10] However, procedural steps for other individual components have yet to be clearly laid out and reviewed by the appropriate communities.

One can typically find an inventory of preservation program components and their relationships in the planning documents, procedure manuals, and thesauri of subject terms used in this and allied fields. A detailed but concise map comprehensively listing the components of preservation is required, just as blueprints are necessary for building a house. And, if the *components* of preservation—binding, repair, reformatting, etc.—may be thought of as rooms within a house, the *facets* of these components may be likened to locations *within* a room. A closet or a sleeping alcove in a bedroom, for example, can be compared to subdivisions of preservation microfilming such as queuing, filming, or quality control. Mapping preservation in toto, as well as the facets of its individual components, affords MIS planners the ability to prioritize the development of modules and allows developers to be mindful of the relationships between and among the various elements.[11, 12] This design activity will show us what the *house* and its *rooms* should look like, after they have been built.

The term, "component module," despite its seeming redundancy, will be used to express the compound notion that:

    1) A Preservation Management Information System is
       composed of several preservation management information
       subsystems, i.e., "modules," and

    2) Each module is the automated representation of an individual "component," function, activity, or subroutine of
       a preservation program or administrative structure.

This paper proposes that component modules may be developed either cooperatively or independently; in either case, set standards for communication of the information common to each module are essential. These modules may stand alone or together, and may be used in any combination to reflect the needs of any preservation organization.

TRANSFORMING LOCAL PROCEDURE INTO GLOBAL DESIGN

The component modules of the Preservation MIS are capable of running appliances. These appliances or programs may generate binding slips or microfilming targets, monitor and regulate environmental conditions, or index and deliver literature supporting preservation, much like common household devices turn on light bulbs, brew coffee, monitor home security, or access cable TV. If appliances run by one institution are to be run by another, they must share a common structure for which standardized procedure is a prerequisite. It must either exist beforehand, or be agreed upon as a product of the design process.

AVIAC's work on binding data elements, for example, demonstrates the necessity to rethink aspects of earlier automation. The automated binding systems such as ABLE (Automated Binding Library Exchange), with which most librarians are familiar, do not interface with library online public access catalogs (OPACs). These systems assume a work environment separate from catalog and circulation systems, so that bibliographic information must be duplicated in the binding system, and binding status cannot be communicated to library patrons by the OPAC. AVIAC's proposed standardization defines a structure that remedies this problem.[13]

Because one institution may require elaborate procedures but another needs something much simpler, individual data elements should be designated as either mandatory or optional. A series of mandatory data elements will define the structure of a base system, while optional data elements allow for enhancement and differentiation. Local Preservation MI systems, then, may differ from one another but still achieve communication and data exchange.

Proliferation of Preservation MIS modules representing a single component or supporting a single activity should be kept at a minimum. Systems should differ only at the level of operating system, programming language, or shell (the application in which programming is done): interfaces should be as similar as possible. Preservation staff can expect to change MI systems as often as they move to a new institution; however, they should be able to operate different systems supporting the same activity as readily as they can operate faucets in different houses.

DEVELOPING A PRESERVATION VOCABULARY

Common structures and shared systems require uniform terminology, if information is to be shared or fully exploited. If Preservation MIS component modules are to be used in various locations, there must be agreement upon terms used to describe the same activities. Several early proposals for Preservation MI systems used classification schemes as a means of standardizing terminology. Public Archives Canada's PHOCUS successfully normalized the lexicon of photographic conservation, in language-neutral Universal Decimal Classification, converted from English or French thesauri terms.[14] It is likely that MIS programming will process information in similar fashion, converting standardized natural language input to standardized object code, to allow consistent interpretation of recorded data.

Though many sources publish thesauri, few products have been authorized by professional organizations, and even fewer approved through a national standards review process. Often multiple, differing thesauri attempt to govern use of terminology in a single component field of preservation.

And, authorized thesauri only infrequently conform to the structure required by the American National Standards Institute (ANSI).[15] Structured thesauri have the potential to provide Preservation MIS with both consistent terminology and indication of its context and application, but terminology has yet to be standardized.

A CHIP OFF THE OLD BLOCK:
THE CLIENT-SERVER RELATIONSHIP

The Preservation MIS must also be thought of as a component module of a much larger library MIS. Just as elements within the Preservation MIS must demonstrate interconnectivity—a brittle books processing module must communicate with the imaging module into which it feeds—the Preservation MIS must interface with other library MIS modules. In particular, the Preservation MIS should pass information to and from acquisitions, cataloging, circulation, and collection management systems. Data elements in each of these systems that contain or are capable of containing preservation information must be identified, if information is to be exchanged or shared and duplication avoided.

However information is shared, whether within or among component modules of the Preservation MIS or between the Preservation MIS and other library systems, the exchange occurs within what is called a client-server relationship. This association assumes that information resides in the MIS where it is generated and therefore most useful; when it must be employed beyond that location, it can be delivered ("served") to another MIS or component module (the "client"). The relationship is economical because it reduces duplication and thus saves time and disk space. For example, using standardized formats[16] Preservation MIS component modules (acting as clients of cataloging MIS or bibliographic utilities) are served various types of information—author, title, barcode number. This information facilitates management and tracking of items selected for preservation review or treatment. Conversely, Preservation MIS component modules, acting as servers to other management information systems, supply information about condition, status, and so forth—information created as a result of review or treatment.[17]

Before the recent proliferation of Preservation MIS component modules, it was thought that preservation-related data could be accommodated by a single field in either the U.S. Machine-Readable Cataloging format (US-MARC) for bibliographic objects, or the Canadian Heritage Information Network (CHIN) format for museum objects. An early proposal for what eventually became the USMARC 583 (Preservation Actions) field suggested this type of consolidation.[18] New thought, however, has afforded MI systems a more sophisticated ability to extrapolate data and share information. The University of Florida's FILMLOG system, for example, formats technical information generated during preservation microfilming as USMARC 007, 533, 265, and 583 fields, for export to bibliographic systems.[19]

PREREQUISITES TO DESIGN: AN OUTLINE

Systems analysis and design processes have been discussed at length in the literature.[20] This paper has attempted to relate that discussion to the design of a Preservation MIS. It is a small effort, compared to the actual work of design. The outline of prerequisites to design, which follows, is simple—but the work it implies is tremendous.

   I. Market survey conducted to determine need

  II. Rationale written for the Preservation MIS, as well as its component modules

 III. Partnerships established, assuming:

    A. Cooperative development

    B. Economy of resources

 IV. Partners commit to:

    A. Compilation of documentation, including:

      1. Planning documents

      2. Organizational charts

      3. Workflow charts, policies, and procedures

      4. Workforms

      5. Procedural standards and material specifications

      6. Thesauri

    B. Inventory of preservation program organization, expressing:

      1. Structured hierarchy

      2. Mapped relationships, which may be used to document communication between:

        a) The Preservation MIS and other library and vendor MI systems

        b) Component modules of the Preservation MIS

        c) Facets of component modules

        d) Subroutines of facets

    C. Critical evaluation of current operations

    D. Standardization of procedures and terminology

    E. Design of systems characterized by:

      1. Compatibility with operations

      2. Flexibility to:

        a) Accommodate new procedure

        b) Accommodate change

        c) Allow delimitation or expansion in order to reflect local preservation program organization

3. Component/modular construction with:
   a) Standardized parts
   b) Mandatory and optional implementation schedules
   c) Juxtapositions based upon workflow and relatedness of activities, subroutines, etc.
4. Client-server relationships, compatible with other MIS and information sources
5. Use of standardized data interchange to assure the construction of linked or integrated systems

CONCLUSION

This discussion assumes that a system's design will provide a well-considered superstructure for building the system itself, and that design, therefore, must precede development. But, it also recognizes that preservation is not as affluent as many other library and archival communities; average annual preservation expenditures among ARL libraries is below 5 percent of total budget. It seems likely, therefore, that the Preservation MIS will be built much as the poor man builds his castle, room by room, component module by component module. And, it seems just as likely that preservation programs will build different component modules, in various orders, at divers times, to meet the needs and abilities of each.

The work to follow will require coordination and commitment to the creation of systems that can be used beyond the programming institution, or linked in such a way as to contribute to an integrated Preservation MIS. It will require great will simply to evaluate and document current operations, as well as to standardize them and the terms used in their execution.

NOTES

1. A proposal for a system consistent with this discussion is also available: Erich J. Kesse, "A Suggested Preservation Management Information System Architecture" (Paper, available electronically from the Conservation On-Line (CoOL) information service based at Stanford University). For additional information about access to this paper via CoOL, contact the service administrator, Walter Henry, at his current address: WHENRY@LINDY.STANFORD.EDU. For an electronically mailed copy of this paper, contact the author at his current address, ERIKESS@NERVM.NERDC.UFL.EDU.
2. Mention of automated Preservation MIS (component modules) is significantly lacking from national preservation planning documents. Library automation itself is a development of the last 25 years and, as such, has served acquisitions and catalog management well. Preservation MIS were first envisioned in the early 1980s, and programming developed slowly thereafter. Listed chronologically, these early proposals are documented by: (A) Pamela W. Darling, "Management Options for Preservation" (Paper presented to a break-out session at the American Library

Association's Collection Management Institute, New York, N.Y., 1982). This paper envisions an automated system integrated with USMARC bibliographic records that documents collection management and preservation information and is capable of analyzing this information to support or prompt decision making. (B) Jeffrey Abt, "A Computer-Based Approach to Conservation Administration," in *Preprints of Papers Presented at the 12th Annual Meeting of the American Institute for Conservation of Historic and Artistic Works* (Washington, D.C.: American Institute for Conservation of Historic and Artistic Works, 1984), 1-10. This paper describes microcomputer-based systems design (specifically, proposed features and function) for records of conditions and treatments. (C) Erich J. Kesse, "The Preservation Management Information Field" (Proposal submitted by the University of Florida Libraries to the Library of Congress' USMARC and Network Development Office, 4 December 1984). This proposal calls for integration of coded preservation information into USMARC cataloging and implies use of an interfaced search engine to index and analyze this information for management purposes. While not directly related, the USMARC 583 field, developed by the Library of Congress in association with preservation specialists, is an out-growth of this proposal. (D) Nancy E. Elkington, "The Design and Implementation of a Database Management System for Preservation Information" (Paper presented to the 2nd Annual Conference of the Library and Information Technology Association, Boston, Mass., 1988). This paper examines microcomputer-based applications required to facilitate specific preservation activities. (E) Erich J. Kesse, "A Sketch for a Preservation Management Information System" (Paper presented to the Research Libraries Group, Mountain View, Calif., March 1989). This paper is the first detailed outline of a comprehensive Preservation MIS. It calls for system design with integrated, relational database construction, based on an inventory of management activities divided along lines of common organizational structure for preservation. Abstracted in: Research Libraries Group, "Preservation Information Management System" (Paper released to Research Libraries Group Preservation Committee members by RLG, Mountain View, Calif., 1990). (F) Gay Walker, "Automating the Future: Preservation and Programs" (Paper presented to the American Library Association's Preservation of Library Materials Section program "Bring on the Empty Horses," San Francisco, June 1990). This paper envisions a future MIS which provides both management information about preserved items and electronic access to the preserved items. It inventories and attempts to prioritize management activities that might be automated. Unlike Kesse, Walker assumes that the MIS will be constructed component by component, without a fully developed master plan. (G) Washington Research Library Consortium, "Proposed Preservation & Collections Conservation Expert System" (Proposal to National Endowment for the Humanities Office of Preservation, Lanham, Md., 1 June 1992). This proposal is one of the first plans to envision the translation of preservation activities and decision-making to a rule-based logic unnecessary for the design of expert systems. The proposal remains unfunded; in the judgment of some, it failed to divide work into manageable components.
3. Walter Henry, "Conservation OnLine (CoOL) Delivers Full Text via Internet," *Abbey Newsletter* 16 (December 1992): 102-103. Other online information resources include the Getty Conservation Institute's Conservation Information Network (for a description see the Institute's *Newsletter* 2 (Winter 1987): 1-2) and several electronic list services, among them the Conservation Distribution List (also administered by Walter Henry) and the Research Libraries Group's Preservation List (RLG Pre-L) and PREFIS.

4. Colin Boreham, *Feasibility Study for a National Conservation Treatments Data Base* (Canberra: National Library of Australia, Automated Data-Processing Systems Branch, 1983). For a description of similar applications see *Computer Technology for Conservators: Proceedings of the 11th Annual IIC-CG Conference Workshop, May 13-16, 1985, Halifax, Canada*, ed. John Perkins (Halifax: International Institute for Conservation, Atlantic Regional Group, 1986).

5. Research Libraries Group, *Guide to the Preservation Needs Assessment Package* (Mountain View, Calif.: Research Libraries Group, 1993). The Package is similar to CALIPR, developed by the University of California at Berkeley for the California State Library. See also Barclay Ogden and Maralyn Jones, *CALIPR: An Automated Tool to Assess Preservation Needs of Book and Document Collections for Institutional or Statewide Planning*, version 2.1 (Sacramento: California State Library, 1991).

6. University of Florida Libraries, "FILMLOG" (Unpublished application programming disk and demonstration documentation presented to the Research Libraries Group's workshop "Great Collections Preservation Microfilming Project, Phase 2," Gainesville, Fla., 15 March 1990). FILMLOG automates the processing, cataloging, and management procedures used in preservation reformatting; it was the first system to map and automate these procedures. Similar systems, some based on the FILMLOG model, are in use in the libraries at Harvard University and Stanford University, as well as the New York Public Library and the Southeastern Library Network (SOLINET).

7. A description of these systems may be found in the transcript of "Bring on the Empty Horses," a program presented by the American Library Association's Preservation of Library Materials Section in San Francisco, June 1990. To date, few decision-support systems are used in preservation.

8. The role of procedures in MIS design is described, albeit in relation to museum collections management, in *Museum Documentation Systems: Developments and Applications,* ed. Richard B. Light, D. Andrew Roberts, and Jennifer D. Stewart (London: Butterworths, 1986).

9. System and Procedures Exchange Center (SPEC) Kits are compiled periodically by the Association of Research Libraries, Office of Management Services (Washington, D.C.); some focus on preservation issues. Preservation SPEC Kits include "Basic Preservation Procedures" (SPEC Kit 70), "Brittle Books Programs" (SPEC Kit 152), and "Preservation Guidelines in ARL Libraries" (SPEC Kit 137).

10. See Automation Vendors Information Advisory Committee, Working Group on Communication of Binding Data Elements, "Binding Data Elements" (Unpublished third draft standard, prepared for submission to the National Information Standards Organization, March 1993).

11. In "A Sketch for a Preservation Management Information System" Kesse suggests a map of preservation in toto.

12. Klaus Hendriks and Diane Hopkins, with their map of photograph conservation, suggest a model for mapping components: "Establishing Nodes for a Conservation Information Network," *Preprints of Papers Presented at the 12th Annual Meeting of the American Institute for Conservation of Historic and Artistic Works* (Washington, D.C.: American Institute for Conservation of Historic and Artistic Works, 1984), 63-69; Public Archives Canada, Picture Conservation Division, *PHOCUS* (Ottawa: Public Archives Canada, 1985).

13. For additional discussion, see Bruce Jacobsen, "Automation of Bindery Preparations," *New Library Scene* 8:2 (April 1989): 15-17.

14. Public Archives Canada, Picture Conservation Division, *PHOCUS*.
15. National Information Standards Organization, *American National Standard Guidelines for Thesaurus Structure, Construction and Use*. ANSI/NISO Z39.19-1993 (New York: American National Standards Institute, 1993).
16. Standardized information (i.e., data) exchange formats include: (A) National Information Standards Organization, *American National Standard for Information Retrieval Service Definition and Protocol Specification for Library Applications*. ANSI/NISO Z39.50-1988 (New Brunswick, N.J.: Transaction Publishers, 1988). This standard has been adopted for exchange of data among library information systems. A 1992 version has been approved but has not yet been published. (B) National Information Standards Organization, *American National Standard for Information Sciences—Bibliographic Information Interchange*. ANSI/NISO Z39.2-1985 (New York: American National Standards Institute, 1986). This standard has been adopted for exchange of data among bibliographic information systems using USMARC. (C) American National Standards Institute, *American National Standard for Electronic Data Interchange*. ANSI X.12-1991 (New Brunswick, N.J.: Transaction Publishers, 1991). This standard has been adopted for exchange of data among business information systems.
17. Preservation information has typically been placed in the 007 (Physical Description [Microforms]), 533 (Photoreproduction), and 583 (Preservation Actions) fields in USMARC bibliographic cataloging and the 5750 (Current Condition), 5810 (Treatment) and related fields in Canadian Heritage Information Network (CHIN) museum object cataloging.
18. Erich J. Kesse, "The Preservation Management Information Field" (Proposal submitted by the University of Florida Libraries to the Library of Congress' USMARC and Network Development Office, 4 December 1984).
19. University of Florida Libraries, "FILMLOG."
20. Analysis and design processes are discussed by Diane Hopkins, "Systems Analysis and Design: Overview," in *Computer Technology for Conservators: Proceedings of the 11th Annual IIC-CG Conference Workshop, May 13-16, 1985, Halifax, Canada,* ed. John Perkins (Halifax: International Institute for Conservation, Atlantic Regional Group, 1986), 41-62.

PART 4:
PRESERVATION PLANNING, CONDITION SURVEYS, AND NEEDS ASSESSMENT

Limited funding and collection growth make it impossible (and probably inadvisable) to preserve everything. How then does a library decide what to save, and what urgency to assign to those items deemed to have continuing research value? The papers in this section cover a variety of approaches to collecting preservation-related management information; computer support and analysis is important in all of them. John Dean suggests that information based on the analysis of collections and the preservation unit's capacity for work can be combined with knowledge about collection value to set preservation priorities; he believes an approach to funding that emphasizes the essential integrated nature of preservation with other library operations will be most successful. Dean's paper examines the forces that have caused preservation units to be established and the types of management information that are important in sustaining and furthering such programs. Rather than stimulating senior library management with what he calls "crisis literature" and its inflated estimates of the number of embrittled volumes in American libraries, he advises preservationists to demonstrate the manageability of the problems in their institutions, as revealed through objective studies of the collections. Among the survey types he reviews are sample surveys, preservation needs surveys, condition surveys, and action surveys.

Nancy Schrock describes a condition survey conducted in four Massachusetts public libraries. Since most condition surveys have occurred in academic libraries, she observes that we know little about the condition of public library collections, so different from academic libraries because of their heavier circulation and weeding. Schrock's study profiles the condition of public library book collections, analyzes causes of damage, and suggests strategies for collection maintenance; random sampling is the selected survey technique. Schrock suggests that the resulting data are not only useful locally, but can give public libraries with similar collections information useful in shaping their own preservation programs. Further, the survey methodology is an effective model for use in other libraries.

Martha Hanson and Jeannette Smithee write about their experiences with a preservation needs assessment survey in 10 New York State institutions, including public libraries, academic libraries, and historical agencies. Assuming (like Dean) that libraries cannot preserve everything, the authors point out that needs assessments can help libraries set priorities, match preservation solutions to preservation problems, and develop a reasonable strategy for action (including cost estimates). Hanson and Smithee stress the importance of feasibility as a factor in drafting a preservation action plan—does the institution have the resources and technical capabilities to complete the plan? They observe that the sort of concrete data generated by a needs assessment survey can help librarians justify the reallocation of scarce resources to preservation.

Microcomputers and commercial software can be valuable survey tools. Stuart Kohler examines the usefulness of the computer in manipulating data and refining the decision-making process necessary for developing objectives, priorities, and methodologies for preservation. He explores important hardware issues (including questions of performance and speed), profiles four off-the-shelf software packages that can be easily adapted for survey use, discusses the elements to be included in survey forms and database records, and describes how to construct a test database. Kohler also offers some valuable advice about data quality and quantity, helpful in establishing a balance between minimum and ideal requirements for an acceptable survey.

Managing Collection Information
for Preservation Planning

John F. Dean

Director, Department of Preservation and Conservation
Cornell University

INTRODUCTION

Libraries, particularly academic research libraries, appear to be in a state of crisis and face great difficulty in resolving a number of fundamental problems related to the scarcity and allocation of resources. For example, many libraries confront the difficult decision of whether to convert their bibliographic records to machine-readable form, or to try to reduce cataloging arrearages. The latter is especially vexing, with many libraries reporting backlogs equal to 10 percent of their collections, some titles having been there for 10 years or more.[1] The lack of storage space for collections is also a serious problem for libraries. The host of new buildings opened during the late 1960s and early 1970s has been all but filled for some time, and the immediate prospects for new construction seem unlikely. Thus, more attention is being paid to the concept of off-campus, high-density storage, or to electronic alternatives to concrete and steel.

Given this environment, the establishment and continuing development of preservation programs in libraries are fraught with numerous difficulties and challenges. The three most obvious and immediate needs are for money, staff, and space, commodities that seem to be in increasingly short supply, even for more traditional and proven library departments. As relative newcomers on the library operational scene, preservation departments frequently have to fight harder for resources than better-established units; in addition, they must constantly justify their existence and defend strategies often not easily understood by colleagues. In many cases, preservation departments are launched to take advantage of the availability of grant funding, but this conditional status imposes a level of stress that is unreasonable for a new program. For these and a variety of other reasons, it is important for preservation administrators to articulate and quantify preservation goals in an objective fashion, to identify the dimensions of their institutions' preservation needs, and to develop realistic and cost-effective strategies that emphasize the essential integrated nature of preservation with all other library operations.

It is obvious that preservation planning cannot occur in a vacuum. No matter what the source of funding or the consortial context, the impact of a preservation program on the library must be carefully assessed, and the many changes to which the institution is constantly subject must be taken into account. This paper will discuss some of these issues, examine the impetuses that have led to the establishment of preservation programs, and address the types of management information that are influential in driving and sustaining programs.

THE PLANNING PROCESS AND THE CREATION OF PRESERVATION PROGRAMS

The many reports of the national brittle book crisis and the widespread alarm that they caused in library and archival circles helped to stimulate the drive toward the creation of preservation programs. But, as Sally Buchanan and Sandra Coleman noted in their report on the Stanford survey, many of the figures on which the reports were founded were "only estimates" and not at all based on objective surveys.[2] In particular, Buchanan and Coleman cited a Library of Congress (LC) report that stated rates of embrittlement at LC of 30 percent, Columbia at 30 percent, New York Public Library at more than half its collection, and Harvard at 40 percent, but the figures were apparently largely hypothetical, undocumented, and based on unknown sources. Yet the literature blared the news of the crisis: "The Columbia University Library indicates that it will cost $34 million to preserve the 30 percent of its collection already in danger of irreversible damage";[3] "Research libraries foresee 'terrific crisis' as rate of book deterioration speeds up";[4] and, from the *National Enquirer*, "Millions of valuable books deteriorating in nation's libraries."[5] While objective studies of most collections have occurred after preservation programs were already in place, there is little doubt that flaunted anecdotal figures helped draw attention to one of the preservation problems that in turn led to programs' being established.

Another factor influential in the introduction of preservation programs may be the rather vague and unquantified sense that library treasures are in peril and a preservation program will in some way rectify the accumulated damage of centuries. More frequently for academic research libraries, it seems, peer pressure within a group of institutions, combined with the availability of grant funds, has caused the creation of preservation programs. Ironically, it has been less common for library administrators to establish programs as the result of a perceived need to manage existing standard operations in a more efficient and cost-effective way.

The Association of Research Libraries (ARL) Office of Management Studies' Preservation Planning Program (PPP), initiated in 1980, provided a valuable tool for libraries to use in determining their preservation needs. The "PPP" approach, stressing broad staff participation and cost-benefit analysis, is certainly the most logical and systematic way to develop a preservation program. Unfortunately, many library administrations, perhaps under the spell of the crisis literature, still regard preservation as a black hole that will consume all available funds, and have failed to avail themselves of this opportunity. It falls to the preservation profession to alter this impression by demonstrating the manageability of the problems which are revealed through objective studies of the collections and standard operations. Another and much rarer reason for the establishment of a preservation program, is the direct and dramatic effect of substantial and continuing outside funding.

THE NEW YORK STATE EXPERIENCE

As the result of New York state legislation in support of preservation, 11 comprehensive research libraries within the state were granted annual funding, beginning in 1984, to support the establishment and development of preservation programs. The initial annual sum, at $90,000 per library, was substantial enough to provide realistic encouragement, and the 11 libraries each submitted five-year plans as required by state regulations. The state's requirements for the first five-year plans, covering the period 1985 through 1990, called for a number of commitments from the requesting libraries, as well as the completion of a detailed questionnaire on the state of each library's collections. As nine of the 11 libraries had no recognizable preservation program in place, any meaningful quantification of the range of problems was clearly difficult to accomplish; as a result, most of the five-year plans were somewhat speculative. It is interesting to note that, although many of the libraries indicated that the collection information would be forthcoming once their programs were established, a recent informal survey indicated that to date very little in the way of needs assessment had been done, although most of these libraries regard it as a high priority.

CORNELL'S STRATEGIES FOR PRESERVATION PLANNING

Cornell University's first five-year plan concentrated heavily on the direct establishment of strategies and operations known to be effective in dealing with the preservation problems that were quite evident in the Cornell collections, as well as a highly optimistic plan for advanced conservation training. As most of the central university funds devoted to preservation were allocated to commercial binding, the first target of study was that portion of the collections most affected by these expenditures. The rationalization of these binding funds resulted in substantial cost savings which, coupled with the New York state annual funding and a timely Andrew W. Mellon Foundation grant, enabled a coherent program to be developed from scratch. The second five-year plan, submitted in 1990, represented a more sober and considered projection of the program's development. In particular, these five main concerns, certainly not unique to Cornell, were articulated:

1. The need to maintain the collections responsibly by instituting satisfactory environmental controls, thereby reducing damage and deterioration
2. The need to replace materials too damaged and deteriorated for normal use
3. The need to safeguard new book and periodical purchases by the design of appropriate contractual binding standards and specifications and the development of efficient management systems to implement them; and the creation of cost-effective in-house binding systems for those new materials suited to this approach
4. The need to respond quickly and effectively to those materials damaged by reader use, through the establishment of repair systems
5. The need to preserve and restore to satisfactory condition materials whose retention in original format is important

Because the general intent of the Cornell program was the development of a comprehensive preservation effort, work to establish a broad approach for the program's direction began almost immediately. This approach has centered on two main strategies:

- To preserve library materials damaged as the result of use, to process all new unbound materials in a timely fashion, and to ensure the cost-effective commercial binding of periodicals
- To begin a collection-by-collection preservation program, concentrating initially on those collections considered to be of great national significance (the R.L.G. Conspectus level fives, of which Cornell has 102)

The first strategy addresses those basic needs common to every institution and represents a minimalist approach to preservation for which all libraries must provide resources. The second strategy is largely based on the support of grant funds. Both require rigorous management control, careful cost accounting, and the continuous gathering and assessing of collection information. Because of the Cornell Library's flexible accounting systems, savings in allocated preservation budget lines are allowed to "roll over" (that is, cross from one budget year to the next), and to be transferred from one account to another with relative ease. Thus, for example, unspent funds in the commercial binding budget may be accumulated for more than one fiscal year and, if needed, be used to reinforce salaries. Clearly, the chief result of this flexibility is to encourage staff to pursue cost savings, to nurture an entrepreneurial spirit, and to require a virtual analytical approach to preservation management.

MANAGEMENT INFORMATION: BEGIN WITH BINDING

Periodicals: A Logical Starting Point

In reviewing the collection information needs for any new preservation program, it seems important to begin by examining current practices and expenditures, before making expensive and possibly indiscriminate survey forays into the collection. As noted, commercial binding is an appropriate area for investigation as it is likely that it may be the only sustained preservation allocation for many libraries.

In a recent study of the preservation expenditures of ARL libraries derived from 1989-1990 statistics, the 115 member libraries reported that of the $34,080,614 spent on preservation (excluding salaries and wages), $24,555,458 was expended on contract binding/conservation.[6] According to this study, for many of the smaller ARL Libraries contract or commercial library binding appears to be the only preservation expenditure. While the top five libraries spent an average of $5.93 per serial title on binding, the last five spent $8.30 per serial title. In contrast, the overall preservation expenditures for the top five averaged $4.82 per volume based on total holdings, while the last five spent only eight cents.

Most libraries require commercial library binders to bind three categories of materials: periodicals, newly acquired unbound materials, and volumes damaged by use (rebinds). However, any study of commercial binding needs should begin with periodicals, as it is only possible to observe the performance of bindings on a title over an extended period of time, and the most relevant data to determine title use is that derived from patterns of use *after* binding. In a study to determine levels of use and the most appropriate form of binding that was conducted at the Johns Hopkins University, a random sample of 400 bound titles for the year 1970 was chosen. Another 20 bound, high-use titles, mainly abstracts and indexes, were excluded from the study. With only a few exceptions, all bound periodicals were eligible for circulation, and the three main survey elements were: the number of times circulated, evidence of use, and evidence of binding wear or stress.

Of the 400 titles surveyed, more than 87 percent (352 titles) showed no evidence of circulation or in-library use, while the remainder had been used very little. The only damage to the bound volumes was significant sagging of the textblocks between the squares and consequent loosening at the joints, the result of simply standing on the shelf. The main conclusions of the study were:

- Most periodicals, even "heavily used" titles, are little used *after* binding.
- Binding styles designed for extremely heavy use (typically the former Library Binding Institute "class A") are unnecessarily damaging to the text, unsuited to the appar-

ent archival needs of periodicals, and too costly.
- Demonstrated low use levels indicate that binding some titles was questionable.
- A new form of binding, incorporating the chief requirements suggested by the study, should be designed.

Accordingly, a quarter buckram, double-fan adhesive, flush binding was developed. This binding enables the textblock to stand on the shelf in a perfectly stable, non-sagging fashion, consumes the minimum amount of inner margin, and opens easily to facilitate reading and copying. At the time of the original specification, the late fall of 1975, the quarter buckram binding was 50 percent less costly than the LBI class A binding.[7]

New Monographic Materials

An analysis of patterns of use of newly acquired, unbound monographic materials is much more problematical. With the possible exception of items needed for direct support of the curriculum, such as reserve materials, it is difficult to justify the use of commercial binding funds on the basis of anticipated use. Yet a decision to shelve paperbacks unbound and unsupported can cause considerable damage, stemming from routine stack maintenance handling and negligent browsing. Since a number of studies have demonstrated rapidly increasing acquisitions costs, and the increasing percentage of monographic purchases that paperbacks represent, it is apparent that some cost-effective approach to making these materials shelf-worthy must be found.[8]

One solution that time has proven highly effective is paperback stiffening, a method developed at the Manchester Central Library, England, in 1961 and refined at the Johns Hopkins University in 1974. The technique involves establishing a flexible woven hinge to more securely fasten the cover to the textblock and adhering a thin board to the inside of the cover to reinforce the book. If subsequent high use damages this structure, the injuries will be detected at the circulation desks and a commercial binding decision can be made at that point. Very few stiffened paperbacks, less than one-half of 1 percent, will need further treatment, a reflection of the general low use of research library materials.[9] Further and significant advantages of this in-house technique are that the unit costs are low (less than $1, including both time and materials), and an efficient operation can process materials within 48 hours, an important point when most automated systems show new materials as "on shelf" the moment they clear cataloging.

Rebinding Damaged Volumes

Similarly, the commercial rebinding of books damaged by reader use can be largely avoided through sensible, in-house book repair techniques. Generally, books suited to in-house repair have sound paper and textblocks. If the paper is brittle, the book is a candidate for replacement, and if the book has a broken leaf attachment structure, it is certainly a candidate for commercial library binding. Studies at the Cornell University Library indicate, however, that 96 percent of books damaged by reader use can be repaired in the Library. The repair techniques used at Cornell involve the sewing of first and last few sections, back-relining, case reconstruction, and the application of laser-printed title labels.[10] The production requirement for this method is four per hour per technician, and the objective is to return all books to the shelf within 48 hours. In terms of cost, the uniform nature of the process and the books' speedy return to the shelf obviates the need for specification and documentation. Cost comparisons demonstrate that the preparation costs for the commercial binding of these materials (circulation charge and discharge, specification, shipment documentation, and inspection) are similar to the cost of actual repair.

The early analysis of commercial library binding costs and procedures inevitably leads to the establishment of basic preservation operations that not only generate significant dollar savings to be applied to the further advancement of the program, but almost incidentally build the essential infrastructure on which the program can begin to develop. Even if a preservation program does not proceed beyond this point, it may still be highly successful in addressing the immediate needs of the library, and there may seem to be little advantage in pursuing a needs assessment approach except for non-operational requirements such as environmental upgrades and disaster planning. Such an approach is wholly reactive however, and if the library preservation program is to satisfy the broader and unarticulated needs of the scholar, it must show initiative and begin to explore the "guts" of the research collection.

VENTURES INTO THE COLLECTION: APPROACHES TO SAMPLE SURVEYS

The Yale Survey

There are many reasons why librarians feel the need to seek a broad picture of the physical condition of their collections, ranging from the simple and understandable desire to "do something," to the need to prepare a well-reasoned action plan. The rationale for the large sample condition survey at the Yale University Library provides a clear statement of objectives:

> [The survey] was designed to yield a detailed description of the collections in the discrete units of the Yale system; to examine the complex relationships between the nature of materials, their condition, and the environment in which they are housed; and to estimate how many volumes require immediate attention, how many will need attention soon, and what kind of attention will be needed.[11]

The authors further point out that by identifying the extent of the preservation problems, the level of effort and consequent costs to resolve them can be articulated in the form of a long-term plan. The Yale survey is an important landmark in collection condition assessment, and because of its large scale it is very unlikely to be repeated. The survey reviewed a sample of 36,500 volumes from the collection of 7,725,424 volumes and consumed 3,800 hours. The unusually large size of Yale's sample is justified because "the structure of the sample needed to examine the books in a large academic library is more complicated than those of surveys previously conducted."[12]

Drott's Method of Sample Selection

The size of the sample to be surveyed has been a matter of some concern to librarians, especially as some statisticians tell us that the relationship of the sample size to the size of the population (collection) is irrelevant. Carl Drott, the writer most widely cited by librarians, sets forth the principles on which sample size is based by describing a system involving confidence level and tolerance, two elements of "error measure." Drott reproduces a "Confidence and Tolerance Determine Sample Size" table which allows the calculation of an appropriate sample.[13]

The table is used by deciding on the level of confidence desired in the result and the degree of tolerance. Confidence is the measure of how certain the surveyor is that the result falls within the limits of tolerance, and tolerance is a measure and expression of the range of accuracy of the result. Thus a tolerance of 1 percent would be expressed as a plus or minus to condition the result statement. For example, "Brittle books represent 20 percent of the collection, plus or minus 1 percent (i.e., between 19 and 21 percent)."

The sample size selected from the table is not entirely dependent upon confidence and tolerance. It is valuable to estimate the approximate percentage of the most significant category to be surveyed; thus one may decide that brittle books represent the most significant category and estimate that no more than 30 percent of the collection is brittle. The decimal .30 is subtracted from 1.00 and the two fractions multiplied together: 1:00 - .30 = .70; .30 x .70 = .21. The resulting .21 is multiplied by 4.00 (Drott formula) to produce a correction factor of .84. If it is decided that a survey should have a confidence level of 95 percent with a tolerance of 1 percent, the table establishes a sample size of 9,604, which is then multiplied by the correction factor to produce a revised sample size of 8067 (9604 x .84). Drott cautions that the table should only be used for sample sizes larger than 30, but less than 10 percent of the total population. All statisticians point out, however, that the larger the sample, the more confidence we can have in the accuracy of the results.

Random, Systematic, and Fractional Sampling

The method of sample selection is of vital importance to the design and validity of sample surveys, and for random sampling, each item in the collection must have an equal chance of being included in the sample. This ensures that the random sample is representative of the entire population. There are a number of ways that randomness can be assured; the most objective use tables of random numbers, such as the Rand Corporation's *A Million Random Digits with 100,000 Normal Deviates*.[14] Although many library preservation surveys have used tables of random numbers, the samples have usually been further conditioned by "stratification," by which a proportionate number of items from each stratum (subject area, collection, branch library, etc.) have been surveyed to produce more coherent and particular results. Given the complexities of modern research library collections, the variety of formats and multiplicity of use patterns, careful stratification seems essential if the results are to have any utility.

Other methods of sample selection commonly used by librarians are systematic and fractional sampling. Systematic sampling typically involves drawing the requisite number of items at a fixed interval from a list. For example, a sample of 400 to be drawn from a shelflist card file of 100,000 would involve pulling every 250th card, beginning at a random point in the file. Another and less tedious approach would be to take the linear measure of the cards in the shelflist and divide this by the sample number, thus a 1,000-inch shelflist would yield a sample card every 2.5 inches. Fractional sampling involves the same basic procedure, except that the sample card would be selected at random from within the interval (i.e., from within each 2.5-inch group. The validity of systematic and fractional sampling is entirely dependent upon the unbiased ordering of the list; it is generally assumed that conventional library shelflists are ordered in an unbiased fashion.[15]

The Preservation Needs Surveys

The types and numbers of questions to be answered by a sample survey obviously depend upon the range of data that is gathered, and the ultimate purpose of the survey. If the survey incorporates a decision-making or prioritizing model, such as the Research Libraries Group Preservation Needs Assessment Package (PreNAPP), an attempt is made to combine risk factors that place the surveyed item at jeopardy (lack of fire protection, inadequate environmental controls, absence of a disaster plan, etc.), with vulnerability (high frequency of use, poor security, and high value) and condition. PreNAPP provides an automated data manipulation system designed to produce a report on the general preservation problems of the collection, with a view to assessing areas of need and consequent action. Because PreNAPP derives its data from an extremely small sample (400 items) and employs rather simplistic data elements, the results should be regarded as only generally indicative of a course of action. When PreNAPP was applied to Cornell University's collections, some anomalies emerged that tended to weaken confidence in the results. For example, none of the 400 items randomly selected from the approximately 4 million shelflist cards had brittle paper, although other surveys indicate that the proportion of the collection that is brittle is between 15 and 20 percent.

Condition Surveys

Condition surveys are designed to identify the physical condition of the collection in a much more specific manner, often combining observations on damage and deterioration with incidence and type of use. For example, the Yale survey required basic information on place and date of publication, and whether or not an item was eligible for circulation. The condition portion of the questionnaire consisted of 12 primary queries, each with a number of subsidiaries. The condition queries on the Stanford questionnaire relating to paper condition, binding condition, and board and cover condition were further divided using a 0-2 condition definition.

The Harvard University Preservation Office has recently developed an excellent survey system that produces lists of random samples and a database that features tabulation and analysis capabilities. The survey instrument has 21 primary condition categories, each with a number of subsidiaries. By manipulating different combinations of condition, a precise action statement can be derived from the data. In addition, general description data (publication date, collection name, subject, place of publication) provide context, and some costing information can be derived from the record of the number of pages and the item's dimensions.[16]

Action Surveys

A variant of the condition survey is the action survey, which expresses the preservation needs of the collection in terms of actions that will secure, replace, protect, or treat the items examined. For example, instead of reporting that an item has brittle paper, the item will be directly identified as a reformatting candidate. The Cornell University Department of Preservation and Conservation uses an action survey system that has evolved from a model used successfully for over 40 years. The standard information applicable to all items includes:

- Call number
- Publication date
- Publication place
- Volume number (if applicable)

- Total volumes in the title (if applicable)
- Number of pages (omit if a set)
- Year of last circulation

There are six action categories:
- Reformat
- Commercial Bind
- Basic Repair
- Basic Bind
- Enclose
- Conservation Treatment

These six categories have a number of subsidiary elements. As the questionnaire shows (Figure 1 on next page), the Cornell system is designed to identify costs as precisely as possible, thus all appropriate elements (such as level of staff involved in a particular action) are indicated. The explanatory notes accompanying the survey, which is now conducted entirely with laptop computers, include:

Reformat

This category is used for those items that need to be replaced or supplemented by a facsimile (microform, photocopy, digitized image). Because many items are returned to the shelf even after they have been reformatted, it is important to know whether or not the sewing will need to be cut because of overly tight inner margins to facilitate reformatting, as this incurs a cost. On line D, the indication of "Brittle" means that the paper will not withstand a double corner fold, whereas the indication of "Acidic" means that a spot test has shown that the paper is acidic but not brittle. Thus, data gathered indicate two levels of priority (brittle and acidic), number of pages (a cost factor in reformatting), size (indicated through one of five size classification symbols used as part of the call number at Cornell), and whether or not there will be a cost for returning the item to the shelf.

Commercial Bind

This category identifies those items that are best addressed by the commercial binder. On line C, an indication that the item is a serial suggests that the Commercial Binding Office will have a record, especially if combined with "First Bind" (i.e., a surveyed item that has never been bound). A "Rebind" in this category will invariably indicate that the item is not rare and that the leaf attachment structure is broken.

Basic Repair

This category describes those items normally repaired immediately following circulation (i.e., non-rare, non-brittle, sound textblock). "To Binding" indicates the normal spine replacement technique, and "To Leaves" indicates

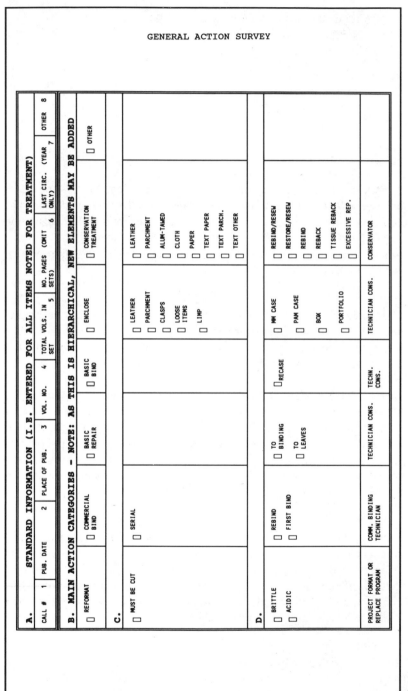

Figure 1

that leaves are damaged and need repair or possible replacement. "To Binding" and "To Leaves" may be indicated separately or in combination.

Basic Bind

Presently this category identifies in-house basic cloth binding for items that may be rare, and which generally have sound paper and textblocks. A rare item for recasing in cloth would typically have a deteriorated, but non-original binding of little value.

Enclose

The descriptive portion of this category on line C is used to provide some indication of why an enclosure is appropriate and what other work may be needed. For example, parchment and leather bindings will need to be furbished as well as enclosed.

Conservation Treatment

In general, this category is intended to identify work to be performed by conservators. Line C provides a limited set of descriptions, the first five of which indicate binding material, the last three the material of the textblock. The six action elements on line D represent the main types of conservation action; they are a conscious limiting of a large number of possible treatment actions.

Rebind/Resew indicates an item that will be given a new binding (because the original is too deteriorated or not contemporary with the text), and which has broken sewing. It is assumed that all books to be resewn will be washed, alkalized, resized, and receive moderate paper repairs (i.e., fold reinforcement, first and last leaves supported).

Restore/Resew means that the original binding must be restored and replaced after the textblock has been treated, as described above.

Rebind is somewhat analogous to recase, in that the original sewing is retained but a new binding is applied because the original cannot be saved or is a secondary binding. All leaf repairs are performed *in situ*.

Reback is for items that have generally sound sewing structures and that need to have the original bindings restored by rebacking in the appropriate material. Other binding support, such as corner reinforcement, may also be performed.

Tissue Reback is applied to books with light structures (generally smaller volumes with fairly thin boards) that have quite sound material at the surface but which are broken in the outer joint. In most cases, fine bindings produced from the mid-18th century on are appropriate for this treatment.

Excessive Repair applies to textblocks that are severely damaged (e.g., wormed or mold-damaged) and which require special efforts to render them fit.

The Cornell survey is designed to address both sample and comprehensive survey needs, and conducting surveys is the responsibility of the Conservation Liaison Specialist, also charged with identifying candidates for treatment and all the related documentation. A comprehensive survey, in the context of the Cornell program, is the continuing process of examining library materials at the shelf (mainly in the Special Collections vaults) and identifying items for treatment. The application of the survey model permits lists of items requiring particular forms of treatment to be generated from the database, which enables the cost-effective batch processing of even the most complex forms of conservation treatment. A similar approach, but with a different instrument, is taken for the survey of graphic materials and manuscripts, with a computer-based survey instrument serving both as a means of identifying needs and costs for collection assessment, as well as a tool for treating the collection in a cost-effective fashion. The overall strategy in Cornell's comprehensive survey of Special Collections materials is to identify candidates for treatment or reformatting, based on the knowledge that these materials are of great significance to the programs of the University. In addition to this continuing survey of the "general" Special Collections, particular collections are targeted as appropriate subjects for grant-funded proposals.

All surveys of library collections, whether sample or comprehensive, must take into account patterns of use and have some mechanism for the inclusion of items that are charged out and thus temporarily off the shelf during the survey. Pollsters are very conscious of those members of a sample population that do not respond to questionnaires, as nonrespondents can be very different from respondents. Books that are in use are directly analogous to these nonrespondents and, given the generally low use of research collections, are certainly different from most of the collection. Even precise data on the apparent preservation needs of a collection are irrelevant unless user need and documented use are factored into the final strategy design.[17]

DOCUMENTATION

Surveys, particularly of the type used by Harvard and Cornell, frequently provide the main fabric and rationale for a proposal to a funding agency; clearly, the data collected and processed must be accurate and capable of addressing and answering a wide range of questions. Proposals to funding agencies are quite comparable to commercial contract bidding. If the preservation strategy recommended is not appropriate and the unit costs are unreasonably high, the "bidding" library will not be funded. On the other hand, if the plan of work is too ambitious and the unit costs are too low, the library may be funded but unable to complete the project without doing considerable damage to other library operations.

Consequently, grant proposals, and the survey and costing efforts that make up their main substance, probably contain more accurate descriptions of collections, their value, patterns of use, and condition, than can be obtained for any other less cogent purpose. The proposal's plan of work provides a blueprint for action, determining costs, degree of effort, production schedule, and predicted outcome. It also establishes reporting protocols that require an ongoing evaluation of the project and the performance of its staff. Most library preservation departments now take advantage of the power and flexibility of computers to track, using file and spreadsheet systems, their progress in fulfilling the commitments of a grant. In addition, because of stricter institutional budget control requirements, every aspect of the library's "cost share" must be similarly charted to provide a constant and auditable record.

As grant funds for a comprehensive approach to the nation's preservation problems become more freely available, preservation administrators will respond by designing sophisticated models for describing a greater variety of problems within specific collections, along with a broader range of strategies for their resolution. This "whole collection" approach, which incorporates all formats of research materials (books, manuscripts, photographs, graphic arts, etc.), and all appropriate preservation strategies will encourage administrators to apply the rigorous principles of grant project management to all standard preservation operations.

CONCLUSION

More than any other library management enterprise, preservation must constantly justify its existence. Library administrators are not likely to be swayed by panegyrics on the ethics of preservation, but their support can be gained by objective and quantified demonstrations of need, and the overall cost-effectiveness of sound preservation management. The links between the improved bibliographic access provided by increasing numbers of machine-readable records, and the need to fulfill the promise of those records by providing physical accessibility, must be stressed, as must the role that grant-funded preservation plays in continuing to build bibliographic databases.

Preservation administrations are beginning to realize that, given the obesity of research collections and their continuing exponential growth, it is not possible, or even advisable, to preserve everything. Preservation management information, based on careful analysis of the collections and preservation operations, then integrated with management information on collection value and utility, should drive the selection mechanisms for preservation. For many preservation administrators, the struggle for recognition within their own libraries and the proactive stance that must be adopted to secure grant funding to drive the local and national programs have forged a determination that has placed preservation in the forefront of technological change. As Ross Atkinson noted when referring to preservation in a recent paper on digital technology, "Who would have thought three or four years ago that the library function, which is by definition the most conservative of all library operations, would be the one which would become increasingly engaged with cutting edge technology?"[18]

NOTES

1. Grace Agnew, Christina Landram, and Jane Richards, "Monograph Arrearages in Research Libraries," *Library Resources & Technical Services* 29 (October-December 1985): 347.
2. Sally Buchanan and Sandra Coleman, "Deterioration Survey of the Stanford University Libraries Green Library Stack Collection," in *Preservation Planning Program Resource Notebook* comp. Pamela W. Darling, rev. ed. by Wesley L. Boomgaarden (Washington, D.C.: Association of Research Libraries, Office of Management Studies, 1987).
3. "The Preservation Crisis," *Journal of Academic Librarianship* 6 (November 1980): 290.
4. Jack Magarrel, "Damage in the Stacks: Research Libraries Foresee 'Terrific' Crisis as Rate of Book Deterioration Speeds Up," *Chronicle of Higher Education*, 30 May 1978, 9.
5. Quoted from the *National Enquirer*, 14 February 1978, in Pamela Darling, "Creativity vs. Despair," *Library Trends* 30 (Fall 1981): 179.
6. John F. Dean, "Commercial Binding and In-House Alternatives" (forthcoming).
7. John F. Dean, "The Binding and Preparation of Periodicals: Alternative Structures and Procedures," *Serials Review* 6 (July-September 1980): 87-90. A more detailed description (also by Dean) appears in "Serials Binding: Options and Problems," *Proceedings of the UK Serials Group Conference, 26th-29th March, 1984*, ed. Brian Cox (Guildford: UK Serials Group, 1985).
8. John F. Dean, "The In-house Processing of Paperbacks and Pamphlets," *Serials Review* 7 (October-December 1981): 81-85.
9. Herman H. Fussler and Julian Simon, *Patterns in the Use of Books in Large Research Libraries* (Chicago: University of Chicago Press, 1969). Fussler and Simon note that the frequency of use of books in a large research library may be as low as once in 50 years.
10. For a full description of these techniques see: John F. Dean, "The Complete Repair of Bound Volumes," *Serials Review* 13 (Fall 1987): 61-67.
11. Gay Walker, et al., "The Yale Survey: A Large-Scale Study of Book Deterioration in the Yale University Library," *College & Research Libraries* 46 (March 1985): 113.
12. Ibid., 127.
13. M. Carl Drott, "Random Sampling: A Tool for Library Research," *College & Research Libraries* 30 (March 1969): 119-25.
14. Rand Corporation, *A Million Random Digits with 100,000 Normal Deviates* (Glencoe, Ill.: Free Press, 1955).
15. Ray L. Carpenter and Ellen Storey Vasu, *Statistical Methods for Librarians* (Chicago: American Library Association, 1978). This work provides a very useful discussion of statistical methods within the context of libraries.
16. Described in "Physical Condition of the Collections [Task Force B]," *Preservation Planning Program*, rev. ed. (Washington, D.C.: Association of Research Libraries, Office of Management Services, 1993).

17. Fussler and Simon, 127. The authors note that "past use of a title over a sufficiently long period is an excellent and by far the best predictor of the future use of that title."
18. Ross Atkinson, "Three Questions" (Paper presented at the American Library Association Preconference, "Electronic Technologies: New Options for Preservation," New Orleans, 14 June 1993).

A Collection
Condition Survey Model
for Public Libraries

Nancy Carlson Schrock

Conservator and Consultant
Bookbinding and Library Conservation

Preservation has become an integral part of operations in academic and research libraries, but public libraries have been slow to see its relevance for high-use circulating collections that are weeded heavily. What is the condition of our public library collections? Does the systematic weeding they typically receive actually eliminate the need for a preservation program? And if not, then what type of preservation program would be most appropriate? The answers to these questions are increasingly important as statewide preservation planning efforts seek to involve public libraries, and online networks subject more and more materials to heavy use through interlibrary loan. programs.

Surveys can be an effective way to determine condition and identify causes of damage. However, the majority of surveys have been conducted by academic libraries, where they focused on the problems of acidity and embrittlement; their results are not applicable to general collections in public libraries. The only published survey of book condition in a public library was reported by the Wellesley Free Library in 1989.[1] Nearly 22 percent of the Wellesley book collection was damaged, and the survey findings were used to justify additional funding from the capital budget to initiate a program of replacement, repair, and weeding.

In 1991, the Massachusetts Board of Library Commissioners awarded an LSCA Title I grant to the Wellesley Free Library to replicate its 1988 survey, and to gather comparative data from three other public libraries within the Minuteman Library Network.[2] The goals of the project were to profile the condition of public library book collections, analyze causes of damage, and suggest strategies for their maintenance. These efforts coincided with development of a Massachusetts statewide preservation program.[3]

At the time of the survey, the Minuteman Library Network (MLN) membership included 22 public and two academic libraries in eastern Massachusetts. All members share technology, resources, and expertise through an online catalog and an extensive interlibrary loan program. During 1988, members drafted cooperative collection development policies, and were one of the first consortia in Massachusetts to do so.

The municipalities represented by MLN fall into three groups: population centers of 40,000-75,000 citizens; suburban towns with populations of 15,000-40,000; and small communities of 7,000-15,000. The six cities and large towns, formerly manufacturing and industrial centers, have a mix of old New England, suburban, and newly arrived ethnic groups; their libraries focus on popular reading, literacy, and outreach programs. The suburbs have a highly educated population who require strong reference and nonfiction collections. Both city and suburban libraries have holdings of 100,000-250,000 volumes.

The small towns are in a state of transition from self-contained rural communities to bedroom suburbs of Boston and the high-tech industries of Route 128. Their collections average 35,000-60,000 volumes and focus on popular reading, relying on interlibrary loan to meet increasing demands for more extensive nonfiction material. Most of the libraries were founded in the 19th or early 20th centuries and retain older material; some house the historical collections of their towns. All have active children's programs.

Project staff wanted to survey the types of holdings found throughout the network, so they selected Framingham Public Library to represent the large population centers; Medfield to represent the small towns; and Concord, along with Wellesley, to represent the suburbs. The results for individual participants could then serve as models for other similar libraries in the network, while the aggregate sample would cover the range of materials found system-wide.

Concord Free Public Library. 230,000 volumes. An active suburban library with older collections whose primary roles are reference and research. Many of the materials held are unique and are more typical of items traditionally found in academic libraries.

Framingham Public Library. 178,000 volumes. A large suburban library oriented toward current reading needs in English and Spanish, with heavy weeding, active outreach, and high circulation. Framingham is the largest town in the state and has a significant Hispanic population.

Medfield Public Library. 40,000 volumes. A small public library that focuses on popular materials and a children's learning center. Medfield's population is expanding as young families move into new housing in this formerly rural community.

Wellesley Free Library. 205,000 volumes. A large suburban and subregional library with a significant reference collection, heavy circulation, and high interlibrary loan statistics.

SURVEY METHODOLOGY

After a review of surveys conducted during the last five years, the LSCA project staff decided to use the methodology developed for the Wellesley Free Library survey of 1987. The needs assessment programs of PreNAPP and CALIPR were judged to be too general for the detailed condition data that were needed. Moreover, reusing the original methodology produced consistent data that helped Wellesley evaluate the impact of preservation on the condition of their book collections.

The LSCA survey was based on the methodologies used at Yale University[4] and Stanford University,[5] modified for public library collections. The descriptive categories of Yale were modified to describe binding types, eliminating enclosure type and leaf attachment. The binding types reflect those found in public libraries, including publishers' bindings with dust jackets, children's library bindings (reinforced side-sewn hardcovers), and plastic laminates. Rather than analyzing data by subject matter, the survey broke down holdings by collection type, which corresponds to the audiences of public libraries:

- Adult Fiction
- Adult Nonfiction
- Children's and Young Adult
- Non-Circulating (Reference)

As at Stanford, the condition characteristics were ranked 0-2:

---

0 = good condition; no damage

1 = fair condition; minor damage;
    candidate for minor repair

2 = poor condition; major damage;
    candidate for rebinding, replacement, weeding

Condition characteristics were expanded to include distortion of the textblock, dust jackets, mutilation, and environmental damage. By combining characteristics, the survey was able to project the percentages of the collections that were in good, fair, and poor condition, while the data for individual condition characteristics isolated the types and causes of damage. (See DATA MANAGEMENT heading on page 214.)

LSCA CONDITION SURVEY FORM

Library:_____Wellesley _____Framingham _____Medfield _____Concord
Sample No.: _____

ITEM DESCRIPTION:

Bar Code: _____
Call No.: _____
Publication Date: _____
Year Entering the Library: _____
Circulation: _____
Collection: _____

PHYSICAL DESCRIPTION:

Binding Type

_____ Hard cover
_____ Original trade binding
_____ Dust jacket
_____ No dust jacket
_____ Library rebinding
_____ Leather binding
_____ Children's library binding

_____ Soft cover
_____ Original trade
binding (paperback)
_____ Plastic laminate
_____ In-house process
_____ Pamphlet binding
_____ Spiral binding
_____ Other

Condition

_____ Dust jacket (0-2).
(Leave blank if no jacket)
_____ Boards/covers (0-2)
_____ Hinges (0-2)
_____ Spine (0-2)
_____ Distortion (0-1)
_____ Pages
detached/torn/loose (0-2)
_____ Fold test (0-3)
_____ pH test (0-2)

_____ Repair
_____ Appropriate
_____ Inappropriate
_____ Mutilation (0-2)
_____ Food/drink/stains
_____ Razored
_____ Scotch tape
_____ Torn
_____ Underlining/writing
_____ Environmental damage (0-2)
_____ Animals
_____ Burns
_____ Insects
_____ Mold
_____ Soil
_____ Water damage
_____ Yellowing/foxing

Surveyor: _____ Date: _____
1/26/92

SAMPLING

The samples were drawn randomly to meet the objective defined by the statistical consultant: "To select a sample from the collection of each library that would faithfully mirror the conditions in each collection as a whole."[6] A sample of 900-1,000 items was selected in each library because this generally produces a confidence level of 95 percent with a confidence interval of 2-3 percent. Thus, if survey results for such a sample size show that 35 percent of the books in a library exhibit highly acidic paper, a library can predict with 95 percent certainty that 32-38 percent of its collection is highly acidic.

A key requirement of random sampling is that each item in the population (the whole collection) has an equal chance of being chosen for the sample. Since public libraries typically circulate a considerable proportion of their fiction and children's books at any one time, selecting from shelf location does not produce a reliable sample because the most heavily used items may never appear on the shelves. Therefore the sample was drawn from the shelflist, using two sets of random numbers to indicate drawer number and location within the drawer (a specified number of inches measured from the front). Since some drawers were not completely full, it was necessary to over-sample to compensate. Depending upon the estimated percentage of empty space in drawers, surveyors were given 1,100-1,200 locations, which generated the necessary 900-1,000 hits. Items were retrieved from the shelves or recalled if in circulation. When a card indicated multiple volumes or copies, all were surveyed to eliminate arbitrary choices. This occurred infrequently, and the statistician determined that it had little effect on the complete sample.

Sample size and sampling methodology were consistent among all four libraries, so that comparisons were valid and data from the institutions could be combined. Confidence intervals were computed for the results of individual libraries, using a standard statistical formula based on the percentage of a characteristic found in the sample and the size of the sample. Because the four library collections were of unequal sizes, results from each library were weighted by the ratio of the number of volumes in that library to the total number in all four libraries. Results for the combined sample of 4,000 public library books had confidence intervals of ±1.7 percent to nearly 0—producing an extremely accurate profile of book condition in the Minuteman Network. (See Appendix.)

DATA MANAGEMENT

Survey data were entered directly into an IBM-compatible laptop computer using the database management program Alpha 4, customized for the project by a systems consultant.[6] Alpha 4 software was selected for the project because it combines the capabilities of dBase with the user-friendly interface of a Macintosh program. It has options for calculation and summary fields that were used to generate 21 standard reports with averages and percentages for each of the libraries, as well as the combined results.

The portable computer proved to be an efficient and effective method of entering data. Two surveyors worked as a team; one person surveyed while the other entered the information into the computer. Data consistency was monitored by the project manager, who proofread all entries for the first library surveyed, and entries for all damaged books in the other three libraries. One of the surveyors had done the initial Wellesley survey in 1987, which contributed to the consistency of the comparative data for the two Wellesley surveys. The two surveyors each worked six months, 17 hours a week, to pull the shelflist sample, locate volumes, survey condition, and enter data for 4,000 books. Once trained, they could survey a library in six to seven weeks, provided that the shelflist was current and in good condition.

SURVEY RESULTS

The final results were analyzed, noting common trends and significant differences between libraries and types of collections. The survey findings formed the basis of preservation planning documents prepared for the individual libraries by the project's conservation consultant. Data from all libraries were combined to profile the condition of public libraries in the Minuteman Library Network.[8] In addition, badly damaged items were searched against the network's database to calculate the frequency of multiple copies within individual libraries and within the network. This information was used to estimate the percentage of badly damaged items that could be weeded and the percentage that required repair, if the titles were to remain available to MLN members.

PROFILE OF COLLECTIONS

The majority of the books in the libraries were new, with 40-50 percent published in the 1980s or later. Nevertheless, all libraries retained a core collection of older materials. Concord had the oldest collection, Medfield the youngest. [FIGURE 1] A comparison of the age of the Wellesley collections in 1987 and 1992 indicated that heavy weeding played a major role in collection management: 40 percent of the 1970s publications were discarded during the interim five years between surveys. [FIGURE 1A]

The distribution of books within the collections reflected the differing audiences of the four libraries. Since Medfield and Framingham focus on circulating collections, their holdings were strongest in fiction and children's literature. As a small rural/suburban library, Medfield had the smallest percentage of volumes devoted to reference and nonfiction. Wellesley's position as a subregional library center and Concord's emphasis on research materials for the study of local authors were reflected in the higher percentages of

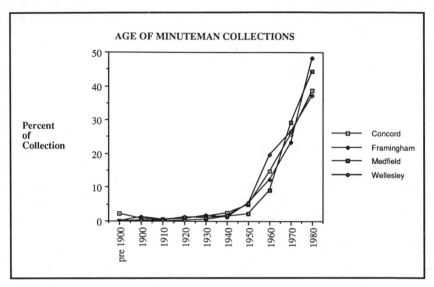

Figure 1

nonfiction held by these libraries. Framingham had the largest percentage in the non-circulating category, because their local history collection was included. [FIGURE 2]

The majority of the books were still in the original hardcover trade bindings in which their publishers issued them. Unlike academic libraries, the public libraries did little commercial rebinding of monographs. The libraries purchased 10-20 percent of their acquisitions in soft covers. Medfield and Framingham, with their emphasis on popular fiction, purchased more paperbacks, while

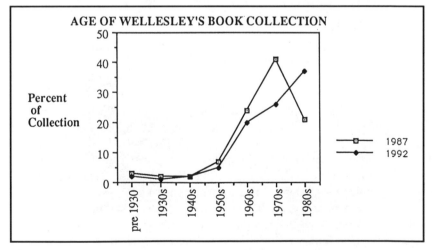

Figure 1A

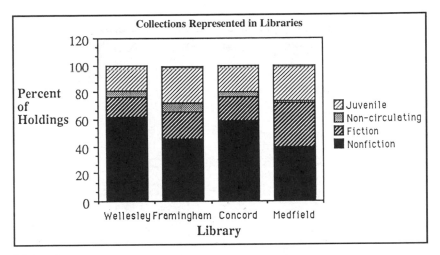

Figure 2

Concord and Wellesley, with their older collections of nonfiction, did more rebinding. Children's books, particularly picture books, are available in reinforced side-sewn bindings, called "children's library bindings" in this survey. They were used extensively in all four libraries. [FIGURE 3]

CONDITION OF COLLECTIONS

The surveyors examined the condition of the samples from several viewpoints: paper (its acidity, its brittleness, whether it was torn), binding (cover, spine, whether the pages were attached), and overall condition (mutilation, environmental damage, distortion). Within each of these categories,

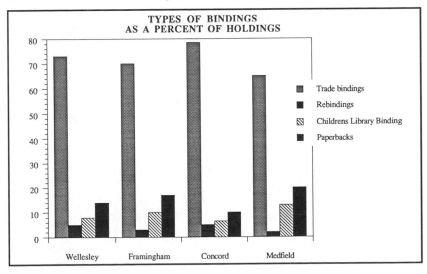

Figure 3

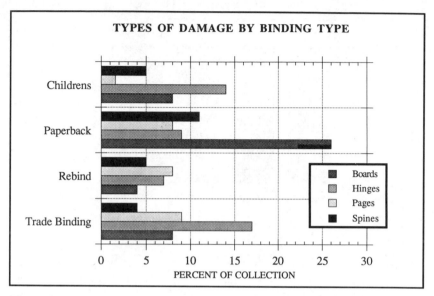

Figure 4

materials were ranked according to their condition: good, minor damage (needs simple repair), or major damage (needs extensive treatment, replacement, or withdrawal).

Although 61 percent of the books had acidic paper, brittle paper was not a serious problem in the public libraries. Medfield had no brittle paper in its sample, reflecting the youth of its collections (less than 1 percent predated 1940). Wellesley and Framingham had 2-3 percent brittle. Concord, with the oldest collection (7 percent pre-1900 and 14 percent published before 1940), had 9 percent embrittlement. (Even this percentage is far lower than the 25 percent estimate for most research collections.) Brittle material was typically found in pre-1940 publications and in mass-market paperbacks more than 20 years old.

The types of bindings the libraries had selected over time affected the overall condition of their collections. Sturdy commercial rebindings were in the best condition, while paperbacks were in the worst. Hardcover trade bindings were in fair condition, but their covers and hinges had suffered twice as much damage as the buckram rebindings. Children's library bindings were in surprisingly good condition.

Types and levels of damage were linked to binding type. The covers and spines of paperbacks were in the worst condition. Loose or broken hinges (the structures that attach the textblock to the cover) were major problems for trade bindings and children's books, but damage to spines was low for all hardcovers. This may be because of the routine use of dust jackets, which tend to protect the headcap when a book is pulled from the shelves. [FIGURE 4]

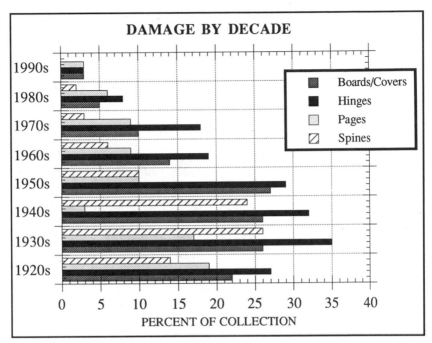

Figure 5

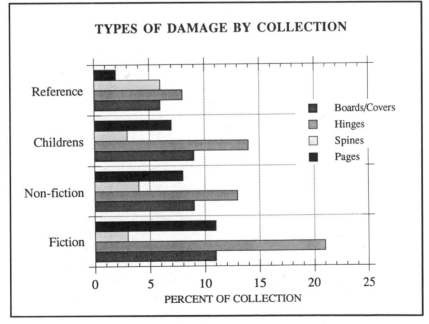

Figure 6

When injuries were analyzed by age, older books showed more signs of damage. Hinges deteriorated first and in every decade were the most commonly damaged area of the book. Covers and spines were found to be in progressively poorer condition as the collection aged. [FIGURE 5] When damage was graphed by collection, fiction appeared to be in the worst condition. [FIGURE 6]

ANALYSIS: CAUSES OF DAMAGE

The data about book condition pointed to several causes of deterioration: binding type, collection, shelving practice, and heavy use. In general, older materials were in poorer condition, but certain categories of material seemed better able to survive aging. Binding type, for example, had a definite impact: libraries are forced to purchase much of their book stock in trade bindings produced for the retail market (where buyers may read a book once or twice), not sturdy enough for the library market where 50 or more people may borrow a copy. Paperbacks are even more fragile (none of the libraries laminated or stiffened paper covers, which might have made a difference). In contrast, commercial rebinding is a sturdy option, but it requires an additional investment of library funds. It was rarely used by the libraries that were surveyed, and never systematically.

Shelving and circulation practice also had an impact, especially on the fiction collection. Fiction books were newer and should have been in better shape than many other materials but were actually in the worst condition. They were heavily used and often returned in book drops. They were also the collection that had the most physical distortion of the textblock (62 percent of fiction compared to 7 percent of nonfiction and 8 percent of children's books). Distortion is frequently caused by mis-shelving—storing volumes fore-edge down, allowing books to lean at a slant for an extended period of time. Heavy and oversized volumes are particularly susceptible to this type of damage. Several libraries stored books on their fore-edges on book trucks, in "new book" displays, and on bottom shelves. Eliminating these practices can make a difference. Wellesley reduced the distortion of its fiction collection from 48 percent to 39 percent after a five-year program to improve shelving and repair. In contrast, 76 percent of fiction in Medfield and 61 percent in Concord and Framingham were distorted.

Wear and tear also take their toll on high-use collections in public libraries. All libraries had similar rates for mutilation and environmental damage. Damage from mutilation ranged from 15-17 percent (minor injuries), to 1-3 percent (major injuries). The causes of this damage were:

- Food 11%
- Underlining 7%
- Tears 6%

Although the percentage of damage was consistent among all libraries, the causes were not. Wellesley had the most underlining (9.2 percent), while Medfield had the most food damage (14 percent). Perhaps people eat while reading fiction and underline while reading non-fiction. Nonetheless, an equal portion of the public was careless, regardless of the community. Environmental damage was also consistent from library to library. The major signs of injury were water (5 percent), soil (2 percent), and yellowed paper (4.5 percent). About 90 percent of the books surveyed were found to be unaffected by environmental damage.

IMPACT OF PRESERVATION IN WELLESLEY

By replicating the 1987 survey, Wellesley Free Public Library became the first institution to document statistically the impact of a concerted preservation program on the condition of its collections after a period of five years. As a result of the first survey, the town allocated money from capital funds for replacement and rebinding of items with major damage and long-term significance to the collections. An elementary repair facility with four work stations was equipped in the basement and staffed by volunteers from the Women's Service League, trained and supervised by library staff. By the end of fiscal year 1992, 3,496 volumes had been rebound and 1,841 volumes replaced; volunteers and library staff had executed 29,804 mends on 11,900 volumes. The survey found that 7 percent of the holdings had been repaired in 1992, compared to 1 percent in 1987.

The impact of the preservation program is evident in other 1992 findings. The percentage of books in good or excellent condition jumped from 78 to 83 percent, while the percentage of items with major damage at Wellesley was the lowest of the four libraries (6.5 percent, compared to 11 percent for Framingham, 12.6 percent for Medfield, and 20.3 percent for Concord). All library staff were trained by a conservation consultant to recognize damage, route volumes with minor damage from circulation to repair, and incorporate an evaluation of physical condition into weeding decisions. Guidelines for commercial binding were developed; these include prebinding selected paperbacks with long-term value, recasing oversized materials, and a "no trim" policy for publishers' bindings to ensure that the original dust jackets can be reused so that the books remain attractive to borrowers. Volunteers repaired books with minor damage and, by catching damage when it is minor, they prevented major damage from developing. A few experienced volunteers are able to perform more involved treatments.

The following graphs show the decline in the percentage of damaged materials in the Wellesley Free Library. Not only has the amount of damage decreased, but there is less discrepancy between the relative condition of the different collections. This is particularly notable in the fiction collection,

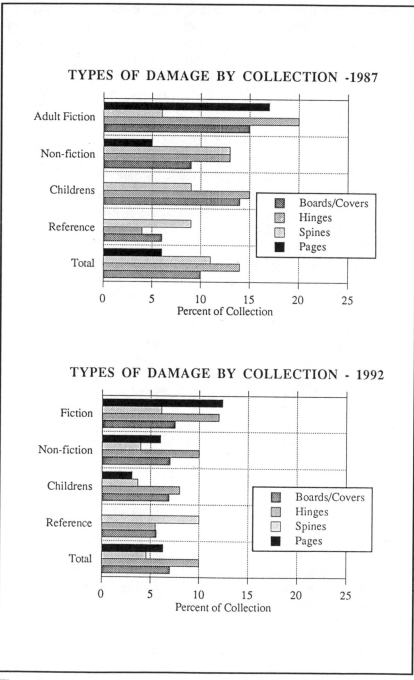

TYPES OF DAMAGE BY COLLECTION -1987

TYPES OF DAMAGE BY COLLECTION - 1992

Figure 7

which used to be the material in the worst condition. Weeding, rebinding, and the elimination of poor shelving and circulation practices that caused distortion have all contributed to the improvement. [FIGURE 7]

PRESERVATION PLANNING FOR INDIVIDUAL LIBRARIES

To compare the amount and type of treatment required to preserve the collections, the treatment characteristics were combined, eliminating overlap, to compute the percentages of the collections that were in excellent condition, good condition with some wear (but needing no treatment), affected by minor damage (suggesting in-house repair), and affected by major damage (requiring rebinding, replacement, or withdrawal).

All libraries had similar percentages for "good with some wear" (12-15 percent), reflecting similar rates of damage from mutilation, environment, and wear and tear. Since nearly 40-50 percent of each collection was 10 years old or less, it was not unexpected that 63 percent or more of each collection would be in excellent condition. However, the percentages of the collection with minor and major damage varied. [FIGURE 8]

The books in the Wellesley Free Library were in the best condition, even though Framingham and Medfield had newer collections. Most significant was the low percentage with major damage (6.5 percent), a result of their preservation program initiated after the 1987 survey.

Concord, in contrast, had the oldest collection and the greatest proportion of materials with major damage (20 percent). Many of these older items were stored in the basement and were not allowed to circulate beyond the reading

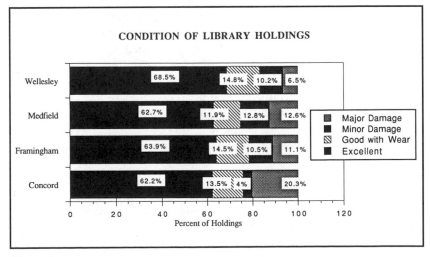

Figure 8

room. Three years ago, Concord instituted a repair program staffed by a binder who can handle the more complex treatments required of older materials, but it will take years to catch up with the backlog of items with major damage. Concord must also develop policies to deal with the 9 percent of its collection that has paper too brittle to be used.

The collections in Framingham and Medfield exhibited similar percentages of minor and major damage, despite the 130,000-volume difference in their size. They had similar mixes of fiction and children's books, high circulation, and problems with book distortion. Their programs should emphasize preventive maintenance, improved shelving, and simple repair techniques, such as hinge tightening.

PRESERVATION IMPLICATIONS FOR THE MINUTEMAN NETWORK

Since the Minuteman Network's online catalog provides its members with access to the titles in all consortium libraries, in theory books with major damage could be discarded rather than repaired, rebound, or replaced, when other copies were available. To test this premise, the surveyors and consultants conducted a brief survey of sample items identified as having major damage, after librarians had a chance to review them for discard. Although the sample sizes (64, 117, 119, and 204) were not large enough to produce statistically significant results, the findings did indicate trends that suggest the potential impact of network participation on individual preservation programs.

Framingham and Medfield, city and rural libraries that emphasize current reading, could rely upon MLN to supply missing titles if items were damaged. On average, eight to 12 other network libraries have a total of 12 to 17 copies. With its branches and policy of buying multiple copies of fiction, Framingham had duplicates of 30 percent of damaged items within its own system. Its staff discarded 14 percent of the damaged items while repairing many others. Medfield had no duplicates in-house, but discarded 25 percent of the damaged items identified during the survey because it had no facility for repairing items with major damage. Only 2 to 5 percent of titles within the two libraries were unique, while another 9 to 15 percent had one to three other copies in the network. For these libraries, weeding is a viable preservation decision for handling damaged volumes.

The situation was different in Wellesley and Concord with their larger nonfiction, reference, and research collections. In Wellesley, 26 percent of the titles were unique and another 41 percent had only one to three copies in the network. In Concord, 33 percent were unique and another 53 percent had only one to three copies in the network. For both libraries, on average, three to four other network libraries had a total of four to five additional copies.

Reflecting Wellesley's aggressive weeding campaigns of the past few years, every title was judged worth retaining, with badly damaged items being repaired, rebound, or replaced, rather than weeded. Concord discarded 10 percent. For Concord and Wellesley, a larger percentage of titles will need to be repaired or replaced if they are to remain accessible to the network. These libraries provide the subject depth lacking in libraries like Framingham and Medfield.

Surprising were the high percentage of items that had circulated one or more times since the libraries had gone online, even though the volumes were damaged: 97 percent in Framingham, 88 percent in Medfield, and 80 percent in Wellesley. It was not unusual for some books to have circulated 40-50 times, with a few children's books surviving 100 returns. Unlike academic libraries, public libraries do not typically purchase for future research needs, but to fulfill the demands of their current users. Space constraints also demand that shelf space be allocated to titles that people want to borrow.

Relying upon the existence of copies within other network libraries to justify discarding worn out items is viable only if the other copies are in usable condition. However, increased resource sharing, accelerated by current municipal budget cutbacks, will result in higher damage levels to individual items, as members elect to weed and rely on fewer items to meet the demands of more users. Effective interdependencies are possible only if member libraries make a commitment to take better care of their books, especially titles that are unique or represent subjects identified as a library's primary responsibility in MLN's cooperative collecting policy.

The final survey report recommended that network libraries institute preservation programs for the physical maintenance of holdings on four levels:

- Simple repair and maintenance for high-use materials in all libraries, so that local citizens retain access to materials that are in good condition for as long as needed
- Commercial rebinding and more complex repair for libraries that retain their collections for an extended period of time and lend these materials to other network members
- Replacement of titles that are unusable yet needed to support information access within the network
- Identification of unique or historically significant items that warrant conservation or special attention

If libraries take responsibility for building subject collections as part of a network collection development policy, they should invest in the care of these books, including repair or rebinding, particularly if fewer than three copies of a book remain in the system.

AFTERMATH AND RESULTS

Survey reports were submitted to the four participating libraries, along with recommendations for improving the condition of book collections within each site through proper shelving, handling, and repair. Wellesley used the data to substantiate the need for renewed funding for replacement and rebinding as part of the town's capital budget; it continued its active volunteer program in conjunction with the town's service league. Framingham improved the materials and procedures used by its repair technician. Concord used the data to justify continued funding for two part-time technicians, who had begun on a temporary basis. Medfield began to upgrade its repair program by adopting improved materials and procedures for book repair that emphasize preventive maintenance and early intervention for books with minor damage. With its small budget, Medfield will request support from the Friends of the Library for equipment and volunteers. For all four libraries, quantifiable data made it possible to present a cogent case for preservation to staff, town government, and local citizens.

A summary report was also submitted to MLN member libraries, and the conservation consultant gave a presentation to the board. In fall 1993, librarians from the four survey libraries led panel discussions about the project and its preservation implications at sites throughout Massachusetts. A proposal is presently before the Minuteman Network to incorporate physical condition responsibilities into the shared collection development policy. If the proposal is accepted, member libraries will pledge a higher level of care for materials in those areas in which they have elected to collect in depth.

On the state level, the Massachusetts Board of Library Commissioners has begun to sponsor workshops in basic repair, care and handling, and decision-making for physical treatment as part of its efforts to build a statewide preservation program. Staff education should enable librarians to incorporate considerations of physical condition as they make decisions about treatment, replacement, and weeding.

CONCLUSIONS

The LSCA project produced an effective survey methodology that gathered a range of data about the condition of book collections in MLN libraries. Its findings indicate patterns of use and patterns of deterioration that differ from those in academic libraries. Although the paper in the public libraries that were surveyed was found to be acidic, embrittlement was not a problem because so few volumes were retained permanently. Thus there was little need for reformatting. Books were heavily used and heavily weeded. Funding was limited.

Instead of focusing on brittle books or permanent retention, efforts in public libraries should emphasize preservation in support of circulation and network-wide access. This should include preventive maintenance and minor repair, focusing on the hinges that deteriorate first, to keep the publishers' trade bindings in circulation as long as possible. Still, it is clear from the findings that trade bindings, even hardcovers, cannot survive the 50+ uses that public libraries give them. Commercial rebinding, frequently used in the 1950s and 1960s, has survived better than any other binding type. It should be reinstated in the 1990s for specific categories of materials. These might include nonfiction volumes that are expected to remain in the collection beyond five or 10 years, or books that are damaged and in demand.

Survey results can also generate consciousness-raising among library users and win citizen support. Towns have made an enormous investment in their libraries' collections, and librarians have a responsibility to maintain these capital assets. The results of the LSCA survey helped libraries raise funds for repair and rebinding.

In summary, condition surveys meet an important local need. When done systematically and accurately, their results also contribute to national efforts. The data from the four combined surveys accurately profile the types of book collections and binding types found in the Minuteman Network. Public libraries that have comparable holdings can use the findings to guide their programs. The methodology can also serve as a model for future surveys by other libraries, helping to accumulate more information about public library collections. For example, given the increasing reliance of public libraries on paperbacks and the poor quality/high cost of hardcover best-sellers, it would be useful to survey libraries that have elected to treat their paperbacks by applying laminates or reinforcing the inner covers with pressboard. Knowing how well these techniques last with use would help libraries make cost-effective preservation decisions at the time of acquisition. By responding to such real needs in libraries with circulating collections, preservation can play a vital role in maintaining general collections so that they may be used by local readers and shared with others in local, state, and regional networks.

Wellesley/Framingham/Concord/Medfield Condition Survey

	Wellesley			Framingham			Concord			Medfield			All		
	Number	Percent	Error	Number	Percent	Error	Number	Percent	Error	Number	Percent	Error	Number	Percent	Error
Average Circulation	13			21			8			11			53		
Publishing Date															
Pre-1900	0	0.0	0.0	0	0.0	0.0	68	6.8	1.6	0	0.0	0.0	68	1.7	0.5
1900-1909	3	0.3	0.3	13	1.3	0.7	16	1.6	0.8	0	0.0	0.0	32	0.8	0.3
1910-1919	2	0.2	0.3	5	0.5	0.4	16	1.6	0.8	1	0.1	0.2	24	0.6	0.3
1920-1929	12	1.2	0.7	7	0.7	0.5	20	2.0	0.9	2	0.2	0.3	41	1.0	0.3
1930-1939	9	0.9	0.6	17	1.7	0.8	23	2.3	0.9	5	0.5	0.5	54	1.4	0.3
1940-1949	18	1.8	0.8	12	1.2	0.7	49	4.9	1.3	15	1.6	0.8	94	2.4	0.5
1950-1959	50	5.1	1.4	56	5.5	1.4	71	7.1	1.6	22	2.3	1.0	199	5.0	0.6
1960-1969	194	19.8	2.5	126	12.3	2.0	178	17.8	2.4	87	9.2	1.8	585	14.8	1.0
1970-1979	260	26.6	2.8	243	23.8	2.6	248	24.8	2.7	278	29.4	2.9	1,029	26.1	1.2
1980-1989	365	37.3	3.0	497	48.6	3.1	248	24.8	2.7	422	44.7	3.2	1,532	38.8	1.2
1990-	66	6.7	1.6	46	4.5	1.3	64	6.4	1.5	112	11.9	2.1	288	7.3	0.8
Total	979	100.0		1,022	100.0		1,001	100.0		944	100.0		3,946	100.0	
Collections															
Nonfiction	604	61.6	3.0	462	44.8	3.0	550	54.9	3.1	380	40.9	3.2	1,996	50.6	1.7
Fiction	160	16.3	2.3	215	20.8	2.5	168	16.8	2.3	301	32.4	3.0	844	21.4	1.3
Noncirculating	36	3.7	1.2	72	7.0	1.6	30	3.0	1.1	20	2.2	0.9	158	4.0	0.7
Juvenile	181	18.5	2.4	283	27.4	2.7	178	17.8	2.4	229	24.6	2.8	871	22.1	1.4
Basement	0	0.0	0.0	0	0.0	0.0	76	7.6	1.6	0	0.0	0.0	76	1.9	0.5
Total	981	100.0		1,032	100.0		1,002	100.0		930	100.0		3,945	100.0	
Hard cover	852	86.8	2.1	853	82.7	2.3	903	90.1	1.8	756	79.4	2.6	3,364	84.8	1.2
Soft Cover	130	13.2	2.1	179	17.3	2.3	99	9.9	1.8	196	20.6	2.6	604	15.2	1.2
Total	982	100.0		1,032	100.0		1,002	100.0		952	100.0		3,968	100.0	

December 1, 1992

Appendix page 1

Wellesley/Framingham/Concord/Medfield Condition Survey

Binding Type	Wellesley			Framingham			Concord			Medfield			All		
	Number	Percent	Error	Number	Percent	Error	Number	Percent	Error	Number	Percent	Error	Number	Percent	Error
Original Trade Binding (Hard)	719	73.2	2.8	718	69.6	2.8	782	78.0	2.6	618	64.9	3.0	2,837	71.5	1.5
Library Rebinding	51	5.2	1.4	33	3.2	1.1	53	5.3	1.4	19	2.0	0.9	156	3.9	0.7
Leather Binding	0	0.0	0.0	0	0.0	0.0	6	0.6	0.5	0	0.0	0.0	6	0.2	0.1
Children's Library Binding	80	8.1	1.7	106	10.3	1.9	65	6.5	1.5	125	13.1	2.1	376	9.5	0.9
Original Trade Binding (Paper)	0	0.0	0.0	152	14.7	2.2	61	6.1	1.5	13	1.4	0.7	226	5.7	0.9
BT Plastic Coating	22	2.2	0.9	7	0.7	0.5	27	2.7	1.0	0	0.0	0.0	56	1.4	0.4
In-house process	105	10.7	1.9	5	0.5	0.4	1	0.1	0.2	169	17.8	2.4	280	7.1	0.6
Pamphlet Binding	1	0.1	0.2	4	0.4	0.4	6	0.6	0.5	7	0.7	0.5	18	0.5	0.2
Spiral Binding	2	0.2	0.3	6	0.6	0.5	1	0.1	0.2	1	0.1	0.2	10	0.3	0.2
Other	2	0.2	0.3	0	0.0	0.0	0	0.0	0.0	0	0.0	0.0	2	0.1	0.1
Total	982	100.0		1,031	100.0		1,002	100.0		952	100.0		3,967	100.0	
Dustjackets	608	61.0	3.0	646	62.6	3.0	625	62.4	3.0	652	68.5	3.0	2,531	63.6	1.6
Repair Done	69	6.9	1.6	60	5.8	1.4	82	8.2	1.7	62	6.5	1.6	273	6.9	0.9
Repair Appropriate (Y)	39	3.9	1.2	20	1.9	0.8	18	1.8	0.8	19	2.0	0.9	96	2.4	0.5
Mutilation															
Total 0	802	81.8	2.4	851	82.5	2.3	813	81.2	2.4	757	79.6	2.5	3,223	81.3	1.3
Total 1	167	17.0	2.4	163	15.8	2.2	154	15.4	2.2	168	17.7	2.4	652	16.4	1.2
Total 2	11	1.1	0.7	18	1.7	0.8	34	3.4	1.1	26	2.7	1.0	89	2.2	0.5
Total	980	100.0		1,032	100.0		1,001	100.0		951	100.0		3,964	100.0	
Food	83	8.3	1.7	103	10.0	1.8	114	11.4	2.0	133	14.0	2.2	433	10.9	1.0
Razor	2	0.2	0.3	3	0.3	0.3	3	0.3	0.3	1	0.1	0.2	9	0.2	0.2
Scotch Tape	7	0.7	0.5	16	1.6	0.8	17	1.7	0.8	18	1.9	0.9	58	1.5	0.4
Torn	33	3.3	1.1	44	4.3	1.2	77	7.7	1.7	64	6.7	1.6	218	5.5	0.7
Underlining	92	9.2	1.8	75	7.3	1.6	72	7.2	1.6	48	5.0	1.4	287	7.2	0.9

October 3, 1992

Appendix page 2

Wellesley/Framingham/Concord/Medfield Condition Survey

	Wellesley			Framingham			Concord			Medfield			All		
	Number	Percent	Error	Number	Percent	Error	Number	Percent	Error	Number	Percent	Error	Number	Percent	Error
Environmental Damage															
Total 0	894	90.5	1.8	919	89.1	1.9	862	86.1	2.1	842	88.4	2.0	3,517	88.5	1.1
Total 1	77	7.8	1.7	96	9.3	1.8	109	10.9	1.9	96	10.1	1.9	378	9.5	1.0
Total 2	17	1.7	0.8	16	1.6	0.8	30	3.0	1.1	14	1.5	0.8	77	1.9	0.5
Total	988	100.0		1,031	100.0		1,001	100.0		952	100.0		3,972	100.0	
Animals	0	0.0	0.0	3	0.3	0.3	1	0.1	0.2	4	0.4	0.4	8	0.2	0.1
Burns	0	0.0	0.0	0	0.0	0.0	1	0.1	0.2	1	0.1	0.2	2	0.1	0.1
Insects	0	0.0	0.0	0	0.0	0.0	0	0.0	0.0	0	0.0	0.0	0	0.0	0.0
Mold	0	0.0	0.0	1	0.1	0.2	2	0.2	0.3	1	0.1	0.2	4	0.1	0.1
Soil	12	1.2	0.7	6	0.6	0.5	44	4.4	1.3	21	2.2	0.9	83	2.1	0.5
Water	32	3.2	1.1	32	3.1	1.1	48	4.8	1.3	75	7.9	1.7	187	4.7	0.6
Yellowing	48	4.8	1.3	44	4.3	1.2	65	6.5	1.5	21	2.2	0.9	178	4.5	0.7
Dust Jackets															
0 - No damage	528	85.6	2.8	530	82.0	3.0	505	80.8	3.1	601	92.0	2.1	2,164	85.2	1.6
1 - Minor damage	89	14.4	2.8	100	15.5	2.8	106	17.0	2.9	43	6.6	1.9	338	13.3	1.6
2 - Discard jacket	0	0.0	0.0	16	2.5	1.2	14	2.2	1.2	9	1.4	0.9	39	1.5	0.5
Total	617	100.0		646	100.0		625	100.0		653	100.0		2,541	100.0	
Distortion															
None - good condition	900	90.4	1.8	856	83.0	2.3	825	82.3	2.4	658	69.1	2.9	3,239	81.4	1.2
Distorted	96	9.6	1.8	175	17.0	2.3	177	17.7	2.4	294	30.9	2.9	742	18.6	1.2
Total	996	100.0		1,031	100.0		1,002	100.0		952	100.0		3,981	100.0	
Boards/Covers															
0 - No damage	925	93.0	1.6	921	89.2	1.9	890	88.9	1.9	851	89.5	2.0	3,587	90.1	1.0
1 - Minor damage	64	6.4	1.5	95	9.2	1.8	94	9.4	1.8	84	8.8	1.8	337	8.5	0.9
2 - Major damage	6	0.6	0.5	16	1.6	0.8	17	1.7	0.8	16	1.7	0.8	55	1.4	0.4
Total	995	100.0		1,032	100.0		1,001	100.0		951	100.0		3,979	100.0	

October 3, 1992

Appendix page 3

Wellesley/Framingham/Concord/Medfield Condition Survey

	Wellesley			Framingham			Concord			Medfield			All		
	Number	Percent	Error	Number	Percent	Error	Number	Percent	Error	Number	Percent	Error	Number	Percent	Error
Hinges															
0 – No damage	894	89.9	1.9	882	85.6	2.1	810	81.2	2.4	789	83.0	2.4	3,375	85.0	1.2
1 – Minor damage	86	8.7	1.7	99	9.6	1.8	109	10.9	1.9	107	11.3	2.0	401	10.1	1.0
2 – Major damage	14	1.4	0.7	49	4.8	1.3	78	7.8	1.7	55	5.8	1.5	196	4.9	0.7
Total	994	100.0		1,030	100.0		997	100.0		951	100.0		3,972	100.0	
Spines															
0 – No damage	948	95.4	1.3	976	94.8	1.4	947	94.6	1.4	928	97.7	1.0	3,799	95.6	0.7
1 – Minor damage	42	4.2	1.3	50	4.9	1.3	38	3.8	1.2	16	1.7	0.8	146	3.7	0.7
2 – Major damage	4	0.4	0.4	4	0.4	0.4	16	1.6	0.8	6	0.6	0.5	30	0.8	0.3
Total	994	100.0		1,030	100.0		1,001	100.0		950	100.0		3,975	100.0	
Leaf (page) attachment															
0 – text intact	931	93.7	1.5	955	92.5	1.6	921	92.1	1.7	846	89.1	2.0	3,653	91.9	0.9
1 – pages loose	53	5.3	1.4	59	5.7	1.4	54	5.4	1.4	66	6.9	1.6	232	5.8	0.8
2 – pages detached	10	1.0	0.6	18	1.7	0.8	25	2.5	1.0	38	4.0	1.2	91	2.3	0.5
Total	994	100.0		1,032	100.0		1,000	100.0		950	100.0		3,976	100.0	
Paper Acidity															
0 – Not acidic	388	39.0	3.0	403	39.1	3.0	342	34.1	2.9	407	42.8	3.1	1,540	38.7	1.6
1 – Slightly acidic	262	26.3	2.7	210	20.3	2.5	299	29.8	2.8	299	31.5	3.0	1,070	26.9	1.5
2 – Highly acidic	346	34.7	3.0	419	40.6	3.0	361	36.0	3.0	244	25.7	2.8	1,370	34.4	1.6
Total	996	100.0		1,032	100.0		1,002	100.0		950	100.0		3,980	100.0	
Paper Condition															
0 – Flexible	966	97.4	1.0	1,009	97.8	0.9	912	91.2	1.8	951	100.0	0.0	3,838	96.6	0.7
1/2 Brittle	26	2.6	1.0	23	2.2	0.9	88	8.8	1.8	0	0.0	0.0	137	3.4	0.7
Total	992	100.0		1,032	100.0		1,000	100.0		951	100.0		3,975	100.0	

October 3, 1992

Appendix page 4

Wellesley/Framingham/Concord/Medfield Condition Survey

	Wellesley			Framingham			Concord			Medfield			All		
	Number	Percent	Error	Number	Percent	Error	Number	Percent	Error	Number	Percent	Error	Number	Percent	Error
POOR CONDITION:															
Hinges 2/Boards 2	0	0.0	0.0	4	0.4	0.4	10	1.0	0.6	4	0.4	0.4	18	0.5	0.2
Boards 2/Spines 2	0	0.0	0.0	1	0.1	0.2	1	0.1	0.2	0	0.0	0.0	2	0.1	0.1
Spines 2/Distortion 2	1	0.1	0.2	0	0.0	0.0	2	0.2	0.3	1	0.1	0.2	4	0.1	0.1
Hinges 2/Distortion 1	6	0.6	0.5	13	1.3	0.7	25	2.5	1.0	22	2.3	1.0	66	1.7	0.4
Pages 2	10	1.0	0.6	18	1.7	0.8	25	2.5	1.0	38	4.0	1.2	91	2.3	0.5
GOOD CONDITION W/O DISTORTION:															
Hinges, Spine, Pages=0	782	78.5	2.6	809	78.4	2.5	759	75.7	2.7	710	74.6	2.8	3,060	76.8	1.4
Hinges, Spine, Pages, Envi.=0	736	73.9	2.7	750	72.7	2.7	698	69.7	2.8	661	69.4	2.9	2,845	71.4	1.5
Hinges, Spine, Pages, Mutil.=0	676	67.9	2.9	703	68.1	2.8	661	66.0	2.9	627	65.9	3.0	2,667	67.0	1.6
GOOD CONDITION WITH DISTORTION:															
Hinges, Spine and Pages=0	57	5.7	1.4	113	10.9	1.9	105	10.5	1.9	175	18.4	2.5	450	11.3	1.0
Hinges, Spine, Pages, Envi.=0	50	5.0	1.4	96	9.3	1.8	88	8.8	1.8	156	16.4	2.4	390	9.8	0.9
Hinges, Spine, Pages, Mutil.=0	51	5.1	1.4	91	8.8	1.7	80	8.0	1.7	153	16.1	2.3	375	9.4	0.9

October 3, 1992

NOTES

1. Anne L. Reynolds, Nancy C. Schrock, and Joanna Walsh,"Preservation: The Public Library Response," *Library Journal* 114:3 (15 February 1989): 128-32.
2. The grant, entitled "Model Collections Condition Survey: A Methodology for Statewide Preservation Planning," was awarded to the Wellesley Free Library by the Massachusetts Board of Library Commissioners. Anne Reynolds, Director of Wellesley Free Library, served as project director. Project staff included Nancy Schrock as Preservation Consultant, Joanna Walsh as Systems Consultant, and Kendon Stubbs as Statistical Consultant. The surveyors were Priscilla Cobb and Halle Lyon.
3. Massachusetts Task Force on Preservation and Access, *Preserved to Serve: The Massachusetts Preservation Agenda* (Boston: Massachusetts Board of Library Commissioners, 1992).
4. Gay Walker and Jane Greenfield, "The Yale Survey: A Large-scale Study of Book Deterioration in the Yale University Library," *College & Research Libraries* 46 (March 1985): 111-32.
5. Sally Buchanan and Sandra Coleman, *Deterioration Survey of the Stanford University Libraries, Green Library Stack Collection* (Stanford, Calif.: Stanford University Libraries, 1979).
6. Kendon Stubbs, "Sampling Methodology for the Wellesley/Framingham/Concord/Medfield Preservation Project," in *Results of a Model Collection Condition Survey, Federally Funded with LSCA Title I Funds through the Massachusetts Board of Library Commissioners*, Appendix C, October 1992. Available from the Massachusetts Board of Library Commissioners, 648 Beacon Street, Boston, MA 02215.
7. Joanna Walsh, "Report of the Systems Consultant," in *Results of a Model Collection Condition Survey, Federally Funded with LSCA Title I Funds through the Massachusetts Board of Library Commissioners*, Appendix B, October 1992. Available from the Massachusetts Board of Library Commissioners, 648 Beacon Street, Boston, MA 02215.
8. Copies of the full survey reports for the individual libraries and the project summary are available from the Massachusetts Board of Library Commissioners, 648 Beacon Street, Boston, MA 02215.

Regional Preservation Needs Assessment: The Central New York Preservation Needs Assessment Project

Martha Hanson

Preservation Administrator
Syracuse University Library

Jeannette Smithee

Assistant Director
Central New York Library Resources Council (CENTRO)

INTRODUCTION

In 1992, 10 Central New York institutions participated in the state's first regional preservation needs assessment survey, the Central New York Preservation Needs Assessment Project (PNAP). The PNAP process showed that libraries and historical agencies of varying sizes whose collections include many different formats could successfully develop preservation plans; furthermore, this work was accomplished in a short period of time by staff with little previous preservation experience. The project introduced participants to four important concepts:
- The benefits of random sampling as a management tool
- The theory behind matching preservation solutions to preservation problems
- Matrix calculations as a simple but powerful tool to determine priorities for action
- The impact of feasibility as a factor when drafting a plan for action.

PNAP demonstrated a cost-effective method for libraries and historical agencies to assess preservation needs cooperatively.

BACKGROUND

PNAP was a cooperative project sponsored by the Central New York Library Resources Council (CENTRO), one of the nine Reference and Research Library Resources Councils in New York state. CENTRO's purpose is to facilitate resource sharing among its 60 members which include academic and special libraries, as well as public and school library systems. PNAP was initiated by the Council's Preservation Committee (made up of representatives from member libraries) whose responsibility is to gather and disseminate information about local, regional, and national preservation efforts, and to promote cooperative activities and projects.

PNAP was funded through a Discretionary Grant from the New York State Program for the Conservation and Preservation of Library Research Materials. The New York State Legislature established this program in 1984 to provide funding for libraries and other organizations engaged in efforts to preserve deteriorating research materials. The program allocates resources through its three components:

- Annual funding for 11 comprehensive research libraries in New York state (the "Big 11"), to support library conservation/preservation activities
- Funding for Big 11-coordinated preservation projects that contribute to the development of cooperative programs in the state
- Funding for other projects that contribute to the preservation of significant research materials in libraries, archives, historical societies, and other agencies within New York state (the Discretionary Grant program)

PNAP was the result of more than a year of planning by CENTRO's Preservation Committee and followed five years of its having sponsored well-attended workshops on a variety of topics. In 1990, while developing their first three-year plan, Preservation Committee members came to a painful conclusion: despite five years of work, the Committee had little understanding of the nature and scope of Central New York's preservation problems. Hindsight showed that the Committee's first five years of efforts, while well-intended, lacked coherence and failed to provide meaningful information that could be used to establish priorities for regional action.

The Preservation Committee realized that, in order to determine the character and extent of preservation problems in Central New York, it would be necessary to conduct regional needs assessment projects. The objectives established for these projects were:

- Identify the preservation needs of CENTRO member library collections
- Set priorities for institutional action
- Generate comparable quantitative data about regional preservation needs

A regional needs assessment would also lay the groundwork for cooperative projects to support the development, implementation, and maintenance of institutional preservation programs in Central New York.

WHY NEEDS ASSESSMENT?

The library profession is learning that the cost of owning materials does not stop with the acts of acquiring and cataloging them. Merely to buy and catalog items does not assure that they will exist forever: in fact, many will deteriorate within decades of their acquisition. Fortunately, many institutions are now acknowledging that, in order to ensure access to their collections for the foreseeable future, they must provide resources to preserve them. But the costs for an institution to preserve all its materials are prohibitive and diminish resources available to meet other pressing needs. At a time when acquisitions and other budgets are shrinking, many libraries find themselves in the difficult position of attempting to introduce preservation activities into a well-established institutional culture, and to justify to that culture the need to reallocate scarce funds from more traditional functions to preservation.

Assuming that institutions cannot afford to preserve everything in their collections, how do they determine the nature and scope of preservation problems? Decide what materials are not only most likely to be lost, but are also important enough to preserve? Establish priorities for preservation action? Estimate the dollar cost of meeting these priorities? A preservation needs assessment provides answers to these and other fundamental questions.

There are a variety of approaches to conducting a preservation needs assessment, but all seek to provide meaningful documentation that institutions can use to justify resources for preservation. An effective needs assessment will reveal the nature and scope of preservation requirements, help establish priorities, and develop a reasonable strategy for action (including cost estimates) based on these priorities and the institution's ability to meet them.

To date, most needs assessment activities have been designed for individual institutions; there are few models for conducting a cooperative needs assessment project. A literature search of *Educational Resources Information Center (ERIC)*, *Library and Information Science Abstracts (LISA)*, *Library Literature*, and the OCLC Online Union Catalog confirmed that there have been only a handful of documented regional or statewide projects; in the past few years, important regional or national needs assessment efforts include those launched by the Amigos Bibliographic Council, OCLC, and the National Library of Medicine.[1] In addition, several states have initiated regional or statewide needs assessments.[2] Most of these cooperative efforts have focused on gathering information about the status of preservation activities among a group of institutions, rather than on the needs of the collections held by the institutions. The one exception is California's 1992 statewide preservation planning project which used an automated needs assessment instrument called CALIPR (a special-purpose dBase IV program for IBM-compatible microcomputers developed at the University of California at Berkeley that requires a hard disk and 1.8 MB memory) to assess the preservation needs of book and document collections in California.[3]

CHOOSING THE NEEDS ASSESSMENT MODEL

In 1991, the CENTRO Preservation Committee's search for suitable regional cooperative needs assessment models yielded only unpublished Library Services and Construction Act (LSCA) projects developed and conducted by Barclay Ogden, Head of the Conservation Department at the University of California, Berkeley. These included the "Greater Bay Area Preservation Planning Project" (1989/90) and the "Preservation Program Development Shared Consultancy" (1990/91).[4] The Bay Area Project involved 15 libraries of various types. Its goal was to identify the preservation needs of a variety of types of collections in the Bay Area, and its immediate objectives included:

- Assessing the current and future preservation needs of the collections
- Setting priorities for the needs that were identified
- Laying the groundwork for cooperative plans to address these needs

The Shared Consultancy Project aimed to provide fundamental training for staff in 12 libraries that had been involved in the Bay Area Project, to address the preservation needs identified in the project. By the end of the Shared Consultancy, participants had developed disaster preparedness plans, written preservation plans with long- and short-term goals, and completed a cooperative proposal for a preservation project to treat endangered materials in the region.

The Bay Area projects appealed to CENTRO's Preservation Committee for several reasons. In particular, these included the random sample-based needs assessment survey, a decision-making model for preservation management, the inclusion of institutions similar in profile to those of the CENTRO members, and a process that resulted in implementable preservation plans for participants. Most preservation needs assessments conducted in libraries and archives have been condition surveys. Although condition surveys provide valuable information about the nature and scope of preservation problems, typically they have not included mechanisms to allow an institution to discriminate among competing needs and establish priorities (assuming insufficient funds to meet all preservation needs). What distinguished the Bay Area model from other projects was that it established priorities through the inclusion of three new factors: exposure, risk, and value.

The backbone of the 1990 Bay Area Project was a random sample assessment survey from which the participants made inferences about their collections' needs. Theoretically, each institution could have examined every item in the collection or portion of the collection it chose to assess (the "target collection"). However, an inventory is an expensive way for an institution to gather the preservation management information it needs to characterize the nature and scope of its preservation problems; random sampling is a much more cost-effective strategy.

Based on information gathered from 100 items randomly selected from their target collections, participants in the Bay Area Project made estimates about the preservation problems of these materials. Although one might think that to achieve a specific confidence level an institution's sample size ought to be proportional to the collection size, probability theory indicates that this is not the case. In fact, the goal of a preservation needs survey is not absolute precision, but rather attaining a level of accuracy that will point to major concerns that should be addressed, in order to maintain the serviceability of an institution's collection. The Bay Area Project used samples of 100 items from each participant's collection, believing that 100 items would provide estimates with a confidence level sufficient to proceed with broad-based institutional and regional planning efforts. Samples of 400 items would have provided estimates with slightly higher precision, but sample sizes larger than 400 provide little additional information.

To prepare for selecting the random samples, each participant in the Bay Area Project created an appropriate sampling frame to ensure that any item in the target collection had an equal probability of being selected. In order to develop a frame, participants first identified whether or not the target collection was represented by a computer file, a card file (shelflist), or a written inventory. For example, if an institution's entire target collection were represented in an online catalog, the sampling frame was created by a computer-generated random list of bibliographic records. If an institution's entire target collection were represented in a single manual shelflist, a sampling frame was created from randomly selected shelflist cards. However, if an institution's collection were represented in several scattered finding aids, the li-

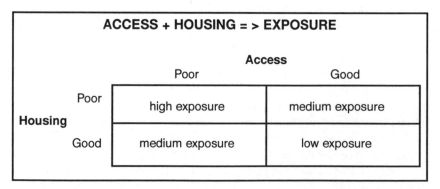

Figure 1 *The level of exposure (high, medium, or low) is determined by the severity of the combination of housing and access problems. Materials that are housed well and are seldom used are at much lower exposure than materials that are poorly housed and used frequently.*

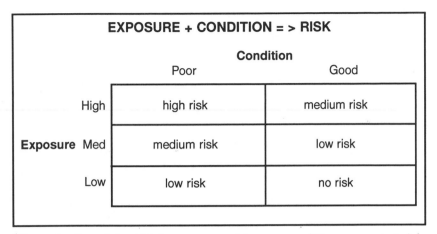

Figure 2 *Materials at high exposure and in poor condition are most at risk. Materials with low exposure and in good condition are, in relative terms, at no risk.*

brary created a sampling frame by location (or map, showing where items were physically housed) and selected random physical locations rather than random bibliographic records or shelflist cards.

Once participants developed their respective sampling frames, they pulled the sample items and gathered information about each one by completing a 13-question survey form. The survey gathered data about access, housing, condition, and value.[5] Survey questions about access asked whether items were missing or in frequent use (making them more vulnerable to damage and loss). Queries about housing sought information about automatic fire protection, the physical environment, and temperature and relative humidity. Together, these access and housing questions determine the degree of "exposure" the item has to damage by readers or the environment. [FIGURE 1]

Condition questions examined physical damage or deterioration. The ranking for exposure, combined with the questions about condition, indicated a relative urgency for an item's preservation—its "risk." The Bay Area Project defined risk as the vulnerability of materials to damage or loss. [FIGURE 2]

Finally, the survey assessed the relative value of materials, with the expectation that among materials equally at risk, items of moderate value would be given a lower preservation priority than high-value materials. Value questions on the survey assessed an item's uniqueness or rarity, its value as an artifact, or its importance to the institution's collection. The combination of risk and value determined "preservation priority." [FIGURE 3]

Because the items examined were part of a random sample where any item in the collection had as much chance of inclusion as another, the information collected in the areas of access, housing, condition, and value could be generalized to the collection from which the sample had been selected,

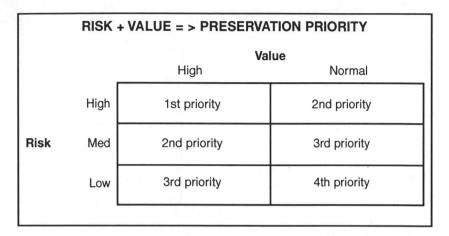

RISK + VALUE = > PRESERVATION PRIORITY

		Value	
		High	Normal
Risk	High	1st priority	2nd priority
	Med	2nd priority	3rd priority
	Low	3rd priority	4th priority

Figure 3 *Preservation Priority can be determined by relating the risk to value. Items with high value and high risk will become the highest priority for preservation action. Items for which there is no risk defined will not have a preservation priority since no action is needed.*

suggesting appropriate solutions to the problems identified by the questions. A series of "rules" was used to combine answers to different survey questions and identify suitable preservation approaches. For the Bay Area Project, solutions were calculated manually using matrices; the calculations are now done much faster by the CALIPR software. Examples from the CALIPR manual of matching solutions to preservation problems include:

- If Y(es) is answered to "Used in the past 5 years?" the solution is User Education
- If Y(es) is answered to "Missing parts or pages?" and "Deteriorated text/image?" the solution is Replace/Reformat
- If Y(es) is answered to "Broken into pieces, have them all?" and "Uncopyable text/image?" and "Significant artifact value?" the solution is Protective Enclosure[6]

The categories of potential preservation solutions included:

- Inventory Control
- Education
- Fire Protection
- Disaster Plan
- Environmental Control
- Rebind/Repair
- Replace/Reformat
- Protective Enclosures
- Conserve

The range of appropriate solutions was broad so that library administrators making decisions would realize that preservation was more than book repair or microfilming (reformatting) projects. For example, actions affecting the entire collection such as a disaster preparedness plan or a fire protection system might be assigned a higher priority than actions affecting a smaller portion of the collection.

THE PNAP MODEL

The CENTRO Preservation Committee based its Preservation Needs Assessment Project on elements from the Greater Bay Area Preservation Planning Project and the Preservation Program Development Shared Consultancy. The PNAP model included conducting random sample needs assessment surveys, identifying priorities for action, and establishing preservation plans tailored to the resources and technical capabilities of each participating institution. Key elements to the success of the PNAP model are:

- Establishing a short-term, consultant-assisted project strategy
- Enlisting administrative support from each participating institution, before the project's start
- Relying on a random sample needs assessment survey that provides an estimation of the nature and scope of preservation problems
- Using the CALIPR software to establish a rank order of institutional priorities for action and/or treatment
- Providing realistic estimates of dollar costs for meeting priorities
- Establishing preservation plans based on an institution's ability (in terms of resources and technical skills) to meet priorities
- Developing collective priorities for planning future regional action

IMPLEMENTING PNAP

The goals of the Central New York Preservation Needs Assessment Project were to introduce a systematic process for identifying the preservation needs of different types of libraries and historical agencies in the Central New York Region, and to provide CENTRO with comparable quantitative data about the nature and scope of regional preservation needs, in order to assist in planning to meet those needs. PNAP's immediate objectives were to guide each participating institution through the needs assessment process, assist each institution in developing its preservation plan from the survey's findings, and lay the groundwork for plans to implement regional preservation activities. The Participants in PNAP included one four-year college, one medical college, two community colleges, four public libraries, and two historical agencies.[7]

Phase I

The Central New York Preservation Needs Assessment Project consisted of three phases, each introduced with a one-day seminar conducted by project consultant Barclay Ogden (administrators for the 10 participating institutions had attended an introductory meeting and committed their libraries to the project at the time the grant proposal was written). Phase I included a random sample survey of participants' target collections. The first training seminar offered an overview of preservation needs assessment and practical advice on options for sampling the target collections. Participants also examined several books selected as a practice survey sample. They answered questions about these volumes such as "Missing parts or pages?", "Broken into pieces, have them all?", "Deteriorated text/image?", and "Uncopyable text/image?", then manually completed matrix worksheet calculations leading to appropriate preservation actions and priorities. This exercise helped them understand the reports and calculations that the CALIPR software would produce for their actual surveys.

Next, participants selected the collection or portion of a collection they wished to survey (their "target collection") and provided information to CENTRO about it. The target collections varied in size and scope; most participants selected a discrete portion of their collection as a target (e.g., the local history collection, special collection, or institutional archives). The inclusion of a high proportion of local history and special collections was not planned, but offered CENTRO an opportunity to look more closely at the needs of these valuable regional resources.

The techniques of random sampling used for PNAP are those described for the Bay Area Project. The random samples were generated from online systems for two participants and pulled from shelflist card files by three others; the historical agencies and libraries sampling primarily non-book items created a location map for their collections and used a random number table to identify locations for items in the sample.

Over the next four weeks, every institution conducted a needs assessment survey, creating a sampling frame and selecting the sample items using an appropriate random sampling technique to obtain a 100- (or 400-) item sample drawn from the target collection. Staff, students, and/or volunteers located and examined each survey item and completed access, housing, and condition questions on the survey forms. [FIGURE 4] Some condition questions and all value questions were answered by a librarian. No library required additional staff for its survey.

PRESERVATION NEEDS ASSESSMENT SURVEY

Bibliographic Identification

Library Name _____   Building/Department _____

Call No.   _____   Author   _____

Title   _____   Imprint   _____

Format   B   D   F   T   P   O

Access Data

Y N 1.   Missing?
Y N 2.   Used in past 5 years?

Housing Data

Y N 3.   Lacks automatic fire protection?
Y N 4.   Lacks disaster response plan?
Y N 5.   Stack conditions not to standard?

Condition Data

Y N 6.   Missing parts or pages?
Y N 7.   Broken into pieces, have them all?
Y N 8.   Deteriorated text/image?
Y N 9.   Uncopyable text/image?

Value Data

Y N 10.   Probably only copy in New York State libraries?
Y N 11.   Significant artifact value?
Y N 12.   Part of a comprehensive collection?
Y N 13.   If lost or unusable, WILL replace, repair, or reformat this edition?

Figure 4

A copy of the CALIPR software was purchased for each PNAP participant; data from the survey forms were entered to generate institutional reports arranged by format. Data entry and report generation took about one hour for a 100-item survey. Most institutions used CALIPR directly, but CENTRO entered the data for the few that lacked microcomputers. Based on the results of the institutions' surveys, CALIPR calculated the preservation problems, solutions, and priorities for each format surveyed.[8] Because this was an exploratory needs assessment, participants' target collections and samples were not limited to books. Items in the following formats were included in the PNAP survey: Books, Unbound Documents, Film (including microforms and photographic films), Tape (including computer tapes, audio, and video tapes), Photographs (printed on a paper base), and Other. Books, however, were the predominant format.

CENTRO then created regional summary reports from the CALIPR reports for all formats sampled by the 10 participants. These extrapolated each institution's sample results to estimate the total number of items in its target collection affected by the particular preservation problem. The summary reports also suggested total numbers of items in the region affected by particular preservation problems. At the conclusion of Phase I, the participating institutions had sampled and surveyed collections representing an estimated total of 627,500 items, including books, unbound documents, films, photographs, and magnetic tapes. CALIPR provided statistically reliable data for estimating the numbers of items in the target collections with particular preservation problems, assigned appropriate preservation action/treatments to the preservation problems identified in the survey, and displayed a rank order of preservation priorities for action/treatment. The regional summary of preservation needs and priorities identified similarities and differences for the target collections of the 10 participants. Additional needs assessment surveys must be done in order to generalize results to other collections.

Phase II

Phase II stressed management strategies for addressing preservation needs. During Phase II participants developed plans based on needs identified in the survey, as well as institutional capabilities. At the second seminar the participants reviewed and interpreted summary reports of preservation problems, solutions, and priorities identified by the survey. They also prepared for the site visits to be conducted prior to developing their institutional preservation plans.

Site visits were conducted by PNAP project liaison Martha Hanson, Preservation Administrator at Syracuse University Library. During these visits she met with the PNAP participant to:

- Review the CALIPR survey needs assessment reports

- Observe the current preservation operations (if any) and procedures for identifying damaged materials
- Review costs for various preservation actions and treatments
- Determine (with the help of a Feasibility Checklist) a strategy for action on preservation activities identified by the needs assessment
- Meet with the director to discuss preservation goals and preservation project management
- Tour the building, if time allowed[9]

The site visits were viewed by participants as an important bridge between the "numbers" generated by the needs assessment survey and the decisions for action to be included in their institutional preservation implementation plan.

A significant strategy in this phase was the introduction into the planning process of the factor of "feasibility" (each institution's ability to meet its preservation priorities). The feasibility factor included the dual elements of capability and resources. To determine capability, these questions were asked:

- Is there a technical solution available to solve the preservation problem?
- Are there management skills within the institution to handle the responsibility for a particular task or project?
- Do external services exist that can carry out the work?

To determine the resource availability, these question were asked:

- Is staff available to perform the work?
- Is space available to perform the work?
- Is money available to pay for staffing, services, supplies, or equipment?

Participants determined feasibility for each preservation priority by using a decision-making matrix that combined the factors of capability and resources to determine a feasibility number. Then, by multiplying each survey preservation priority number by a feasibility number, participants arrived at program implementation strategy numbers, which formed the basis of their preservation plans. [FIGURE 5]

Each participant drafted a preservation plan reflecting the feasibility of the institution's taking action on the preservation priorities identified by CALIPR survey results. As a result of incorporating feasibility, some needs identified by CALIPR as high priorities become lower program implementation goals. It is important to stress that, although CALIPR established preservation priorities for collections, each participant drafted a plan that reflected his or her institution's ability to meet those priorities. The identification of an institution's preservation priorities did not always translate exactly into its program implementation strategy.

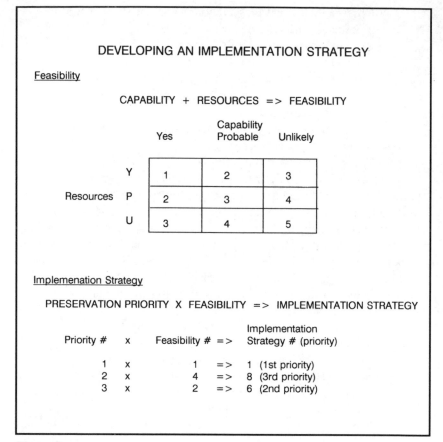

Figure 5

Phase III

Phase III consisted of a one-day seminar to plan for collective action. The planning phase involved the participants in a process of determining regional priorities for potential cooperative action; identifying the individuals, committees, or agencies that could assume responsibility for each action; determining the feasibility of carrying out each action; and determining the priorities for cooperative action. The discussion and decision-making by PNAP participants provided direction for future planning by CENTRO's Preservation Committee. The Committee used PNAP results to indicate the regional needs and priorities for cooperative action when it revised the "Central New York Library Resources Council Preservation Committee Three Year Plan 1993/1994-1995/1996," and to develop a 1993-94 Discretionary Grant proposal, "Central New York Preservation Program Implementation Consultancy."

SUMMARY OF RESULTS

The Central New York Preservation Needs Assessment Project produced six major results:

1. The identification of institutional preservation problems, solutions, and priorities
2. The development of institutional preservation plans
3. The identification of collective preservation problems, solutions, and priorities
4. The identification of collective priorities for cooperative action
5. The establishment of CENTRO priorities for cooperative action
6. Publication of *Preservation Needs Assessment: A Management Tool*

To go into more detail about each of the major results:

1. Identification of Institutional Preservation Problems, Solutions, and Priorities

The first tangible results of the project were printed CALIPR reports that displayed a summary of preservation problems, solutions, and action/treatment priorities for items in various formats surveyed in the target collections. These reports presented a rank order for preservation activities required by the target collections.

2. Development of Institutional Preservation Plans

All 10 institutions completed preservation plans for their target collections; these included priorities for action/treatment, realistic estimates of the dollar costs for meeting the priorities, and a timetable for action. The participants based their plans on the preservation priorities established by CALIPR and on their own institutions' abilities to meet those preservation priorities.

Estimating realistic costs for implementing the preservation actions was an important consideration in determining an institution's ability to take action. In order to calculate costs, participants needed to know how many items in their target collections had a particular preservation problem. Since CALIPR survey reports were based on a random sample survey, they provided statistically reliable data for estimating the number of items in the larger target collections with certain specific needs. With this information, participants proceeded to estimate costs for each priority/treatment suggested by CALIPR, then work through the process of determining the feasibility of their respective institutions meeting these priorities.

It is important to note that CALIPR utilizes a strategy that addresses very visible problems in order to justify an institution's reallocation of scarce resources to preservation: the PNAP survey gathered information to justify the need for action *right now*. For example, the PNAP survey's condition questions identified damage already done, not anticipated damage that could arise from anticipated use. Already damaged materials prove the need for preservation resources because they document threats to current library service, rather than service to the unknown readers of the future. The plans drafted by PNAP participants reflected CALIPR's strategy, by presenting convincing arguments about the need for immediate action and the associated costs.

3. Identification of Collective Preservation Problems, Solutions, and Priorities

The target collections sampled for the needs assessment survey represented an estimated total of 627,500 items, including books, unbound documents, photographs, films, and magnetic media. [FIGURE 6] They were selected by participants to address a need important to their institution and because of their suitability as manageable short-term projects. Although the sample represents only a small portion of the Central New York Region's total library holdings, it is a significant portion because it included a high representation of special collections and archival materials. In fact, nine of the 10 institutions chose to target their special collections or historical documents collections for assessment. As a result, the aggregation of data for these 10 institutions has provided CENTRO with a preliminary assessment of the collective preservation needs of Central New York's unique resources. Of the 627,496 items surveyed:

9,997 items had problems associated with inventory control or security. However, identification of inventory control problems was only possible for those samples drawn from a computer-generated list or manual shelflist. These lists included all items that "should be" in the collection and a survey item that could not be located was considered "missing." Some of the participating historical agencies and libraries drew their samples directly from the stacks or shelves; the survey sample included only items that were there and did not determine whether items were missing or lost.

72,688 items, many of which were high-value materials, were not covered by written emergency plans for their salvage in case of disaster.

15,840 items lacked fire protection and were at high risk of complete loss in case of fire or flood. The majority of these were unique materials.

518,032 items lacked environmental control. The majority of the collections surveyed were at risk of deterioration owing to the poor environmental conditions in which they were housed.

148,739 items would benefit from programs of staff and user education because of sustained heavy usage and subsequent wear. Education programs help to minimize the damage from rough use, such as abusive photocopying and fore-edge shelving.

15,083 items needed rebinding or repair in order to sustain further use.

7,157 items needed conservation treatment in order to sustain further use.

69,811 items needed replacement or reformatting in order to sustain any further use.

14,404 needed protective enclosures in order to sustain further use.

TARGET COLLECTION FORMATS		
Colgate University Library: Special Collections	Books	12,000
Fayetteville Free Library: Local History Collection	Books Unbound Documents Film Photographs	113 14,400 50 2,000
Herkimer County Community College Library: College Archives	Books Unbound Documents Photographs	1,000 9,100 1,000

Oneida Community Mansion House:
     Archival Materials Relating to the
     History of the Oneida Community
	Books
	Unbound Documents
	Photographs
		4,000
		500
		3,500

Onondaga Community College Library: College Archives	Books	963
Onondaga County Public Library: Local History Department	Books Unbound Documents	35,000 1,000

Onondaga Historical Association:
     Entire Collection Relating to
     Onondaga County History
     (including 115,000 glass plate
     negatives)
	Books
	Unbound Documents
	Film
	Photographs
	Magnetic Tape
	Other
		9,000
		10,000
		26,750
		100,000
		100
		115,000

Skaneateles Library Association: General Circulating Collection	Books	35,000

SUNY Health Science Center Library:
     Entire Collection Including Serials,
     Monographs, and Special Collection
     (History of Medicine)
	Books / Serials
	Unbound Documents
	Film
	Photographs
	Magnetic Tape
	Other
		164,600
		300
		69,800
		300
		4,000
		20

Utica Public Library: Local History Department	Books	8,000

Figure 6

4. Identification of Collective Priorities for Cooperative Action

In order to identify emerging regional preservation problems, solutions, and priorities in Phase III, the PNAP participants viewed the Phase I survey results for particular preservation actions from two perspectives: the number of items affected and the number of institutions affected. The regional summaries included relative priorities for preservation actions, as shown in the example for books. [FIGURE 7]

5. Establishment of CENTRO priorities for Cooperative Action

After identifying collective problems, solutions, and priorities, the participants established priorities for cooperative action. At the Phase III seminar, participants worked through a process of determining feasibility and establishing priorities for cooperative action. As a result of the process, participants decided to establish collective priorities based on the number of institutions affected by an action, and to concentrate on the book format for their initial cooperative planning efforts. This was done because the target collections were of varying sizes and it seemed more important to stress actions that affected many institutions, rather than larger collections held by a few institutions. The book was selected because it was the only format held by all of the participating institutions.

The group identified actions that institutions planned to take, regardless of cooperative activity, and then recalculated the collective priority. The new chart, which omitted actions such as User Education, best done by individual institutions, included those collective priorities for which cooperative action was desired or needed. The group also identified actions to omit from the

---

REGIONAL SUMMARY

Books
269,676 items in target population, ten institutions reporting

Action	Collective Priority: (# Items Affected)	Collective Priority: (# Instit. Affected)
Inventory Control	7 (9,927)	4 (5)
Disaster Plan	3 (30,758)	4 (5)
Fire Protection	6 (11,840)	5 (2)
Environmental Control	1 (185,927)	3 (7)
Education	2 (95,934)	1 (10)
Rebind/Repair	5 (12,992)	2 (8)
Conserve	8 (6,669)	3 (7)
Replace/Reformat	4 (18,627)	3 (7)
Protective Enclosure	9 (5,772)	4 (5)

Figure 7

planning effort; actions that required cooperation to launch; potential individuals, committees, or agencies to carry out cooperative actions; and the feasibility of completing the actions.

As in previous phases of the PNAP process, priority numbers and feasibility numbers were used to determine implementation strategy, this time for collective regional action rather than individual institutional action. The categories of preservation action ranked highest for cooperative action by CENTRO were Rebind/Repair, Replace/Reformat, Disaster Preparedness, and Protective Enclosures.[10]

6. Publication of *Preservation Needs Assessment: A Management Tool*

The PNAP project final report, *Preservation Needs Assessment: A Management Tool*, was published to document the project's activities and results, and to serve as a guide for future needs assessment projects. It includes a description of the project and samples of the documentation and reports from the three phases of the project. Copies of the publication were distributed in New York state to library systems and others interested in coordinating regional preservation needs assessment projects.[11]

PROJECT EVALUATION

The Central New York Preservation Needs Assessment Project (PNAP) met its goals by successfully guiding participants through a systematic process to identify the preservation needs of their institutions, and by providing CENTRO with comparable information about the nature and scope of regional preservation needs. At the completion of the project each participating institution had a documented preservation plan for addressing the preservation needs identified for its target collection. CENTRO had collected data about preservation needs in the region and identified priorities for needed cooperative preservation action. The Council and two of the participating institutions submitted applications for 1993-1994 Discretionary Grants, based on needs identified by the project.

The PNAP process demonstrated that, in a short period of time, libraries and historical agencies of varying sizes, with collections representing a variety of formats, and staff with little previous preservation experience, could successfully complete preservation plans. PNAP also demonstrated a cost-effective method for a regional group of libraries and historical agencies to assess preservation needs cooperatively. Some of the factors in the success of the PNAP project were:

- The guidance and expertise of Project Consultant Barclay Ogden
- Individual site visits

> • The use of two-participant teams from most institutions, reinforcing learning the techniques for sampling, determining priorities, and feasibility
> • A short project time period, maintaining momentum between phases

Only a few procedural changes would be made in repeating the project. The major change would be to allow more time for preparation of institutional survey sampling frames (including site visits, if necessary).

NEXT STEPS

Based on the priorities for cooperative action established by the PNAP participants, CENTRO developed a proposal for a "Preservation Program Implementation Consultancy." The proposal, which was subsequently funded by the Discretionary Grant Program of the New York State Program for the Conservation and Preservation of Library Research Materials, focuses on the three areas identified as collective priorities by the Preservation Needs Assessment Project. These are Disaster Preparedness Planning and Implementation, Preservation Program Implementation Management Strategies, and Preservation Techniques Refresher.

PNAP was a practical project to enable the participants and the region to make informed decisions about what to do next. Interestingly, some of the institutions that targeted a special or local history collection, thinking that they needed to institute an item-specific repair or conservation project, were shown that instead they should address concerns such as disaster planning, environmental controls, or fire protection which affect their entire collection, not just the special collection surveyed. Otherwise, project participants were cautioned that the survey results applied only to the target collections. Several participants, in their institutional plans, included plans to repeat the process for other portions of the library.

The PNAP project results were only "a first glimpse" for the CENTRO region. CENTRO plans to repeat the PNAP process with other libraries and historical agencies in Central New York. The value of the Preservation Needs Assessment Project as a cost-effective tool for preservation planning has been demonstrated by the first 10 PNAP participants. There are, in the CENTRO region, 9 academic libraries, 31 special libraries, approximately 50 small public libraries, 3 county historical agencies, and over 50 smaller historical agencies that were not reached by this first PNAP project. The collective preservation priorities for the region will be revised and refined as the process is repeated to include other collections. The CENTRO Preservation Committee will incorporate the revised regional priorities in planning future cooperative preservation projects.

NOTES

1. AMIGOS Preservation Service, *Final Performance Report, AMIGOS Preservation Service* (Dallas: AMIGOS Bibliographic Council, 1993); Tom Clarenson, Margaret Child, and Darryl Lang, "The RONDAC Preservation Survey," *Conservation Administration News* 47 (October 1991): 14, 27, 29; Greater Northeastern Regional Medical Library Program, *Preservation Needs Assessment of U.S. Health Sciences Libraries* (New York: New York Academy of Medicine, 1989).

2. Wesley L. Boomgaarden and Edward T. O'Neill, "A Study of the Magnitude and Characteristics of Book Deterioration in Ohio Libraries," *Preservation Issues* 6 (December 1991); John H. DePew, *An Investigation of Preservation Service Needs and Options for Florida Libraries: A Final Report* (Tallahassee: Florida State University School of Library Science, 1990); Patricia A. Morris, "PALM-COP: A Statewide Preservation Effort in South Carolina," *Conservation Administration News* 40 (January 1990): 10-11, 30; Gregor Trinkaus-Randall, *The Massachusetts Preservation Needs Assessment: An Analysis* (Boston: Massachusetts Board of Library Commissioners, 1993).

3. Barclay Ogden and Maralyn Jones, *CALIPR: An Automated Tool to Assess Preservation Needs of Book and Document Collections for Institutional and Statewide Planning*, version 2.1 (Berkeley: University of California, 1992).

4. Barclay Ogden, "Greater Bay Area Preservation Planning Project" (Paper prepared for a 1989/90 LSCA Title III project, Berkeley, Calif., October 1989); Barclay Ogden, "Preservation Program Development Shared Consultancy" (Paper prepared for a 1990/91 LSCA project, Berkeley, Calif., 1990).

5. Ogden and Jones, 7-9, 30-33.

6. Ogden and Jones, 29-30.

7. The participants were Colgate University, Fayetteville Free Library, Herkimer County Community College, Oneida Community Mansion House, Onondaga Community College, Onondaga County Public Library, Onondaga Historical Association, Skaneateles Library Association, State University of New York Health Science Center—Syracuse Library, and Utica Public Library. Project Director Jeannette Smithee (Assistant Director, Central New York Library Resources Council), Project Consultant Barclay Ogden (Head, Conservation Department, University of California at Berkeley), and Project Liaison Martha Hanson (Preservation Administrator, Syracuse University Library) provided guidance and assistance to the 10 participating institutions during the four-month project.

8. Ogden and Jones, 29-33.

9. *Preservation Needs Assessment: A Management Tool* (Syracuse: Central New York Library Resources Council, 1993), 37-44.

10. Ibid., 11-12.

11. Copies of *Preservation Needs Assessment: A Management Tool* (50 pages) may be obtained at cost ($10) from the Central New York Library Resources Council (CENTRO), 763 Butternut Street, Syracuse, NY 13208.

Computer-Assisted Preservation Surveys

Stuart A. Kohler

Information Technology Librarian
Norwich University Libraries

INTRODUCTION

It is well-documented in the conservation/preservation literature that a thorough survey of collections is a primary step in planning a major preservation initiative.[1,2] Gathering data on the current physical condition of collections is vital for assessing need and allocating resources to address the preservation requirements of a library or archive. It is unlikely that an institution will have resources sufficient to provide preservation treatment for every item in its care, so difficult choices must be made in selecting what is to receive treatment, and in what order. A carefully planned and conducted condition survey will assemble the data necessary to make such evaluations.

DATA COLLECTION: QUANTITY VS. QUALITY
Quantity: How Much Data Is Enough?

Often there is a conscious or unconscious desire to collect as much information as possible during a condition survey, although only in some instances is this practice justified by the immediate purpose at hand (generating data to help establish preservation priorities). It is important to keep in mind that there are costs associated with collecting data, paid in time and data manipulation, and to establish a balance between the minimum requirements for an acceptable survey and the ideal. For example, it is certainly possible that excess data collected today could prove useful tomorrow for some other purpose—interesting correlations could be made, for example, between various nonphysical elements (such as time and place of origin for the material) and physical condition.[3] Collecting auxiliary data may also serve to enhance catalog descriptions and be of great value to scholarly research.

For the majority of institutions, however, collecting information outside the scope of a tightly focused preservation survey is a luxury which must be given a lower priority: just amassing the data required to make preservation decisions for a large collection is likely to prove an enormous task for most institutions.

Quality: Why Is It Important?

The issue of collecting too much or too little data is frequently mistaken as a principle concern in conducting a preservation survey. Although it is important to establish the scope of data collection at the outset, the more important issue is the quality of the data collected. Regardless of the range of data to be included in the survey, the quality of data is paramount. Data that lack specificity will yield vague and inconclusive results. In general, the more precise each data element, the more useful it will be for analysis. A good test for quality is the question, "What specific decision will this information help me make?" (Examples of levels of specificity are given on page 264 in the section DATA SPECIFICITY AND TIME-DEPENDENCY.)

THE PERSONAL COMPUTER AS SURVEY TOOL

One of the great assets in undertaking a large-scale preservation survey is the personal computer. PCs provide a highly advanced tool for the manipulation of large amounts of data, permitting sophisticated analysis at a much higher level than is possible using traditional paper-form data collection. The static nature of manually collected information greatly limits its usefulness; manual surveys typically result in a single set of data in the form of a stack of paper. Since it is possible to arrange this stack in only one order at a time, multi-layered evaluations require either multiple copies of the survey forms, or an additional system to keep track of summaries created when the forms are arranged according to different criteria.

It is important to bear in mind, of course, that while computers are unsurpassed in their ability to arrange and rearrange information, they do not analyze data; as we shall see, only people have the capacity to analyze collected information.

COMPUTER HARDWARE

Practically any functioning personal computer with a hard disk drive will meet the minimum hardware requirements for a computer-assisted preservation survey. Older machines, however, cannot provide the performance and speed that newer, more powerful ones offer. If one is faced with conducting a survey in an institution that has no computer equipment on hand, what follows can be a general guide.

A basic personal computer consists of a screen or monitor, a central processing unit (CPU), a keyboard, and, optionally, a pointing device known as a "mouse." A printer is necessary to create paper copies of database reports, which are the results of data manipulation.

CPUs are classified by the power of their microchips, essentially the "brain" of the central processing unit. Presently an 80386 chip (or a "386 CPU") should be considered "standard"—purchasing earlier, slower chips would be an investment in old technology and definitely not cost-effective. With the development of the much more powerful 586 generation of chips, some vendors may even consider a 486 machine (the next step beyond the

386) to be standard equipment. (If one wishes to work within the Microsoft Windows environment, a 386 machine is a minimum requirement. Be sure to check the system requirements of specific Windows database products.)

Data are stored in a subunit, the disk drive, located inside the CPU case. Disk drives, or hard drives (distinguishing them from the drives that use removable "floppy" disks), are rated by storage capacity in megabytes (MB) of data. Standard sizes are roughly 40, 80, 120, 320 megabytes and higher. If a new purchase is being considered, an 80 MB drive should be ample, leaving room for other institutional uses of the computer. A minimum of 20 MB of free space is appropriate for most surveys. (Older machines that were equipped with two floppy drives ("dual floppies") are inadequate for a computer-assisted preservation survey.) Monitors may be black-and-white or color. Color is generally considered to be easier on the eyes, and many database products use color to highlight or clarify data displays.

When purchasing computer equipment for the first time, it is wise to buy a complete setup, since individually acquired pieces are not always compatible (all disk drives do not work with all CPUs). One last caveat applies to printers: database software products support (that is, can be used with) a variety of makes and models of printers. Before selecting a printer, especially a "bargain" printer, one should ensure that it is either a brand recognized by the software chosen for the survey or that it emulates one of the printers the program supports.

DATABASE SOFTWARE

Simply put, a database is an electronic file of information. The two basic elements of a database are fields and records. Taking a paper analogy, we might consider a paper-based conservation survey form. Each blank to be completed on the paper form corresponds to a data field in the database. If each paper form contains information about one item, one discrete group of items, or a single unit of any kind, then each form is analogous to a single record in the database. Five blanks on a form, then, would represent five fields; five paper forms would constitute five records in the database.

The number of PC database software products on the market is large and continues to grow. A new generation of databases for the Microsoft Windows environment promises users a more intuitive interface between themselves and the machine, although there is no need to migrate to Windows simply to conduct a preservation survey. The criteria for selecting database software include:

1) Maximum number of records per database
2) Maximum number of fields for each record in the database
3) Maximum number of indexed fields per database
4) Ease of report generation

5) Ease in creating data input forms

6) Text-string searching capability

Most popular database products easily handle the number of records and fields required for a preservation survey. Similarly, it is unlikely that required indexing will exceed standard software capabilities. Indexes are used to arrange data in ordered form, so that all the records in the database may be sorted alphabetically (in either ascending or descending order), according to the values entered into indexed text fields. Indexed fields may also be used to locate specific information (material prior to 1850, for example, if the date field is indexed).

Ease in generating reports and creating data input forms is a more subjective assessment and will vary widely from one database product to another. One valid criterion, however, is that it should not be necessary to hire a database specialist to generate simple columnar reports from collected data. The usual reports to be generated will display a limited number of selected fields that conform to specified conditions (e.g., a list of items and locations for materials that have aggressive iron gall ink on brittle substrates).

The ability to search for specific sequences of letters or characters can be a powerful tool in locating desired information. Frequently such searches employ "wildcard" characters—symbols the software interprets to represent one or more characters. Accordingly, searching for the string of characters "*frame*" (where the asterisk is a wildcard character) in a miscellaneous notes field will locate each instance of the words "frame," "framed," and "unframed." Nevertheless, one should avoid excessive reliance on this type of text-string searching because of the toll it takes on speed and performance in data manipulation. In designing the database, it is important to create as many specific fields as possible, avoiding lengthy "narrative" entries that are hard to search. Searching performance may also be increased by the use of controlled vocabulary, which may be either coded entries (1=severe, 2=moderate, 3=minimal, for example) or standardized lists of descriptors (so that "marginalia" rather than "margin notes" will be used in every instance). However, this strategy requires scrupulous maintenance of a master list or thesaurus and additional training and supervision of the data collectors, if it is to be effective.

In the final selection of a particular database, one would be well advised to choose something familiar, preferably a product that is already in use in one's own institution. There is certainly no shortage of fee-for-service database consultants, but the level of sophistication needed to conduct a PC-based preservation survey is also within the reach of most computer users.

As examples of the variety available in database software, four products are described below. The four programs were chosen because they are representative of different categories, and their selection represents a necessarily subjective decision. First, dBase IV is included because for years it was considered to be the "industry standard" for database formats; as of the third quarter of 1992, dBase dominated the personal computer database arena with a 65 percent market share. This means that there are many copies of this product currently in use, and it is quite likely that it will be found in many institutions. Q&A was chosen as an easy-to-use DOS environment product. FileMaker Pro is included as a familiar Macintosh database. Finally, Paradox for Windows appears in order to include a database designed specifically for use in the Microsoft Windows environment. Accordingly, it should be kept in mind that these are not the only, or necessarily the best, database software available. A case could be made to include many other products.

1. *dBASE* (Borland, formerly Ashton-Tate); list price: $795; mail order: $485

System Requirements: IBM PC, PC XT, AT or 100 percent compatible; or, IBM compatible 286 or 386 systems. 640 K RAM; one floppy disk drive; monochrome or color monitor. Supports any printer with at least 80 columns.

The following comments are based on the enhanced user interface provided with dBase IV:

The first step in using dBase is creating the database definition (the structure of the database that contains information about each element—field name, field type, field length, whether the field is to be indexed, and so forth). The user is prompted to define 1) field name, 2) data type, 3) width (with decimal places, if the field is numeric), and 4) whether the field is to be indexed.

The next step requires the user to define the form to be used for adding/editing records. There is an option for a "Quick Layout" that automatically includes all fields in the definition. Fields are easily rearranged with "mark" and "move" commands.

To add information, the user selects first the desired database, then the form to be used. This same form is also used to display data, one record at a time.

To query the database, another form is created by the user which includes the desired values. This aspect of dBase IV is not particularly intuitive and at this point most users resort to querying by means of a command line language (the "dot prompt"). Text-string searching is possible, but somewhat difficult. The syntax of the query is extremely exacting, and some practice is needed to develop a facility and familiarity with querying.

Although the user interface also guides users through creating reports, the difficulties are similar to those of setting up queries. In short, for both querying and reporting, novices are likely to require assistance and training in the use of dBase.

Summary: dBase fulfills the requirements of a database that can be used for a preservation survey; if it is already available in one's institution, its use should be considered. If, however, one is contemplating the purchase of a database product specifically for a computer-assisted survey, the moderate-to-steep learning curve may not justify the purchase of dBase.

2. *Q&A* (Symantec); list price: $499; mail order price: $295

System Requirements: IBM or compatible; DOS 2.0 or higher; 512 K RAM (640 preferred); hard disk; monochrome or color monitor. Supports Microsoft Mouse or 100 percent compatibles.

The database definition is created by laying out the desired fields on the input form. Once the form is created, the same form is used for adding or editing records, as well as searching or querying the database. Querying is done using Query By Example (QBE), a searching mechanism found in many products which is designed to facilitate data retrieval. With QBE, the user types in the data value for which he or she is searching, and Q&A then retrieves all records containing that value. Q&A supports both simple text-string searching and conditional searching (e.g., date < 1850).

Simple reports are easily and quickly generated: the user merely lists the fields to be included in the report. In this way, a document may be generated that only includes the fields required, saving time and paper by not printing entire records when a subset of the fields will suffice. Searches may also be saved at the time the report is defined; this is a time-saver, because the same complex query can subsequently be run automatically, whenever enough new data have been collected and an updated report is desired.

A report style that is generally characteristic of high-end databases, the crosstab report, is available in Q&A. Crosstab is an abbreviation for cross-tabulation, which permits the construction of a table based on three different variables. Crosstabs are considered very powerful analysis tools, often used to reveal subtle relationships that would otherwise be difficult to identify. One example would be creating a report that presents an analysis of frequency of use, curatorial value (the significance of the item to the collection), and format ("map" or "manuscript," for example). Without cross-tabulation, only two of these three variables could be analyzed at one time.

Q&A also provides two additional query aids, the Query Guide and the Intelligent Assistant. The Query Guide assists the user in formulating the request by prompting him or her to select phrases that Q&A then uses to construct the query and search the database. It may be customized to include user-supplied phrases, helpful for specifics such as collection names, stack areas, etc.

The Intelligent Assistant (IA) takes guided querying one step further by permitting natural language searching of the database. The IA comes with a built-in vocabulary of about 600 words and phrases; this vocabulary can be enlarged by the user. An IA profile must be set up by the user, identifying fields to be automatically included in a report based on a condition in a single field, alternate field names, and similar "personalization" of IA queries.

In addition to its database component (File), Q&A includes word processing (Write) as well; there is also a mail merge capability (useful, although not a necessary component for a preservation survey). Tools are included to build customized versions of the program, including the ability to record long, commonly used series of keystrokes for "playback" using a single keystroke or macro, and the capability to tailor the menus used to help guide users through the system.

Summary: Q&A is an outstanding database product. Its low learning curve (several hours, using manuals and tutorial) and sophisticated features make it a powerful tool accessible to beginning computer users. It would be an excellent choice for a computer-assisted preservation survey.

3. *FILEMAKER PRO* (Claris); list price: $299; mail order price: $185

System Requirements: A Mac Classic or later machine. Claris recommends one MB of memory if running System 6.05, two MB of memory if running System 7.

Macintosh systems are considered by many to set the standard for intuitive graphical user interface applications. FileMaker Pro databases are easily created, simply by specifying database fields. Particularly useful is the ability to define a field that will present possible values in a scrolling list. The first input form layout is automatically created after the fields are defined; other layouts may be devised graphically, using the mouse to resize and position the field. The size on the layout screen determines field size, giving the user a visual representation of how much space is available for data entry. Searching follows the same form as data entry and QBE is used to query the database. Reporting is relatively easy for columnar reports and is also WYSIWYG (What You See Is What You Get—what appears on the screen is what will be printed out).

4. *PARADOX FOR WINDOWS* (Borland); list price: $795; mail order price: $475

System Requirements: IBM-compatible 386 CPU. 4 MB of RAM. Requires hard disk with 15 MB of free space for program files. VGA color monitor is recommended. Requires MS-DOS version 5.0 or later and Microsoft Windows version 3.1 or later.

Although Paradox for Windows has much in common with the original

DOS version, the newer product takes full advantage of the benefits of working within the Windows environment. Help and error messages are clear and generally guide inexperienced users through the process of building a database (called a "table").

After selecting "file, new," the user is prompted to define table type, choosing either a Paradox or dBase style. Both offer the basic set of field types, although Paradox supports additional types such as graphic, permitting the inclusion of scanned or imported graphic images. The only basic field type absent from the Paradox style is "logical" (yes/no, true/false), but this type of field is available in the dBase-style table. The next step in the definition process is choice of field name, field type, field size, and key (will this field be indexed?). Where there are specific decisions to be made, a right click on the mouse or tapping the space bar brings up a list from which to select. Definitions are also easily modified after initial creation.

Querying is Query By Example, after one designs a query form which is a simple process of selecting the fields to be displayed for the resulting data set. Similarly, designing a report form customizes the output for reports generated to screen or printer. In both query and report forms, there is an option to select a "quick form"; this builds a usable form automatically. Sorting (creating temporarily arranged lists) is also a simple option, selected from the menu of options which is always displayed across the top of the screen. The documentation seems to be clear and well-written.

Summary: If one wishes to work in the Microsoft Windows environment (and can meet the necessary hardware requirements), Paradox for Windows will be an excellent choice.

THE SURVEY FORM

Even before turning on the computer, it is wise to plan a form on paper. This serves two purposes: 1) creating the form that will be used to collect the data, and 2) defining the database fields. This same model may serve as the data entry form from which collected information will be keyed into the database. Taking the time to design on paper will avoid many of the hazards of structuring the database "on-the-fly" (some databases are much less forgiving of errors or changes made in the definition stages than others).

Direct data input is an alternative to collecting information on paper forms and using the forms to enter data. A laptop or notebook computer capable of running the database software can be taken into the stacks and used to key information; at a later time, the data are transferred to the desktop computer serving as the survey's primary computing site. If this method of data collection is adopted, procedures need to be established to ensure that the temporary or "working" databases on the laptops are deleted, to avoid duplication of records in the master database.

The better organized the form, the easier it will be to identify data elements overlooked in the initial definition stages. Because of the uniqueness of each library and archive, no single form will be appropriate for every institution. However, there are six common data collection categories that are necessary to the basic structure of any survey database. Each of these categories includes a number of subdivisions made up of individual fields; fields may, in turn, have subfields. The six categories are:

1) Specific Descriptor
2) Storage Location
3) Physical Description (media, substrate, etc.)
4) Physical Condition
5) Treatment Proposal
6) Treatment Priority

Each of these six categories will be stratified, and the number of fields and subfields assigned to each will depend on the needs of the institution conducting the survey. For example, the specific descriptor for archival materials can include catalog name, series, acquisition number, and/or a short, written description of the material; for library materials information such as title, call number, and/or accession number is appropriate. The Physical Description section (3) can include as few as three or four fields, or 20 or more fields. The most basic set of Physical Description fields includes format, size, and medium. At the next level of detail, a group of format subfields might incorporate terms such as book, letterpress book, multi-volume set, manuscript, typescript, computer printout, pamphlet, periodical, broadside, printed form, blueprint, architectural drawing, map, newspaper, work of art, photograph, photocopy, notebook, scrapbook, and "other."

These subfields may themselves be further divided: work of art, for example, could be broken into print, drawing, etching, engraving, water color, etc. In the context of a rare book collection, much more information might be collected about binding materials and structure; subfields could include such terms as leather (full, half, or quarter), vellum, cloth, paper boards, as well as unusual attributes such as fore-edge paintings. Each item (except "other") in the list will be a check-off on the form and a yes/no (or "logical") field in the database; "other" can be a short text field, 15 to 25 characters long.

Size may simply be a text field including measurements (height by width), or two separate fields (height and width), or a set of subfields including standard terms such as quarto, octavo, folio, etc. Media fields can range from a basic set of printed, ink, pencil, and artistic media terms, to a more complete group including such characterizations as ink—carbon, ink—iron gall, ink—colored, pencil—lead, pencil—grease, water color—single, water color—multiple, gouache, hand-tinted, and "other."

Physical Condition (4) gathers the information needed to determine treatment priorities. This set of fields could include such designations as boards—

detached, spine—detached, sewing damage, torn headcap, red rot, tears/losses, stains—water, stains—mold, active mold, fire/smoke damage, aggressive ink, brittle, missing/loose leaves, fasteners, insect/rodent damage, gum/wax seals, mends—paper, mends—linen tape, mends—glassine, mends—silking, mends—pressure sensitive. Most of these conditions may be further subdivided according to severity, using either a simple major/minor distinction or a graded system numbered one through five (with 1 being the worst and 5 being the least serious condition). The simplest implementation of this type field is to make it one character in length and use the number or a code letter to indicate severity. (The use of graded conditions will be discussed further in the section of this paper dealing with time-dependent functions.)

Treatment Proposal (5) need be no more complex than an indication of full treatment, simple rehousing, or no treatment required. If one wishes to provide a more detailed conservator-style proposal, subfields might include disbinding, rehousing, phase boxing, binding repair, rebinding, humidification, flattening, unframing, surface cleaning, washing, mending, lining, encapsulation, and "other."

Treatment Priority (6) is an evaluation of urgency from the perspective of physical condition, or as a combination of physical condition and two additional pieces of information, Frequency of Use and Curatorial Value. These last two items are sometimes considered to be outside the scope of a preservation survey. Usage statistics and estimation of significance to the collection is the purview of the librarian, archivist, or curator, rather than that of the conservator, although an argument favoring the inclusion of such information in a preservation survey has been clearly made in the literature.[4, 5] Indeed, the most meaningful evaluation of preservation priorities cannot fairly discount these two elements. Treatment of a document that is extremely brittle but never used should not take precedence over a moderately brittle document that is frequently consulted. Likewise, assessment of an item's value as intrinsic, legal, exhibit, or strictly informational may help set preservation priorities.[6]

Consideration might be given to performing the survey as a series of surveys, each having its own form. The initial assessment can be reduced to the Identification and Storage Location sections (1 and 2) listed above, and a Physical Condition section (4), scaled back to a basic yes/no answer to the question, "Does this material warrant a more detailed preservation survey"? Proceeding through a large collection in successive sweeps may improve efficiency and help set priorities within the survey process itself.

SYSTEM TESTING

The next steps include using the database software to create the files for the database definition and data input forms, testing the system with sample data, and generating trial reports. In most database products, the creation of the database definition and data input forms follows quite easily once one has prepared the form on paper, as described above. To reiterate, it is preferable to have many small fields of a few characters in length than to rely heavily on large text fields; the use of the latter requires more data manipulation to identify multiple conditions and create sorted lists.

An adequate test database uses 100 to 250 records. This is a large enough sample to begin testing various sorting and reporting operations. It will give an indication of how all the pieces fit together, as well as identify data fields that were overlooked in the planning stages. It is highly likely that data fields will be added on the basis of collecting real data from the actual collection. Discovering and adding these fields before large-scale data collection begins is considerably easier than attempting modifications of the database structure later on.

In this testing phase, one should intentionally include as many different material types and conditions as possible. In institutions with fairly uniform collections (books in a library, for example), selecting material by random sampling may prove useful in assembling a representative sample. Procedures for random sampling are well-documented in the literature.[7] It is important to bear in mind, however, that random sampling is the method of choice when the goal is to gain a generalized, overall picture of the collection's condition. Data collected in such a survey will not be a valid basis for establishing specific preservation priorities because a particular item of great value and/or poor condition might not be selected in a random sample and therefore would not appear on any list generated. Also, for many institutions (especially archives) random sampling may not produce useful results even for the test database. In this setting, it is important to have as complete a range of different material types and conditions as possible. Accordingly, reliance on the knowledge of experienced staff to locate various sorts of materials may prove to be the most efficient strategy.

DATA SPECIFICITY AND TIME-DEPENDENCY

Simply collecting vast amounts of information (even preservation-specific) on a particular collection will not necessarily help preservation administrators or custodians arrive at a concrete plan of action. The real advantage of utilizing a computer lies in its ability to manipulate data elements in a variety of ways, to refine the decision-making process inherent in developing objectives, priorities, and methodologies for any preservation initiative. One of the most meaningful types of data that may be collected in a preservation analysis concerns "time-dependent elements," or physical characteristics that are inherently unstable and therefore affected by the passing of time. One of the best examples of such an element is the presence of pressure-sensitive tape.

Simply indicating that documents or book pages have been mended with pressure-sensitive adhesive tape does not yield meaningful data, unless there are so few taped items that all such documents or pages may be scheduled for treatment at once. This is usually not the case, so that noting the condition or aging characteristics of the tape is important.[8] Tape falls into one of three broad categories: new, in the midst of its aging cycle, or at the end of its chemical life. While it may have done significant damage that is difficult if not impossible to reverse, tape at the conclusion of its aging cycle is capable of little if any further chemical activity and is therefore unlikely to do any additional harm; in a rather curious use of the term, one might even consider such tape as "stable." New tape, on the other hand, at the beginning of its cycle of chemical changes, has usually caused little damage and is relatively easy to treat. Between "new" and "completely aged" lies the most critical condition, in terms of preservation intervention; inaction on the part of the custodian will permit the process of deterioration to continue until the damage becomes permanent or irreversible.

Obviously the priority of treatment in this example is clear: pressure-sensitive tape in the aging category is the first concern; new tape is second, and third would be the completely aged tape which has little or no chemical activity left. One way to collect data in a manner that will facilitate its retrieval according to the suggested priorities is to create a text field of seven characters in length for pressure-sensitive tape (such as "ps-tape") and allow "new," "aging," or "aged" as acceptable values for the field; a more efficient method in terms of retrieval is to create three one-character fields (logical or text) for the three conditions and use them as "check boxes."

Similar evaluation of time-dependencies can be applied to aggressive inks; iron gall ink, for example, is frequently seen to accelerate the deterioration of the paper substrate on which it rests. The degree to which the substrate has been attacked may indicate the need for immediate stabilization or (if the injury is extreme) suggest that no further damage is likely to occur. Furthermore, time-dependency is not always chemical in nature. An example of a time-dependent physical condition is a large map with significant tears and losses which is frequently consulted. Each time this item is used, additional damage is likely to occur in the handling; the need to stabilize it as quickly as possible is readily apparent. In this case, frequency of use is a critical factor in establishing a time-dependency, since a low-use item in the same condition would not merit urgent attention.

CONCLUSION

By employing specific, meaningful data elements in the preservation survey, the personal computer may be used to identify, combine, and present in sorted order both time-dependent preservation concerns and more traditional physical conditions. Frequency of use is an important criterion. Another useful element is significance to the collection (i.e., intrinsic, legal, exhibit, or information-only value). The advantage of computer sorting and reporting is that these activities reveal complex relationships between and among different data elements. Paper-based attempts at such evaluations would be difficult at best, and likely involve additional forms for tabulations, if not multiple copies of each paper form, placed in various groupings to identify the various interrelationships.

The goal of this discussion has not been to provide a manual for conducting a computer-assisted preservation survey, but rather to note the advantages of collecting meaningful data elements with the knowledge that effective decision-making tools may be produced by manipulating the resulting database in a variety of ways, using a personal computer. Working with the data in this way will help establish realistic priorities in planning the preservation program.

NOTES

1. John N. DePew, *A Library, Media, and Archival Preservation Handbook* (Santa Barbara, Calif.: ABC-CLIO, 1991), 238-39.
2. Mary Lynn Ritzenthaler, *Archives & Manuscripts: Conservation; A Manual on Physical Care and Management* (Chicago: Society of American Archivists, 1983), 67-68.
3. Gay Walker, et al., "The Yale Survey: A Large-Scale Study of Book Deterioration in the Yale University Library," *College & Research Libraries* 46 (March 1985): 113. In the design of its large-scale survey, Yale purposely included nonphysical characteristics "to expand the profile of the deteriorated volumes and to suggest reasons for their deterioration."
4. Christinger Tomer, "Selecting Library Materials for Preservation," *Library & Archival Security* 7 (Spring 1985): 1-5.
5. Lisa B. Williams, "Selecting Rare Books for Physical Conservation: Guidelines for Decision Making," *College & Research Libraries* 46 (March 1985): 153-57.
6. The concept of intrinsic value was developed by a committee formed by the National Archives in 1979. The official report was published in 1982 and is highly recommended for further reading on the subject of value: National Archives and Records Service, *Intrinsic Value in Archival Materials*, Staff Information Paper no. 21 (Washington, D.C.: National Archives and Records Service, 1982). A significant portion of this publication is included as Appendix J in Depew, 419-21. As a thought-provoking piece related to this discussion, see also James M. O'Toole, "On the Idea of Permanence," *American Archivist* 52 (Winter 1989): 10-25.
7. M. Carl Drott, "Random Sampling, A Tool for Library Research," *College & Research Libraries* 30 (March 1969): 119-25. Also, see Appendix A in Walker, "The Yale Survey," cited above.
8. Robert Feller published an excellent article on the life cycle of pressure-sensitive tapes, and the reader is encouraged to consult the full text of that article for his complete discussion: R. L. Feller and D. B. Encke, "Stages in Deterioration: The Examples of Rubber Cement and Transparent Mending Tape," in *Preprints of the Contributions to the Washington Congress, 3-9 September 1982* (London: International Institute for Conservation of Historic and Artistic Works, 1982), 19-23.

PART 5:
PRESERVING SPECIAL FORMATS

As recently as 10 years ago, most library and archive collections consisted of paper-based print materials; the music library probably collected sound recordings. Today's collections include many different formats, with correspondingly different preservation needs. In her paper on salvaging flood-damaged microfilms, Sharon Gavitt explores whether there is an appropriate role for freezing (a common recovery technique with books and paper). If freezing wet microfilms causes no further damage to them, Gavitt points out that it offers many valuable advantages: salvage activities (washing and re-processing) can be deferred to a more opportune time; films are protected from further damage, such as mold growth; fewer staff are needed to accomplish the work at hand. In her paper, Gavitt describes a study in which three different approaches to thawing and recovering film samples were tested; the study showed no visible differences between microfilm processed immediately after soaking and that processed after freezing and thawing, suggesting freezing to be a sound recovery measure for this material type.

In his paper on the preservation of motion picture films, Anthony Slide asks the questions, what does it cost? and, who is paying? Slide stresses the urgency of the problem (large numbers of films on disintegrating nitrate stock) and takes to task the film industry, guilty of spending little or nothing from its own pocket for preservation but accepting federal dollars for this purpose, restricting access to preserved titles by claiming the rights of copyright holder. He suggests several solutions to the problems associated with motion picture preservation and access (make access by the public a condition for federal funding; identify and save "missing" films; periodically re-copy both nitrate and safety film onto new stock; store films under sound environmental conditions) and considers the elements involved in the preservation (versus restoration) of motion pictures.

Several of the papers in this volume touch on the difficulties of preserving electronic media. Jan Michaels examines the intellectual and technological problems associated with saving electronic information. She observes that our society as yet attaches little importance to electronic information, which it views as disposable. At the same time, publishers of electronic resources appear to have only vague ideas about how today's documents will be accessed 50 years from now. Among the many problems associated with saving electronic information that Michaels discusses are provenance and authenticity, out-dated playback equipment, defunct software packages, and brief shelf-lives. She also makes a convincing argument for the responsibility to preserve not just the information electronic resources contain, but some of the carriers of that information (CD-ROMs, magnetic tapes) as well.

Observations on the Effect of Freezing and Thawing Microfilm[1]

Sharon Gavitt

Archives Conservation Specialist I
New York State Archives and Records Administration

FLOOD-DAMAGED MICROFORMS

In a tragic accident, 20,000 gallons of water flowed from ruptured air conditioning pipes onto books and microforms in the Cultural Education Center at the Empire State Plaza, Albany, New York, on Friday, December 21, 1991. The Cultural Education Center houses collections from the New York State Archives, Library, and Museum, including at least 5.5 million service copy microforms and countless masters. As a result of this flood, thousands of microfiche and about 200 rolls of microfilm were soaked with water. These microforms included both diazo and silver processes.

The initial response to this disaster was quickly to inquire about appropriate salvage treatments for wet microforms, in order to save as many of them as possible. At the same time a labor-intensive rescue effort, in which staff volunteers dried microfiche using paper towels, was begun. Many of the damaged microfilm rolls were processed through a Prostar II microfilm processor which is normally used to develop, fix, wash, and dry silver gelatin microfilm. Over the weekend the remaining rolls of wet microfilm were washed off-site at the exhibit fabrication facility in a Creonite Process KM3 photographic sheet film and print processor. This photographic processor normally accommodates the chemical processing (developing, fixing, washing, drying) of exposed commercial photographic film and print paper sheets up to 52 inches in size. It takes approximately 10 minutes per roll to process microfilm through a Prostar II. The Creonite sheet film and print processor was adapted to accommodate 35mm film by using special spools and a dowel.

Photo processor chemicals were removed from the Creonite and replaced with water, creating a deep-water wash environment. The water temperature was set at 82 degrees F (wash) and 120 degrees F (dry). As the microfilm quickly moved out of this processor, it had to be spooled by hand. The film came out clean and flat, but about four to five hours were required to complete the processing of 40 rolls of silver gelatin microfilm. This resulted in increased immersion time for the microfilm rolls still waiting to be treated. The increased immersion time did not visibly alter the microfilm. After rescue efforts, the rolls of microfilm appeared to be cleaner and, more importantly, they were readable, making the operation a success.

We also learned that the type of storage box is a factor to consider when setting recovery priorities: plastic boxes (if the water can seep in) act as mini-immersion tanks for the film; this effect can continue even after the boxes are removed from the water. However, if firmly closed, these boxes are watertight and actually float. Thus, films stored in cardboard or insecurely closed plastic boxes should be salvaged first.

FREEZING MICROFILM: AN APPROACH RIPE FOR STUDY

Freezing is a common procedure in the salvage of books and paper. Used with microfilm rolls, it might have allowed more time to work on them at a later date, preserving them from further damage such as mold growth. Freezing can also prevent the need to depend on so many staff members to work immediate and long hours, performing a tedious task. By conserving staff energy and postponing some of the salvage steps to a more opportune moment, one can give greater attention to rescue methods, methods that should require less staff time. Freezing film also allows more time to gather supplies and equipment, as well as contact disaster response services.

After the disaster, I decided to conduct research to determine whether or not anyone had explored the possibility of freezing microfilm. Written correspondence and telephone conversations with preservation experts in the areas of photography, microfilm, motion picture film, and imaging revealed a lack of information in this specific area. A thorough literature search for research, experimentation, and standards was completed, confirming that observation. Hendriks and Lesser reported the results of an experiment involving water immersion and various drying methods for still photographic negatives and prints.[2] Many of the drying techniques used involved freezing. However, Hendriks and Lesser did not include microfilm in their experiment, and for that reason rolls of microfilm are the focus of this study.

According to Hendriks and Lesser, black-and-white film negatives can be left in clean water for up to 72 hours. (Their work also corroborates the empirical findings of this study that vacuum freeze-drying may leave behind residue and dirt from the water on the film.) A case study by Henry Klein recorded the results of trying to salvage microfilm after allowing it to air-dry rolled. The film was unusable, because unwinding it caused severe damage to the emulsion.[3]

This study compares the effects of short- and long-term water submersion on microfilm, as well as the effects of freezing, thawing, and drying using various approaches such as vacuum freeze-drying, the Prostar II microfilm processor with water, and the Prostar II microfilm processor using the developer, fix, and wash cycles. Possible concerns were sticking of the emulsion, shrinking of the base, and severe mottling or spotting, making the microfilm unreadable or possibly difficult to duplicate. The benefits of freezing, thawing, and drying by these means include preventing mold growth; reducing water immersion time (especially valuable with microfilm that may have been immersed for an unknown period); postponing rescue efforts; and (in the case of vacuum freeze-drying) eliminating rewinding.

SAMPLES AND VARIABLES

For this study, 35mm silver gelatin and diazo microfilm roll samples on a 5 ml polyester base were used. Each microfilm roll sample had been exposed and its images chemically processed approximately one year earlier. Since that time, rolls had been stored in a temperature- and relative humidity-controlled environment and enclosed in their original Kodak film boxes. The microfilms included in the experiment were either expendable extras or films rejected by our microfilm unit because they did not meet minimum splicing standards for preservation. Some of the samples were shorter than others, so all of them were cut to a uniform size and weighed on a gram scale before and after drying, to help determine shrinkage and weight change. Ambient temperatures (in the laboratory environment, in the water used both during immersion and in the processor, and in freezing and drying) were important variables to be considered. The pH of the water that was used and microfilm immersion times were also significant. Using both diazo and silver gelatin film provided an opportunity to compare the effects of freezing and drying on both processes.

PROCEDURES

All of the microfilm samples were immersed *without* boxes in 300 mls of tap water filtered through an AMF Cuno Filter Model CT 102 single-pressure five-micron filter cartridge system which removes micron-sized mineral particles from the water. Using a Fisher Accumet Model 230A pH ion meter, the pH of the water was established at 8.4 and the temperature 70 degrees F. Some sample rolls of each film type, silver gelatin and diazo, were immersed for five hours; others were immersed for 72 hours. [TABLE 1] Before freezing, the microfilm rolls were allowed to drain for about two minutes; all of the samples were frozen for 72 hours at zero degrees F in a walk-in Mesler freezer. To compare before-and-after image quality, photocopies of selected images on each sample roll (as well as images from a roll of microfilm duplicated from the sample following the experiment) were printed using a Canon NP Reader/Printer 680. Also, densitometer readings using a Macbeth TD 502 densitometer were taken at three different sections of each roll of film, varying the samples from dark to light. The consistent positioning of the densitometer was maintained for before-and-after readings by circling the beam of light on the film with a black film marker.

Samples

1. Silver film, 5-hour soak, Processor (water)

2. Silver film, 5-hour soak, Processor (developer, fix, wash)

3. Silver film, 5-hour soak, Vacuum freeze-dried

4. Silver film, 72-hour soak, Processor (water)

5. Silver film, 72-hour soak, Processor (developer, fix, wash)

6. Silver film, 72-hour soak, Vacuum freeze-dried

7. Diazo, 5-hour soak, Processor (water)

8. Diazo, 72-hour soak, Processor (water)

9. Diazo, 72-hour soak, Processor (developer, fix, wash)

10. Diazo, 72-hour soak, Vacuum freeze-dried

Table 1

THREE DRYING METHODS

1. Microfilm Processor—Water

The Prostar II microfilm processor, owned by the New York State Archives and used during the December 21, 1991 water disaster, was selected for use in this study. Because microfilm ranges from 100 to 400 feet long, the literature recommends that wet microfilm rolls be professionally treated using film processors.[4] The processor was used in this study to determine whether or not freezing created changes (such as blocking or sticking of the emulsion) that would prevent the film from passing through it. After freezing and before processing, the frozen microfilm samples were thawed in filtered water for about an hour. The temperature of the water in the processor was 99.5 degrees F, and in the dryer 136 degrees F.

Problems that occurred during processing included taped splices and leaders coming undone, and very slight sticking at the edges of silver gelatin rolls. The microfilm was otherwise quite readable and able to be copied.

2. Microfilm Processor—Developer, Fixer, Wash Cycles

This drying method was used to determine whether or not processing frozen microfilm through the Prostar II using chemicals instead of water would have an obvious effect on the film. If not, the film could be put through this processor without draining the chemicals and refilling the equipment with filtered water. The frozen microfilm samples were thawed for 10-30 minutes in water with a temperature of 65.5 degrees F and then put through the processor's full cycle, using fresh chemicals. The water temperature was 101 degrees F and the dryer was 145 degrees F.

An obvious problem occurred with one roll of silver gelatin microfilm that was immersed in water for 72 hours before freezing: brown spotting. This roll was rewashed in the processor but some of the spotting remained on the film. It seems that processing with 100 percent filtered water may produce less image spotting than using the developer, fix, and wash cycles.

3. Vacuum Freeze-Drying

If it is successful, vacuum freeze-drying eliminates salvage steps like thawing in filtered water and respooling for correct film direction. First frozen in the Mesler freezer, microfilm samples were then vacuum freeze-dried for three weeks using a unit manufactured by VirTis that was located in the freezer. The vacuum pressure was set at 5 microns.

Surprisingly, the microfilm rolled apart easily; it was flat and the emulsion did not stick. Faint tidelines did occur occasionally on the film, possibly because of alkaline water deposits, but these generally did not interfere with readability.

TESTING AND RESULTS

Densitometer readings taken before water immersion and after drying indicated little change in most samples, particularly in the lightest image areas. [TABLE 2]

Weight, length, and temperature variables were abandoned as possible tests for this study. The microfilm technician had to cut the microfilm and add a leader for each roll of film put through the processor; thus, weighing the pieces might have produced an inaccurate measurement. Vacuum freeze-dried film should have yielded an accurate pre- and post-drying weight measurement, but we could not compare this with film put through the processor. This having been said, weights seemed to be approximately 0.10 to 0.01 of a gram less after drying than before. The leader splicing may also have rendered length measurements inaccurate. Finally, the temperature of the Prostar II processor ran on the high side although, visually, the film did not seem to have been affected. There was no visual evidence of mold growth on microfilm immersed in filtered water at 70 degrees F.

Visual inspections of microfilm samples included the use of a light table and magnification, as well as viewing on a Canon NP Reader/Printer 680. Inspections were conducted before, during, and after each step in the experiment.

Densitometer Readings:
Select Examples,
Before and After

Silver Gelatin Film:
Sample 1—Processor
0.73 / 0.76
0.53 / 0.55
0.48 / 0.51
0.09 / 0.08
0.25 / 0.25

Sample 2—Vacuum Freeze-Dried
1.27 / 1.29
1.61 / 1.67
1.01 / 0.99

Sample 3—Processor
1.05 / 1.05
1.54 / 1.51
0.97 / 0.97
0.78 / 0.81

Sample 4—Vacuum Freeze-Dried
1.20 / 1.26
0.28 / 0.29
1.0 / 1.09
0.49 / 0.51

Diazo Film:
Sample 1—Processor
1.42 / 1.46
0.30 / 1.33
1.34 / 0.29

Sample 2—Vacuum Freeze-Dried
0.08 / 0.08
0.68 / 0.65
0.93 / 0.92
0.12 / 0.14

Table 2

1. *Diazo Film*: For diazo film, reducing immersion time seems to be more critical than freezing. Observations during this study showed that after immersion and before freezing, the diazo film formed emulsion blisters, sporadically dispersed throughout the film, creating a bumpy planar distortion. About 30-50 percent of the surface area of film immersed 72 hours and approximately 2-10 percent of the surface area of film immersed five hours were affected—indicating that the longer the immersion time, the greater the possibility of emulsion blisters forming. With the exception of the areas affected by emulsion blisters, frozen diazo films put through the microfilm processor generally appeared flat.

The vacuum freeze-dried microfilm rolls stuck very slightly when first unrolled but continued unrolling easily. Microfilm was unrolled and checked immediately after being removed from the vacuum freeze-dryer. Probably because of the radical temperature change (from 0 degrees F to 70 degrees F), slight condensation occurred during the initial inspection of the film, particularly as one got closer to the core. The film appeared flat and the image area was readable and in good condition. A faintly visible cloudy, milky residual cast occurred on the film, which may have been caused by alkaline water residue. Readability of diazo microfilm put through the processor and through the vacuum freeze-dryer was the same.

2. *Silver Gelatin Film*: After drying, pencil thin, barely visible tidelines occurred on the silver gelatin microfilm rolls along the top and bottom edges, but the film separated easily during processing. Silver gelatin microfilm that was immersed for 72 hours and dried in the microfilm processor that uses water contained some amoebae-like water stain areas that had a translucent sooty appearance. This white haze did not appear in the image area of the microfilm. Cockling of the film base as it unrolled into the microfilm processor increased as one got closer to the hub, making some distortion slightly visible, but this cockling disappeared after processing. Occasionally, silver microfilm immersed in water for 5 hours and vacuum freeze-dried showed large white areas, but the image they covered was still somewhat readable. This white area occurred on only two frames of one microfilm sample. The cause of this type of splotching could be film-to-film contact, sediment, or chemical residue. Generally, silver film put through the processor that uses chemicals appeared flat and clear.

Duplicated Rolls

After they had been immersed and dried, sample rolls were duplicated, and the duplicates were analyzed. Emulsion blisters did not appear on the duplicated microfilms made from the diazo test samples. Duplicates made from diazo films that had been immersed for 72 hours showed some very slight mottling. The image area on all of the diazo duplicated films was readable.

The freeze-dried diazo sample appeared darker than the duplicates made from that sample, yet both had good readability.

Visually comparing the silver gelatin duplicates with the actual test rolls showed good readability of all the microfilm specimens. The film was smooth and flat. The only visible distinction between the rolls was that test sample rolls were pinkish black and the duplicated rolls were greenish black. The brown spots and stains evident on the silver roll that was immersed for five hours and put through the processor did appear on its duplicate.

Photocopies

Photocopies made from sample microfilm rolls before and after the test (as well as photocopies made from post-experiment duplicated rolls of film) were compared to determine the "copyability" of immersed and dried microfilm. The copies were made at three random points on each roll, using a microfilm reader/printer. Various exposures, light to dark, were taken of each frame sampled.

The visual analysis of photocopies made from both diazo and silver gelatin microfilm showed virtually the same clarity and readability for both pre- and post-study image areas. This was true for each exposure made for the test. Photocopies made from post-experiment duplicated microfilms had a heavier image definition but were nonetheless quite readable. The emulsion blisters were actually accentuated on photocopies made from post-study duplicated films, obscuring the image definition. [FIGURE 1] This was particularly true for diazo film immersed for 72 hours and processed through the Prostar using water. With diazo samples an emulsion blister occasionally appeared on the photocopy made from the post-experiment duplicate film, as well as photocopies from diazo films that were vacuum freeze-dried. In some cases, the bold quality of the photocopy made from a duplicated film appeared out of focus and required a lower exposure than did the pre- and post-experiment photocopies. Overall exposures of F34 and F54 seem to be the best for obtaining good image quality and copyability.

An isolated case in which a silver gelatin roll was washed for 72 hours and processed through the Prostar using chemicals showed dark spots obliterating some image areas on the photocopies made from post-experiment duplicate films. [FIGURE 2] After a second run through the processor using water only, the obfuscation was removed and the image clarity returned. [FIGURE 3] This clarity was revealed when another photocopy was made. The results point to the conclusion that the visual obstruction may have been dust, dirt, or chemical residue, ruling out the possibility of scratches or lifting of the emulsion.

A silver gelatin microfilm roll immersed in water for five hours and vacuum freeze-dried evidenced occasional white blotching which showed up on

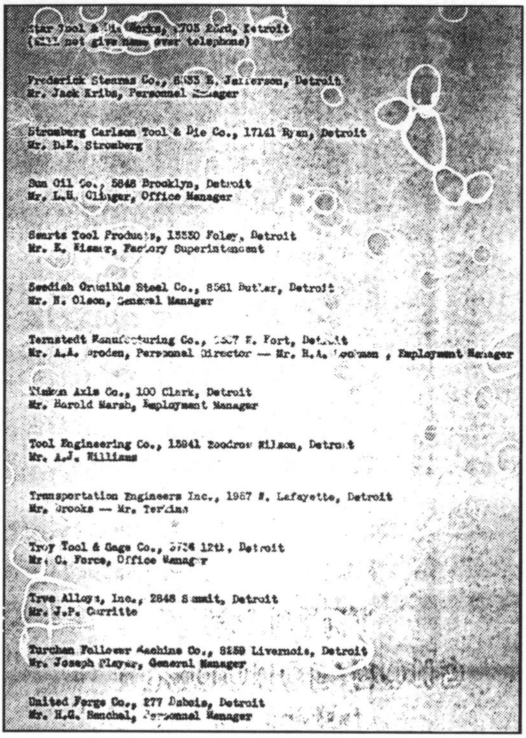

Star Tool & Die Works, 2703 23rd, Detroit
(will not give name over telephone)

Frederick Stearns Co., 6533 E. Jefferson, Detroit
Mr. Jack Kribs, Personnel Manager

Stromberg Carlson Tool & Die Co., 17141 Ryan, Detroit
Mr. D.E. Stromberg

Sun Oil Co., 5848 Brooklyn, Detroit
Mr. L.H. Clinger, Office Manager

Swarts Tool Products, 13330 Foley, Detroit
Mr. E. Wismer, Factory Superintendent

Swedish Crucible Steel Co., 8561 Butler, Detroit
Mr. E. Olson, General Manager

Ternstedt Manufacturing Co., 1507 W. Fort, Detroit
Mr. A.A. Broden, Personnel Director — Mr. H.A. [illegible], Employment Manager

Timken Axle Co., 100 Clark, Detroit
Mr. Harold Marsh, Employment Manager

Tool Engineering Co., 13841 Woodrow Wilson, Detroit
Mr. A.J. Williams

Transportation Engineers Inc., 1987 W. Lafayette, Detroit
Mr. Brooks — Mr. Perkins

Troy Tool & Gage Co., 5734 12th, Detroit
Mr. C. Force, Office Manager

True Alloys, Inc., 2848 Summit, Detroit
Mr. J.P. Corritte

Turchan Follower Machine Co., 8259 Livernois, Detroit
Mr. Joseph Player, General Manager

United Forge Co., 277 Dubois, Detroit
Mr. H.G. Henchel, Personnel Manager

Diazo microfilm emulsion blisters—post-experiment copy (F50 exposure)

Figure 1

the test roll, *post*-drying. [FIGURE 4] This blotching vanished when a copy was made from the post-drying *duplicate*. [FIGURE 5]

For one silver roll, which was washed for 72 hours and then vacuum freeze-dried, the post-drying dimensional stability on the photocopy appeared *better* after the experiment than before. However, the photocopies made from the duplicated roll require longer exposure times to make them readable; at the same time these accent the imperfections on the microfilm. To reproduce a clear copy from the duplicated film seems to surpass the capabilities of this microfilm reader/printer.

MICROFILM SERVICE

Kodak Quality Control Laboratories will rewash, dry, and return rolls of water-damaged film to institutions that use Kodak film and labs. However, they impress upon the customer that restoration means returning films to a condition that makes them usable for information retrieval, not to their original quality. Kodak also states that restoration of the film will not guarantee archival quality, and that silver duplicates must be made from rescued microfilm.[5]

Silver gelatin micro-film with dark spots obliterating image area—post-experiment copy (F39 exposure)

Figure 2

Same silver gelatin microfilm as Figure 2 after rewashing in processor. Spots removed and image area is now visible (F 39 exposure)

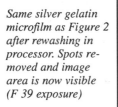

Figure 3

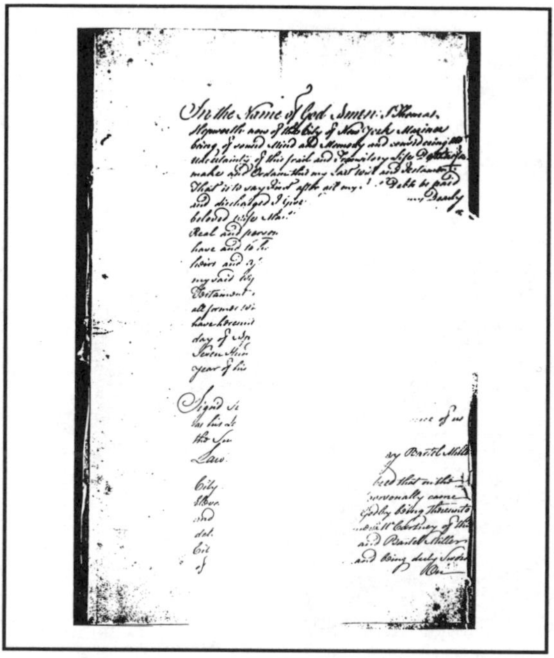

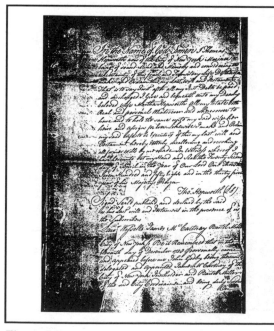

Silver gelatin microfilm after being vacuum freeze-dried showing white obstruction (F35 exposure)

Figure 4

Same image as Figure 4 using after experiment duplicate microfilm copy—white area vanished.

Figure 5

CONCLUSION

Based upon this study, the visual differences between microfilm that was processed after freezing, and microfilm that was processed immediately after it was soaked, were undetectable. Noticeable image damage occurred as the result of immersion, both before freezing and during processing. The few instances of splotching and mottling described in this paper did not interfere with image readability, especially when the film was duplicated or copied on a microfilm reader/printer. After close and carefully documented observation, this study concludes that microfilm can be frozen as a disaster recovery measure, but duplicated copies should be made from the salvaged roll for archival purposes. Advantages to consider when freezing microfilm include curtailing possible damage to film immersed for more than 72 hours, postponing rescue efforts to a more favorable time, and preventing mold growth. Future study of the effects of freezing and mold growth on film, as well as the long-term quality of "restored" microfilm, is appropriate. Finally, the results of this experiment may awaken institutions to the importance of reassessing the location of their microfilm storage facility, with an eye to potential sources of water damage. A savings of salvage operation time and money for microfilm replacement will make this effort worthwhile.

ACKNOWLEDGEMENTS

I would like to thank James M. Brown III, the State Archives Microfilming Supervisor, and David LaPlante from the State Museum Exhibit Preparation Unit, for their assistance with this project.

NOTES

1. The opinions expressed in this paper are the author's; they do not necessarily reflect those of the New York State Archives and Records Administration.
2. Klaus B. Hendriks and Brian Lesser, "Disaster Preparedness and Recovery: Photographic Materials," *American Archivist* 46 (Winter 1983): 52-68.
3. Henry Klein, "Microfilm Resuscitation—A Case Study," *Journal of Micrographics* 9 (1976): 229-303.
4. Hendriks and Lesser, 53.
5. Eastman Kodak Company, *Water-Damaged Film*, Document QC0004 (Mt. Prospect, Ill.: Kodak, n.d.).

The Challenge of Film Preservation in the 1990s

Anthony Slide

Independent Film Scholar

THE AMC FILM PRESERVATION FESTIVAL

The response to the first Film Preservation Festival presented by the cable television network American Movie Classics (AMC) on the weekend of March 12-14, 1993 was in many ways indicative of the problems facing film preservationists in the 1990s. The Festival showed a variety of films preserved in recent years, including *The Last of the Mohicans* (1920), *Hell's Angels* (1930) and *Becky Sharp* (1935), together with informative presentations about preservation, while viewers were encouraged to telephone an 800 number, order VHS tapes of their favorite films, and generally contribute to the saving of America's film heritage. The proceeds were to go to this country's five leading archival film institutions: the International Museum of Photography at George Eastman House, the Library of Congress (LC), the Museum of Modern Art (MOMA), the National Center for Film and Video Preservation at the American Film Institute, and the UCLA Film and Television Archive.

The event was sponsored by the Film Foundation, established in 1990 by director Martin Scorsese and others with the explicit goal of raising a minimum of 30 million dollars for film preservation. Despite the "big name" filmmakers (including Woody Allen and Steven Spielberg) associated with the Foundation, its efforts at fund raising to date have been nothing short of abysmal. It was Martin Scorsese's intent that the AMC Film Preservation Festival would bring in $150,000 from the general public and a further $150,000 from the film industry. While exact figures have not been made public, it is understood that approximately $115,000 was contributed by the television audience. Scorsese sent out personal letters to 75 prominent figures in the film community, including studio heads and executives who will ultimately benefit from the preservation of their films. This appeal to the industry raised the grand sum of $5,000, of which $3,000 came from Jeffrey Katzenberg of the Walt Disney Studios.

FILM PRESERVATION:
WHAT DOES IT COST AND WHO IS PAYING?

The Costs of Preserving Films

In that it costs approximately $15,000 to preserve one black-and-white feature film in 35mm and between $30,000 and $60,000 to preserve an average 35mm color feature film, it is obvious that the Film Preservation Festival was a financial disaster for the archival film community. Routinely, the major American film archives receive an average of $100,000 a year from the National Endowment for the Arts (NEA). Nitrate stock, on which all films made before 1950 were shot, is unstable, highly inflammable, and continues to decompose at an alarming rate, while financial resources slowly disappear. Ironically, money for film preservation is disappearing faster than the films that need to be preserved or restored. What little cash is available from the private sector tends to be given for the preservation of a specific film or group of films, often with sentimental appeal to the donor but in no immediate need of preservation.

It is the so-called "orphan films," those which no producer or studio claims and that lack viable commercial potential, that are in the most immediate danger. Unless funding is found for their preservation, these films will be lost to future generations. They lack glamour, and their directors and stars have no cult following, no audience recognition. In some cases, the cost of their preservation is higher than the cost of their production.

Government Funding vs. Public Access

It has become increasingly obvious to observers of the film preservation scene in the United States that major Hollywood studios and production companies have taken unfair advantage of the government funding for preservation available through the National Endowment for the Arts. Rather than finance the preservation of their assets themselves, these companies have waited until the process was paid for by the taxpayer. Then, because they own the copyrights to such films, they are able to block access to the preserved or restored product by others and release the films to television or home video, promoting them as recently restored. Film preservationists find themselves in an untenable situation in that, while fully cognizant of the commercial exploitation of their work, they can offer no protest because the copyright owners have the potential simply to remove their films from the protection of the nation's archives and thus derail the preservation of America's national heritage.

As onerous as the cost of preserving or restoring a film is the cost of storing nitrate films. In an effort to avoid shouldering such expenses, copyright holders have often donated or deposited their nitrate film holdings with the various American film archives. When films are donated, those who own the rights to them typically retain copyright and control of access, while often using the gift as a tax write-off. Thus a system has developed in which copyright owners benefit financially from giving their films to archives, while at the same time preventing access to the films by other parties and requiring the American taxpayer, through the National Endowment for the Arts, to finance the storage and preservation of these controlled assets.

The National Film Preservation Act

Some donors have even been able to circumvent U.S. copyright laws which place a maximum copyright term of 75 years on any film: a number of major Hollywood studios donated films to the Library of Congress but required a deed of gift allowing them control over the films in perpetuity. These and other revelations came to light when the Librarian of Congress held hearings in Los Angeles and Washington, D.C. in February and March 1993, as authorized by the National Film Preservation Act of 1992 (Public Law 102-307). These hearings marked a new and, it is hoped, important step forward by the National Film Preservation Board, created by Congress in 1988.

Despite its title, the Board (which is made up of representatives from various institutions in the film industry) has nothing to do with film preservation, but rather annually selects 25 films that are culturally, historically, or aesthetically significant for addition to the National Film Registry.[1] This is a meaningless activity heavily influenced by politics. For example, D.W. Griffith's *The Birth of a Nation* (1915), arguably the most important film of all time, was not added to the Registry until 1992 because of objections to its perceived racism, and then only after two productions cast with (*Carmen Jones*, 1954) or produced by (*Within Our Gates*, 1920) African-Americans were added in the same year.

Perhaps because Librarian of Congress James Billington (unlike the major American film archivists) has no direct tie to or reliance on the film industry, he has proven to be a strong advocate of a national film preservation program and an ardent critic of the film industry. He has described industry executives as "misguided and shortsighted," and complained that the support of the Hollywood studios for preserving old films does not extend beyond cocktail party chatter.[2] Billington would like to see the film industry contribute significant resources toward film preservation. Others at the hearings argued for a film preservation tax, to be levied on all theater tickets and home video sales and rentals.

The Proper Role of the Film Studios

There is an immediate need for producers to support the preservation of their films in national libraries, archives, and similar institutions. Further, when a copyright owner profits from the preservation of one of his or her films through its subsequent release on videotape or laser disk, either a royalty should be paid to the preserving archive, or the copyright owner should reap no profit until the full cost of preservation has been earned and returned to the agency that funded the work.

Studios argue that there is little need for public preservation of their films, claiming that they handle the preservation of their assets internally. Sadly, such preservation activities do not meet archival standards and are typically linked to a film's commercial potential. With the honorable exceptions of the Turner and Walt Disney organizations that have long ago adopted an enlightened film preservation program, Hollywood studios understand little if anything about what constitutes preservation. Rather than go to a specialized laboratory equipped for preservation requirements, studios turn to major laboratories with whom they have long-term contracts; such laboratories are only able to handle the mass production of multiple-release prints.

PRESERVATION AND ACCESS: THE CHALLENGE OF THE COMMITTEE FOR FILM PRESERVATION AND PUBLIC ACCESS

One group presenting a major challenge to film archivists is the Committee for Film Preservation and Public Access, an independent organization which correctly argues that preservation without access is pointless.[3] While archives generally offer space and equipment for a scholar or student to study an individual film, they often have no provision for films to be screened for larger groups in theaters or seminar rooms. Archivists have typically been unable (because of restrictions imposed by donors or copyright owners) or unwilling to permit preserved films to be released on videotape for general consumption. One archivist at the Museum of Modern Art has argued that films were not meant to be seen on video, and therefore the Museum will not permit any of its preserved films to be transferred to and screened in this format. (This is a nebulous argument, in view of the home video revolution of recent years.)

Whether archives' restrictions are donor-driven or self-imposed, access is an immediate challenge facing all of them, with the Committee for Film Preservation and Public Access arguing that immediate or eventual availability should be a requirement for all Federal funding for film preservation. Among the titles to which the Committee points as examples are *A Farewell to Arms* (1932) and *Meet John Doe* (1942), both preserved by the Library of Congress in superior, complete versions. Both are in the public domain, but because of restrictions by one-time copyright owners these versions cannot be screened publicly. Similarly, *For Whom the Bell Tolls* (1943) has been restored by the UCLA Film and Television Archive, but the copyright owner refuses to permit that version to be released on video.

The perspective of copyright owners, donors, and some archivists on films in public archives is reminiscent of the attitude toward the printed page in the Middle Ages, when only the privileged were privy to the beauty of language. It was once the serfs who paid the taxes, but were prohibited from reading. In the 1990s, it is the American taxpayer who funds film preservation, but is denied access to that for which his or her tax dollars have paid. Film preservation cannot operate in a vacuum, and films can only come alive when they are seen. Archivists and preservationists of the 1990s have an obligation not only to preserve films, but to present them to the public.

FINDING "MISSING" FILMS: THE EXAMPLE OF BRITAIN'S NATIONAL FILM ARCHIVE

In 1980, primarily as a publicity stunt, the American Film Institute issued a list of the "10 Most Wanted" films: *Frankenstein* (1910), *Cleopatra* (1917), *The Kaiser, the Beast of Berlin* (1918), *Little Red Riding Hood* (1922), *Greed* (1923), *That Royle Girl* (1926), *London After Midnight* (1927), *Camille* (1927), *The Divine Woman* (1928), and *Rogue Song* (1930). The response was disappointing, in that a print of *Frankenstein* was uncovered (its existence was already known), together with a two-and-a-half minute clip from *Rogue Song* and a few feet of *Cleopatra*. The other films on the list remain lost.

Recognizing the need to preserve its national heritage rather than simply films of glamorous appeal, in 1992 Britain's National Film Archive published a book titled *Missing Believed Lost*, authored by film historian Allen Eyles and the Archive's Keeper of Feature Films David Meeker. It pointed out that Alfred Hitchcock's second feature film as director, *Mountain Eagle*, is lost, but it also documented lost films by obscure British directors such as George Pearson, Walter Forde, and Bernard Vorhaus, and featuring performers little known on the international scene, such as comedian Max Miller. The project was financed by British-based millionaire J. Paul Getty, Jr. who, unlike his American counterparts, has contributed vast sums toward film preservation. Of the 100 films discussed in *Missing Believed Lost*, some 10 have been located since publication of the book.

If nothing else, the British endeavor illustrated yet again the need to find and preserve the lesser productions of motion picture history, a challenge that fund raisers in the United States have difficulty addressing. As Clyde Jeavons, curator of the National Film Archive, explained to the *New York Times*, "We're still in the primeval history of the moving image, and to have lost anything is a tragedy. It's rarely the well-known classics; it's the middle-of-the-road material, which makes up the bulk of cinema history."[4]

PRESERVATION VS. RESTORATION

The need some feel to glorify the film preservation process is nowhere more obvious than in the interchangeable use of the words *preservation* and *restoration*. To announce that a film has been *preserved* is considered old-fashioned and unexciting. It is now necessary to *restore* a film. A studio executive picks up the telephone and orders a laboratory to make a new print of a 20-year-old film for screening at a revival house. Without fail, the advertising will announce the presentation of a newly-restored print. To the layman, such distinctions might not seem important, but not only does the common use of the word *restore* belittle the work of the preservation technicians who really do restore films, it also raises questions about the responsibility a preservation specialist accepts in tackling the "restoration" rather than the preservation of a motion picture. (For more on this topic, see FILM RESTORATION: PROBLEMS OF DEFINITION AND APPROACH heading, next page.)

The preservation of a film generally involves its transfer from volatile nitrate film stock to so-called safety film, which has an acetate base. It also means safeguarding original or master elements (in the case of a film made after 1950, a negative or a finegrain [positive]) through storage in temperature- and humidity-controlled vaults. The FIAF (International Federation of Film Archives) Preservation Commission recommends that films be stored at a temperature of 23 degrees F and 30 percent humidity, but adds, "Archivists should not be disheartened by the low temperature recommended above, but always keep in mind that every degree the temperature is lowered is beneficial. For example, a reduction of approximately $6°$ C will double the useful life of almost any material."[5]

The physical preservation of a film is a relatively simple, if expensive, process, and dependant on the extant original elements. If the original picture and sound negative exists, new master materials in the form of finegrains must be made. If a positive print or a finegrain (a positive master element) is the only existing material, a new negative can be manufactured. Laboratory procedures do not permit making a negative from a negative. Similarly, it is not possible to make a viewing print from a finegrain: first a negative must be made, and from that a positive print.

If the film was shot in 35mm negative, each element that must be produced before a viewing print can be made constitutes one step (or one generation) farther from the original master material. The more elements that must be made before a print can be struck, the more degraded such a print will be. Original nitrate prints when projected look beautiful, not only because they were struck from negatives closer to (or perhaps even from) the original camera negative, but also because Eastman Kodak utilized more silver in the manufacture of its film stock in the first half of the 20th century, resulting in more vibrant blacks and whites. It is physically impossible to reproduce the look of an original nitrate print, but the dedicated preservation specialist must attempt to create a negative from which a print can be struck that approximates the appearance of nitrate as closely as possible.

FILM RESTORATION:
PROBLEMS OF DEFINITION AND APPROACH

Restoration, on the other hand, involves far more than the mere copying of a film for preservation. Films consist of two separate and distinct elements, picture and sound, and these materials can easily become separated or exist in different forms. As a result, for example, while a 35mm picture negative may survive, the soundtrack negative can be lost. To restore the film, the preservation specialist must locate a soundtrack from another source, perhaps a 16mm positive print, and match that with the picture negative. If a frame or two of the negative is gone, then the soundtrack must be edited to match the picture; similarly, if there is a cut in the soundtrack, the restorer must edit the picture negative to match.

In many instances, a producer cuts a film for reissue and destroys the sections he or she has removed. To restore the film to its original form, one must seek out the missing pieces, which may be gone in negative form but may have survived in the shape of an original release print. Because a print is inferior to a negative, the restorer tries to work as much as possible with the negatives, or masters, but resorts to sections from a release print to fill in the missing parts.

Not only is the restoration process a complicated technical one, it also raises serious ethical questions. To what extent can and should a restorer tamper with the film? Who decides what represents the definitive version of a film? Purists argue that the film should be restored to the director's "cut," the length and form of the film as established by its maker, but often the production company changes a film before its first screening, and the film as seen at its premiere is not as it was edited by its director.

Should a film preservation specialist consider a restoration nothing more than an academic exercise, or should he or she also be aware of the need for a contemporary audience to enjoy the film-going experience? For example, when a scene is missing in picture form but exists as a soundtrack, should the restorer allow the sound to play while the audience looks at a blank screen, or should he or she edit a series of stills, perhaps not even from the missing portion of the film, in an attempt to provide visuals to match the soundtrack?

The Special Problems of Silent Films

Problems also abound in silent films. If a subtitle is missing, should the restorer write one based on what he or she believes the original title stated? If a scene from a silent film is missing, ought the specialist write a title to link it to the next scene, or incorporate extant still photographs of that scene? The most prominent of all American silent film directors, D.W. Griffith, displayed a penchant for revising his films after their initial presentation; as a result, it is often difficult to determine how one of his motion pictures looked at its premiere, compared to how it was seen by audiences a month later: a serious question arises as to what was the director's cut of the film.

Peter Williamson at the Museum of Modern Art has restored two of Griffith's films, *Intolerance* (1916) and *Way Down East* (1920), and major questions have arisen among both scholars and the audience as to the validity of such restorations. The star of *Way Down East*, Lillian Gish, was offended by the introduction of still photographs from missing scenes into the restoration of her film, believing that this destroyed the flow of the production. *Intolerance* is one of the most controversial of all film restorations. Based on individual frames of film from the start of each scene that were deposited with the Library of Congress for copyright purposes and an extant copy of the original music score, the restoration of *Intolerance* has outraged many devotees of D.W. Griffith who argue that the restored version is not the film as Griffith intended it to be seen.[6] The fact that the restoration was undertaken by the Museum of Modern Art gives it a benediction or sanction from that prestigious organization that is at odds with the general reaction to the finished product.

The Ethics of Restoration: A Variety of Viewpoints

The preservation program at the Museum of Modern Art was headed for many years by Eileen Bowser, who joined the Museum staff in 1954 and retired at the beginning of 1993. She is outspoken in her definition of film restoration:

> As far as the Museum of Modern Art is concerned, our chief goal in doing film restoration is to try and get as close as we can to what the audience saw on opening night. I don't think we have any interest in what might be popular. I think that belongs more to the commercial world than the world of archives. In other words, we have the interest of a film historian to try the best we can to recreate that original experience, although, of course, we're not the same audience at all, and we know that.[7]

The best known exponent of film restoration in the United States is Robert Gitt, the Preservation Officer of the UCLA Film and Television Archive. He became prominent in 1984 with the restoration of *Becky Sharp* (1935), the first three- or full-color Technicolor feature, followed two years later by the restoration of *Toll of the Sea* (1922), the first Technicolor two-color feature film. He has a number of pungent comments to make on film restoration:

> A part of restoration that people don't talk about is restoring the technical quality of the picture sound and color to the level of quality when the film first came out. Restoration is not only a matter of restoring the director's cut, missing scenes, or putting a film back to its original length.
>
> I am most in favor of restoring films to how they looked when they first came out. Restoration becomes controversial when it is a question of restoring a film to the way it looked before release, its preview version or whatever. If you do that, then you should also restore the film to how it looked when first seen by the general public so that the contemporary audience can compare the two.
>
> Sometimes to restore a film you have to be prepared to make modifications in order for it to play smoothly to an audience today, thereby restoring it to how the director would want it to look if he was around today. As an example, if I am working from the best surviving materials on a film and one frame has an ugly blemish across the face of a performer, if you can cut out that frame without creating a jump in the action, you should remove it because the film will look better to the audience. In dealing with a director like Sergei Eisenstein where every frame counts you wouldn't do this, but in the average Hollywood film, where dialogue and performance are the main centers of focus, I don't think it's a serious problem to take out a first or last frame of a shot. And in most cases, the director of the film would not be aware of what you have done.
>
> It's a question of judgment. You should always explain what you have done, and never try and fool anybody. My goal is not to put in every frame of the film if that is going to make the film look bad. I'm more interested in the film as a work of art than as part of the field of academic discussion.[8]

If there were not already sufficient controversy over the technical issue of film restoration, a further dispute has arisen between preservationists working in public archives and independent film restoration experts, who work on an individual basis for major studios and charge substantial fees for their skills: there is a natural suspicion between the two groups. Commercial restraints and demands are the overriding influences on the independents, led by Robert Harris who was responsible for the 1988 restoration of *Lawrence of Arabia* (1962) and the 1991 restoration of *Spartacus* (1960). Some commercial restorations, such as the 1992 rehabilitation of Orson Welles' *Othello* (1952) which replaced the original soundtrack with one featuring stereophonic sound and effects, are disturbing to purists within the archival film community, particularly when such enhancements are not made clear to the viewing public.

Cooperation: A Valuable Product of Restoration Efforts

One positive side effect of film restoration has been the development of closer working relationships within film's archival and preservation communities. To restore a film, preservationists must seek out all extant elements, and this means communicating with their fellows not only in the United States but also throughout the world. Mutual work on a project can also result. In the late 1920s, Warner Brothers released many hundreds of short subjects that utilized the Vitaphone process, with the sound on a separate disk. The picture negatives were donated to the Library of Congress, but the disks were believed lost until their recent discovery by the UCLA Film and Television Archive at Warner's Burbank Studios. The Library of Congress has slowly been making the picture elements available, and Robert Gitt at UCLA has been synchronizing them with the disks and transferring the sound to film. The results benefit not only the archival community, but also allow contemporary audiences to appreciate the many musical and vaudeville performers whose work has survived only in those Vitaphone short subjects.

SAFETY FILM: SAFE OR NOT?

On the technical front, the archival film community faced a major setback in the late 1980s, and one that will continue to be a challenge in the years to come. With reason, film preservationists had assumed that their primary responsibility was the transfer of film from volatile, unstable nitrate film stock to acetate-based safety film. Nitrate film had a lifespan of less than 50 years, whereas safety film was "guaranteed" to last for at least 200—or so it was assumed.

For a number of years, preservationists had been noticing the pungent odor of acetic acid emanating from some safety films, evidence of film stock deterioration. Because of the smell, the phenomenon has come to be known as the vinegar syndrome, a warning of the grim reality that safety film may be as unstable as nitrate. The deterioration of cellulose triacetate (the technical term for safety film) was first noted by Eastman Kodak in the 1950s, in connection with Indian government film that had been stored in a hot, humid climate. Kodak began laboratory studies of the problem in the 1960s, and in

1991 revealed that safety film deterioration "derives from the same chemical mechanism (hydrolysis) and the same triggering factors in the environment (heat and humidity) that nitrate decomposition does."[9] Without the hoopla and publicity surrounding nitrate film decomposition, we now see that safety film has also been decomposing with the same finality.

The late Henri Langlois, the irascible founder of the Cinémathèque Française, had always argued that to preserve nitrate film one should copy it onto new nitrate film stock. At the time this was a laughable suggestion, but now it seems not without merit. Whereas the major thrust of the archival community had been to transfer nitrate film to safety film and then dispose of the nitrate as quickly as possible, in the 1990s it is as important to safeguard the nitrate film, storing it under ideal conditions of low temperature and humidity, until it can be copied onto a medium more stable than today's safety film.

In addition to Eastman Kodak's testing, the Belgium-based Agfa Company conducted a scientific study in 1987. Two years later, scientists at England's Manchester Polytechnic undertook a second study, financed by the National Film Archive and Eastman Kodak.[10] This confirmed the earlier findings on the potential deterioration of cellulose triacetate film, linking injury to improper storage and the metal cans in which the film was housed (which, it was noted, acted as a powerful catalyst).

All of these studies confirm that safety film may have a life of 50 years or less. Further, archivists must now consider the necessity of storing safety films not in cheap and easily obtainable metal cans but in glass (which is chemically inert), acid-free paperboard, or stable plastic containers. Because of the durability of metal cans, it was possible to stack up to six reels of film, one can on top of another, in storage spaces. Plastic or paperboard boxes cannot tolerate the weight of this number of rolls of film; as a result, archivists must reconsider and increase storage capabilities. (Films must be stored flat rather than on their side.) The regular monitoring of safety film is now as important as the continual watch over nitrate holdings because (just as with nitrate film) once a piece of safety film shows signs of deterioration, such deterioration (in the form of a gas emitted by the film) can spread to and affect other films in the same storage area.

Preservationists and Eastman Kodak continue to work on the problem, watched from the sidelines by a nervous film industry that must also consider the potential danger of the vinegar syndrome to its commercial library holdings. In December 1992, Eastman Kodak announced the introduction of a molecular sieve, described as "a kind of sponge which, when packed in a film can like the small pillow-like packets often used in hardware packaging, absorb moisture and damaging contaminants released during the natural aging of stored film."[11] This molecular sieve's potential for damage control remains uncertain and undetermined.

VIDEOTAPE: AN ARCHIVAL ALTERNATIVE?

The transfer of film to videotape is, of course, not considered an archival alternative for preservation in that videotape has a lifespan of as little as five years, and has its own inherent preservation problems. However, experiments with high-definition and digital video formats offer some hope for the future. It is relatively inexpensive to copy a film to video rather than to film, and the loss of quality from one generation to another is substantially reduced. Many "orphan films" that are today considered unlikely contenders for preservation because of their low rating in film history might at least be copied to video, with the valid argument that video is better than nothing.

CELEBRATING FILM'S 100TH BIRTHDAY

The 1990s mark the 100th anniversary of the birth of the motion picture. The exact year of its nativity is, of course, open to argument, but in no other decade would it be more appropriate to urge a solution to the preservation problems facing what is (again arguably) America's only home-grown art form. It has been estimated that all the extant nitrate film in the United States could be copied for $100 million, a sum that is relatively small and which many distinguished figures in the film community could contribute with no noticeable change to their lifestyles.

The governments of many small countries, including the Scandinavian bloc, have made funds available to preserve the entire film output of their nations. British film production is not insubstantial, and yet 73 percent of all British films produced between 1929 and 1975 are safeguarded at the National Film Archive. But in the United States, it is claimed that 75 percent of all U.S.-made silent films are now lost, and that 50 percent of all American films made before 1950 no longer exist.

This is a sorry record but one, of course, for which film archivists should not be expected to shoulder the blame. Furthermore, it is sad to say that, if a generous film industry executive or government agency were to make $100 million available tomorrow for film preservation, there is no guarantee that the job could be done in a timely fashion. The number of qualified technicians is small, and they are outnumbered at all American archives by bureaucrats. Film preservation requires not only funding but also specialized laboratories. Most commercial laboratories can handle only the simplest preservation work. The majority of U.S. laboratories are no longer capable of dealing with black-and-white film, the medium in which most films in need of preservation exist. The Library of Congress is the only U.S. public film archive with its own in-house laboratory. The other archives must rely on just four laboratories—three in Los Angeles and one in New Jersey—equipped and staffed to meet archival needs and standards.

The future is grim and the challenges many for film preservation. As we celebrate film's 100th anniversary in the 1990s, unless significant action is taken there will be little left to celebrate a century from now, at the time of film's bicentennial.

NOTES

1. The National Preservation Board is made up of representatives from the Academy of Motion Picture Arts and Sciences, the American Film Institute, the American Society of Cinematographers, the Directors Guild of America, the International Federation of Film Archives (FIAF), the Motion Picture Association of America, the National Association of Broadcasters, the National Association of Theatre Owners, the National Society of Film Critics, the Department of Cinema Studies of New York University, the Screen Actors Guild, the Society for Cinema Studies, the UCLA Department of Film and Television, the University Film & Video Association, and the Writers Guild of America, together with two delegates at large (currently Roger Mayer of Turner Entertainment and director John Singleton). No working film archivist serves on the Board.
2. Quoted in Brooks Boliek, "U.S. Librarian Lectures Studios on Preservation," *Hollywood Reporter*, 1 March 1993, 1.
3. Members of the Committee for Film Preservation and Public Access include the author, film historians William K. Everson and Leonard Maltin, law professor L. Ray Patterson, and film director Joe Dante.
4. Quoted in Matt Wolf, "Britain's Film Archivists Hunt for the Missing Links," *New York Times*, 3 January 1933, H18.
5. Henning Schou, *Preservation of Moving Images and Sound* (Brussels: Preservation Commission of the International Federation of Film Archives, 1989), 26.
6. The most detailed and exhaustive argument in opposition to the restored version of *Intolerance* is Russell Merritt, "D. W. Griffith's *Intolerance*: Reconstructing an Unattainable Text," *Film History* 4 (1990): 337-75.
7. Eileen Bowser, interview with the author, 4 February 1991.
8. Robert Gitt, interview with the author, 5 May 1993.
9. Eastman Kodak Company press release, n.d.
10. These three studies (Kodak, Agfa, and Manchester Polytechnic) were privately circulated; none has been published.
11. Eastman Kodak Company press release, n.d.

Here Today, Gone Tomorrow? Why We Should Preserve Electronic Documents

Jan Michaels

Preservation Policy and Planning Officer
National Library of Canada

THE COMMUNICATIONS REVOLUTION

It seems to me a curious thing that no one has named a computer or a system or a database Aquarius. I say it's curious, because one would think that somewhere someone would have connected the extraordinary revolution in communication to the dawning of a new age. We have Apples and Artfls and BITNETS, but nothing grand, nothing momentous-sounding. Perhaps the closest simile for the extraordinary transformation through which we are living is Ted Nelson's Xanadu project, with its promise of an earthly paradise. I don't mean to imply that electronic information, global networks, or even virtual realities can create a virtual heaven here on earth; however, we are at the beginning of an extraordinary new era paralleling the invention of the printing press, or perhaps even writing itself.

This paper discusses preservation of electronic published information and why it is important. It is the tremendous respect I have for the cultural transformation through which we are living that prompts me to write it: unless we act quickly, we will lose much of the history of our early forays into electronic communication. I will not discuss the thorny issue of what is, and what is not, published electronic information ("The recent furor over 'cold fusion'. . .developed entirely outside the scholarly-journal process,"[1] for example), nor whether it is the responsibility of a library or archive to preserve it. However, continued understanding of evolving and potentially important scientific fields of study—the results of which are being updated daily—is enabled only through the *recording* of scholarly communication. This record is critical to scientific inquiry, as well as to the history of science. Certainly, whether the information appears in a "prepublication phase of scientific inquiry in which ideas and findings are discussed informally with colleagues"[2] or in an electronic peer-reviewed journal, someone should be thinking about saving it: I leave the *who* for another time. What is unquestionable is that the preservation of electronic information is critically important.

SCHOLARLY INFORMATION:
DO WE ONLY WANT THE NEW?

It is strange that relatively few libraries have thought about the preservation of electronic information. I believe that there are several reasons for this. One relates to the increasing influence of computer and information scientists in library science. Computer science brings an additional professional perspective to the library. This field specializes in information, as opposed to knowledge in the broader sense. It is based in that which is timely and current. Equipment and software often become outdated in less than three years. The computer scientist needs what is fastest, what is most advanced.

This is not true, however, of all the sciences. The Research Libraries Group (RLG) study, "Information Needs in the Sciences: An Assessment," involved interviewing and consulting 131 people either doing teaching or research, or closely connected to scientific research, in eight scientific disciplines. These disciplines included physics, chemistry, biology, geoscience, astronomy, engineering, mathematics, and computer science. In a striking finding, computer science was uniquely identified as the only field in which items older than 10 years had no perceived relevance. Scholars in all other sciences expressed a permanent need for earlier materials.[3]

Contrast the needs of the computer scientists to those of the physicists. Physicists were found to be among the most active and enthusiastic users of electronic networks.[4] At the same time, however, a significant number of monographs dating from 1850 onward and printed on highly acidic paper were judged to be quite important by these scientists.[5] The fragility of both electronic and paper media "may ultimately pose a threat to the orderly reporting and maintenance of the records of research results."[6]

Chemists are in a similar position. "Fast access to current literature certainly ranks first among chemists' information needs, but access to retrospective literature is probably a close second."[7] This is not surprising, since chemical and physical properties do not change over time. Thus far, full-text databases have had little success with chemists; the authors of the RLG report, Gould and Pearce, cite several reasons for their lack of enthusiasm: the journals offered online are also those most commonly available in print; the cost of online access is high; finally, and most significantly, online journals do not include diagrams and illustrations, and some of the most important information is therefore lost.[8] This attitude toward online information may change when illustrations can be embedded in electronic texts.

Compare also computer scientists and geoscientists, who require access to an exceptionally wide range of materials, widely dispersed in terms of time and place of publication, sources, and formats.[9] And what of astronomers, for whom "many observations recorded in the Middle Ages are as useful as those made yesterday"?[10] Even old engineering publications are important: "When petroleum became more expensive in the mid-1970s, for example, research in other fossil fuels going as far back as the 1920s was heavily consulted."[11]

Mathematicians are a step further removed. The RLG study found that "most mathematicians prefer a departmental library devoted only to mathematics because it makes browsing easy. They like to know they will find the green book halfway down aisle three that they have consulted before."[12] This is directly in contrast to computer scientists, who responded that they prefer electronic communication to print.[13] The point is *not* that books are more important than electronic data.[14] The point is, that access to information is important. Often that access is tied to physical characteristics that enable an item to be located easily. More importantly, often the information required may be decades or centuries old. If the information is electronic rather than paper-based, on whose virtual bookshelves will it sit?

ELECTRONIC INFORMATION: WHY DON'T WE TAKE IT SERIOUSLY?

The sciences are not the only areas to have been bitten by the electronic byte. Numerous databases in the arts, humanities, and social sciences are online. Project Gutenberg, for example, begun in 1971, has as its goal "to provide a collection of 10,000 of the most used books by the year 2000, and to reduce. . .the effective costs to the user to a price of approximately one cent per book."[15] The intent is to have all materials available to all patrons, from all locations, at all times.

When this author asked a number of electronic publishers how they thought people would be able to access today's documents 40 years into the future, most respondents discussed online availability—"the net will save it"—or they indicated that because many people subscribed to their publications, many copies would survive—perhaps some as printouts on permanent paper. This somewhat cavalier attitude toward contemporary information may be related to the general disillusionment we as a culture seem to be suffering: little that is electronic seems to possess real importance. Perhaps this perspective is directly related to electronic information's relative immaturity:

> The currently low intellectual level of the net is purely the result of incidental initial conditions. The medium was created by engineers and computer scientists, and they (along with students, reared on video games, with little knowledge, and a lot of time on their hands) are the ones who have been setting people's expectations and standards so far, giving the impression that the net is just a global graffiti board for trivial pursuit. But this initial condition . . . is surely destined to rectify itself as the net's demography

changes and the serious demonstrations of its scholarly potential start to appear.[16]

But, as we all know, this begs the question. Even if the calibre of network
communications will only improve, we must still capture examples of yesterday and today's primitive steps, as well as the first signs of genius. There are
many sad precedents for loss of the commonplace: for hundreds of years,
children learned their alphabets from hornbooks. These are now among the
rarest of 17th-, 18th- and 19th-century artifacts. The National Library of
Canada does not own any. The world-famous Osborne Collection of Early
Children's Books in Toronto only owns five. Can we really assume that
serendipity will be kinder to electronic information? In 1984, Gordon Neavill
wrote an important article called "Electronic Publishing, Libraries, and the
Survival of Information." In it he says:

> So far as I am aware, proponents of computer-based
> electronic systems have not addressed the issue of the
> long-term survival of information. Perhaps they are an-
> chored intellectually in the world of print more than they
> realize. In our familiar print-based environment, the distri-
> bution and the survival of recorded information are so
> closely linked by the physical object in which information
> is recorded that we ordinarily don't think of them as sepa-
> rate issues. The distribution of recorded information neces-
> sarily involves the acquisition of the physical objects in
> which information is recorded. With the acquisition of
> these objects, the survival of information follows automati-
> cally, as long as the objects are retained. In an environment
> in which recorded information is distributed without a
> physical container, the link between distribution and sur-
> vival is broken. The survival of information in an elec-
> tronic environment becomes an intellectual and
> technological problem in its own right.[17]

PRESERVING ELECTRONIC MEDIA: WHAT ARE THE CHALLENGES?

Besides chronicling the past, the new electronic revolution is enabling
publishers to do things previously thought impossible. In " 'The Electronic
Archive': Scientific Publishing for the 1990s" William Gardner describes
what electronic scholarly publishing will be able to achieve: "The near future
will provide revolutionary technologies for the interactive display of scientific information with motion, color, sound, and three dimensions."[18] Instead
of simple audiotapes of conference proceedings, integration of audiovisuals
will be possible in one medium. He insists that electronic publishing "must

provide improved facilities for retrieving information, while continuing to serve as a permanent archive of the society."[19]

From multimedia it is but one step to hypermedia, where animation, electronic models, moving pictures, and sound are linked to conventional text. When hypertext or hypermedia databases and documents become widespread, the problems of electronic preservation will have to be faced by libraries and other repositories. These publications will compound the problems already faced by those responsible for the preservation of electronic publications, because there will be, and can be, no print equivalent. Once a work is authored specifically for the electronic medium, it will be difficult to convert it to a human-readable medium, without the loss of a major part of that work's character. Thus, these works must be preserved in electronic form.[20]

The *Online Journal of Current Clinical Trials* is an electronic journal that has already considered preservation issues. The publisher saves it on computer, with daily backups. The intention is to keep five years of it online, with the rest archived in a separate file. In addition, an archival-quality microfiche is made and each subscriber receives a copy once a year. For now, the microfiche is the prime means by which the journal is preserved. In a telephone conversation the managing editor, Maria Lebron, acknowledged that working with microfiche is less than ideal.[21] The great searching facility electronic publishing provides is missing on microfiche; an important element of the publication has been lost. This significant loss can be compared to that of much art work when a book is microfilmed.

Other publications cannot even be replicated on microfilm:

> The Brookhaven national labs have a database of three dimensional images of organic molecules that are posted and peer reviewed online. These graphic images are approximations based upon x-ray diffraction data and may be rotated in three dimensions; no two-dimensional print images could adequately represent this data.[22]

Thus, even if information technology creates new formats for new kinds of knowledge, these formats supplement today's print collections—they do not substitute for them. Each format must be uniquely appropriate to the content and the use of the knowledge it expresses.[23]

THE MEDIUM IS [PART OF] THE MESSAGE

Electronic publishing's remarkable new facility—its interactivity, its incredible speed, its global potential, its ability to shapeshift and to make sounds—will substantially restructure our culture. In the nineties, "information" seems to be valued above "knowledge," a term increasingly perceived as old-fashioned. Over the course of Western history, the source of wisdom has been defined as the tree of knowledge, then the book of knowledge, and now as information technology. Information technology is simply another point in the continuum of knowledge. As Peter Lyman suggests, "Information technology includes cultural values as well as hardware or format; the conceptual tools that shape the way knowledge is defined are technologies."[24] Our culture values the facility information technology brings us—the brain is no longer described as a muscle, but as a computer. Only through the hindsight of history will we be able to appreciate the true impact of this technology on our culture, our values, and our perceptions.

Whatever information delivery medium comes next, one thing is certain: its technology will be radically different from any of its predecessors, just as electronic technology is drastically different from paper and paper is different from clay. One of the major advantages of computer-based electronic systems, malleability of information, has as its corollary the potential transience of information. Nothing inherent in the technology of computer-based electronic systems ensures that information in the system will survive.[25] And yet survive it must, as a record of our culture and (on a more mundane, practical level) because it could be used as legal evidence. When information is liberated from the confines of a physical container, it is rendered vulnerable. It can be altered or revised without offering any clue that a change has been made. It can even be altogether purged, and thus forever lost.[26]

"WHAT IS LITERATURE?" INFORMATION TECHNOLOGY TANGLES THE QUESTION

The implications of all of this for scholarship are mind-boggling. "Blue sky" writings on the wonders of the computer age often describe the scholar of the future at his terminal, instantly able to call up any book or article from the world's literature. Wrong. . . . Instead, proliferation of texts available in multiple forms, with no clear line between early drafts and final printed versions, may overwhelm any identification of "the world's literature."[27]

How do we prove that one scientist reported his or her findings first, or that one poet rather than another wrote a sonnet, if we have not saved an original copy in an unadulterated way? What is an original electronic copy? How could we prove one in a court of law, if called upon to do so?[28] If computer-based electronic information systems are to become complete knowledge systems, not just handy devices for quick reference, personal or corporate record keeping, and short-term storage of current materials, it will be necessary consciously to design and build into them mechanisms to ensure the long-term survival of information. It is especially important that this be done if such systems are to play a significant role in formal scholarly communication.[29]

Academics, frustrated at the high cost of journals and the long delays in publication and cataloging, are asking in increasing numbers whether it would not make more sense to publish the information electronically. These journals' writing, editing, and peer review are already largely supported by universities through the salaries of faculty authors: academics are not paid by publishers to do these things. Since publishers still charge the university libraries for the final product, in essence universities are paying twice. With electronic journals available via networks, universities have the opportunity to act as their own publisher and so reduce costs.

INCUNABULA VERSUS CD-ROMS: WHEREIN LIES CULTURAL VALUE?

The widely held perception that electronic material, unlike printed information, is not a physical object, must also be re-examined. One can create strong arguments that a specific CD-ROM or magnetic tape or floppy disk (the medium itself—not just the information it contains) is important. And one can argue that a proportion of these physical objects should be preserved in their original format for posterity. Surely it is important to preserve the floppy disks used by Stephen Hawking to write his books, notes, and papers, or the CD-ROM version of the *Oxford English Dictionary* (*OED*). These are, after all, cultural property.

The idea of cultural property has developed largely from international law and dates from the 1860s. One definition suggests that "objects must 'embody creative quality, documentary significance, or impact on human consciousness' to qualify as cultural property."[30] Surely electronic publications and some physical embodiments of these publications meet all these criteria; just as some books are irreplaceable, some disks must be, too. What is the difference between an incunabulum and the earliest CD-ROMs? Incunabula are only multiple-print copies of unique manuscripts. There is nothing magic in them—or is there?

Paul Banks says "yes," and explains why:

> By definition, authenticity cannot be duplicated. Other characteristics, such as ultimate chemical composition, that may be important in technical studies, dating, and authentication, require use of the original. . . . In addition to their possible value as physical documents, they may have great meaning because of people or events associated with them.[31]

The same can be said of modern electronic media; here, structural and tactile information are also important. The magic silveriness of a CD-ROM disk contrasts markedly to a dull old reference book and certainly is part of the history of the technology. The shock of the new when CD-ROMs were first introduced must have been as striking as the introduction of chromolithography was to book illustration.

Just as it is important to show our children our favorite Golden Book or to save our grandmother's cooking-sherry-stained cookbook, just as it is important to preserve Glenn Gould's original magnetic tape recordings of the Goldberg variations, or examples of the first Penguin paperbacks, or "little big books," so it is important to retain some of the early forays into electronic publishing in their original. All of these can be pictured in the mind's eye by anyone much over the age of 30. One can still smell them, or feel them, or recall the impatience engendered by their slow loading. Is this not both knowledge and information? Is the first CD-ROM issue of *Hansard* less important than the first print version? I do not think so.

ARCHIVING THE ELECTRONIC: WHAT EXACTLY DOES IT MEAN?

Having acknowledged the need to save these resources, what are the current views and beliefs about the preservation of electronic information? Many authors seem to assume that, somehow, the information will just survive. They describe, for example, a "knowledge management process [which] embraces the entire information-transfer cycle, from the creation, structuring, and representation of information to its dissemination and use."[32] However, there is no indication of how this process will enable knowledge to continue to be accessible in the year 2094.[33] Others articulate their assumption that "someone" will be responsible for storage, but to date this supposition is largely baseless.[34, 35] Michael Strangelove's 1992 *Directory of Electronic Journals and Newsletters*, an online publication, lists 22 electronic serials that "are either defunct, inactive or are simply no longer available. . .in e-text form."[36] Who has stored them? Where do they now exist?

I don't think that we can rely on publishers to preserve the information that they market. Many librarians assume that, should they need another copy of a CD-ROM or videodisk—should it wear out, and should it still remain important—they can just buy a new one. This supposes, of course, that the item is still for sale and that the publisher is still in business. Even when "archiving" is mentioned in the library literature on electronic publications, it is generally used as a technical term, far removed from the library preservation lexicon. In the data processing field "to archive" means to transfer inactive information from a relatively expensive online storage device to cheaper storage, such as magnetic tape.[37] Thus "archives" store dormant information and are thought of in terms of a 40-year lifetime, at the outside.

This is far different from the research library's definition of archival, which "implies permanence, an archival medium being one that will retain its original information-bearing characteristics indefinitely."[38] So, when Edward

Jennings writes about his electronic journal, *EJournal*, and says, "We also started talking. . .about using the list server for distributing and archiving the journal,"[39] what exactly does he mean? Is this preservation? (An additional problem is that decisions about what should be saved are made inconsistently. Unfortunately, the "preservation function" on BITNET is not automatic: one editor might decide to preserve only current issues while another might preserve the entire backfile.[40]) Neavill sums up the problem very nicely:

> Three categories of information could be in danger. Formal contributions to scientific or scholarly literature for which there is little or no apparent demand might eventually be purged from the system. Nonscholarly writings that have served the primary purpose for which they were created and are no longer in demand would in all probability be purged, precluding their later use by scholars for secondary purposes. Finally, the continual updating of electronic reference works could mean the loss of noncurrent information.[41]

He goes on to caution: "But librarians, scholars, and commercial information vendors should now be searching for a means of ensuring the survival of noncurrent information in online directories and other regularly updated electronic reference works. The printed versions of these works will begin to disappear in the very near future."[42]

LET'S SEE. . .
WHERE DID I PUT THAT 1994 CD-ROM DRIVE?

There are some interesting parallels to electronically published media in terms of its reliance on technology, its impact on society, and society's cavalier attitude toward its care and retention. Some salutary lessons can be learned: perhaps we can prevent history from repeating itself. Audio media—tapes, records, early cylinders, and compact disks—"are dependent on complex technology whose rate of obsolescence. . .rapidly increas[ed] in the 1970s and 1980s. . . . Recordings may be received by an archivist for which playback equipment is no longer available, and cannot be reconstructed because the complex electronic circuitry is impossible to reproduce."[43] In the last 40 years alone, we have seen household use of 78s, 33s, 45s, reel-to-reel tapes, eight-track tapes, cassettes, and CDs. How many homes still have 78 rpm record players, or record players at all? What happened to eight-track tapes? (Many country and western singers *only* recorded on eight-track.)

None of these recording media can be heard unless one has machines that can play them—they all rely on technology. The electronic publishing technology is changing even more quickly than sound recordings, and the associated playback technology is more expensive and more complicated. Alan Ward, the author of the first book devoted to sound archive administration, addresses this directly: "Sound archives are easier to authenticate, preserve and use than machine-readable textual archives."[44]

Fortunately, many early sound recordings have survived, partially because 78 recordings are really rather robust. Early silent films have not been so lucky. It is reckoned that 80 percent of silent films are missing and, while the loss rate drops when we reach the time of the talkies, about one in three British movies from the 1930s—the most productive decade for filmmaking—is still unaccounted for. "Many, particularly the silent films, were intentionally destroyed," explains Clyde Jeavons, curator of England's National Film Archive. "They were considered worthless, particularly when the talkies came in." Others have been lost because they were made on a nitrate base and have turned to powder.[45] Nearly 40 John Ford westerns are missing, as well as important works by film directors such as Alfred Hitchcock, Erich Von Stroheim, Josef Von Sternberg, Fritz Lang, Ernst Lubitsch, and Charlie Chaplin. Are we about to consign current authors, writers, thinkers, or scientists to the same fate?

"REFRESHING" AND "EXERCISING": NEW PRESERVATION NOMENCLATURE

Preservation of electronic publications poses an extraordinarily difficult challenge. The information they contain is imbedded in media that have very short shelf-lives. Assertions such as "The library now faces, for the library collection itself, the one-time 'retrospective conversion' issue it faced in the past two decades to automate the card catalog"[46] are naive: there are real and massive problems associated with the preservation of electronic media. Those advocates of putting everything online—retrospective conversion of everything in print—have missed some important points, not the least of which relates to the costs associated with refreshing all this information: because of the instability (or unknown stability) of modern electronic media, documents must be recopied regularly, and tapes "exercised" even more regularly. If we think mass deacidification of acidic books is daunting, imagine what it would mean if we also had to "refresh" them every five to 20 years. We would say that such a preservation approach was not economically viable.

Lou Burnard of the Oxford Text Archive is aware of these problems and is grappling with them. The Oxford Text Archive is a service to scholarship, hosted and funded by Oxford University Computing Services since 1976. The archive, which contains electronic versions of literary works by many major authors in Greek, Latin, English, and a dozen or more other languages, offers scholars long-term storage and maintenance of their electronic texts, free of charge. It contains collections and corpora of unpublished materials prepared by field workers in linguistics, as well as electronic versions of some standard reference works such as dictionaries. It also holds copies of materials prepared by individual scholars and major research projects, world-wide. The texts themselves are held on magnetic tape on the Computing Services VAX cluster.[47]

In an Internet communication, Mr. Burnard writes:

> Yes, we are well aware of the fact that mag tape doesn't last forever. In our environment, computers don't last for-ever either! We don't try to archive media—just what's on them. That means we have problems with some common PC formats: the rule is that we only archive what can be transferred from the PC disk to the mainframe. So word-processor files have to be converted, and we don't guaran-tee to do so without loss of information. In the 20 years we've been in operation, we've endured five changes of mainframe system and three changes of tape format. Everything is still held on tape with a five-year cycle; how-ever, as we now have a lot of cheap disk storage, we are moving copies onto disk, and backing the disk up to car-tridge independently.[48]

We are all familiar with the problem of the short life of electronic media, but, just to refresh our non-electronic memories (!) it is safe to say that, while opinions of experts vary, there is a great deal of consistency in assuming a useful, reliable life of three to 10 years for WORMs (Write Once, Read Many Times) and CD-ROMs, and five years for floppy and hard disks. As Lou Burnard mentioned, the machines used to read the texts are also of rela-tively short useful life. One member of an Internet discussion group put it this way:

> The major problem in data preservation is not so much the media as the machines—obsolescence is a far greater hazard to long-term storage than degradation. Where will you find a Macintosh or PC fifty years from now? Will it work? Who will repair it? With what parts? For instance, over the last few years it has become increasingly difficult to find working PDPs and people to run them, 8" floppy disk drives, 8-track tape players, many kinds of microfilm readers, and even record players.[49]

To compound our difficulties, electronic media present a new twist that is not paralleled by sound recordings or films: for the latter, one needs only the medium and the machine. With electronic media, one also needs software.

The unique designs of proprietary hardware and software create problems of technological obsolescence. When we move from a simple DOS or ASCII file to a complex electronic document or database with embedded smart codes, the problem of incompatible hardware and software becomes acute. Generations of incompatible electronic hardware and software increase the need to think of preserving the content of electronic data over time, rather than preserving discrete computer tapes, disks, or other storage devices.[50] In addition,

> There is no guarantee. . .that. . .backward compatibility will be continued in all future products. In fact, the history of magnetic recording suggests that backward compatibility provides a bridge between one or, at most, two generations of equipment. Eventually, support for older formats is phased out. As an example, low-density magnetic tape formats, such as 200 or 550 bits per inch, are no longer supported by newer magnetic tape units. Even the 800 bits-per-inch recording format, which was widely used in the 1970s, is no longer supported by some newer tape drives, most of which operate at 1,600 and 6,250 bits per inch. In addition, backward compatibility does little, if anything, to address problems of obsolete media. Eight-inch diskettes, for example, have been almost entirely supplanted by smaller sizes. Since the mid-1980s, 3.5-inch diskettes have been steadily replaced by the 5.25-inch size in new microcomputer configurations. . . . It has been suggested that libraries may have to maintain hardware "museums" to ensure the future utility of magnetic tape and diskette collections. As an additional complication, computer-processible information recorded on magnetic media is designed to be processed by specific systems and application software. Even more than hardware, such software may be updated or otherwise changed in a manner that can render previously recorded information unusable.[51]

CONCLUSION

We may be lucky. It is just the dawning of the age of Aquarius, and I believe that we still have time. We must act quickly. To ensure the survival of electronic documents, roles and responsibilities must be defined, standards developed, and expectations clarified. Manufacturers need to be brought on board, to improve media longevity. Let us think seriously about these issues. Then, let's do something. It's urgent.

NOTES

1. Sharon J. Rogers and Charlene S. Hurt, "Point of View," *Chronicle of Higher Education*, 18 October 1989, A56.

2. Stevan Harnad, "Scholarly Skywriting and the Prepublication Continuum of Scientific Inquiry," *Psychological Science* 1 (November 1990): 342.

3. Constance C. Gould and Karla Pearce, *Information Needs in the Sciences: An Assessment* (Mountain View, Calif.: Research Libraries Group, 1991).

4. Ibid., 7.

5. Ibid., 5.

6. Ibid., 7.

7. Ibid., 14.

8. Ibid., 15.

9. Ibid., 44.

10. Ibid., 48.

11. Ibid., 55.

12. Ibid., 65.

13. Ibid., 72.

14. Although this is the case. The published text is an important key to the interpretation of the author's intent. This holds true for fiction, poetry, and scientific publications, whether their medium is paper, disk, or ROM. Thomas Tanselle, a leading American bibliographer, observes, "Anyone seriously interested in trying to understand what a text means, therefore, must start by questioning the reliability of the particular edition being used. Despite the efforts of the 20th-century bibliographers, too many readers still do not understand that for any work of any period the conditions of its printing may affect the content of its text." He goes on to say that "readers of any piece of writing, if they are serious, will wish to have as much evidence as possible about what the author intended to say." In discussing the editorial attention given to philosophers and scientists (including Darwin and Einstein) he insists that "what must come to be more understood is that the very meaning of scientific texts is at stake." ("Physical Bibliography in the Twentieth Century," in *Books, Manuscripts, and the History of Medicine*, ed. Philip M. Teigen (New York: Science History Publications, 1982), 57-59, 76-77.

15. Michael S. Hart, "Project Gutenberg: Access to Electronic Texts", *Database* 13:6 (December 1990): 7.

16. Harnad, 343.

17. Gordon B. Neavill, "Electronic Publishing, Libraries, and the Survival of Information," *Library Resources & Technical Services* 28 (January-March 1984): 79.

18. William Gardner, "'The Electronic Archive': Scientific Publishing for the 1990s," *Psychological Science* 1 (November 1990): 337.

19. Ibid., 334.

20. Michael William Day, *Preservation Problems of Electronic Text and Data*, Occasional Papers no. 3 (Loughborough: Library Association, East Midlands Branch, 1990), 15.

21. Maria Lebron, telephone conversation with author, October 1992.

22. Peter Lyman, "The Library of the (Not-So-Distant) Future," *Change* 23 (January-February 1991): 37.

23. Ibid., 39.

24. Ibid., 37.

25. Neavill, 77.

26. Ibid.

27. Ithiel de Sola Pool, "The Culture of Electronic Print," *Daedalus* 111 (Fall 1982): 27-28.

28. One potential solution to the problem of proving precedence without requiring the

document to exist in print has been developed by Stuart Haber and Scott Stornetta at Bell Communications Research (Bellcore). They have devised a digital time-stamping system that essentially notarizes electronic documents. The digital stamp not only indicates the time of creation, but also certifies the document's content. (Barry Cypra, "Electronic Time-Stamping: The Notary Public Goes Digital," *Science* 261 (9 July 1993): 162-63.

29. Neavill, 79.
30. Paul N. Banks, "Preservation, Library Collections, and the Concept of Cultural Property," in *Libraries and Scholarly Communication in the United States: The Historical Dimension,* ed. Phyllis Dain and John Y. Cole (New York: Greenwood Press, 1990), 92.
31. Ibid., 91.
32. Richard E. Lucier, "Knowledge Management: Refining Roles in Scientific Communication," *EDUCOM Review* 25 (Fall 1990): 21.
33. Other examples of the survival of electronic information being assumed: "Standards—for network protocols, document architectures, retrieval systems, and computer displays—will be the key to making the connections work." (Mark Kibbey and Nancy H. Evans, "The Network *Is* the Library," *EDUCOM Review* 23 (Fall 1989): 16. Or, as Kaufman and LeClercq, indicate, "Amidst the exclamation points and question marks, the preservation challenge—how and by whom electronic journals will be archived—has been generally ignored." (Paula Kaufman and Angie LeClercq, "Archiving Electronic Journals: Who's Responsible for What," *Information Issues* 2 (Fall 1990): 2). These same fears are explored further by Margaret A. Cribbs: "While the conversion to electronic information processing allows for far more facile retrieval, editing, and storage, there remains a risk of losing stores of data through lack of foresight in electronic information management." She continues, "So may an electronic publisher purge unsold works from a database. . . . Further, electronic publishing allows for the unfettered purging of past issues of indices, price lists, and the like; and lastly, it allows for data stores to vanish when a publisher goes out of business. Repercussions of this loss of material span all disciplines of intellectual endeavor including literary, scientific, philosophical, and historical. . . . A very seldom mentioned issue in information management [is] the lack of proper care in the storage of that information, i.e., the passive destruction of data." (Margaret A. Cribbs, "The Invisible Drip . . . How Data Seeps Away in Various Ways," *Online* 11 (March 1987): 15-26).
34. Robert Kost, "Technology Giveth . . ." *Serials Review* 18:1-2 (1992): 69.
35. Brett Butler, "The Electronic Library Program: Developing Networked Electronic Library Collections," *Library Hi Tech* 9:2 (1991): 24-25.
36. Michael Strangelove, *Directory of Electronic Journals and Newsletters,* ed. 2.1, July 1992, 14. Available as an electronic text from a public access file server, consisting of 2 files: Get EJournL1 Directry, Get EJournL2 Directry. This reference itself is an indicator of problems in the preservation of electronic information. The cited e-mail edition is available concurrently with a print edition (ARL, ISSN 1057-1337), but these are not the same publication. The challenge for you, the reader, is to access the electronic document, since conventional library searches locate only the older printed version; online, the printed title has been superseded by a more recent edition!
37. William Saffady, "Stability, Care and Handling of Microforms, Magnetic Media and Optical Disks," in *Library Technology Reports* 27:1 (January-February 1991): 72.
38. Ibid., 73.

39. Edward M. Jennings, "EJournal: An Account of the First Two Years," *Public-Access Computer Systems Review* 2:1 (1991): 97.
40. Kaufman and LeClercq, 1.
41. Neavill, 81.
42. Ibid., 84.
43. Alan Ward, *A Manual of Sound Archive Administration* (Brookfield, Vt.: Gower, 1990), 109.
44. Ibid., 8.
45. Richard Brooks, "Hunt is On for Hundred Missing Movies," *The Observer* (London), 13 September 1992, 9.
46. Butler, 28.
47. Lou Burnard, "Sidebar 2: Oxford Text Archive," *Library Hi Tech* 9:3 (1991): 14.
48. Lou Burnard, Internet communication to the author, 14 October 1992.
49. Mari Stoddard, Internet communication to the author.
50. Kaufman and LeClercq, 3.
51. Saffady, 59.

PART 6:
PRESERVING SPECIAL COLLECTIONS

Just as different formats have their own peculiar preservation needs, so do special collections. Often the difficulties associated with special collections derive from the fact that each contains a multitude of different formats: the librarians or archivists who manage them must understand the preservation needs of a variety of material types. In their paper on the care of music materials, Kathleen Haefliger and Suzanne Kellerman review both the past and present of preserving scores and other items; their central point is the importance of reconciling the collection's needs with the ways in which musicians use the many types and formats of musical information. The authors profile current efforts in music preservation in a group of major research libraries and examine a number of preservation approaches including reformatting (microfilming, preservation photocopying), mass deacidification, and digitization.

Leslie Kopp argues that dance is the most difficult of the arts to document. In her paper on preserving the materials of dance she includes a dizzying number of formats—news clippings, still photographs, film, videotape, programs, playbills, posters, sound recordings, costume and set designs, performance logs, correspondence, and so forth. Like Haefliger and Kellerman, she stresses the importance of understanding how dance companies use these archival materials, in order to inform preservation decision-making. Kopp examines a menu of some 40 possible approaches to the problems of documenting dance and preserving the resulting documentation.

Scrapbooks and albums represent preservation problems for which no completely satisfactory answers exist. Sherelyn Ogden suggests that the four most common causes of deterioration include the materials from which scrapbooks and albums are made; the structure of their bindings; the materials from which the items attached to their leaves are made (as well as the size and weight of these items); and the method of attachment of the items to the leaves. Ogden cautions that there are many trade-offs to be considered in treating scrapbooks and albums, and that decisions must be made collaboratively between the custodian or owner of the book and the conservator. She presents six examples of specific scrapbook and album projects, showing why different approaches are appropriate for different materials that will be put to different uses.

Preserving Music Materials: Past and Future

Kathleen Haefliger
Music Librarian
The Harid Conservatory

L. Suzanne Kellerman
Preservation Librarian
The Pennsylvania State University

INTRODUCTION AND SCOPE

The history of preservation shows a careful attempt to balance preservation efforts with the reader's need to use material with relative ease; our current term for such a concept is accessibility. Ease of access has driven the decision-making processes of music librarians since the time this specialty was first identified. The maxim that form follows function has inevitably informed music librarians' preservation decisions, and also influenced many of the other day-to-day administrative decisions in a music library. In the context of music librarianship, this adage means that we must reconcile our collections' preservation needs with the ways in which musicians use the various types and formats of musical information. As we shall see, this harmonizing of access and preservation may be more challenging in music collections than in the general library.

The goal for all librarians in their preservation efforts is and must remain access, coupled with the preservation of physical resources or their intellectual content. By tracing the history of the various preservation solutions for music materials from the earliest writing on the subject through contemporary approaches, this paper explores the rationale for a special awareness and need for preservation in the music library. The major emphasis will be on preservation efforts aimed at the written record—in particular, music scores. This is because the literature of music appears in a format similar to or the same as other paper-based documents, and responds largely to the same preservation treatments as book materials.

The authors will only touch briefly on the numerous preservation problems inherent in maintaining and preserving the history of recorded performance, as embodied in music libraries' collections of sound records (78 rpms, long-playing albums, cassettes and other magnetic tapes, and the newest compact disk sound storage systems). A solid body of literature on the preservation of recorded sound has been developed, including the seminal report by A. G. Pickett and M. M. Lemcoe, *Preservation and Storage of*

Sound Recordings (published by the Library of Congress in 1959), which still serves as a primer for audio collections. The efforts and publications of the Association of Recorded Sound Collections have greatly influenced and enhanced the literature on how best to preserve, reformat, and maintain audio collections.

As suggested above, the use that musical scores receive mandates specialized solutions, in order properly to preserve and maintain the materials while also allowing the musician ease of access. These special needs of musicians can best be outlined by describing the various uses they make of scores, and the preservation treatments (beginning with appropriate bindings) that best serve these needs.

To complement our historical review, the authors have surveyed several current efforts in music preservation in a select group of major research libraries. These efforts, which involve digitization as well as the latest technology for retarding paper deterioration, are linked to traditional preservation methods by a great synapse or bridge which, when crossed, reveals a brave new world where preservation and access begin to merge. The dual function of digital preservation projects (whether these projects were primarily intended as preservation models or not) creates an exciting new paradigm for preserving humankind's musical culture, simultaneously advancing both musical preservation and access.

EARLY MUSIC LIBRARIES AND PRESERVATION EFFORTS

In 1902 Oscar T. Sonneck was appointed head of the newly formed music division of the Library of Congress (LC) by its chief, Herbert Putnam, and almost immediately he proposed the M, ML, and MT Library of Congress classification schedules that are now used in the vast majority of music libraries.[1] Remarkably, even preceding LC's establishment of a separate music division, by 1900 three other major research music collections had already been established; these were in the public libraries of Boston and New York City, and the private Newberry Library in Chicago.[2] Establishing the viability of music librarianship at such an early stage in the history of American libraries meant that music librarians became an organized body quite early in the century. At the first documented symposium on music librarians, the question of preservation (as represented by binding decisions and the proper physical treatment of circulating music scores) was already a pressing one.

This symposium (published in the August 1915 music number of *Library Journal*) featured reports from almost all geographic areas of the country on the state of public library music collections, and the ways in which music librarians were solving problems inherent in the administration of their collections.[3] While there seems to be no record of whether the symposium was an actual gathering of librarians or merely a collection of written reports, the essays' conversational tone suggests their authors were addressing an audience. Bessie Goldberg reported that she read her paper on the Chicago Public Library's new music room at the American Library Association's (ALA) Berkeley meeting on June 4, 1915, before it was published as part of the symposium reports.[4]

Binding was a pervasive concern of this group of librarians from such large libraries as New York Public (NYPL), as well as smaller institutions like the Richmond (Indiana) Public Library. Since there is no ALA record of this symposium as a meeting, it is difficult to know how the writers were chosen, and whether this group represented the majority of those public libraries with music collections. Their reports address a number of similar interests, arranged as if the writers were responding to a questionnaire. *Library Journal* printed the contributions chronologically, according to the founding date of the institution, revealing that the first music library collection was that of the Brooklyn Public Library. While it was still a subscription library in 1882, a trustee suggested the library purchase 400 volumes of music for circulation; this collection proved extremely popular. Most of the symposium reports included circulation figures for the libraries' music score collections; by 1915, Brooklyn reported an annual circulation of over 7,000 for the main branch alone, suggesting the immediate popularity of music collections in the early years of this century.

HOW MUSICIANS USE SCORES, OR, WHY FORM MUST FOLLOW FUNCTION

We will return to the broader binding concerns of this group of pioneering music librarians, but first (to fully appreciate that form indeed follows function) it is important to understand how musicians use scores. All musicians require that music lie flat on a performance stand, since players' hands are occupied in touching and manipulating keys or valves, whether they are playing a wind or brass instrument, strings, keyboard, and so forth. As a musician works at perfecting a piece of music, he or she repeats it numerous times, constantly flipping its pages back and forth; thus the leaves must turn easily. Then, there is the real-time demand for speed: one should be able to turn a page without skipping a beat and destroying the rhyth mic continuity. If the music is bound too tightly, or if it is stiff, a musician can easily tear the music while turning a page quickly during an allegro tempo. (In a corollary to good binding, music librarians have always encouraged publishers to use durable, permanent papers of substantial stock and weight, since slick or limp pages also will not withstand the wear and tear of performance).[5]

Ensuring that music receives proper binding is the first and most basic requirement for a preservation program, since scores receive much heavier use than a book that is read straight through, or even one that is studied extensively and whose pages are turned back and forth in reference queries. Music classics are learned and relearned by many people, many times over. In the early 1900s there began the regressive tendency to study only a few of the classics (the so-called "chestnuts"), adding to the wear and tear on certain pieces. Thus, we must provide durable, long-lasting buckram bindings for classics, as well as other scores that will be heavily used.

Music for chamber ensembles (in fact, for any group that calls for more than one instrument) requires another special binding treatment. Such music is published in the form of score and parts; the *score* contains the complete musical composition, consisting of all instruments' parts vertically arranged in real time, as they would sound simultaneously in performance. With this complete score is a set of *parts*, each supplying the single staff line for each instrument. This composite of score and parts extends from a two instrument ensemble, such as a violin and piano sonata, all the way to the most extensive combinations performed by major symphony orchestras, which often supply over 100 separate parts to their individual members.

Circulating music libraries typically purchase music scores and parts up through the nonnet (a score with nine separate instrumental parts). The special requirements to keep this compositional package together include placing the score in a solid binding, and putting its lightly-bound parts in a pocket that is usually located on the inside back cover of the bound score.

There are several advantages for libraries in binding scores and parts this way, but this pattern is not universally followed. When each part is very thick (perhaps the thickness of a regular score, which happens when a group of ensemble pieces like Joseph Haydn's *17 Famous String Quartets* is published together) it is desirable to bind the part as a separate monographic score, and use the features of volume numbering and labeling to keep the four parts together as an entity on the shelf. In this instance, a reader must either charge out all four parts separately, or each participant in the string quartet may withdraw his or her own instrumental part.

A horror for any music library is a misunderstanding by a commercial bindery that results in a score-and-parts piece being returned with the parts neatly bound-in, following the score, or (worse yet) inserted in the center of the music, or interleaved among the score's pages. Of course, this renders the music useless for performance and means that either it must be disbound and rebound properly, discarded altogether, or limited to use as a study aid, the parts now useless appendages to the volume, taking up precious shelf space. The ability to read music and knowledge of the performance formats in which it is issued reduces the chances this costly and ignorant error will occur; they are among the many reasons music librarians should be trained in music theory, literature, history, and performance. (Such training is usually demonstrated by having achieved a college or university degree in music studies.)

MUSIC BINDING: HISTORIC CONCERNS

Returning to the "Symposium on Music in Libraries," we see that the insight demonstrated by those first articles is remarkable. In the first mention of binding in this seminal collection of articles, Mr. Charles Farrington of Brooklyn demonstrated a librarian's understanding of how music is used by describing a binding approach that remains a concern of music librarians today: "the volumes were bound in light board covers, *sewn flexible* so that when opened upon the piano they would *lie flat*."[6] (Emphasis added.) Thus the importance of sewing that permitted the score to lie open on a music stand was recognized from the very beginning. This type of sewing is called "music sew" or "sewing through the fold" and is a current binding style.

The concerns expressed in the 1915 symposium were confirmed in articles on music binding (though they were not numerous) that followed throughout the century. Louisa M. Hooper, librarian of the Brookline (Massachusetts) Public Library, explained her institution's binding policy for chamber music. She describes both the chamber music practices mentioned above (score bound-in, parts residing in a pocket), as well as the use of a fabric strap to hold the parts together (however, this was not as secure as a pocket when one reached for the volume on the shelf).

Louisa Hooper also mentions using "Gaylord's covers for single pieces of music" (apprising us of one early manufacturer of music binding supplies), as well as "press board" covers.[7] For bound part-volumes of chamber music, the library bought boxes made by Schirmer for commercial use (this we assume to mean, for commercial music stores' shelving and display purposes). These were placed on the shelves for circulating materials, where patrons might help themselves. Current binding terminology describes such boxes as drop-front portfolio cases. At the Haverhill (Massachusetts) Public Library opera scores and other "heavy books" were treated by binding them in leather and sewing the scores on tapes to open flat; however, staff confessed to using "cheap pamphlet binders for thin and little-used books" (scores) and left sheet music unbound "at present."[8]

Other institutions placed a higher value on sheet music. At the Hartford (Connecticut) Public Library the staff extolled a valuable collection of "old songs and music covering the years from about 1830 to 1870. This is especially interesting, as it contains many songs published during the Civil War times, which are not found in most collections."[9] This progressive attitude toward the contemporary musical artifacts of American life was not universally shared; given the passage of time and changes in our perspective on American music-making in the 19th and early 20th centuries, we are grateful that some librarians recognized the historical value of sheet music.

The Brooklyn Public Library mentioned that sheet music cost about 75 cents to bind, but it is hard to know whether the item so treated was a single piece of sheet music, one song, one piano composition, or a collection of various composers' works bound together for protection. Some libraries described the practice of grouping together a composer's works in several genres, for the convenience of their users. Thus, one might find a Beethoven volume that included not only his piano sonatas and bagatelles, but also vocal selections from *Fidelio*, plus various oratorios and piano arrangements from the symphonies. Cataloging such a mishmash must have been a nightmare; furthermore, such collections often bore "homemade" title pages with made-up names such as "Beethoven Piano Works." (These collections also may have contributed to the concept of certain uniform titles used in cataloging records that describe the *contents* of the volume at hand, rather than the musical *genre* of the pieces included. Our present day practice, for example, of assigning [Selections] or [Piano music] may have its origin in such practices.)

The reasons for binding disparate pieces of sheet music together were certainly practical; this approach not only ensured that all those loose pieces would be protected in a single secure volume but also meant that, together, they could achieve a thickness appropriate for binding and spine lettering. The Los Angeles Public Library confirmed this practice by explaining that "all scores are flexibly bound, sheet music being made up into books at least one fourth of an inch thick."[10] Thus, the struggle between providing both collocation and protection to a group of related items by binding them together in durable buckram covers, and the desire to treat each publication as a separate entity in accordance with the formative principles of bibliographic description, are embodied in the sheet music dilemma.

The St. Louis Public Library's approach to music collections differed from the norm. Mr. Arthur Bostwick asserted that the music library existed to serve the needs of *readers*—those who want to sight read the music, perusing it in a manner similar to reading books on travel, history, or fiction. "We wish to encourage the reading use of music and we believe we are doing so," although "[we] do not buy trashy or worthless music any more than novels of similar class." The collection was not primarily intended for the individual who wanted to perform the music, although such persons were welcome to use any music they found there.

Mr. Bostwick's contrary and controversial views extended to sheet music as well. He defiantly states, "We circulate no sheet music any more than we circulate single short stories. . . . Our music books are all bound volumes," he explained, "containing five or more pieces, when they are short." St. Louis also bound different musical settings of an author's or poet's words into single volumes, and claimed to be the first library to have facilitated access in this manner. The library also constructed bound collections of modern dance music such as tangos, one-steps, maxims, and "the peculiar and characteristic syncopation known as 'rag-time.'"[11]

BINDING EXPERIMENTATION CONTINUES

An interesting "innovation" is described in an early guide to *Music in Public Libraries* (1924) by the British writer Lionel Roy McColvin. He suggests that scores be bound in different colors for the different classes of music, facilitating shelving and easy identification. He developed a comprehensive scheme by type of composition, so that (for example) chamber music was bound in maroon cloth; sacred music, black; oratorios, cantatas, etc., brown; musical comedy, green; wind instruments, yellow; string instruments, red; and so forth.[12]

By 1927 American librarians recognized this practice in the first ALA-sanctioned pamphlet on *The Care and Treatment of Music in a Library*, edited by Ruth Wallace of Indianapolis Public. "Many libraries use a color scheme in binding, such as blue for piano music, brown for vocal music, red for opera scores, and so on. This makes it possible to see at a glance the extent of a certain class in the collection, and helps to detect misplacement of books."[13] An improvement over the earlier score-and-part binding practices described above was to include a flexible paper cover that protected the parts of chamber music and other multiple-part pieces. For choral music, Wallace cites the use of a special method of hinging called "Gambleizing." "The characteristic feature of this hinge," she writes, "is the way in which it is sewed, allowing the pages of the music to open flat and at the same time providing a good reinforcement along the back."[14]

An alternate method of linking the separate part-volumes for string quartets and other substantial chamber music parts is also illustrated and described in this pamphlet. It calls for binding each part separately, but including an envelope flap on the outside back cover into which the front cover of the next part can fit. This dovetailing of the parts meant that they are connected on the shelf and cannot be separately removed, a feature alerting a user that all the parts are needed to perform the piece of music.

The Music Library Association was formed as a separate library organization in 1937. Within the first year of its history it addressed the ever-present issue, "Binding Problems in Music: Methods and Costs." Dorothy Lawton, who was in charge of the circulating Music Library at The New York Public Library, wrote a paper that was published in the very first series of *Notes*, MLA's official organ. She reviewed the various types of binding for music and their purposes, summarizing practices already established, which have been identified and described in this paper. For several reasons, Lawton was very cautious about the use of spiral bindings. They did not permit any spine lettering and pages could easily be torn out. She was also concerned about the potential for injury to a reader, if the ends of the wire became loose, although she mentioned that the latest type spirals, made of cellophane or similar material, promised to be more satisfactory. Although on the one hand she claimed never to bind orchestral parts, like Ruth Wallace she indicated New York Public sewed parts onto a flexible paper folder, for protection. Perhaps this procedure was performed in-house, since she had cause to complain about the costs of binding materials.

Although she pointed out its high cost, Lawton naturally felt binding was absolutely necessary to preserve and extend the life of costly scores that might serve the library for 20 years or more. Even within The New York Public Library, it was shocking that the tally for music materials consumed two-thirds of the annual binding appropriation. Lawton cited rising costs to account for this erosion: "At the beginning of the N.R.A. [National Recovery Administration Act, 1933] bindery materials and labor advanced forty percent." In 1937, the average cost for binding was $1.25 per volume, but Lawton points out the fallacy in this statistic: while musicians might think a score and parts implied one composition at $1.25, in reality the bindery charged $1.25 for each part, as well as the portfolio if one was included. Thus, a string quartet whose purchase price was $4.00 ended by costing the library $11.50. The high cost of binding reinforced the practice of retaining even "shabby" books. An additional factor, Lawton felt, was the frailty of the paper on which music was printed; along with narrow margins, it often prevented rebinding.

When items were out-of-print or hard to obtain, yet valuable and needed by the library, procedures that we now associate with fine book conservation were adopted: the back edges of leaves were guarded with bond paper, which made them strong enough for re-sewing. Ever mindful of costs, Lawton remarked on how expensive this process was; however, it was worth it when music or books might otherwise have been lost. (She does not mention the costs of staff time for this laborious procedure, or that used in flexibly binding orchestral scores; however, these were almost certainly part of the economic equation in figuring the true costs of maintaining music collections.) For all the cost liabilities, Lawton pointed out that brightly colored, clean, and fresh-looking music scores seemed to have a very positive effect on circulation; perhaps in some fashion the readers were "judging the music by its covers"![15]

MID-CENTURY APPROACHES

By mid-century most binding practices were codified; in part, economic considerations drove the choice of binding. Surprisingly, The New York Public Library decided to case strong, new scores without first taking them apart and re-sewing them, and although a page occasionally became loose, the cost savings of $1.25 per volume was considered worth the sacrifice of hand-sewing.[16] For inexpensive songs and piano music, NYPL began to use the first-reported clear plastic cover; it resembled today's "crystal" book jacket. Everyday library use revealed one drawback to all types of plastic covers (with pockets, these were also recommended for chamber music): plastic covers stuck together on the shelves because of their taped edges. When interfiled with cloth bindings, however, they worked well, allowing readers to see at a glance the original covers (this was especially appealing for sheet music). New York Public also expressed an awareness of staff costs. Mention was made of the amount of work required to prepare scores for binding and to complete post-bindery operations, including the time-consuming activities of hand-lettering spines and attaching pockets or date-due slips.

By 1966 the Music Library Association's *Manual of Music Librarianship* included a chapter on binding, authored by Catherine K. Miller, former Music Supervising Librarian for New York Public. Noting that neither the American Library Association, the Music Library Association, nor the Library Binding Institute (LBI) had yet established official standards for music binding, Miller did an extensive review of the literature and cited the most common practices throughout the century.[17] By this time oversewing had become standard book-binding practice, but she cautioned against its use for music, since it draws the book firmly together at the spine, preventing it from lying flat when opened. Thus, the 1915 recommendation to hand-sew music through the folds, the most satisfactory and durable of all signature attachment methods, was still valid. (This sewing method also allows for rebinding.)

In a complete revision of Lionel McColvin's guide, Jack Dove describes advances in binding technologies that occurred after the second World War, including the use of the strong new cold adhesives that eliminated much signature sewing of books, but not of music. Experimentation with new plastic materials resulted in several innovative ways to treat sheet music inexpensively. Dove notes that covers can be laminated for protection, the first mention in music literature of the lamination process. Another method called for encasing sheet music in a regular pamphlet cover with a clear plastic front, allowing the graphics to be easily viewed. The attachment was made either through sewing or stapling through the fold.[18] (However, staples could later rust and prove damaging to the materials they initially served to protect.)

PRESENT PRESERVATION PRACTICES

Today there is only one individual in America who holds a full-time preservation/conservation position in a music library; he is Ted Honea, Supervisor of Binding and Conservator at the Sibley Music Library, Eastman School of Music. In his 1985 article in *New Library Scene* he reconfirms all the best music binding preservation procedures. Certain practices, once accepted because they were economically feasible but now recognized as damaging to long-term preservation goals, are deemed inappropriate in all cases. These include side sewing in which the entire score is sewn together along the spine's edge, and oversewing in which the signatures' folds are sliced off, reducing the item to a stack of single pages that are then machine-sewn. For music materials, oversewing has been replaced by double-fan adhesive binding, whereby a synthetic polyvinyl acetate adhesive is applied to the thinnest spine margin on either side of the page then (while it is still wet) reinforced with a spine cloth. Double-fan adhesive binding allows for rounding and backing, increasing strength and openability, and also permits rebinding, since the amount of inner margin consumed is minimal.

Although there are no published standards for library binding of music, Honea provides a summary of his own developmental standards, based on his wide experience in the field; he covers two main types of score binding: single scores, and sets of parts. While his practices generally conform to those described above, he cautions practitioners about certain specific techniques (including machine sewing, which perforates pages). He has also developed a special method for binding substantial music parts (such as the piano scores for chamber music). When these contain more than one signature they are either French sewn (a cordless technique in which each section is sewn to the next using a kettle stitch-like loop), or sewn following Honea's own sewing technique called *interlock*, which also attaches the spines of several sections to one another.[19]

The sewn signatures are then attached to the case, with the usual pocket for single-section parts inside the back cover. Stubbing is added at the back of the volume to increase the width of the spine, permitting it to encompass both the score and parts and accommodating the thickness of the parts in the pocket. Circulation of the score-and-parts package encourages the borrower to return the entire composition complete. This eliminates the problem for circulation staff that occurs when only one or two of the parts can be found on the shelf (the others being checked out); it puts the responsibility for collecting and reassembling all the parts on the borrower, who checked the item out intact. (The situation of multiple performers, each wishing to return his or her own part separately, is the bane of the circulation librarian. A bound-in score and its parts effectively eliminates this access problem for the music library.)

Honea's wish for a library binding standard for music was partly satisfied by the Library Binding Institute's eighth edition of *Standard for Library Binding* (1986), which is especially sympathetic to music binding. It represents the first attempt to consider libraries' preservation needs, as they relate to binding. Considered in light of sound preservation practice, methods like oversewing and side sewing are recognized as inconsistent with the need for flexible bindings whose contents can be reproduced on a photocopier, and still serve a durable life:

> The LBI standard for library materials acknowledges
> that the diverse nature of library materials, the destructive
> effects of repeated handling and inhospitable environ-
> ments, and the ubiquitous photocopy machine, have com-
> plicated the task of the library binder. Where strength was
> once the only yardstick against which library binding was
> measured, flexibility has become equally important.[20]

Thus, the traditional but more time-consuming and costly practice of
sewing through the fold, as well as double-fan adhesive binding and recasing, are being incorporated into routine music binding practices.

The renewed awareness of the need for music preservation, both in terms
of binding and other techniques, prompted a program on the topic at the
1991 conference of the American Library Association in Atlanta, Georgia.
"Knowing the Score: Preserving Collections of Music," sponsored by the
Association for Library Collections and Technical Services (ALCTS), included presentations on special considerations for sound recordings and
moving images, as well as practical preservation options for the conservatory library. The papers also emphasized binding techniques and other
archival methods for treating music materials; they were presented by prac-
ticing music librarians or preservation officers.[21] The program was also
sponsored by the standing Preservation Committee of the Music Library
Association; that group continues its concerted efforts for music preservation awareness and adoption.

Today there is increasing awareness that libraries face the real possibility
that large portions of their paper-based collections may be extinct and unusable unless preventive action is taken, and music collections are no exception. For decades, binding has been the established option for preserving
paper-based collections; it has proven to be the most cost-effective approach for extending the life of original items. Nonetheless, it cannot be the
preferred preservation method when paper is acidic or brittle. Alternative
means that can save the original's intellectual content are needed for deteriorating materials.

A survey of selected music libraries in large American research institutions conducted in the spring of 1993 revealed that microfilming and replacement photocopying are the preservation options of choice for
reformatting brittle scores and music books; a few libraries have initiated
the use of mass deacidification and digital technology, the latest advances
in retarding or compensating for paper deterioration. The final section of
this essay will deal with advanced preservation problems, where it is critical that action be taken as soon as possible and the latest technology may
be helpful in maintaining, preserving, or extending our base of musical
knowledge.

PRESERVATION MICROFILMING

A tried and tested option, preservation microfilming for music began in the 1930s when Harvard, Yale, The New York Public Library, and the Library of Congress started converting selected titles from their collections to film.[22] Since then, microfilm has become the established archival medium for preserving brittle materials because "microforms rely upon simple, stable technology for creation, reading and printing [and] have a well-established longevity when created and stored in conformity with national standards."[23]

A description of the Library of Congress' preservation efforts will best capture the range of projects that have been undertaken, and the underlying rationale for filming. The first efforts at LC were driven by the recognition that important manuscripts and rare materials in British and European institutions might be destroyed or lost, as a result of the devastation of World War II. The photoreproductions made in the late 1930s and early 1940s enabled many items to remain intellectually available, even when originals were indeed destroyed. After the war the Library's efforts continued, but preservation decisions were made largely on an item-by-item basis. There was no systematic selection process, nor were there well-designed bibliographic controls.

Monetary support for preservation efforts in the Music Division began in 1971. By 1985 more than half a million dollars had been spent on preservation, with emphasis on microfilming. Major collections targeted for filming in the 1960s included the Albert Schatz Collection of opera librettos; original music manuscripts of American composers like Barber, Bernstein, Copland, and Cowell; and full orchestra scores of operas in both published and manuscript forms. Later projects identified additional American resources, such as hymnals, military band music, folklore materials, early scores from silent and sound motion pictures, a selection of fragile copyright deposits from 1870 to 1885, and the marches of Sousa and other American composers. European resources were not neglected: In the early 1980s the Library completed a project to preserve the entire collection of music printed or copied in manuscript before 1700, and all books about music published before 1800.[24] Encouraged by LC's efforts, many other large research libraries began to film their rare and fragile music materials.

In conjunction with Eastman Kodak, the Sibley Music Library at the Eastman School of Music (with one of the world's largest academic rare book music collections) developed a microformatting project that has had a pervasive influence on musicological study in the United States, in the 1960s and beyond. In 1957, the library at Eastman produced an extensive series of micro-opaque cards that were made available for purchase. Their distribution to leading music research libraries meant that students and scholars could consult the major incunabula and early 16th- to 18th-century music writings and scores, in the comfort of their own institutions.

Similarly, commercial microfilm publication of important complete editions of such composers as Schubert, Beethoven, and Handel as well as earlier Renaissance works by Josquin, Palestrina, and numerous others, added to the availability of music libraries' historical resources. These films were bought extensively by those libraries that had not collected the paper editions when these were first published in the late 1800s. The reproductions extended the intellectual depth of music study at institutions everywhere; they also contributed to the burgeoning of documented music scholarship.

Nonetheless, there were certain problems that impeded the use of such films for music performance and study. Because the images in these early microfilm sets were so large (the Breitkopf & Härtel *Complete Works of Schubert* is a good example) the microfilm reader/printer technology of the time was incapable of producing usable performance-size prints. Students were compelled to produce two prints (the top and bottom half of a page of music), then piece them together; even so, the resulting sheet was approximately 11 x 17 inches, very cumbersome for a music stand or piano rack, as well as slick and unpleasant to the touch. This process was so difficult that the scholarly desires of the less persistent may have been effectively squelched. Newer filming equipment, which allows for more flexible reduction ratios, has helped to solve this problem for all but the oldest films.

Brittle books programs as part of preservation departments in research libraries continue to support and produce microfilms of important resources in deteriorated condition. New York Public, Duke, Northwestern, Columbia, the University of Texas at Austin, and Berkeley are only a few of the institutions that have undertaken responsible music filming projects. It is projected that in the near future filming the Denkmaler Editions that document the great music resources of Europe will become a priority. With OCLC and the Research Libraries Information Network (RLIN) spearheading efforts to eliminate duplicate filming through the bibliographic control of master negatives, we can anticipate that all major fragile sources will eventually be filmed; at the same time, access to these treasures will be facilitated.

PRESERVATION REPLACEMENT PHOTOCOPYING

Another brittle books recovery technique is preservation photocopying, which produces copies directly onto acid-free paper through means of xerography. Although not considered by some to be a long-term preservation option, it may be the most appropriate for some materials, including music scores, because of their performance use. Copies are usually about the same size as the original and provide the same information. John DePew in *A Library, Media, and Archival Preservation Handbook* suggests that photocopying "is particularly appropriate for high-use monographs (particularly those of fewer than 100 pages), current reference sets, serial volumes needed in hard copy to complete a set, and items requiring reference to extensive notes, indexes, or graphic materials."[25]

Gloria J. Orr in her article "Preservation Photocopying of Bound Volumes: An Increasingly Viable Option" explains that while preservation photocopying has evolved slowly over the years, this technology can now generate archival-quality copies on a variety of copiers, provided acid-free paper and stable toner are used.[26] Although no national standards for preservation replacement photocopying exist, in 1990 the Association for Library Collections and Technical Services published a four-page leaflet entitled *Guidelines for Preservation Photocopying of Replacement Pages* which outlines procedures for producing copies.[27]

At the Sibley Music Library preservation replacement photocopying is part of the brittle books program. A commercial vendor is used to produce facsimiles of lengthy scores, while staff, directed by Ted Honea, are responsible for duplicating scores of 20 pages or less, in-house. For the majority of scores, the original volume is used; however, in a few cases a microformat edition has been the basis for creating a durable photocopy on permanent paper. Northwestern University also engages in preservation replacement photocopying. Although the work is done on an item-by-item basis and there is no systematic identification of titles suited to this approach, our conversations with the librarian indicated how much the library has benefitted from this preservation option. A commercial corollary to this practice is the new "publishing on demand" service that is currently offered by such established music publishers as Schirmer, and Boosey and Hawkes. When items are permanently out of print (and sometimes when they are only temporarily out of print), each company provides reproductions of selected copyrighted scores by custom order.

MASS DEACIDIFICATION

For library materials that are printed on acidic paper but not yet embrittled, deacidification is an option worth considering. Deacidification is a chemical process of neutralizing the acid content found in paper; thus mass deacidification refers to treating large acidic collections en masse. This preventative measure also deposits an alkaline buffer in the paper, safeguarding it against future deterioration. This process does not reverse deterioration that has already taken place, but rather extends the life remaining in the paper at the time it is treated. Reports from independent laboratory testing indicate that deacidification can extend the life of paper by as much as three to five times, if it has not yet seriously deteriorated.[28] Mass deacidification technology offers music libraries the benefits of preserving materials in their original format, which can facilitate use when original size and medium are important.

Although several research libraries are investigating mass deacidification by conducting test runs or pilot projects, some have actually signed contracts for this service; Northwestern University is "the first library to concentrate these efforts on a music collection."[29] As reported in the May-June 1993 issue of the *MLA Newsletter*, Northwestern targeted its comprehensive 20th-century score collection, primarily because of the importance of the materials. In June 1992, the university signed a contract with Akzo Chemical, Deer Park, Texas, to treat their materials using the diethyl zinc (DEZ) gas process.[30] A total of 11,127 music volumes (both miniature and full scores) were treated. Following the close of Akzo's plant in April 1994, the library developed plans to continue its project by working with Preservation Technologies, Inc., in Glenshaw, PA. Don Roberts, Head Music Librarian at Northwestern, views their experience as a positive one. "Our experience so far at Northwestern demonstrates that MD [mass deacidification] is feasible and appropriate for our score preservation needs. . . . [We] have averted the potential catastrophe of a collection of distinction turning brittle and unusable. We believe that the collection will now be preserved until the time when an appropriate digitization technology becomes viable."[31]

DIGITAL TECHNOLOGY

Digital image reformatting is the newest preservation option available for deteriorating library collections. This type of reformatting involves digital scanning of text or graphics from paper or microfilm, creating bitmapped (binary) images. The captured images can then be viewed on-screen (as an electronic facsimile of the original) or transferred to another medium (such as an optical disk) for storage. Scanned and stored images can be viewed at an access/view workstation, or transmitted to an output device (a printer) for production of a paper facsimile. Digital image technology offers three major advantages: it combines the positive storage and duplication features of microfilm, provides a new avenue for producing preservation replacements, and offers significantly enhanced accessibility heretofore unknown to collection retrieval.

At the University of Tennessee at Knoxville (UTK), digital scanning of a unique music collection is underway. In 1993 UTK began its demonstration project to capture images from a deteriorating collection of scholarly music materials relating to Gottfried Galston and Ferruccio Benvenuto Busoni.[32] This archive documents the relationship between two prominent pianists (Busoni is also a major composer of the period) and contains almost 1,500 piano scores covering the major repertoire for virtuoso pianists, at a time when virtuosity was in vogue. It also contains books, letters, correspondence, photographs, newspaper clippings, and musical and literary manuscripts. An early phase of the project concentrated on digitizing and disseminating a diary by Galston and letters to and from Busoni, unique items all. Now these items will be made available to musicians everywhere; because of advances in digitization, they may even be offered through electronic network transfer.

Another important use of digital technology relates to sheet music, so ubiquitous in American musical history but still considered a problematic area for preservation, control, and access. The importance of sheet music rests not only in its documentation of contemporary taste (especially that for popular music), but also in its cover designs, which sometimes have greater artistic weight than the music itself. At Duke University, recognition of the importance of a collection of approximately 20,000 pieces of sheet music led to a project described by Lois Schultz, music cataloging librarian and project director.

The impetus for this scanning project was a challenge from the university's library director that staff make the institution's numerous uncataloged backlogs publicly available within 24 months. Since there was little systematic access to the sheet music collection, programmer and musicologist Juraj Horacek devised a prototype database for scanning covers, then providing online Internet search access. Color scanning (demanding more sophisticated equipment) is a special feature of this project; the music is indexed by author, composer, performer, and title. Information about cover graphics is also being added, using terms available in the LC thesaurus for graphic materials, as well as names of illustrators, engravers, and lithographers. Lois Schultz indicated that while the university also plans on scanning the musical content of these pieces, copyright permissions and concerns have not yet been resolved.

Duke's long-term goal is to scan and provide copies of complete scores, probably in response to individual requests, as items are identified and selected through database searches. Indexing features include keyword searching; the authors tried several such searches including the term "wimmen," used in a humorous 19th-century pieces. Although the index is available over the Internet, the actual graphics cannot yet be obtained. Even when the necessary hardware is in place, each searcher will need his or her own equipment on which MIME (image, sound, and text viewer software available from Archie) has been mounted. Currently, images can be downloaded as TIFF files and sent to a Macintosh computer for reproduction. Duke's direction, where indexing and access precede the scanning of the entire item, represents a shift in priority. Rather than distributing a complete group of images to every interested institution (for example, as large microform sets are disseminated), the university will maintain a central database. Duke's extensive indexing makes it possible to identify and reproduce only those images an organization or individual wants.

An exciting access project at Case Western Reserve, developed by Jim Barker of the Computer Services Department and Richard Rodda, musicologist, utilizes digital scanning technology to make available the reserve music scores and the music listening assignments for an undergraduate music course, across a campus network. By linking music as realized on recordings with the score (all this enhanced by the music history instructor's analysis and commentary), a student is given access to all the elements needed for music study through his or her dormitory workstation.

The music score application of the Library Collections Services Project involves four-bit gray-scale scanning of selected music scores, which are tied to a digital library of recordings. Since students might not always want to view the score on their screens, laser printers are used to reproduce the scanned images as paper prints. Students may also download the network files on CD-ROM disks to use at locations other than network stations. Funding for this advanced project was provided in partnership with IBM, and the computer center envisions a much more extensive program in the future, involving access to dance and other academic disciplines.

Though the primary focus at Case Western is not preservation, preservation is still the result, since handling originals (as well as making reproductions directly from them) is reduced or eliminated. Furthermore, the enhanced access the project provides is breathtaking. High-resolution scanning at 600 dots per inch (dpi) is becoming a "standard"; this will provide quality access images for years to come. How to manipulate the database becomes the choice of the user. He or she can browse the complete contents, or emphasize any one aspect, perhaps tying it together with another component. Thus, for music study, a student can compare the rhythm of a classical work with, say, a neoclassic piece by Stravinsky. This is an excellent example of where preservation and access merge.

Indiana University has also developed the first phase of a plan for computer-enhanced information delivery in support of music study and research. David Fenske, Indiana's music librarian, expresses a cautious viewpoint of scanning technology; instead, he has chosen to concentrate on audio dissemination of reserve listening, using a Novell server, and to defer linking this information with score digitization for the present. Fenske feels that since, at present, scanning digitizes only graphic representations of scores, this technology offers no great advance over the photocopier. A music score documents a real-time continuum of sound, duration, rhythm, and pitch, which cannot (he believes) be adequately captured by a graphical picture, as represented in a scanned image. The synchronization of score and sound in real-time delivery requires a great deal of dedicated band-width when sent across a network, and this creates an additional constraint. It is planned that later phases of Indiana's project will include delivery of score, sound, text, video, and motion graphics, but for now the university has chosen to wait until advanced digital technology that captures the musical essence of the score becomes available.

CONCLUSION

The common thread in all these music preservation efforts, from 1915 through the current projects at Indiana and Case Western, is ease of access, combined with preserving intellectual content for future generations. As the most basic preservation option in music libraries, binding provides extended life and has enabled the development of research collections. Today, music librarians and preservationists pursue other options as well, seeking to retard paper deterioration through deacidification, or reformat through microfilming, photocopying, and digitization. While preservation approaches will continue to change over time, the maxim that form follows function, as it applies to the preservation and performance of music, has exerted a great influence and will continue to inform conservation decisions for the future. Until the time when orchestra musicians appear on stage with computer screens on their music stands, the need for paper copies of music scores and parts will endure. Nonetheless, the new, exciting access features of digital technology are extending the musician's intellectual realm, as well as his or her understanding of complexities and interrelationships in music.

NOTES

1. Jon Newsom and H. W. Hitchcock, "Oscar (George) T(heodore) Sonneck," in *New Grove Dictionary of American Music*, vol. 4 R-Z (New York: Macmillan, 1986), 262.
2. Mary W. Davison and Donald W. Krummel, "Libraries and Collections," in *New Grove Dictionary of American Music*, vol. 3 L-Q (New York: Macmillan, 1986), 45.
3. "Symposium on Music in Libraries," *Library Journal* 40 (August 1915): [563]-94.
4. Ibid., 582.
5. Refers to MLA/MPA Joint Committee: Music Library Association/Music Publishers Association. In the early 1980s a joint committee consisting of appointed members of the Music Library Association and the Music Publishers Association met to discuss preservation issues of mutual interest. Successful joint efforts include a standard for the use of acid-free permanent paper and the widespread adoption of such papers in the music score industry.
6. "Symposium," [563].
7. Ibid., 565.
8. Ibid., 566.
9. Ibid., 564.
10. Ibid., 569.
11. Ibid., 566-67.
12. Lionel R. McColvin, *Music in Public Libraries* (London: Grafton & Co., 1924), 51.
13. Ruth Wallace, *Care and Treatment of Music in a Library* (Chicago: American Library Association, 1927), 48.
14. Ibid., 50.
15. Dorothy Lawton, "Binding Problems in Music: Methods and Costs," *Notes*, 1st series, 1 (November 1937): 24-28.
16. Gladys E. Chamberlain, "Binding," *Library Journal* 76 (1 November 1951): 1776.
17. Catharine K. Miller, "Binding and Circulation," in *Manual of Music Librarianship*

(Ann Arbor, Mich.: Music Library Association, 1966), 58-64.

18. Jack Dove, *Music Libraries* (London: Andre Deutsch Ltd., 1965), [44]-47.

19. Ted Honea, "Music . . . A Binding Challenge," *New Library Scene* 4 (June 1985): 1, 8-10.

20. Paul A. Parisi and Jan Merrill-Oldham, eds., *Library Binding Institute Standard for Library Binding*, 8th ed. (Rochester, N.Y.: Library Binding Institute, 1986), iii.

21. "Knowing the Score: Preserving Collections of Music" (Program at the American Library Association Conference, Atlanta, Ga., 30 June 1991).

22. Nancy E. Gwinn, ed., *Preservation Microfilming: A Guide for Librarians and Archivists* (Chicago: American Library Association, 1987), xxii.

23. Janet E. Gertz, "Preservation in Microfilming for Archives and Manuscripts," in *Advances in Preservation and Access*, vol. 1, ed. Barbra B. Higginbotham and Mary E. Jackson (Westport, Conn.: Meckler, 1992), 165.

24. Gail L. Freunsch, "Music Preservation Microfilming Project Marks Its Fifteenth Anniversary," *Library of Congress Information Bulletin* 44 (17 June 1985).

25. John N. DePew, *Library, Media, and Archival Preservation Handbook* (Santa Barbara, Calif.: ABC-CLIO, 1991), 188.

26. Gloria J. Orr, "Preservation Photocopying of Bound Volumes: An Increasingly Viable Option," *Library Resources & Technical Services* 34 (October 1990): 445-46.

27. Association for Library Collections and Technical Services, *Guidelines for Preservation Photocopying of Replacement Pages* (Chicago: American Library Association, 1990), [1]-[4].

28. Peter G. Sparks, *Technical Considerations in Choosing Mass Deacidification Processes* (Washington, D.C.: Commission on Preservation and Access, 1990), 3.

29. "Lasting Concerns," *MLA Newsletter* 93 (May-June 1993): 6. "Lasting Concerns" is a regular column on preservation issues prepared by the Music Library Association's Preservation Committee.

30. Ibid.

31. Ibid., 26.

32. Tamara J. Miller, "Case Study: University of Tennessee Project" (Paper presented at the ALCTS "Electronic Technologies: New Options for Preservation" Preconference, New Orleans, La., 24 June 1993).

Documenting Dance and Preserving the Collections

Leslie Hansen Kopp

Executive Director
Preserve, Inc., Jacob's Pillow

RECORDING THE MOST EPHEMERAL ART

Dance is, with little argument, the most difficult of the arts to document. A tradition handed down from generation to generation, dancer to dancer, this ephemeral art leaves few tangible records: news clippings of reviews, still photographs, perhaps a film or videotape. Documenting dance has challenged performers and historians alike; quite often, when the dancers leave the stage, the work is gone. Because the materials that make up the history of dance are so diverse, no one approach to preserving them is sufficiently comprehensive. All the various types of documentation at hand provide invaluable information about a given work; however, despite the available technologies, preservation of the documentary heritage of the performing arts is in a state of crisis.

Every dance company, whether aware of it or not, has an archive. A dance company's documentary records typically include programs and playbills, news clippings, posters, photographs, scrapbooks, videotapes, films, sound recordings, costume and set designs, performance logs, and oral history interviews, as well as correspondence, memoranda, financial records, minutes of the board of directors, school records, and annual reports. Without these archival resources, companies are unable to review previous performances, study past publicity or fund-raising campaigns, plan new programs, revive works long out of the repertoire, provide information for grant proposals, or create press kits.

In recent years, dance companies have become increasingly aware of the value of their historical materials. Today in the dance community, a family that has lost so many members to both age and AIDS, the desire to acquire and maintain archival documents has become acute. What most performers and dance companies do not know is that their archival material—these records of the past—will not last forever; in fact, without proper attention and care, they will not last very long at all. And while preserving dance archives has become an intellectual priority, it is not always a financial reality. Thus, the challenge has become to educate this eager community in the methods of archival documentation and preservation, in order to assure dance a life beyond performance.

PURPOSES AND METHODS FOR DOCUMENTING DANCE

The purposes for which choreographers and dancers document dance are almost as varied as the types of documentation available. Performances are recorded, usually on videotape, as a representation of a work, since no two performances are the same and works are often performed with different casts. Likewise, as rehearsal time is precious, performance videos are used to teach roles to new cast members or understudies and to reconstruct works that have been out of the immediate repertory. Rehearsals are often documented for study purposes while the choreographic process is in progress.

In addition, records of the dance that are not necessarily records of a performance—news articles, critical reviews and still photographs—are used for public relations purposes—to create press kits, to promote bookings and tours, and for grant proposals and fund raising. Those who create the documentation include not only the choreographers and performers, but also dance presenters, specialists in video, photography, or notation, and the major dance repositories. Types of documentation presently employed in the dance field include:

- Camera work (moving and still image, video and film, color and black-and-white)
- Documents on paper created by the dance company (programs, playbills, posters)
- Notation (Laban and Benesh systems, as well as choreographers' notes)
- Scholarly or analytic discussion (reviews and news articles as well as symposia convened by critics, scholars, librarians, and archivists)
- Oral and video history interviews
- Designs of sets, costumes, lighting, etc.
- Publications (books, journals, and periodicals)
- Music scores (often marked with choreographic notes)
- Business records (annual reports, financial records, touring records, correspondence, etc.)

PRESERVATION CONSIDERATIONS

In many ways, the physical conservation of dance materials is more challenging than the creation and collection of those items. Books are silently burning and scrapbooks crumbling because of the acid content in their papers. Rubber cement, pressure-sensitive tape, mucilage, and other adhesives have ruined countless documents and photographs. Film may contain flammable nitrate or be composed of cellulose diacetate. Videotape has proven to be an imperfect tool, as the oxide which holds the image literally flakes off the tape.

An additional concern is created by the technological advancements in the equipment used to record dance—as new formats are created, repositories find they must become museums of technology (copies of videotapes from an older format to a newer format are successive generations apart from the original quality). And what will happen when high-definition television becomes the norm? Will we be satisfied with low-definition dance documentation?

TAKING THE MEASURE OF NATIONAL ISSUES

In 1990, the Andrew W. Mellon Foundation and the Dance Program of the National Endowment for the Arts (NEA) initiated a study of the issues surrounding dance documentation and preservation.[1] Entitled *Images of American Dance: Documenting and Preserving a Cultural Heritage*, the study's immediate purpose was not to inventory holdings or to conduct an in-depth analysis of major repositories and libraries, but rather to learn what comprises the existing system of dance documentation and preservation, how transactions are conducted within the system, and to what extent the needs of the dance community are being met. By focusing on the needs of people who use dance materials, it was hoped the study would better equip both the artistic and archival communities in their efforts to build, strengthen, and extend dance documentation and preservation efforts at the local, regional, and national levels, thereby ensuring that the legacy of dance endures.

Both the Mellon Foundation and the NEA envisioned a study that was directly connected to the dance community, one whose findings and recommendations reflected the needs and experiences of dancers, choreographers, scholars, collectors, and others. In particular, they wanted to be sure that their own concerns about dance archives did not slant the conclusions that had yet to emerge. The study had to explore an array of archival activities, encompass a broad range of dance experience (theatrical, social, folk, etc.), and conclude itself in a relatively short period of time—approximately six months.

Through two phases of research, the study drew upon the input and expertise of seven field researchers located in six cities (New York, San Francisco, Los Angeles, Minneapolis/St. Paul, Salt Lake City, and Washington, D.C.); eight advisors of different ethnic, professional, and artistic backgrounds; and three core staff members. In addition to the 160 interviews conducted in the six research sites, the study reflected conversations with the staff of several major repositories of dance archives, producers of two national dance festivals, and documenters of commercial musical theater. Two follow-up meetings in New York City and Washington, D.C. during the second phase of the research further tested and elaborated the findings.

Virtually everyone with whom the field researchers spoke recognized the importance of creating and preserving comprehensive records of the history and making of dance. At the same time, the dance community is experiencing enormous pressures that both stimulate and complicate this widespread interest. One of these is the proliferation of video technology, which has sharpened the appetite of artists for tapes, both of their own work and the work of others. Another has been the toll that AIDS and the passage of time have taken on at least two generations of artists, including many founders of modern-day forms and teachers of dance traditions. Finally, the chronic shortage of funding continues to hamper efforts to document and preserve dance in all quarters—a shortage that is more painful because it stands in such contrast to the enormous need that has been expressed by the dance community.

DANCE DOCUMENTATION AND PRESERVATION: FIVE KEY CONCERNS EMERGE

While there was some variation in the level and sophistication of dance documentation and preservation conducted at each research site, five principal conclusions, applicable to the field at large, emerged.

1. Great historical, geographic, cultural, and artistic gaps exist in the current record of dance in the United States: ballet and modern dance have been favored over other forms; European-based traditions are more present in the records than non-European; finished work tends to be documented more than the creative process; and most of the personal stories of people who have contributed to the making of dance history are missing altogether.

2. Video technology has profoundly changed the way dance is documented, what is recorded, and how the field thinks about preservation. The majority of artists interviewed indicated a preference for videotape over other documentary approaches, and because it is relatively inexpensive, much more work representing a much wider range of styles and traditions is gradually being recorded. However, the usefulness of this record is often compromised because of the quality of the recordings, and inadequate storage and cataloging procedures.

3. In none of the six study sites was there a fully functioning, institutionalized dance documentation and preservation network. However, in each city, many of the components were in place. Furthermore, in each city numerous smaller, informal networks were thriving, often in response to particular needs and generally relying on the telephone and personal contact for communication.

4. "Access" has become everyone's byword—for artists who create the work and records of it, for repositories that house those records, and for scholars and others who want to use those materials. Furthermore, video-cameras and computers have raised everyone's expectations of what should be available on demand. Among the barriers to easy access are the incomplete record of what collections exist and what is in them; the inadequate and inconsistent organization of those materials; the conflict between the needs of archive users and the limits of physical and intellectual property rights; and the tension between the demand for "hands-on" use and long-term preservation needs.

5. A variety of education initiatives is needed both within and without the dance field to ensure that high archival standards are adopted and maintained; that skilled people are properly preserving works and histories; that resources are allocated to address gaps in the collective record of dance; that dance archives are adequately funded; and that the general public is aware of the importance of dance and dance history in our culture.

The study then proceeded to enumerate a "menu of possible actions," drawing directly on the recommendations of field researchers, a cross-site analysis, and input from the advisory committee. These possible actions (ranging from collaborative efforts between major repositories and ethnically-specific cultural centers, to skills-development workshops in the techniques of video documentation and preservation, and the creation of archival directories) were grouped under the five broad conclusions that emerged from phase one of the research.

A MENU OF LOCAL AND NATIONAL ACTIONS IS DEVELOPED

Further analysis of the research suggested that within this lengthy menu of approximately 40 actions there could be found specific, highly effective actions at the local and national levels. The study recommends a two-pronged set of comprehensive measures—one at the local level and one at the national level. The elaboration of these measures was informed by many concepts:

- The need to empower communities at the grassroots level with the tools and resources to record their own history
- The need to address documentation and preservation systematically, but with as little bureaucracy as possible
- The recognition that there is often a dynamic tension between the creative community's need for hands-on, easy access to materials and long-term preservation requirements

- The need to address complex technological, cataloging, and legal issues at the national level in a coordinated fashion
- The desirability of creating a framework that will encourage the participation of funding sources with both local and national mandates
- The necessity of working both horizontally and vertically, creating building blocks that can be linked to construct a strong local, regional, national, and ultimately, international dance documentation and preservation network

The seven-point package of initiatives on the local level includes the designation of a community documentation and preservation center (possibly based in an existing institution such as a dance service organization, museum, arts center, media arts center, community center, or public library). The facility, activist in character, would engage in such activities as:

- Running a video lending program (of tapes and equipment)
- Housing computers linked with any online services the field has to offer
- Offering skills-development workshops and public education programs
- Engaging in community outreach
- Establishing a formal mechanism for the exchange and sharing of materials and expertise between national repositories and local resources

Additionally, the study recommends the designation or creation of a properly equipped video studio where videotape records of dances can be professionally made; subsidizing the work of professionals engaged in documentation; and the creation of a database of all local dance collections.

Among the initiatives outlined in the eight-point program to strengthen the national dance documentation network are:

- Increased levels of funding to national repositories
- Coalition building among the heads of the major dance repositories, as well as major culturally specific repositories
- Designation of funds to address artistic and cultural imbalances in collections
- Designation of restricted funds to eliminate cataloging backlogs and emergency funds to assist in immediate acquisition, transfer, or documentation of especially endangered artists, formats, and materials
- Standardization of descriptive elements and schemes as a first step in creating a union catalog of dance holdings

and planning for the time when these collections will be accessible via computer by individual users throughout the country and through other international repositories
• Addressing the limits of physical and intellectual property rights that impede dance documentation and discourage access to dance archives
• Strengthening international linkages among repositories
• Encouraging and financially supporting bonds between national and local repositories

The report concludes that dance is poised at a critical moment, at the end of an especially productive century. For the first time, the field has the technology to disseminate widely both new works and the rich history of the art form, and to build basic libraries that reflect the breadth of our dance culture. It emphasizes that documenting, preserving, and passing on the legacy of dance directly supports a broad range of objectives—from supplying artists with crucial working tools to developing new audiences, enlivening dance education, deepening cultural understanding, and fostering and celebrating our national heritage. As such, supporting documentation and preservation falls under the purview of a broad range of philanthropies, including those that may not have specific funding categories for archival activity.

It also offers unique opportunities for collaboration—among grant-giving foundations and agencies, and among these same funding groups and the archival and artistic communities. While the report underscores the fact that the effort to build dance archives cannot rest on the shoulders of dancers and other artists, most of whom are compensated at levels that are low even by eleemosynary standards, it points out that companies and presenters do have a critical role to play in passing on the legacy of dance, by making documentation and preservation an integral and ongoing part of their planning and their work. "Creation in the absence of documentation and preservation only denies the future," the report concludes. "The stakes could not be higher: quite simply, the conveyance of a history, the continuity of an art form, and the preservation of works through which our own renaissance becomes more likely."

LOCAL AND NATIONAL INITIATIVES

The publication and distribution of *Images of American Dance* spawned and reinforced numerous initiatives on national, regional, and local levels. A sampling of these initiatives follows.

The Dance Heritage Coalition is a national alliance administered by a committee composed of representatives of the Dance Collection of The New York Public Library, the Harvard Theatre Collection, the Library of Congress, and the San Francisco Performing Arts Library and Museum. The primary mission of the Dance Heritage Coalition is to identify and develop collaborative methodologies and systems that preserve and make accessible the creative contributions of American dance—past, present, and future. The Coalition collaborates with the dance community, the library and archival fields, scholarly institutions, and individuals in four essential areas: access to materials, documentation of dance, preservation of dance documents, and education.

A major goal of the Coalition is the creation of a national union catalog of dance materials, available on existing national bibliographic networks. Other proposed projects include the development of national strategies for documenting the artistic and historic record of dance, and educational initiatives to improve access to collections. The Coalition is forged by participatory, cooperative projects, rather than by direct membership.

Preserve, Inc. is a national clearinghouse for information about archival documentation and preservation of the performing arts. Established in 1987, Preserve is now located on the campus of Jacob's Pillow Dance Festival. Working directly with artists in residence, Preserve is uniquely positioned to provide the dance community with the tools to collect and maintain its own documentary heritage.

Preserve at Jacob's Pillow offers workshops and seminars on organizing and collecting archival materials; videotaping and viewing facilities for performance documentation and oral and video histories; online access to major dance collection catalogs, listservs of the Dance Heritage Coalition and the Dance Librarian's Discussion Group, and other Internet services; a library of resources, publications and offprints; professional archivists and dance specialists for on-site assistance in evaluation and organization of materials; and a quarterly newsletter communicating information on dance documentation and preservation, a calendar of events, and news reports.

The Cunningham Dance Foundation Archives was the first such company-based collection. Established in 1976 as a pilot project of the National Endowment for the Arts, this comprehensive collection includes programs, press clippings, photographs, posters, costume designs, choreographic notations, films, and videotapes of works created by Merce Cunningham and his collaborators (including John Cage and Robert Rauschenberg). Additionally, the archives maintains card files of performances (both chronological and alphabetical) which document the works and the casts.

The Cunningham Archives is presently undertaking a project to catalog its holdings in a computerized database, which may serve as a model to devise a software program for dance company archives. And, in what will no doubt prove to be a new take on the creation and documentation of dance, Mr. Cunningham is now choreographing on computer with a movement-generating software program called LifeForms, developed at Simon Fraser University.

The Dance Anthology Project at Jacob's Pillow was inaugurated in March 1993 with the award of a Challenge Grant from the National

Endowment for the Arts. Over the next three years, the Dance Anthology Project plans to commission revivals of seminal dance works; commission new works and document the process of their creation; and provide students with access to "etudes," excerpts of important dance works in a variety of styles, ensuring the meaningful exchange of ideas and choreographic intent among generations of dance artists. Many of these projects will be initiated by the artists involved to explore specific preservation goals while others will be developed by the Pillow.

The Paul Taylor Repertory Preservation Project (1993-94) has as its objectives to preserve some 30 dances at risk of being lost through film, video, and Labanotated scores; film dances that are currently part of the company repertory; recreate productions through restoration and construction of costumes and sets; present recreated dances in the repertory of the Paul Taylor Dance Company so they can be performed again for audiences of today and in the future; transfer rapidly deteriorating documents to archival media; and arrange and describe all holdings.

CONCLUSION

Dance exists at a perpetual vanishing point. Its moment of expression is ironically its moment of extinction, and in that moment it encapsulates the rhythms of individuals and groups as they move through time and space. Dance critic Marcia Siegal observed in the introduction to her book, *The Shapes of Change*:

> Continuity in dance must be worked at. The minute you relax your efforts at preserving something you start to lose it. There's no such thing as setting aside an idea or a style or a work for a while and then expecting it to be intact when you come back to it later.
>
> This is also true of a dancer's body and of a critic's memory. Preservation—or the losing battle we fight with it—may in fact be the basic issue of American dance. The immediacy and the ephemerality of dance are its most particular qualities—they are the reason for dance's appeal as well as its low rank on the scale of intellectual values. People are thrilled by it because it is so singular an occurrence. When you have seen a dance, you've done something no one else will do again. But for this very reason scholars can't get hold of it. Dance leaves them with nothing tangible to analyze or categorize or put on reserve in the library.[2]

While it is true that the experience of dance cannot be retained in a repository, the many parts that are documented can create the whole.

Documenting and preserving dance are an imperative for our culture, for unless we take steps to save its history, there is little chance that any dance will survive.

NOTES

1. William Keens, Leslie Hansen Kopp, and Mindy N. Leving, *Images of American Dance: Documenting and Preserving a Cultural Heritage* (Washington, D.C.: Dance Program, National Endowment for the Arts, 1991).
2. Marcia B. Siegel, *The Shapes of Change: Images of American Dance* (Boston: Houghton Mifflin, 1979), xiii.

Experience and Examples in the Preservation of Scrapbooks and Albums

Sherelyn Ogden

Director of Book Conservation
Northeast Document Conservation Center

A pile of broken pages, haphazardly stacked between two tattered covers. This, unfortunately, is the image that comes to mind when most librarians and archivists think of scrapbooks and albums. Nearly every library and archives has at least one of these books in its collection, and many have hundreds. Scrapbooks and albums present unique problems, challenging those responsible for their preservation. Completely satisfactory answers to the scrapbook/ album dilemma do not exist. Those solutions we have are at best a compromise, trading such concerns as ease of use for low cost, or the original appearance of the book for the long-term preservation of the information it contains. Success in preserving these books lies in integrating several factors into a single approach, one that takes into account the value of the book and balances the advice of the preservation specialist with the needs of the book's custodian.

DEFINITIONS

Many of the terms used in preservation have several common variants in meaning. For this reason it is best to begin by defining some basic terms, as they will be used in this paper. "Preservation" includes the "activities associated with maintaining library, archival, or museum materials for use, either in original form or in some other format."[1] This is the definition suggested by the American Library Association (ALA), and it is used broadly to encompass a number of procedures, from duplication to conservation. "Duplication" as it is used here refers to all forms of copying; microfilming, photocopying, and photographic copying are the types of duplication used most often for scrapbooks and albums. "Conservation," again according to ALA, is "the treatment of library or archival materials, works of art, or museum objects to stabilize them chemically or strengthen them physically sustaining their survival as long as possible in their original form."[2]

Scrapbooks and albums are two very similar types of books. In fact, distinguishing between them is difficult because their likenesses are so marked. The *Oxford English Dictionary* (*OED*) defines a "scrapbook" as "a blank book in which pictures, newspaper cuttings, and the like are pasted for preservation."[3] An "album" is described as "a blank book in which to insert autographs, memorial verses, original drawings or other souvenirs."[4] The

OED further characterizes an album as "a book for reception of photographic cartes and views, or of postage stamps, or other things which are collected and preserved. . ."[5]

The difference between these books typically relates to the type of items selected for inclusion in them, and to the organization of the materials within the book. The arrangement of items in a scrapbook often has an informal quality with miscellaneous items attached in the book casually or at random. Albums, on the other hand, are generally more formal; they frequently contain the same type of materials, and these are attached in the book in a deliberate order or position. The distinction between scrapbooks and albums may also relate to differences in their binding. The term "binding" refers to the covers of a book and to the structural elements that fasten its leaves together. Although the bindings of both scrapbooks and albums are usually made of relatively poor-quality materials, the bindings of albums may be made of better components. Also, albums tend to have a more complicated binding structure than scrapbooks and are often more elaborately decorated.

PROBLEMS INHERENT IN SCRAPBOOKS AND ALBUMS

Poor storage conditions, inappropriate handling, and heavy use contribute greatly to the deterioration of scrapbooks and albums, just as they do to the damage of other types of books. Many of the causes of deterioration in scrapbooks and albums, however, are inherent in the books themselves. Four of the most common of these causes are:

1. The materials from which the binding and leaves are made
2. The structure of the binding
3. The material from which the items attached to the leaves are made (coupled with the size and weight of the items)
4. The method of attachment of the items to the leaves

These causes are the reason scrapbooks and albums are quite difficult to preserve—there are no completely satisfactory solutions to the problems that result from them.

The Materials from Which Scrapbooks and Albums Are Made

The materials from which scrapbooks and albums are made vary widely. Often the bindings and leaves have been mass-produced from inexpensive components so that the books would be affordable to a mass market. Usually these materials are of very poor quality and deteriorate rapidly, frequently damaging the items they house. The leaves of a scrapbook or album, for example, are often made of groundwood pulp paper, which becomes acidic and brittle over time. When the leaves become fragile they often break, causing items attached to them to crack or tear as well. Further, acidity migrates from the leaves into the items, hastening their deterioration.

Bindings are also frequently made of substandard materials. Sheepskin was used to cover many scrapbooks and albums in the late 19th and early 20th centuries, because it was inexpensive and readily available. Over time this inferior leather dries out and becomes excessively acidic; it eventually grows powdery and so weak that the binding breaks in areas where it is flexed. Many scrapbook and album bindings are covered in cloth rather than leather, because of the lower cost. Some cloth decays quickly and becomes weak. The outcome is that the covers often tear loose from the book, leaving the items contained in it unprotected.

Binding Structures

Many different binding structures have been used for scrapbooks and albums. Some structures, or particular features of them, create problems. For example, scrapbooks and albums should be bound with built-in compensation that allows for the added thickness of the materials they will contain. If the compensation is insufficient (which often happens) stresses are placed on both the binding and the items, and damage can result. Many scrapbooks and albums use stubs to create the extra space needed for the items. An associated problem, however, is that these can form an edge against which brittle leaves fracture when flexed, causing them to separate from the binding.

Another common structural problem in scrapbooks and albums is the way in which the leaves are attached to each other. Frequently the leaves are held together with cloth hinges that vary greatly in quality. In some books the cloth used for the hinges remains strong over time, while in others it quickly deteriorates and tears, causing leaves to detach. Yet another problem is that the binding structure of some scrapbooks and albums allows items to be affixed too far into the inner margin. This not only damages the items, but the bulk created prevents the scrapbook or album from closing properly and places stress on such critical elements as the hinges, joints, sewing supports, and thread, causing them to break and the book to fall apart. Some scrapbooks and albums lack sewing and are held together with adhesive. The adhesive usually dries out over time and releases, causing the binding to break down.

The Contents of Scrapbooks and Albums

The items contained in scrapbooks and albums may also be problematic. Since these books often contain materials of a transient nature that were intended to last only for a short time, the contents (as well as the bindings and leaves) are frequently made of inexpensive and inferior materials that deteriorate rapidly; newspaper clippings made from groundwood pulp paper may be the most prevalent example. Another problem is that items in scrapbooks and albums vary in size, weight, thickness, and format. Often they are larger than the space allocated for them—they extend beyond the book's edges and are susceptible to damage. Sometimes items are too heavy to be supported by the leaf to which they are attached; these may pull loose from the leaf and become damaged or even lost. Yet another problem is that an item may not be appropriate for inclusion in a book. A poster, for example, may have to be folded several times, often at right angles to other folds, in order to fit. This not only creases the poster, it may also cause cockling, pleating, or bursting at its folds.

Method of Attachment

The method used to attach items in a scrapbook or album may also be a problem. A variety of means have been used, including adhesives, tapes, straps, slits, and ribbons. All vary in quality and long-term stability. Some are very destructive to the materials they affix. Unstable adhesives, which discolor and stain items, are especially problematic. The placement of items, in conjunction with their attachment, may also create problems since pieces are often attached together, one on top of another, or side-by-side, overlapping each other, making it impossible to view them without handling them. This can lead to serious damage if items are brittle.

CONSIDERATIONS IN THE DEVELOPMENT OF A PRESERVATION PROPOSAL

The development of proposals for the preservation of scrapbooks and albums requires collaboration between the custodian (curator, librarian, archivist, owner) of the book and a preservation specialist, most often a conservator. Several factors need to be considered, each weighed carefully against the others. The acceptability of copying the items contained in the book is one of the first factors to consider; microfilming, photocopying, and photographic copying are the primary means of preservation duplication. Microfilming is the method chosen most often (in spite of user difficulty and loss of image detail) because it is generally most cost-effective.

Related to this is another factor—the nature of the value of the book. This is of critical importance. If the book is important solely for the information it contains, duplication is an acceptable option. However, if the book has value because of a particular person, place, or institution associated with it, or if it is significant because of its age, bibliographic importance, design, structure, or artistry, preservation of the original is necessary and duplication alone is inadequate. Sometimes the items in a book will have associational or other special value, but the binding will have none. In this case, if the binding is contributing to the deterioration of the items it shelters, the pieces will be removed from the binding and stored in a way that will not contribute to their deterioration, perhaps in acid-free folders and archival storage boxes.

Security is another factor to be considered, particularly if one is considering removing items from the book and storing them elsewhere, in another format. For example, items that have been removed from acidic book leaves, placed in acid-free folders, and then stored in boxes can be more vulnerable to theft and loss than they were when attached to album or scrapbook pages. This may not be a problem if the items are rarely consulted, but if they are frequently used, security should be taken into account. Use, then, becomes another important factor for consideration. Scrapbooks and albums that are rarely used can often be considered a low priority for preservation, even if they are in fragile condition or highly valuable, whereas books that are frequently used should be given a high priority. Condition is also, of course, a factor to consider. Immediate action may be needed for books in advanced stages of deterioration, but postponed for books in stable condition.

Finally, the costs of various preservation options should be compared. Cost should be considered in terms of both staff time and dollars. Depending on the size, condition, and complexity of the book, costs can range from one or two hours of work (about $50) at the low end for microfilming a scrapbook or album, to hundreds of hours (and many thousands of dollars) at the high end for complete treatment of the items and the original binding.

EXAMPLES OF SPECIFIC SCRAPBOOK AND ALBUM PROJECTS

Duplication in Combination with Treatment

Dan Kempner Scrapbooks

Many institutions own dozens if not hundreds of scrapbooks and albums that contain deteriorated and brittle newspaper clippings made of groundwood pulp paper. Physical treatment of books such as these would require hundreds of hours and thousands of dollars. Even if these resources were available, the wisdom of treating massive amounts of groundwood pulp paper, which will continue to deteriorate at a very rapid rate even after treatment, is questionable. Because these books are usually valuable only for the information they contain, duplication is the most practical preservation measure, with microfilming generally being the most cost-effective approach.

Sometimes, however, scrapbooks and albums of purely informational value contain a few items that have associational or other special importance. An example is the Dan Kempner Collection of scrapbooks belonging to the Rosenberg Library in Galveston, Texas. The library has approximately 60 scrapbooks in the Dan Kempner Collection, each filled primarily with newspaper clippings but also containing magazines, advertisements, letters, and telegrams, all adhered to leaves of very brittle groundwood pulp paper. Some of the materials contained in the books have special significance and need to be preserved in their original form.

Complete conservation treatment for every scrapbook would require removal of the items from the wood pulp leaves using solvents, washing the individual pieces, aqueous alkalization of them by immersion in an alkalizing agent, reinforcement of fragile items by lining with Japanese tissue paper, reattachment of the items to new leaves of acid-free paper, and rebinding in new covers made of archival-quality materials. This level of treatment would have cost tens of thousands of dollars and the library could not afford this. The archivist and the conservator discussed several alternatives that entailed less treatment, and the archivist chose to try one as a pilot project.

For this project all the items in the Dan Kempner Scrapbook Number One were microfilmed. Because ease of use was a special concern, a hard copy of the scrapbook on acid-free paper was produced from the microfilm copy. Those items of special value were identified by the archivist and then removed from the original scrapbook by the conservator and treated as appropriate. Following treatment these items were placed in acid-free folders in an archival storage box. This affordable preservation option proved successful in meeting the library's requirements for use, preservation of information, and conservation of items of special value.

Jerome Robbins Scrapbooks

Sometimes complete conservation of newspaper clippings is necessary. Five scrapbooks of newspaper clippings belonging to choreographer Jerome Robbins were severely water- and mold-damaged while housed in a storage vault. The books had enormous value for the information they contained about dance and the American musical theater. The scrapbooks included a total of approximately 6,200 clippings, as well as programs, invitations, telegrams, and other miscellaneous items relating to some of the most important work of Robbins' career. The bindings were very deteriorated, severely stained and misshapen from water damage and covered in places with a heavy layer of mold. The clippings were extremely degraded, weak, brittle, and pulpy. They had been affixed to leaves with a variety of adhesives and were so stained from the adhesives, mold, and water damage that they were difficult to read; in many instances, they were completely illegible. Major portions of numerous clippings were completely disintegrated. Many clippings had attached themselves to adjacent pages and were irreparably damaged.

Since the scrapbooks were valuable primarily for the information they contained, duplication of the clippings was considered first. However, because of the severity of the damage, the majority of clippings would have required conservation treatment prior to copying. Replacement of clippings with photocopies made from newspapers in good condition was also considered. But, many of the clippings were from esoteric newspapers and other periodicals that were no longer available, even in research libraries. After collaborating with the conservator, the owner of the scrapbooks decided on a combination of treatment, duplication, and replacement, in an attempt to preserve as much information as possible.

The clippings were treated, whenever feasible. Procedures included surface cleaning, removal from the leaves with a variety of solvents, washing, aqueous alkalization, stain reduction, sizing, and reinforcement by lining. Those clippings too deteriorated to sustain treatment were photocopied by a conservator onto acid-free paper. A researcher was hired to obtain copies of clippings that had been partly or completely destroyed by the water and mold damage; unfortunately, copies of only about 45 percent of them were obtainable. The miscellaneous items were treated as needed.

All the pieces contained in the scrapbooks—clippings, photocopies, and miscellaneous materials—were attached to sheets of acid-free paper in their original order. The sheets of paper were then placed between two sheets of polyester film (a clear inert plastic). The film was sealed with an ultrasonic weld. This procedure, known as polyester film encapsulation, provides excellent protection and support for fragile paper, and it was used here because the original clippings were still very fragile even after treatment. The encapsulated sheets were bound in a cloth post binding: custom-made covers were attached to the encapsulated sheets by screw posts, which passed through both the covers and the polyester film. The original bindings were not reused because they were too deteriorated and damaged, and because they were too small to accommodate the encapsulated leaves.

Igor Sikorski Scrapbook

When the binding of a scrapbook or album is itself of special value, the book must be preserved in its original form. Duplication is often useful in this situation, in that it reduces the need to handle the fragile original materials the book contains. Thus, minimal treatment can be adequate for books that would otherwise require more extensive treatment that (in some cases) alters their original form. An example of this is the personal scrapbook of Igor Sikorski, a pioneer in aviation. The cloth stationery binding was in fragile condition, and the items contained in the book were in only fair-to-poor condition.

The book received minimal treatment. The items and the leaves to which they were attached were surface cleaned and nonaqueously alkalized by spraying an alkalizing agent onto the surface of the leaves. This treatment is intended to slow the deterioration of paper, without altering its appearance. The binding was not repaired, because this would have altered it significantly. The cloth cover of the book was intact, but the internal hinges were broken, the sewing and spine linings were loose, and the adhesive used to consolidate the spine had released, causing sections of the book to separate from each other.

Repair of the binding would have entailed disbinding, mending tears in the leaves, resewing, lining the spine, and enlarging the original binding to fit the resewn leaves. This extensive treatment was not necessary, if the book were to receive only occasional handling. Instead, the scrapbook was housed in a cloth-covered, drop-spine box and was removed from routine use. A microfilm copy of the items was made for researchers, the great majority of whom require only the information contained in the book and have no need for the scrapbook as an artifact.

Mary Moody Northen Scrapbook

Duplication was also invaluable in the preservation of the Mary Moody Northen Debut Scrapbook. Compiled by the young daughter of an influential Galveston, Texas, family, the book has great associational value especially to the institution that owns it, a foundation established by the Northen family. The scrapbook bulged with ribbons, cords, tassels, bouquets, dance cards, telegrams, party invitations, and other memorabilia. The book required stabilization, as well as preservation as an artifact. This was a problem, because the structure of the book and the placement of the items on the leaves was causing damage to the items, already deteriorated and fragile. In addition, some of the plant materials were too deteriorated to remove from the leaves without causing further damage.

The decision was made to microfilm the book and restrict research use to the film copy. Even though this minimized handling of the scrapbook, the items contained in the book still needed to be stabilized because of their extreme fragility. The cover of the book was already detached from the leaves. The sewing was intact but was removed to release stress on the items, particularly the bulky ones attached close to the inner margin. Leaves and items made of paper were surface cleaned and nonaqueously alkalized, where appropriate. The leaves were interleaved with polyester film to help support the items when the pages were turned. Plant materials were a special problem, because most of them were so deteriorated they disintegrated when touched. Where plant materials were loose, they were encapsulated in polyester film and reattached in their original position. Where they were still attached to leaves, polyester film was placed over them and fastened into position. Two drop-spine boxes were constructed to house the scrapbook, one for the leaves and items, and one for the binding and pink leather over-cover that originally wrapped around it.

Preservation of Items, But Not the Binding

Berley Studio Albums

In some instances, the items contained in a scrapbook or album do not need the protection of a binding; removal of all the items from the binding and storage in another format, such as acid-free folders and a box, is acceptable. The Fashion Institute of Technology in New York City has over 200 albums of garment sketches in its Berley Studio Collection. These pencil sketches are the originals from which copies were made for distribution to garment designers and manufacturers as design ideas. Covering the years 1919 through 1959, these drawings have special value as unique visual resources and must be preserved in their original form.

Some 37 albums containing over 10,000 drawings received heavy use. The drawings needed to be stabilized to sustain this level of activity. Because of the numbers involved, the work had to be done in the most efficient way possible. The bindings, which had no associational or other special value, were deteriorated and structurally damaged. Further, they contributed to the damage of the drawings: the album leaves to which the drawings were affixed were very brittle and acidic; as the leaves were turned they broke, tearing the drawings.

After deliberation with the conservator, the librarian decided that the drawings did not require the physical protection and security from loss provided by a binding. The albums were disbound. The drawings were surface cleaned, removed from each leaf using moisture and solvents, washed, and aqueously alkalized. Stains were reduced to the degree possible. The most serious tears were repaired, and a few fragile drawings were encapsulated in polyester film. The drawings were returned to the Fashion Institute where they were placed in acid-free folders, with 10 to 15 drawings to a folder, and boxed in acid-free archival storage boxes.

Preservation of Both Items and Binding

Kate Furbish Albums

Sometimes the binding is integral to the value of the book and must be preserved. The album *Flora of Maine* is an example. Treatment of this album was undertaken when reproduction and publication of the book was planned. This album is one of a series of 16 produced by the artist Kate Furbish between 1870 and 1908. It contained 93 drawings and watercolors with identifying labels. The artist not only produced the drawings and watercolors, but also designed the binding and selected all the materials for it, so that the binding as well as the items had special value.

The binding was in relatively good condition though the cloth hinges that attached the leaves to it were very deteriorated, weak and torn in places. The drawings, watercolors, and identifying labels were also fairly sound, but they were adhered to acidic, brittle leaves with discoloring adhesive. The curator decided that, because of the high value of the drawings and watercolors, they and the leaves to which they were attached should be treated as extensively as necessary to preserve them, and to enable the album to sustain increased use, as a result of the attention the book was expected to generate. Since both the binding and the items contained in it had artistic, associational, and informational value, the album was to be preserved in its original form. To achieve these two goals it needed to be disbound, the items treated, and the album rebound, using as many of the original materials as possible to preserve the work of Ms. Furbish.

The album was carefully disbound, causing as little damage to the binding as possible. The drawings, watercolors, and labels were removed from the leaves using steam and water, then surface cleaned and washed. The leaves were surface cleaned, washed, and aqueously alkalized. All adhesives were removed. The drawings, watercolors, and labels were reattached to the album leaves with corners of handmade paper, or by spot-adhering with rice starch paste. The cloth hinges were replaced with new ones of unbleached linen that were thicker but similar in appearance to the originals. The leaves were re-sewn and rebound in the original binding, which was enlarged with goat leather to accommodate the increased thickness caused by the new cloth hinges. The two goals of the treatment were achieved: the drawings, watercolors, and leaves received thorough conservation treatment and were better able to sustain increased use, and the original form of the album was preserved.

BASIC IN-HOUSE PRESERVATION MEASURES

The preservation options discussed above require the expertise of a conservator, duplication specialist, or both, as well as a significant financial investment. A few measures, however, can be taken by the book's custodian (whether personal or institutional) at relatively low cost. These measures will retard deterioration of scrapbooks and albums and will help to stabilize, if not improve, the condition of these books.

Control of Temperature, Relative Humidity, and Light

Maintaining environmental conditions at appropriate levels will significantly extend the useful life of scrapbooks and albums. Temperature, relative humidity, and light all affect the longevity of these books. Control of temperature and relative humidity is of particular importance. Heat accelerates most chemical reactions, including deterioration. High relative humidity provides the moisture necessary to promote these harmful chemical reactions and, in combination with high temperature, encourages mold growth and insect activity. Extremely low relative humidity leads to desiccation and embrittlement of certain materials. Fluctuations in temperature and relative humidity are even more damaging than extremes of these factors. Book materials are hygroscopic, readily absorbing and releasing moisture. They respond to diurnal and seasonal changes in temperature and relative humidity by expanding and contracting. These dimensional changes accelerate deterioration and lead to such visible damage as cockling paper, flaking ink, and warped covers.

Authorities disagree on the ideal temperature and relative humidity for the storage of books. A stable temperature no higher than 70 degrees F and a stable relative humidity between a minimum of 30 percent and a maximum of 50 percent are acceptable guidelines for most institutions. Fluctuations in temperature and relative humidity should be avoided to the degree possible. Achieving these conditions may require installation of adequate climate controls and operation of these controls to conservation standards. Climate control equipment ranges in complexity from a simple room air conditioner, humidifier, and/or dehumidifier, to a central, building-wide system, which filters, cools, heats, humidifies, and dehumidifies the air.

Light accelerates deterioration of book materials by acting as a catalyst in their oxidation. It leads to weakening and embrittlement of cellulose fibers and can cause paper to bleach, yellow, or darken. It also causes media and dyes to fade or change in color, altering the legibility and/or appearance of pages and bindings. Any exposure to light, even for a brief time, is damaging, and the damage is cumulative and irreversible. For these reasons light levels should be controlled in areas where scrapbooks and albums are used and stored. Although all wavelengths of light are damaging, ultraviolet (UV) radiation is especially harmful because of its high level of energy. The sun and mercury vapor, metal halide, and fluorescent artificial lighting are the most damaging sources of light because of the high amounts of UV energy they emit. Extra effort should be put into protecting scrapbooks and albums from exposure to this radiation.

Because total damage caused by light is a function of both intensity and duration of exposure, illumination should be kept as low as possible, and used for the briefest amount of time. Ideally, scrapbooks and albums should be stored in windowless rooms illuminated only when necessary, and then by incandescent light. Time switches should be used for lights in storage areas, to help limit the duration of exposure. Windows should be covered by drapes, shades, blinds, or shutters that completely block the sun. Skylights that allow direct sunlight to shine on collections should be covered, or painted with titanium dioxide or zinc white pigments, which reflect light and absorb UV radiation.

Filters made of special plastics also help control UV radiation. Ultraviolet-filtering plastic films or Plexiglas can be applied to windows to lower the amount of UV radiation passing through them. However, these filters do *not* provide 100 percent protection against light damage. Drapes or similar devices that completely block the light are preferable. Fluorescent tubes should be covered with ultraviolet-filtering sleeves in areas where books are exposed to light. An alternative is the use of special low-UV fluorescent tubes.

Permanent exhibition of materials should be avoided. Since even slight exposure to light is damaging, permanent exposure is deadly. If materials must be displayed, it should be for the briefest time and at the lowest light levels, with the light coming from an incandescent source. Materials should never be displayed where the sun shines directly on them, even if only for a short time, and even if the windows are covered with an ultraviolet-filtering plastic.

Provision of Good Storage

Good storage methods are especially important for the preservation of scrapbooks and albums. Because these books are often large, bulky, and fragile, they are particularly vulnerable to damage caused by poor storage practices. An important measure that can be taken for the preservation of these books is to store them properly and provide good-quality storage containers.

Small scrapbooks and albums in sound condition can be shelved upright between other books of similar size. Large books, however, should be shelved flat to give them the overall support they require. Additional shelves may be inserted at narrow intervals, to avoid stacking books that are shelved flat. (Books should be stacked only when absolutely necessary, and then only two to three books high. Ideally, all books that are stacked should be individually boxed.) Special care should be taken to ensure that call number flags or titles of books that are stored flat are visible so the books can be identified without moving them. Shelves should be wide enough to support the books completely, so that there is no overhang and they do not protrude into the aisles.

Scrapbooks and albums that are damaged should be tied together with a flat, undyed cotton, linen, or polyester tape and then shelved flat. Ideally, they should be placed in a storage container as well; custom-fitted drop-spine and phase boxes are best. Drop-spine boxes are preferable because they provide better support and keep books cleaner, but they are considerably more expensive than phase boxes. A lower-cost alternative to both of these custom-fitted boxes is standard-size archival storage boxes available from commercial suppliers. The disadvantage of these boxes is that, since they are not custom-fitted to the book, the scrapbook or album can shift within the box and possibly be damaged. If all of these boxes are too expensive or take up too much space on shelves, scrapbooks and albums that are infrequently used can be placed in card stock enclosures (which are best for small books) or wrapped in permanent durable paper.

CONCLUSION

Preserving scrapbooks and albums can be complex and challenging; it requires that difficult decisions be made. By their nature, these books are one-of-a-kind. Each preservation solution, likewise, is unique. By matching appropriate preservation options with books, custodians, and preservation specialists can help ensure that these unique materials continue to inform, enlighten, and delight for years to come.

ACKNOWLEDGEMENTS

The author thanks the clients who entrusted the Northeast Document Conservation Center (NEDCC) with the preservation of their scrapbooks and albums and allowed these to be discussed in this paper; Paul Hudon and Christopher Clarkson, for their assistance in preparing this paper for publication; and colleagues at NEDCC, past and present, too numerous to mention individually, for their help with this article and their work preserving scrapbooks and albums. Much of this paper was originally presented in the Book and Paper Session at the 19th annual meeting of the American Institute for Conservation of Historic and Artistic Works, Albuquerque, New Mexico, June, 1991.

SUGGESTIONS FOR ADDITIONAL READING

Bignell, M. "Scrapbooks and Albums." In *Basic Conservation of Archival Materials: A Guide*, pp. 94-97. Ottawa: Canadian Council of Archives, 1990.

DeCandido, Robert. "Out of the Question." *Conservation Administration News* 54:18-19 (July 1993).

DeCandido, Robert, "Scrapbooks." In *Preserving America's Performing Arts: Conference on Preservation Management for Performing Arts Collection, April 28-May 1, 1982, Washington, D.C.*, pp. 68-69. Ed. by Barbara Cohen-Stratyner and Brigitte Kueppers. New York: Theater Library Association, 1985.

Jense, Mary Ann. "On Dog Tails, Dog Ears, and Just Plain Going to the Dogs." In *Preserving America's Performing Arts: Conference on Preservation Management for Performing Arts Collection, April 28-May 1, 1982, Washington, D.C.*, pp. 70-72. Ed. by Barbara Cohen-Stratyner and Brigitte Kueppers. New York: Theater Library Association, 1985.

Preservation of Scrapbooks and Albums. Preservation Basics Leaflet no. 1: National Cooperative Information Project, November 1991.

Smith, Merrily. "Scrapbooks in the Library of Congress." In *Preserving America's Performing Arts: Conference on Preservation Management for Performing Arts Collection, April 28-May 1, 1982, Washington, D.C.*, pp. 73-77. Ed. by Barbara Cohen-Stratyner and Brigitte Kueppers. New York: Theater Library Association, 1985.

Zucker, B. "Scrapbooks and Albums: Their Care and Conservation." *Illinois Libraries* 67:695-99 (1985)

NOTES

1. "Glossary of Selected Preservation Terms," *ALCTS Newsletter* 1:2 (1990): 15.
2. Ibid., 14.
3. *Oxford English Dictionary*, compact ed., 2 vols. (Oxford: 1979), 2678.
4. Ibid., 52.
5. Ibid.

PART 7:
EDUCATION AND TRAINING FOR
LIBRARIANS, ARCHIVISTS, AND READERS

If our collections are to be properly cared for, it is essential that librarians, archivists, and readers understand and apply the principles of preservation, as these relate to their particular connection to the materials in question. In a thought-provoking paper about education for librarians, Sheila Intner examines the issue of including preservation components in non-preservation courses in library school curricula, versus offering "stand-alone" preservation courses. Intner also explores the question of the best place to teach the actual techniques of preservation (paper chemistry, repair and restoration) and the potential value of establishing library school/teaching library partnerships for preservation education. Intner concludes by proposing the elements that should be contained in an ideal curriculum for preservation librarians.

In their paper on educating archivists for preservation, Evelyn Frangakis and Christine Ward examine the changing emphasis in archival preservation from item treatment to a more comprehensive programmatic approach; they focus on the Society of American Archivists' (SAA) nationwide education programs. The authors describe a model for training preservation managers that is presently used by SAA, with support from the National Endowment for the Humanities. Frangakis and Ward make the point that preservation no longer means responding to damage that has already occurred, but rather is more akin to prevention: preservation means actively eliminating those conditions that cause or encourage damage. SAA's approach shows promise as a method of educating professionals, disseminating standards, and promoting the development of preservation programs in archival institutions.

Ann Paietta observes that preservation literature seldom concerns itself with the impact readers and staff have on library materials. Paietta makes the point that careless or poorly trained collection maintenance staff and uninformed readers can undo much valuable preservation work and negate a clean, controlled library environment. In her paper she describes how a library or archive can develop good stack maintenance habits in its staff and raise readers' consciousness about the proper handling of library materials. Paietta suggests that the life of these materials can be significantly extended through comprehensive staff training and reader awareness programs.

While a great deal has been written about emergency planning and recovery, library and archival literature is largely silent about the role of the director or curator in this important area. Barbra Higginbotham and Miriam Kahn observe that the director's responsibilities—leadership, coordination, and public relations—are not only quite different from those of staff involved in the actual work of emergency planning and response, but also critical to a complete and successful recovery when disaster strikes. They make the point that recovery is a lengthy and complex process: one could say that, when the immediate emergency subsides, the real work of the director begins. Kahn and Higginbotham also examine many of the sensitive, human issues involved in rescue operations; they introduce the concept of an emergency response team, empowered to assign work and supervise staff in emergencies.

Educating Preservation Librarians: Perspectives on Curricular Issues and Answers

Sheila S. Intner

Professor
Simmons College Graduate School of
Library and Information Science

INTRODUCTION

Education for preservation librarianship has a relatively brief history, dating from the 1970s when the School of Library Service at Columbia University initiated a specialized program of study that combined three elements: foundations in librarianship; techniques of restoring and revitalizing deteriorated materials; and management of preservation programs within libraries.[1] If one looks beyond librarianship, however, he or she can find long-established programs of study rooted in the more traditional scholarly disciplines from which the ideas embodied in preservation education sprang—art, history, and chemistry, for example. Selected areas of knowledge from these fields were overlaid upon the interdisciplinary framework comprising preparation for general library work (knowledge about scholarly processes and the publishing world, library functions, and the management of library organizations) to form a specialized knowledge base appropriate for those preparing to assume primary responsibility for saving the deteriorating resources in the nation's large research libraries.

The Columbia model (now functioning as part of the graduate library and information science program at the University of Texas at Austin), being the first of its kind, furnished a point from which other schools could add, subtract, shift, and experiment with different combinations of course work, independent research, and pre-graduate practice, while also varying the elements of librarianship, management, the sciences, technology, and preservation procedure that went into the makeup of the specialized program. Many schools added courses in preservation techniques and/or preservation management to their curricula. Some also offered opportunities for pre-graduate practice (variously called internships, practica, guided field study). Others included preservation in their list of continuing education offerings. But few matched or exceeded the scope and coverage of the Columbia (now the University of Texas at Austin) program.

A recent review of preservation education produced general recommendations placing greater emphasis on research and management.[2] Concern has been expressed by knowledgeable observers that too strong a focus on conservation techniques (paper cleaning and repair, hand binding, etc.) and not enough on library management might fail to equip preservationists to integrate and operate effectively within the general library setting, and to impress upon them the importance of considering and successfully relating to colleagues working in the functional areas to which preservation is related, such as collection development, materials processing, and bibliographic control.[3] Another issue raised by practitioners and educators alike is the need for professional schools to educate people to lead library preservation activity even when they plan to work outside the research library community, perhaps in colleges, smaller universities, elementary and secondary schools, and ordinary communities, where budgets and staffing patterns rarely support a full-fledged preservation program headed by a full-time preservationist, yet collections require attention, albeit on a smaller scale.

This paper provides an analysis of a selection of issues that might be considered in designing curricula for preservation education in graduate professional school programs, and offers suggestions on how these might be addressed. The issues explored here include:

- The advantages and disadvantages of including preservation components in non-preservation courses in library school curricula, e.g., technical services, collection development, serials management, media services, etc.
- The advantages and disadvantages of the "stand-alone" preservation course
- The advantages and disadvantages of teaching preservation techniques in the library school (is the library school the appropriate place to learn paper chemistry, repair and restoration, and so on? If not, where should these techniques be taught?)
- The potential value and potential danger in establishing library school/teaching library partnerships for education for preservation
- Elements in an ideal curriculum designed to prepare preservation librarians

The perspective from which these issues are described and discussed is that of the author, a library school faculty member with more than a decade of experience teaching courses in preservation management, collection development, and technical services. The interpretations and judgments expressed herein are solely her own, not those of the school in which she teaches, nor the institutions with which she has previously been affiliated, as is responsibility for all errors of omission or commission, for which she apologizes profusely to the reader.

PRESERVATION COMPONENTS IN
NON-PRESERVATION COURSES

When faculties recognize the need to add a new type of knowledge to the library school program, two immediate responses are possible: add the new knowledge to existing courses, or create a new course in which to teach it. Both methods result in incorporating the new knowledge into the curriculum taken as a whole, but neither ensures that all students will receive the new information unless the designated material is also made a requirement for graduation. Logic and experience suggest that new topics are unlikely to become requirements immediately, although nothing prevents their assuming such recognition and importance over the course of time.

In a number of respects, it is far easier to add the recent knowledge to existing courses than to initiate a new one. For one thing, the existing courses are there, already scheduled to be taught, listed in school bulletins and on other printed course lists so students are aware of them, and schools are able to absorb the new material without having to make any administrative changes. Not only do catalogs have to be amended to account for new courses, but there must also be publicity beyond mere listing (such as alerting faculty advisors to recommend them) in order to develop an audience for the new class. Faculty advisors, who may have spent considerable time with their advisees setting up program models according to each student's intended career goals, must try to remember who might benefit from the course and consult with them again to suggest that it be substituted for one they had already decided to take; this adds an unforeseen burden to faculty workloads. Although the new course will eventually be integrated into the total curriculum, a time lag of a semester or two, or sometimes a year or more, may elapse before this is accomplished.

If new material is added to existing courses and there are no changes to the course lists, faculty changes need not be considered or effected. Existing faculty can continue teaching their courses, perhaps with the addition of guest lecturers who have special expertise in the new subject area. Alternatively, current veterans or newly hired faculty must become interested in the new material and acquire the requisite knowledge; perhaps they may already have pursued such interests in their past education or experience, but had no earlier opportunity to incorporate them into their teaching. Either way, the school budget need not be increased to accommodate new courses or added faculty hours, even though existing offerings are enriched.

From the students' viewpoint, incorporating new knowledge into existing courses also has its advantages. This author finds students under great pressure to select and schedule their courses, as well as to finance their graduate education. There always seem to be many more desirable courses than their programs or their funds will permit them to take. Most graduate students work (at least part-time) while they attend school, thus time for classes and homework is limited at best and must be juggled with work, personal obligations, and other extra-curricular commitments. Because the stress level is already high, increasing the offerings in the curriculum adds another psychological, yet very real, burden on students.

To summarize briefly, then, incorporating preservation into existing courses has the following advantages:

- No administrative changes are required, such as
  scheduling and publicizing.
- No new advising is required.
- No new faculty are required.
- Library school budgets are not affected.
- No new pressures are added to student choices.

The disadvantages of incorporating new knowledge into existing courses should also be identified and assessed. Just as adding a new course to a student's program means deleting another he or she had intended to take, adding new material to existing courses means deleting or compressing other information that was previously taught, or otherwise altering the course plans to make room for it. Two logical cognates for preservation knowledge are courses in collection development and technical services, but it would not be easy to incorporate new material into either one. The scope and coverage of both subject areas have been expanding throughout the last two decades as new problems, issues, and options have emerged.

In collection development, a host of essential topics to be covered in a 14- or 15-week course includes developing written policies; conducting research studies to ascertain user needs; formulating collecting goals and objectives consistent with the library's and the institution's mission, goals, and objectives; considering the options for resource sharing; making the appropriate choices between access and ownership; assessing collections both quantitatively and qualitatively; allocating funds knowledgeably and equitably among competing subjects, departments or branches, audiences, and media; establishing effective selection and deselection processes; and supervising collection development staff. Each of these topics could occupy several lectures, without covering all the material one might wish to include, yet the list is still incomplete, omitting any consideration of vendor/library relations and other acquisitions-related knowledge, or of specific collecting areas.

Similarly, in technical services, subtopics include a variety of issues and problems in acquisitions, cataloging, classification, processing, and circulation, to say nothing of describing both manual and automated systems of various kinds that are available to accomplish each of these functions, as well as the related issues of database design, quality control, training, standards, and evaluation.

Under these circumstances, it is hard to expect that preservation can get much more than a brief mention in courses in technical services or collection development, perhaps as much as one lecture or reading and not likely more than that. Not much can be accomplished within this limited framework.

Another drawback to including preservation as part of existing courses is that the approach will be from one particular perspective—that of the bibliographer or the technical services librarian—rather than balanced from all points of view concerned with preservation qua preservation. The preservation information to be presented must be selected to relate to the other material in the course, because the overarching concern of each course is not its focus on preservation issues but those of the main subject. As a result, only part of the preservation knowledge base will be covered, and that only from a particular point of view.

If faculty members teaching collection development, technical services, or other courses already part of the library school curriculum decide they wish to add preservation material, but they do not themselves have the requisite knowledge, they may turn to practitioners or other faculty colleagues to act as guest lecturers in providing the preservation component. The solution seems simple, but it may not accomplish as much as the "host" instructors believe it will.

Guests, even when given specific topics, do not always stick to the point. Faculty would be ungrateful to criticize guests who wander from the designated theme, since most of them contribute their time generously after working a full day or taking time away from busy schedules, receiving no compensation of any sort. Sometimes when guests focus on what they know best—specific problems affecting their libraries or elements in their own research studies—they cover only narrow areas within the specialty, without relating them either to the rest of the preservation knowledge base or the rest of the material in the course. Instead of painting preservation in broad strokes against the background context of the course in which the lecture is being given, preservation stands alone in isolation from other course work. It might be interesting, but without relevance to the rest of the learning experience the information guest lecturers convey will probably not remain with students for long; even if it is remembered, its application to other areas and other problems being studied in the course may go unrecognized.

Thus, incorporating preservation into existing courses has the following disadvantages:

- Existing material in the course must be deleted or compressed to make room for preservation material.
- Preservation cannot be given much time, so coverage will be minimal.
- Preservation must be approached from the perspective of the main subject of the course, not as a separate body of knowledge having its own dynamics.

• Guest lecturers may not cover material with sufficient breadth or relate it to what students are learning in the rest of the course.

THE "STAND-ALONE" PRESERVATION COURSE

One alternative to adding preservation material to existing courses is to create a new "stand-alone" course in which to teach it. Some of the advantages and disadvantages of doing this are immediately apparent. First, the new course must be added to the curriculum which, in the schools in which this author has taught, is not necessarily a simple process. Usually a proposal for the new course must be prepared, presented to a curriculum committee or to the faculty as a whole (if not both), and voted upon. Depending on the completeness of the proposal and the receptivity of the faculty, further work on the proposal may be recommended before action is taken. It could be a month or longer—as much as a semester in some schools—until the next meeting is called and decision-makers are able to act on the revised proposal.

Most new curriculum proposals come from members of the faculty, but one cannot assume that all will. The impetus for the proposal may come from someone outside the full-time faculty—either an adjunct or an interested practitioner—and his or her efforts to introduce changes to the curriculum will usually require the guidance and assistance of one or more faculty members. Unless members of the faculty have strong working relationships with local practitioners, suggestions from them may be viewed with suspicion. Working librarians may be lacking in knowledge of how the process of curriculum change functions and lose interest or patience if a proposal is not accepted immediately. They may fail to include all the details of course goals and objectives, enumeration of topical areas to be covered, a model calendar of lectures and assignments, a draft reading list, etc. (in other words, a more-or-less complete draft syllabus) that are expected to accompany the proposal. No matter who submits proposals for a new course, getting them approved is usually more than a perfunctory task, although some proposal processes have fewer steps and requirements before final decisions are made.

The addition of new faculty to teach the stand-alone preservation course must be considered carefully. If a current full-time member of the faculty proposes teaching the new course, but that person already has a full complement of classes to teach, the new offering can be added by dropping an existing course for which the person is responsible. Sometimes there is a domino effect—Professor A picks up the new course and drops an existing course. Professor A's dropped course (call it Course A) is gladly picked up by Professor B, who wants to teach it but not Course B, another subject already on his or her course list, so Professor C must be approached to pick up Course B, etc., etc. When all the reshuffling is done, some courses may be left with no one designated to teach them, like the losing marchers in musical chairs who are left standing because all the chairs are occupied. The solution may be to teach the "loser" courses less frequently, rather than not at all. Unless school or university policies prohibit it, instead of teaching all courses in the curriculum once a year, several may be relegated to being taught once in two years, or every third semester, or on an irregular schedule based on the build-up of student demand for them.

Providing instruction for a new stand-alone preservation course may involve hiring a new faculty member, either part- or full-time. If a vacancy already exists on the faculty, this is an opportunity to hire someone who can teach the new preservation course. If the search goes well and a person with the requisite expertise wants the job, there is no problem. But if the search does not produce someone who can and will teach what has been designated for the new faculty member, dislocations will occur until new solutions are found. This would not be a great problem if library and information science faculties had many members who could be counted upon to provide flexible scheduling; but given that most accredited programs have fewer than 10 people who teach full-time (32 out of 51 U.S. library and information science schools), any dislocation presents an urgent and disturbing concern.[4] In the event a veteran faculty member wants to teach the new course, the school can reshuffle existing courses to suit the current faculty, then go out to find someone to fill a slot created by combining the courses current faculty do not wish to teach.

When there are no vacancies on the faculty, schools might supply instructors for new courses in preservation by hiring adjuncts for one course (either the preservation course or another course that would release the person responsible for it to teach preservation). This is a viable alternative to hiring new faculty members with just the right combination of teaching interests, and it empowers the school to take advantage of the expertise of practitioners, who have gained what they know through long years of experience. Working as adjunct professors enables knowledgeable practitioners to contribute to academic curricula without taking on a host of extra-instructional activities, such as research and publication, student advising, and school- or university-wide committee work. In addition to the immediate value of obtaining an instructor for a course, hiring practitioners to teach in professional school programs helps establish and develop closer relationships between them and the schools that hire them, which benefits both parties as well as the field at large.

All of these plans for adding to the faculty assume there is some flexibility in the school's personnel budget. If the money for added teaching hours is lacking entirely, the only solution to the dilemma of how new courses in preservation will be taught is to drop something currently being taught or to rotate several current courses over an extended schedule. Such a solution may not affect individual students in large numbers, but it might anger a few each year because certain courses they wish to take are not offered; eventually, this can create an atmosphere of ill will.

Logistics, budgets, and other considerations aside, offering a stand-alone preservation course is the best way to ensure there is time to cover the material that needs to be conveyed, and that the information is approached from the preservationist's perspective. It enables full attention to be devoted to preservation issues, such as the history and background of preservation efforts, purposes of preservation, sources of preservation problems for different types of materials, solutions to selected preservation problems, methods of preventing deterioration, decision-making for preservation, problems currently being researched, managing preservation units in libraries and information centers, etc. Material covered in class sessions can be augmented with outside readings, homework assignments, field trips, guest lecturers, class projects, and other sorts of enrichment. The added pressure on the curriculum as a whole of offering another new course (or on the course selections of individual students) may be offset by the value to both of having a full course in preservation.

Mention must be made of an important advantage to adding a new faculty member with expertise in preservation that is often overlooked in light of the more pressing financial and administrative issues: full-time faculty are expected to conduct research and produce new knowledge of value to the field. While offering one stand-alone course in preservation might not require hiring a full-time faculty member whose research adds to the body of preservation knowledge, it is a step in that direction. Certainly, incorporating preservation information into existing courses without adding to the curriculum is much less likely to produce such a result.

To sum up briefly, advantages of offering a stand-alone course in preservation include the following:

- If new faculty are hired to teach the course, this enlarges the faculty and is an opportunity to hire a preservation expert whose research will add to the body of knowledge.
- If local practitioners are hired as adjuncts, this provides an opportunity to build new relationships between schools and practitioners.
- Preservation material can be covered more fully than if it is incorporated as part of another course.
- Preservation material can be approached from a preservationist's perspective, not the perspective of collection developers, technical service librarians, etc.
- Opportunities are available to enrich class work with many different kinds of outside activities.

In addition, Nisonger suggests more arguments in favor of establishing

separate specialty courses:
- The needs and wishes of an important constituency [i.e., the preservationists] are met.
- Status of the work is enhanced.
- Recruitment to the specialty is facilitated.
- The knowledge base is legitimatized.[5]

Disadvantages of adding a stand-alone course in preservation are:
- As a new course, it must go through an approval process which may be complicated and lengthy, requiring the efforts of several people.
- A new course requires more faculty hours or, alternatively, dropping or rescheduling current offerings.
- A new course costs more than incorporating material into existing courses.
- Publicizing the new course adds to faculty advising workloads.
- Having more courses in the curriculum increases the pressure on students' course selections, which may eventually result in ill will toward the school in general.

Nisonger adds the following to this list:
- It may not be a propitious time to introduce a new course.
- The constituency for the course may not exist.
- Not enough academic content may exist to warrant a separate course.[6]

The decision to add preservation material to existing courses or to add a whole new course covering preservation alone is rarely a neat, isolated happening on a linear path of curriculum development. It is much more likely that some faculty members will add preservation material to the other courses they teach at the same time a new stand-alone course is added to the curriculum, regardless of who teaches it. Practically speaking, there are compelling reasons why library schools should not limit themselves to an either/or choice. Instead, both stand-alone preservation courses and the addition of preservation components to other courses should be encouraged:
- Students encountering preservation information for the first time in a non-preservation course may unexpectedly discover an area of interest to them, which they can develop later in their academic careers by taking the stand-alone course.
- Having available both types of exposure to preservation information cannot help but reach more people than a stand-alone preservation course, and every librarian should have at least a cursory understanding of the specialty.

• Reinforcing preservation issues in students' minds by exposing them to such issues in several different contexts will do more to sensitize them to the gravity and importance of preservation problems than studying them only from the preservationist's point of view.

Personal observation of new graduates' job searches corroborates the findings of Herbert S. White and Sarah L. Mort, that say students tend to take the jobs that are available, which are not necessarily the ones for which they prepared.[7] Thus, although the number of entry-level preservation jobs in the marketplace is far fewer than the number of reference or cataloging jobs, the possibility cannot be ruled out that library school graduates will be offered—and will accept—preservation jobs for which they did not prepare. The exposure these people may have had to preservation information in courses in technical services, collection development, serials management, rare books, or other subjects in which it might reasonably be included will help meet their unexpected need. As students interview for professional positions, their ability to show a general understanding of current issues in librarianship, preservation included, will also benefit them.

TEACHING PRESERVATION TECHNIQUES IN THE LIBRARY SCHOOL

One specific consideration in conceptualizing preservation education is the notion of teaching technical knowledge having little to do with library or information science per se (e.g., paper chemistry, paper restoration, microfilming, binding) in programs leading to the master's degree in library and information science. A case could be made that such techniques should be taught in other venues, e.g., in departments of chemistry, physics, or art, or in technical schools teaching binding, filming, papermaking, etc. Specialized institutions such as the Northeast Document Conservation Center might implement educational programs taught by members of their staffs for those techniques in which they have experience and expertise, such as microfilming and paper repair. Schools such as Boston's North Bennet Street School, which teaches hand-binding and fine papermaking, could also offer technical education in their interest areas.

The issue is not whether these techniques should be learned by people planning to do hands-on conservation, repair, and binding in libraries—clearly, they must—but, rather, is the library school the appropriate place to teach these techniques, just because they will be applied to library materials instead of to museum materials or to privately-held paintings, rare books, and so forth? This question may be seen by some as analogous to having people come to library school to learn how to operate computers because they plan to become inputters for library database vendors, or to learn how to operate and repair heating and air conditioning units because they plan to become building engineers in large university libraries. No doubt they need the knowledge and will use it for the operation of a library or information center. But is a school of library and information science the appropriate place to learn such skills?

The Columbia University preservation program incorporated conservation skills and underlying technical knowledge into its curriculum with apparent success. For many, the ability to restore the pages and repair the bindings of damaged books went hand-in-hand with the ability to manage staff, plan budgets, and establish new programs. But for others, interest and success in acquiring technical skills were not necessarily paired with the desire to develop and hone managerial skills. A balance between the two would seem to be a critical factor.

Although few would wish to see the acquisition of technical knowledge excluded entirely from the preservation curriculum, one can imagine administrators arguing that students can learn conservation techniques elsewhere—in schools of fine arts, for example—but it would be difficult, indeed, for them to learn library management skills anywhere but a library school. According to this reasoning, library schools should confine themselves solely to the managerial aspects of preservation and ignore techniques. This dichotomy between teaching students "how to do it" and "how to run it" is not unique to preservation, but it presents a genuine dilemma for schools of library and information science about how best to address it in the curriculum.

Briefly, the advantages of teaching conservation techniques in the library school include the following:

- The special needs of materials collected by libraries and archives can be emphasized over objects of art or museum artifacts.
- Preservation librarians should be able to acquire all the special knowledge they need to perform their jobs in the library school program.
- Librarians who manage preservation programs are also expected to perform some, if not all, of the hands-on treatments needed for materials, and they must train others to do so.
- Preservation managers must make decisions about treatment alternatives that require deep understanding of each treatment—understanding that would enable them to perform the procedures themselves.
- In order to work with conservation specialists and consultants, preservation managers must be fully aware of the implications of their suggestions and proposals.

In addition to the arguments presented above—that library schools are not the place to teach highly specialized, hands-on techniques of making, repairing, or restoring paper, bindings, etc., or operating microfilming equipment, and so on, as well as the scientific theories on which these processes are based—the disadvantages of teaching conservation techniques in library schools include the following:

- Library schools are not equipped with conservation laboratories and the cost of installing high-quality facilities would be prohibitive.
- Faculty who teach preservation management do not necessarily have the expertise to teach either the techniques or the scientific theory, requiring that more people be hired.
- Adding more courses to the curriculum exacerbates the pressures on students, faculty, and administrators, with all the negative results that implies.

"TEACHING LIBRARY"/LIBRARY SCHOOL PARTNERSHIPS

In the spring of 1989 at the Simmons College Seminar on Recruiting, Educating, and Training Cataloging Librarians, Robert M. Hayes proposed that library schools and libraries join forces to form teaching partnerships to accomplish the kind of preparation for new catalogers that medical schools and teaching hospitals achieve in preparing new physicians.[8] The analogy is apt. Without some period of apprenticeship or supervised practice, it is difficult, if not impossible, to ensure that a neophyte professional has learned the requisite theoretical knowledge *and* has the ability to put it to work in practice.

In medicine, the stakes are life and death, and people do not want to take chances. In library and information service, the risks appear to be less serious, but since the quality of information service can have far-reaching effects on scholars as well as ordinary individuals, perhaps they are not as unimportant as one would imagine. Clearly, allowing newly graduated catalogers to alter national and international databases without first ascertaining that they can deal effectively with complex bibliographic problems—not merely textbook cases in cataloging— could have a disastrous impact on database quality. Similarly, allowing new preservationists to run programs for entire libraries without first ensuring that they can deal effectively with complicated decisions involving conflicting needs and objectives, could have a negative effect on library collections.

The teaching library/library school partnership supplies two important elements in the education of excellent preservation professionals that cannot be duplicated in the library school alone:

1. Living laboratories in which the theoretical knowledge taught in the library school can be applied to real practical problems in the teaching library
2. Protection for the neophyte preservationists, preventing them from making bad decisions in unsupervised settings where they might cause serious damage to collections, to library budgets, or to their careers and the credibility of preservation processes

At the same time, the library school teaches its students the theoretical knowledge that apprenticeships alone generally do not supply. Rather, the point of apprenticeships is to expose participants to a variety of practical problems as they happen to occur in real-life settings, arming them with numerous experiences from which they might deduce principles, if they are clever and observant, and if their minds are so inclined. Without teaching libraries in which student preservationists can serve guided apprenticeships before graduation, they will have to experiment with little guidance in their first jobs, and their mistakes could prove to be costly for the institutions that dare to hire them.

Not all the groups involved with preservation education—faculty, students, practitioners, experts in other disciplines—agree about the importance of work practice for students, variously known as internships, practica, field study, etc. The debate is not new. In her chapter on the practicum in education for collection development, Elizabeth Futas assesses its advantages and disadvantages this way:

[The "Pro" Side:] Although the classroom is an excellent place to learn the more theoretical aspects of the process of collection development, it is an uneasy and cumbersome place to try to learn, or to teach, the practical aspects of collection development. No professional does collection development in a vacuum. Collection development is a process that needs to have a community at its root. . . . From within the institution there is also the problem of what has already been purchased and what the existing collection looks like. Some evaluation of current offerings help [sic] to determine the policies and processes of what comes next. Nothing but experience can teach you how the process works, no matter how much you talk and discuss it. Therefore a practicum in collection development seems to be an obvious way in which to introduce reality into the realm of the theoretical. . . .

[The "Con" Side:] The process of collection development requires knowledge of specific information about the agency, its clientele, and its environment. Some of the information required to grasp the knowledge so important to the process requires expenditure of a great deal of time and energy on the part of the individual who seeks to build the collection. A professional. . .learns about both in time. And time is something that practicum students. . .do not have. . . . [I]n the shorter practicum experiences, students could spend almost all of their time learning how to do the jobs that the practicum consisted of without ever getting a chance to do them. In fact, they would be consuming the time of the field supervisor and the host library or information agency without ever giving any payback in terms of what they could, in turn, accomplish for that agency.[9]

One might believe that newly graduated preservationists could start acquiring practical experience in manageable doses by taking entry-level positions in smaller libraries and learning what to do there, before moving upward to larger libraries and more responsible positions. In fact, large university research libraries often require a year or two of experience for virtually all job descriptions, making it difficult for new librarians to compete successfully for jobs. (A platitude commonly heard among some research university librarians is "we don't hire entry-level people—let someone else give them their first training.") But at the Simmons College Seminar in 1989, Barbra B. Higginbotham pointed out that small college library cataloging departments do not have master catalogers on staff to provide entry-level people with training for complex problem solving.[10] She suggested the national cataloging networks—OCLC, RLIN, WLN—sponsor a system of educational exchange, whereby small college members could send their entry-level catalogers to large university members' cataloging departments for a training period. Higginbotham also proposed the training be subsidized in part by the network, which would gain measurably in database quality and accuracy with fewer expenditures on after-the-fact cleanup, and in part by the sending institutions, which would benefit by having new staff trained properly by experts. In fact, the sending institutions might go even farther and subsidize some of the receiving institutions' expenses.[11]

Higginbotham's arguments lead one to want similar programs for preservationists. After all, if small college libraries do not have cataloging experts on staff, they are even less likely to employ preservation experts. What is the training program if not the equivalent of a post-graduate internship or practicum? Degree-holding librarians might not have to be concerned about receiving good grades or earning a diploma, but their performance as trainees would undoubtedly be evaluated somehow, and the college that hired them and paid for their training certainly would have a right to request evidence that their performance was satisfactory.

Whether a period of guided practice is implemented before a person receives a master's degree in the form of a student practicum, or afterward, as in-service training, the result is the same. Furthermore, employing institutions do not escape the costs of training people simply because new librarians hold master's degrees at hiring time. The only way employing institutions can escape paying for training is if they avoid it altogether—and they might pay a different and much higher price in failed programs and services (as well as failed librarians) if they follow that path.

There are a number of valuable results to be realized from entering into teaching library/library school partnerships, including the following:

- Learning occurs as part of a cohesive educational program, focusing on predetermined goals and objectives and designated learning experiences.
- Teaching libraries can help design learning programs along with library school faculties, thereby ensuring they include those elements most important to real-life practice.
- Total costs of the practice/learning program are divided among three partners: the student, who pays tuition for the course; the library school, which pays for faculty advisors and curriculum administration; and the teaching library, which pays the cost of on-site supervisors and other associated supplies and equipment for the "course."

After graduation if teaching libraries hire the students they help train, they will recover their investments in the program immediately by having better workers right from the start. If they choose not to hire them, they will, at least, have contributed significantly to the field by developing a new cadre of professionals, receiving some measure of gratitude and good will in return, as well as whatever productive work the student-employees performed. On balance, this does not seem to be a bad bargain.

The perils of forming teaching library/library school partnerships, however, warrant consideration, also. They include the following:

- The teaching library may, indeed, invest more staff time and effort in the students it trains than it can ever recover.
- The library school must relinquish some control over its curriculum to the teaching library—at least in those areas in which the teaching library participates.
- No single teaching library can provide all possible preservation experiences; thus, students will receive a skewed vision of the specialty.
- There may not be enough positions available in local teaching libraries to accommodate all the students who want practical training.

Several of these drawbacks are serious matters, especially faculty loss of control over curriculum—a jealously guarded power—and the potential lack of space for all who want training, forcing both the teaching library and the library school to have to reject some students. The latter problem offers a number of sensitive issues: who should decide who is accepted or rejected? On what basis should the decisions be made—first come, first served? A set of qualifying procedures? Is ill will likely to result from rejection that may reflect negatively on the library school or the teaching library?

Even the former problem has ramifications that demand exceptional negotiating skills to resolve: who has the final say about matters such as "course" goals and objectives, required assignments, contact hours, etc.? Should either partner have veto power? Who should determine the students' final grades, their practice supervisors, faculty advisors, or both? And, if both, what if they disagree? People on both sides of this partnership must have a common vision of what a practice "course" should involve and what it should aim to accomplish, or disagreements between the two institutions may sabotage the plan. One can imagine the disillusionment of students if a plan for practical learning in a teaching library had to be abandoned because practitioners and professors could not agree on details.

ELEMENTS IN A MODEL CURRICULUM

The Columbia program provides one model for preservation education, but it need not be the only one. A different model could be developed to incorporate the idea of the library school/teaching library partnership. Such a model begins with the assumption that the two elements into which an ideal curriculum must be divided are the theoretical knowledge base and the practical knowledge base. It recognizes most theoretical knowledge is learned in formal course work in the academy and most practical knowledge is acquired on the job in the library or information center, but that one can easily imagine learning practical things in a classroom setting or discovering the theory behind an action during the course of one's work in a library, particularly if these objectives are built into the plan. The task of designing a model curriculum lies in deciding with the greatest possible precision exactly what should be learned; how and where the learning should take place must flow from consensus on what knowledge is to be conveyed.

The plan has three elements:

1. A foundation in the theory and practice of librarianship, followed by a concentration on the theory and practice of preservation management in either a library or an archival setting, covering a broad range of materials and formats, including books, microforms, sound recordings, photographs, archival collections,

        manuscripts, and newer electronic media

2. Technical knowledge including collection-wide applications (environmental control, security, and handling and use), as well as preventative strategies (binding, mass deacidification, and the use of surrogate copies) and intervention strategies (replacement, reformatting, and conservation treatments)

3. Practical experience in a library or archive setting by means of structured internships under the direction of master preservationists and administrators[12]

Course listings to satisfy the first part of this model curriculum might include offerings typically part of library and information science programs such as research methods, principles of management, introduction to reference, bibliographic control and organization of knowledge, collection development, and technical services management. The second and more specialized part of this foundations component requires courses in preservation management investigating general issues, such as understanding the physical properties of materials, identifying the causes and nature of damage and potential solutions, planning for preservation, etc., and the specific needs of users and materials typically held either in libraries or in archives, chosen according to a student's career goals.

Technical knowledge would be imparted in another course dealing with paper-based materials as well as film-, magnetic tape-, and analog or digital disk-based materials. Methods of handling, repairing, and restoring the materials would be taught, as well as appropriate methods of duplicating, reformatting, deacidifying, and/or treating them individually and collectively, and understanding the chemical and physical bases for the methodologies.

A legitimate question arises concerning the likelihood that library and information science students will enter the program with sufficient basic knowledge of chemistry and physics to master the specialized material they must cover in one year. It is common knowledge that library and information science students tend to major in the humanities, not the sciences, yet the courses described here clearly depend on good grounding in at least two scientific disciplines—chemistry and physics. Clearly, library schools are not the place to teach science, but students who lack the basics will have to receive the needed instruction at some point before they begin the courses described for this second component of the curriculum. Several methods could ensure the proper science background: requiring it as a prerequisite for entering the program; providing a special "crash" course in "Science for Preservationists" to be taken during the first semester or year of the program; or, requiring that student preservationists without previous exposure take the necessary courses at the undergraduate level without receiving graduate credit for them.

The third and final component in the curriculum plan is a supervised internship at a library or archive having a well-developed preservation program employing master professionals, giving students the opportunity to apply, in practical situations, what they learn in their academic courses. To address the potential drawbacks of internships and ensure a true learning experience for the students, goals and objectives for each internship must be written in terms that lend themselves to subsequent evaluation of the student's performance, and students must document what they learn as part of the experience. Interns can keep diaries, submit periodic reports, or produce other documents such as project proposals, reports, outlines, etc., to furnish the necessary written documentation. To ensure that the internship produces a meaningful result for the host library or archive, students are expected to make a significant commitment and be prepared with knowledge of the setting and its operations before they begin. Just as course syllabi outlining goals and objectives, units of study, assignments, and grading provide an understanding of what an academic course will entail, negotiation of internship "contracts" among students, supervisors, and the program's faculty director, could provide for mutual understanding of the parameters of each internship. An integral part of the plan should be the potential for extending participation in the internship component to libraries and archives in colleges, smaller universities, and public libraries for students intending to serve in those settings—provided a knowledgeable administrator can guide the intern and protect him or her from making unwise decisions or costly mistakes.

This model curriculum emphasizes the managerial responsibilities of preservation librarians and aims to arm them with broadly based theoretical and practical knowledge about library and information center operations. The abilities to draw up budgets and gather planning data for preservation programs are key elements to be taught and learned, as are methods of effective functioning with colleagues at all levels in multi-faceted organizations.

CONCLUSIONS

As preservation problems continue to plague libraries and threaten their abilities to provide society with an organized record of its intellectual development that will last for all time, the need grows for librarians, information specialists, and archivists prepared properly to address them. Visions of proper preparation continue to involve harder work for students and faculty as well as greater involvement on the part of knowledgeable practitioners. At millennium's end, these visions are far from being entirely new directions; they are merely natural developments over the course of time that could easily have been forecast a decade ago, when preservation education emerged and underwent a period of initial development as a discrete field of specialization. The birth pangs over, the work of building both the body of knowledge and the cadre of expert preservationists continues. These two goals can be accomplished together if strong programs of preservation education can be 'built, and if they are founded in the research environment of the university.

SUGGESTIONS FOR ADDITIONAL READING

Bansa, H. "The Awareness of Conservation: Reasons for Reorientation in Library Training." *Restaurator* 7:36-47 (1986).

Brundin, Robert. "Field Experience and the Library Educator." *Journal of Education for Library and Information Science* 31:365-68 (Spring 1991).

Cloonan, Michélle Valerie. "Preservation Education in American Library Schools: Recounting the Ways." *Journal of Education for Library and Information Science* 31:187-203 (Winter 1991).

Coleman, J. Gordon, Jr. "The Role of the Practicum in Library Schools." *Journal of Education for Library and Information Science* 30:19-27 (Summer 1989).

Conway, Paul. "Archival Preservation: Definitions for Improving Education and Training." *Restaurator* 10:47-60 (1989).

Fang, Josephine R., and Ann Russell. *Education and Training for Preservation and Conservation.* Munich: K. G. Saur, 1991.

Feather, John. *Guidelines on the Teaching of Preservation to Librarians, Archivists, and Documentalists.* The Hague: IFLA, forthcoming.

———"Manpower Requirements in Preservation." In *Preservation Administration.* Ed. by I. R. M. Mowat. Brookfield, Vt.: Gower, forthcoming.

Harvey, John F., and Frances Laverne Carroll, eds. *Internationalizing Library and Information Science Education: A Handbook of Policies and Procedures in Administration and Curriculum.* Westport, Conn.: Greenwood Press, 1987.

Higginbotham, Barbra B., and Mary E. Jackson, eds. *Advances in Preservation and Access,* vol. 1. Westport, Conn.: Meckler, 1992.

Hookway, Sir Harry, et al. "Education for Conservation." *Journal of Librarianship* 17:73-105 (1985).

Intner, Sheila S., and Kay E. Vandergrift, eds. *Library Education and Leadership: Essays in Honor of Jane Anne Hannigan.* Metuchen, N.J.: Scarecrow Press, 1990.

Lyders, Josette Anne, and Patricia Jane Wilson. "A National Survey: Field Experience in Library Education." *School Library Journal* 37:31-35 (Jan. 1991).

Nassimbeni, Mary. "Role and Value of Fieldwork in Education for Library and Information Science: A Cross-Site Comparison of Two Case Studies." *South African Journal of Library and Information Science* 58:75-86 (Mar. 1990).

Ratcliffe, F. W., ed. *Preservation Policies and Conservation in British Libraries: Report of the Cambridge University Library Conservation Project.* London: British Library, 1984.

Steig, Margaret F. *Change and Challenge in Library and Information Science Education.* Chicago: American Library Association, 1992.

Turner, J. R. "Teaching Conservation." *Education for Information* 6:145-51 (1988).

White, Herbert S., and Marion Paris. "Employer Preferences and the Library Education Curriculum." *Library Quarterly* 55:1-33 (Jan. 1985).

NOTES

1. When Columbia University's School of Library Service was closed in 1992, the post-MLS preservation management and conservation education program, established under the leadership of Paul Banks in 1981 with funding support from the Carnegie Corporation of New York, the Mellon Foundation, and the National Endowment for the Humanities, did not disband. It moved to the Graduate School of Library and Information Science of the University of Texas at Austin, with Carolyn Harris (formerly head of preservation operations at Columbia University Libraries) as its director. Mention of the original establishment of the program is found in A. Venable Lawson's 1982 annual review of library education, "Education, Library," in *ALA Yearbook 1982* (Chicago: American Library Association, 1982), 114.
2. "Report of the Study Committee on Education and Training for Preservation [of the National Commission on Preservation and Access]," Deanna Marcum, Chair (Unpublished typescript, 1991).
3. "Forging an Education Partnership in Preservation Management: A Proposal," prepared by Sheila S. Intner, Carolyn Clark Morrow, and Robert D. Stueart (Unpublished typescript, 1992), 2-3.
4. *Directory of the Association for Library and Information Science Education, 1992-93* (Raleigh, N.C.: Published annually as a special edition of the *Journal of Education for Library and Information Science* by the Association, 1993). The average number of full-time faculty members not also holding an administrative position in the 51 U.S. accredited schools listed was 9.18 persons. The smallest full-time teaching faculty was four (in five schools); the largest, 27 (in one school). Administrators who also teach were not counted as full-time teaching faculty, since they rarely carry a full teaching load in addition to their administrative duties.
5. Thomas E. Nisonger, "Should Courses in Acquisitions and Collection Development Be Combined or Separate?" in *Recruiting, Educating, and Training Librarians for Collection Development*, ed. Peggy Johnson and Sheila S. Intner (Westport, Conn.: Greenwood Press, 1994), 137-38.
6. Ibid.
7. Herbert S. White and Sarah L. Mort, "The Accredited Library Education Program as Preparation for Professional Library Work," *Library Quarterly* 60:3 (July 1990): 187-215.
8. Robert M. Hayes, "The Challenge of Excellence in Librarianship," in *Cataloging, the Professional Development Cycle*, ed. Sheila S. Intner and Janet Swan Hill (Westport, Conn.: Greenwood Press, 1991), 3-11.
9. Elizabeth Futas, "The Practicum in Collection Development: A Debate," in *Recruiting, Educating, and Training Librarians for Collection Development*, ed. Peggy Johnson and Sheila S. Intner (Westport, Conn.: Greenwood Press, 1994), 145-56.

10. Barbra B. Higginbotham, "Standards, Volume, and Trust in the Shared Cataloging Environment: Training Approaches for the Smaller Library," in *Recruiting, Educating, and Training Cataloging Librarians: Solving the Problems*, ed. Sheila S. Intner and Janet Swan Hill (Westport, Conn.: Greenwood Press, 1989), 355-66.
11. Ibid.
12. "Forging an Educational Partnership," 2.

Archival Preservation Education: An Overview of the Society of American Archivists' Programs and New Directions for the Future

Evelyn Frangakis
Preservation Program Director
Society of American Archivists

Christine Ward
Chief, Bureau of Archival Services
New York State Archives and Records Administration

INTRODUCTION

Archives exist to identify, acquire, preserve, and provide access to those records of our society that have enduring value for research and other purposes. Preservation of such documentary materials is not only a necessity to ensure the continuation of our cultural heritage, but also a fundamental responsibility of the archival profession. This is a charge that is taken very seriously by the Society of American Archivists (SAA), the national professional organization for archivists, archival institutions, and others concerned with the identification, preservation, and use of the historical record. To help its membership meet the preservation challenges of the modern era, SAA provides leadership in developing standards for archival institutions, and develops and supports educational programs for the working archivist.

This essay will examine the changing emphasis in archival preservation education over the last 15 years, focusing on SAA's nationwide programs. It will also describe a model for training preservation managers that is currently being employed by the Society of American Archivists, with funding from the National Endowment for the Humanities (NEH). This education program will be fully evaluated when the project is completed in 1994; however, there are already strong indicators of its promise as a method of educating professionals, as well as a means of disseminating standards for and promoting the development of integrated and fully functioning preservation programs in archival institutions.

The Society of American Archivists is not the only source of preservation training programs for archivists. Regional archival associations offer workshops and sessions at their meetings, and many of the regional conservation centers provide training through their field service programs. However, because of the Society's leadership role in archival matters and its ability to provide a coordinated broad-based program that has member-wide availability, SAA is in a position to promulgate standards across regional and institutional lines and to influence the profession nationally. Undoubtedly, the Society's education activities have had, and will continue to have, a lasting effect on the design of other in-service educational programs for archivists.

In 1986 SAA's Task Force on Goals and Priorities issued a report that confirmed the development of comprehensive professional education programs and the formation of standards for both professional and programmatic proficiency as important to the profession.[1] All these years later, these are still priorities; they have been further endorsed as preservation objectives for the 1990s by SAA's Task Force on Preservation.[2] The development of preservation management program models and the establishment of functioning preservation administration programs in archives throughout the country will represent a milestone in the profession's progress toward systematic program development and institutional competence.

PRESERVATION—AN EVOLVING CONCEPT

Paul Conway, the Society of American Archivists' preservation program officer from 1988 through 1989, observed that "archivists need to define for themselves just what archival preservation entails and assess the capacity of the thousands of archives, large and small, scattered and isolated from each other, to develop and administer sophisticated preservation programs."[3] Beyond building a preservation knowledge base for the profession, and determining just how this knowledge can and should be applied in a wide variety of institutional settings, the profession also requires a means of disseminating that knowledge to archivists already working in institutional settings. At the local level, archivists need help in applying that knowledge to functioning institutional programs, and they require tools for preservation program planning, as well as for monitoring and evaluating the progress of the program and the results of preservation actions.

Over the last 15 years, the meaning of the term "preservation" has changed considerably, resulting in a revision and expansion of the relevant body of knowledge that forms the foundation for the preservation education of the archives professional. Archivists have always placed an emphasis on preservation. T. R. Schellenberg points out that everything an archivist does is concentrated on the dual objectives of preserving valuable records and making them available for use.[4] The term preservation has long been part of the archivist's lexicon; but preservation takes on different meanings, depending on the context in which it is used.

In the past, the concept of preservation implied merely the identification and acquisition of documents, salvation from destruction by virtue of materials' being assumed into a repository.[5] For many years the terms preservation and conservation were used interchangeably to refer to any number of physical actions taken with archival materials, most often treatments carried out on individual documents. During the 1980s the emphasis on individual item treatment began to give way to a more comprehensive programmatic approach to preservation that focused on managing and improving the condition of all archival holdings in an institution through environmental control, proper housing, and improved practices that favor the stabilization and maintenance of the entire collection. This "holistic" approach has come to be known as responsible custody and is described more fully in a report of the Task Forces on Archival Selection to the Commission on Preservation and Access.[6]

In 1990 Paul Conway proposed a new definition that clarified the management concept of preservation; today, it has gained broad acceptance:

> Archival preservation is the acquisition, organization, and distribution of resources (human, physical, monetary) to ensure adequate protection of historical information of enduring value for access by present and future generations. Archival preservation encompasses planning and implementing policies, procedures, and processes that together prevent further deterioration or renew the usability of selected groups of materials. Archival preservation management, when most effective, requires that planning precede implementation, and that prevention activities have priority over renewal activities.[7]

This definition highlights the administrative aspects of preservation, focusing on the allocation of resources and on planning, policy development, and program design; it offers a concept of preservation that is intentionally open-ended and flexible, one as applicable to preserving records in modern electronic formats as to preserving those created on paper. The definition does not specify the actions that constitute a preservation program. These are determined at another level, and the choice of preservation activities is dependent upon such circumstances as the availability of resources and technologies, and the nature of the records involved. Decisions about records selected for preservation action are based upon their value, use, and preservation risk.

Today, new methods, techniques, and tools make it possible to ensure that the archival record, regardless of the format in which it is created, is preserved and remains accessible and usable into the future. Preservation is closely linked to both our responsibility for and our capacity to ensure access to information contained in the record and to retain that information as a record—that is, to ensure that the context surrounding the record's creation, as well as the content of the record, is preserved for future generations.

Archival preservation no longer has an item-level focus, nor is it associated with a set of disjointed and unconnected activities aimed at saving individual treasures in a collection. Preservation no longer means responding to damage that has already occurred. Rather, it is more akin to prevention: preservation means actively eliminating those conditions that cause or encourage damage. It is a coordinated set of activities focused on defining and managing the physical needs of our collections, in order to ensure their availability into the future. Preservation management takes a comprehensive and integrated approach to defining needs, establishing priorities, identifying solutions, articulating goals and objectives, and implementing programs to meet those identified needs.

THE SOCIETY OF AMERICAN ARCHIVISTS AND PRESERVATION EDUCATION

The body of preservation knowledge and approaches to preservation action have been evolving and maturing in recent years, and SAA has assumed responsibility for disseminating this information to its membership. The Society remains committed not only to providing for the professional development of its constituents, but to upgrading the quality of programming within member institutions as well. Sensitive to the needs and priorities of its membership, the Society has designed its educational programs to respond to identified issues and concerns.

For instance, the 1977 Conference on Priorities for Historical Records, funded by NEH and the National Historical Publications and Records Commission (NHPRC), identified a range of problems confronting the archival profession and attempted to translate these problems into program needs in order to begin to set national priorities for action. The participants identified six conservation needs:

- To experiment with mass treatment techniques
- To establish a network of regional conservation centers
- To establish a national conservation program
- To provide training for paper conservators
- To provide conservation education as part of archival training
- To study the use of microfilm as a conservation medium[8]

In 1978, the National Conservation Advisory Council sponsored a meeting of librarians and archivists to identify a set of national conservation requirements. That meeting agreed on the following needs:

- Increased awareness of various aspects of conservation of materials for librarians and archivists
- Continuing education programs for practitioners

• Conservation administration training
• Mandated course work in conservation for professional
  archivists and librarians[9]

Clearly the focus was on treatment, but training for archivists and librarians was also identified as a need even in these early days.

THE BASIC ARCHIVAL CONSERVATION PROGRAM

SAA's Basic Archival Conservation Program emerged in 1980 in response to the training needs identified at these conferences. The original program was designed to bring about improvements in care and handling of collections through training archivists to revise practices and procedures within their institutions, or to implement new ones. The program had three primary objectives:

1. To build communication skills within the organization
   and beyond (with users and others) by increasing basic
   technical knowledge.
2. To disseminate information to assist archival institutions
   in establishing and maintaining realistic preservation
   programs.
3. To help archival institutions to assess needs, establish
   criteria, and evaluate the quality of in-house and contractual services.[10]

From 1980-1987, the SAA Basic Archival Conservation Program, funded in part by the National Endowment for the Humanities, produced 22 three-day basic conservation workshops, training 549 individuals. From 1982-1987, NEH grant support was increased to provide funding to add workshops on the care and handling of photographs. This program sponsored 14 three-day workshops, training 414 persons. All of the workshops were held in archival settings throughout the country. Participants were selected from a pool of applicants, each of whom had responsibility for the care of archives and manuscripts.

In addition to in-service training in basic skills, the program provided a consulting service designed to subsidize, on a cost-sharing basis, on-site conservation surveys. These were carried out over a five-year period by experienced archival administrators. Consultants visited 51 archival programs and prepared reports on general preservation issues and the administration of photographic collections. During this period, two publications were produced for the SAA basic manual series, *Archives and Manuscripts: Conservation*, by Mary Lynn Ritzenthaler (1983) and *Archives and Manuscripts: Administration of Photographic Collections*, by Ritzenthaler, Gerald J. Munoff, and Margery S. Long (1984).[11] Both manuals present a well-reasoned philosophy of archival preservation management and provide information on recommended policies, procedures, and basic techniques.[12]

The program offered greatly needed knowledge and support for archivists in the basic understanding of preservation problems, technical skills, and general program requirements. The expressed objectives of this successful eight-year project were admirably met. The program produced a cadre of trained archivists who understood the major preservation issues facing their profession and who were equipped to deal with the common preservation problems of their own collections. The program laid a solid educational foundation on which the framework for a more advanced curriculum aimed at different levels of personnel in the archival organization could be erected.

The Basic Archival Conservation Program was a great step forward; it recognized that archivists could no longer be passive about their preservation responsibility. It advanced the view that preservation was a matter of taking a long-range approach to collection care, given the large volume of unique, multimedia historical collections housed in small, minimally funded administrative units. The program's philosophy recognized that, because archivists generally work within larger organizational contexts, it was critical that they view their activities comprehensively, within the context of the parent institution's broader mission, responsibilities, and specific limitations. The two manuals that resulted from the program became some of the SAA's best-selling publications and continue to serve the basic preservation information needs of the archival profession.[13] The first manual, *Archives and Manuscripts: Conservation*, has recently been revised and updated to reflect the evolution of preservation theory and practice over the last 10 years.[14]

THE PRESERVATION MANAGEMENT INSTITUTE

In 1987, the Society developed and piloted a two-week training program for archivists at administrative levels higher than those generally held by the participants in the Basic Program. The basic workshops were not designed to provide sophisticated planning or management skills; the piloted management training program proposed to teach archival administrators both the basic principles of preservation and the administrative skills of program planning, implementation, and resource allocation. The program was only partially successful, perhaps because in splitting the focus between basic knowledge and techniques and management issues, it was impossible in the two-week period to address the issues inherent in administering a comprehensive preservation program.[15] The program was, however, important as a pioneering attempt to integrate the teaching of management skills and program administration into its preservation curriculum. The experiences of this pilot program played an important part in the design of the current Preservation Management Training Program.

IMPACT, EVALUATION, AND CHANGE

Even though most of the participants in the Basic Archival Conservation Program were responsible for the care of archives and manuscripts collections, most were not organizationally positioned to effect programmatic or permanent transformation within their institutions. In order to recast policies and programs, archival administrators—those who have the responsibility for developing and implementing policy and allocating resources—had to embrace the concept of preservation and support the integration of preservation activities throughout the archival program. Mary Lynn Ritzenthaler espoused this basic tenant in 1983.[16] The challenge was, and still is, to ensure administrative and institutional acceptance and to create real change. After eight years of the basic workshops, SAA conducted an assessment to determine if either goal had been realized.

In 1987, NEH provided funds for an extensive evaluation of the basic archival conservation training program. The 18-month study, completed in 1989, made it possible for SAA to survey the profession to obtain feedback on both current and future preservation needs. The study also examined the impact that participation in the Basic Archival Conservation Program had had on participants, as well as on the programs at their institutions. The data collected through this study added to a core of information about archival preservation programs and needs gathered in two 1985 studies, one of state archival institutions sponsored by the National Association of Government Archivists and Records Administrators,[17] and the other a census of archival institutions conducted by the Society of American Archivists.[18] Both of these earlier studies and the 1989 study suggested that, for the most part, archival institutions in the United States had poorly developed preservation programs, or none at all.

The basic conservation program evaluation showed that the basic workshop series significantly increased archivists' awareness of the importance of preservation, and provided them with specific knowledge about preservation concepts and techniques that enabled them to improve particular conditions and practices at their repositories. However, although the survey showed some improvement in certain areas, the findings suggested that archives had not actually integrated preservation activities into their programs, let alone developed preservation management programs. The survey further indicated that archivists still approached preservation in a piecemeal manner, "picking and choosing from among the possible activities, instead of working through an ongoing planning process that sets priorities for the unit and for the parent organization. . . . These findings argue strongly that future SAA initiatives should move beyond the basic level and teach how to make preservation a comprehensive management function."[19] Survey responses also indicated that SAA members believed their most urgent need to be training in preservation program planning. A 1990 survey of SAA Preservation Section members corroborated these results.

In recent years, the profession has launched discussions of institutional evaluation and some are considering the issue of accreditation of archival programs. The movement toward establishing archival program standards will undoubtedly force the development and implementation of preservation programming in archival institutions. But standards are not enough. Archivists must have access to the growing and changing body of preservation knowledge, and learn how to apply that knowledge to support the development, implementation, and maintenance of fully integrated preservation programs customized to meet the needs of every archival institution.

One-time workshops cannot provide the training and support necessary to get comprehensive programs up and running in America's repositories. A continuing education program—in-service training that focuses on management skills as they apply to preservation of collections and that provides practical step-by-step support for the implementation of the nascent preservation program within participating institutions—may well be the solution.

THE PRESERVATION MANAGEMENT TRAINING PROGRAM

In 1990, the Society of American Archivists requested funding from the National Endowment for the Humanities for over $600,000 to support a new three-year preservation training program. The goal of the Preservation Management Training Program (PMTP) is the development of comprehensive, systematic preservation programs across the United States, staffed by archivists who are willing and able to lead the profession, teach others how to build programs, increase awareness of continuing needs, and provide information through formal and informal networks.

The program pioneers the concept of preservation as a function of overall archival management and introduces strategies that integrate preservation management activities into the archival program. Participants learn how to assess their collections' preservation needs, develop priorities based on practical and cost-effective solutions, and design action plans with timetables for preserving collections within their institutions. By the end of the training program institutions will have developed and implemented many of the policies and procedures that will serve as the foundation for a functional preservation program.

The program helps institutions and participants to:
- Develop management strategies and skills to organize and implement comprehensive preservation programs
- Increase their technical knowledge of preservation
- Implement several of the key components of a preserva-

tion program at their home institutions, as an integral part
of their training
- Confront the realities of the operational context within
which their programs will exist
- Learn how to balance preservation concerns against other
institutional priorities

COLLABORATION WITH NEH

The SAA Preservation Management Training Program represents an investment by NEH to build model preservation programs in archives across the country and a network to link together these programs and the individuals who run them. Up to 60 institutions will have the opportunity to participate in this innovative training program. Ultimately, these organizations will become models for archival preservation programming. Already 60 applicants, who must have at least part-time preservation responsibilities in their home institutions, have been selected to participate.

This 1992-1994 training program is composed of four series of workshops, offered concurrently and successively in geographic regions (Northeast, Midwest, West, Southeast) across the United States. Patterned on a successful model for training librarians created by Barclay Ogden of the University of California at Berkeley, and building on the curriculum developed by the Commission on Preservation and Access' College Libraries Group in cooperation with SOLINET, each series is composed of three sequential workshops offered at four-month intervals and linked by interim assignments. The interim assignments are designed to assist in the implementation of practical components of the preservation program. Each workshop within a series is six days in length, for a total of 18 training days.

PROGRAM FACULTY

Faculty for the program were selected according to programmatic needs and have experience in archival conservation and/or preservation administration. All faculty are leaders and experts in the preservation, conservation, and management of archives. The primary faculty member is SAA's Preservation Program Director, Evelyn Frangakis. She teaches each of the 12 workshops in the program and is assisted by a different co-faculty member for each workshop. The other faculty members are: Diana Alper (National Archives and Records Administration), Brenda Banks (Georgia Department of Archives and History), Anne Diffendal (Society of American Archivists), Judith Fortson (Hoover Institution), Karen Garlick (National Museum of American History), Maria Holden (New York State Archives and Records Administration), Kathy Ludwig (Minnesota Historical Society), Hilary Kaplan (Georgia Department of Archives and History), Anne R. Kenney

(Cornell University), Jane Klinger (National Archives and Records Administration, Pacific Sierra Region), Mary Lynn Ritzenthaler (National Archives and Records Administration), and Christine Ward (New York State Archives and Records Administration). Each workshop series also has guest lecturers who specialize in the preservation of photographs, sound and moving image materials, and electronic records.

CURRICULUM DEVELOPMENT

All faculty members contributed to the development of the program curriculum. The grant proposal submitted to NEH offered a basic structure, along with issues to be covered, which served as a valuable starting point. Soon after their selection, faculty convened as a formal group in Chicago for three days, for a "train-the-trainers" session designed to fine-tune the curriculum, provide faculty with instruction in teaching theory and methodology, and furnish an opportunity for the faculty to develop as a team.

A professional trainer familiar with non-profit environments was hired to lead this effort. Faculty learned techniques for effective teaching and presentation skills. They gained an understanding of the adult learning process and developed strategies for working with participants from diverse institutions and backgrounds.

The faculty tackled curriculum development at this meeting, working in groups according to their teaching responsibilities for each of three workshops within a series. Each faculty member developed a curriculum unit. This afforded everyone input into the whole program, while assuring the development of a uniform curriculum. Thus, each series conveys the same information in a consistent manner.

The program was designed in accord with acknowledged principles of adult education. A basic premise in the design of the curriculum is that adults learn best in situations that simulate real-life work experiences. In light of this, the format of the workshops consists of a variety of group exercises and activities. There is some lecture, much discussion, break-out group activities, case studies, role-playing exercises, audiovisuals, and more. The learning environment encourages creativity and enthusiasm, and requires energetic and active participation.

SELECTION OF PARTICIPANTS

Participation in the program was selective; nearly 60 institutions across the country were chosen to send a staff member. Since the training program is institution-based, the primary applicant is the institution, who sponsors an individual to attend the workshops on its behalf. The organization must have the appropriate infrastructure to support a preservation program, and the individual must have the authority to implement that program. The SAA recognizes that both individual and institutional commitment are key to the success of the program. Selection for participation in the program is based on the following six criteria:

1. The sponsoring institution recognizes the need to plan, initiate, and support a preservation program and is willing to commit formally to doing so. Thus the institution will support the applicant's time to carry out the course assignments and will build on them to implement an integrated preservation program.

2. The institution is committed to sponsoring the same person to attend the full training program composed of three workshops. Only one participant from any given repository is selected.

3. Preference is given to institutions with at least three full-time staff members who are performing archival functions.

4. The individual applicant has official responsibility for managing preservation activities at the institution, at least 25 percent of their time.

5. Applicants who have had some prior training in the basic elements of preservation are preferred.

6. The applicant is expected to have a minimum of three years of experience managing some aspect of an archival program.

In addition to the criteria listed above, the sponsoring institution must commit to paying the applicant's program-related expenses. The registration fee for the three-workshop sequence is $750 and helps cover costs for tuition, room, most meals, and instructional materials. Sponsoring institutions are also responsible for transportation and some meal expenses of their participants. NEH funding allows the training program to offer substantial support for every participant.

CURRICULUM AND PROGRAM REQUIREMENTS

In undertaking this training program, the organization must be willing to make a long-term investment and commitment to the preservation of its holdings; it is essential that the institution recognize the need to plan, integrate, and support a systematic preservation program. In order to participate in the program, an organization must be prepared to send the staff member to the full series and to allow him or her to undertake assignments between each workshop that will help build and strengthen preservation efforts at the repository. Because participants begin drafting five-year preservation plans during the last workshop, the institution must be willing and able to submit progress reports for five years after its representative completes the training program. SAA will, in turn, conduct a five-year post-program evaluation.

Institutions that embark on this program make a significant commitment of time and staff resources, which results in actual program development during the course of training. During this period, participants have direct access to a network of information and support, including faculty who are leaders in the field and colleagues who share their concerns and experiences.

Prior to the first workshop, participants receive background readings and are required to complete a data-gathering survey of their institutions. This survey heightens their awareness of what policies and conditions generally exist in the repository, as well as who affects preservation in the institution. Participants receive more reading material before each workshop and are also given abundant printed resources during the training sessions. All workshop topics are approached from the management perspective and include the following:

Workshop A:

Preservation program planning
Nature of archival materials (paper, photographs, audiovisual materials, electronic records)
Collection survey methodology and techniques
Environmental control
Disaster preparedness and recovery

Workshop B:

Care and handling of archival materials
Holdings maintenance
Selection for preservation
Conservation
Reformatting
Exhibits

Workshop C:

Integrating preservation into archival functions
Translating planning into operational programming
Resource allocation and funding
Sources of outside funding
Funding applications
National initiatives
General management issues

Participants also undertake requisite assignments between each workshop, which are reviewed in the successive workshop.

Workshop A assignments are:

> General preservation surveys
> Disaster plans or drafts of such
> Environmental monitoring exercise designed to initiate a
> new, or enhance an existing, program

Workshop B assignments are:

> Care and handling guidelines and training materials
> Development of an exhibition policy
> Critique of an exhibit
> A preservation selection exercise
> Development of reformatting project (optional)

Finally, participants are given an assignment to prepare them for the third and final workshop. They are expected to become familiar with the planning process, method of resource allocation, and organizational mission, goals, and priorities of their own institutions. In the third workshop, they immerse themselves in broad management issues related to program development. At this point, participants begin to draft five-year preservation plans for their institutions, positioning themselves to complete and fully implement the plans following the training program. Participants who complete the program and fulfill its requirements are awarded a certificate of Continuing Education, in accordance with the guidelines of the International Association for Continuing Education and Training.

ADVISORY COMMITTEE

The training program has an Advisory Committee composed of these members: Brenda Banks (Georgia Department of Archives and History), Nicholas C. Burckel (Washington University Libraries), Judith Fortson (Hoover Institution), David B. Gracy II (The University of Texas at Austin GSLIS), Howard Lowell (Delaware State Archives), Trudy H. Peterson (National Archives and Records Administration), and Robert Sink (The New York Public Library). The Advisory Committee serves as general program counsel and assists the SAA office in recruitment of institutions for program participation. Some members also serve as training program faculty.

LOOKING FORWARD

The SAA Preservation Management Training Program is unique among archival educational programs in its extended and active training approach. At the conclusion of this educational initiative, there will be a core body of archival preservation programs across the country. Graduates of the program will serve as the future leaders of archival preservation through implementation of their institutional programs, as well as through teaching others to follow in their footsteps and build on their work. If the training program is successful, the model will be available for others to use and improve upon. The newly established institutional preservation programs themselves will become examples for others to emulate.

This is an important and pivotal period for archival preservation. Never before has such an ambitious program been undertaken. It is already clear that this educational program and its graduates will have a lasting and positive impact on the management of archival programs and the preservation of archives nationwide.

READINGS IN ADULT EDUCATION

The adult education literature is abundant; the following books serve as a good starting point.

Brookfield, Stephen D. *Developing Critical Thinkers: Challenging Adults to Explore Alternative Ways of Thinking and Acting.* San Francisco: Jossey-Bass, 1987.

———— *Understanding and Facilitating Adult Learning.* San Francisco: Jossey-Bass, 1996.

Craig, Robert L. *Training and Development Handbook.* 3rd ed. New York: McGraw Hill, 1987.

Cross, K. Patricia. *Adults as Learners: Increasing Participation and Facilitating Adult Learning.* San Francisco: Jossey-Bass, 1981.

Hiemestra, Roger and Burton Sisco. *Individualizing Instruction: Making Learning Personal, Empowering, and Successful.* San Francisco: Jossey-Bass, 1990.

NOTES

1. *Planning for the Archival Profession: A report of the SAA Task Force on Goals and Priorities* (Chicago: Society of American Archivists, 1986).
2. *Preserving History's Future: Nationwide Goals for the Preservation and Use of the Archival Record* (Chicago: Society of American Archivists, 1993).
3. Paul Conway, "Archival Preservation Practice in a Nationwide Context," *American Archivist* 53 (Summer 1990): 205.
4. T. R. Schellenberg, *Modern Archives: Principles and Techniques* (Chicago: University of Chicago Press, 1975), 224.
5. James O'Toole, "On the Idea of Permanence," *American Archivist* 52 (Winter 1989): 11-25.
6. *The Preservation of Archival Materials: A Report of the Task Forces in Archival Selection to the Commission on Preservation and Access* (Washington, D.C.: Commission on Preservation and Access, April 1993).
7. Conway, 206.
8. Mary Lynn McCree and Timothy Walch, "Setting Priorities for Historical Records: A Conference Report," *American Archivist* 40 (July 1977): 291; 345-47.
9. National Conservation Advisory Council, *Report of the Study Committee on Libraries and Archives: National Needs in Library and Archives Conservation* (Washington, D.C.: National Conservation Advisory Council, 1978), 45.

10. "Basic Conservation Education Program," Grant proposal to the National Endowment for the Humanities from the Society of American Archivists, December 1979, RC10105-80, 1-2.
11. Mary Lynn Ritzenthaler, *Archives and Manuscripts: Conservation* (Chicago: Society of American Archivists, 1983); Mary Lynn Ritzenthaler, Gerald J. Munoff, and Margery S. Long, *Archives and Manuscripts: Administration of Photographic Collections* (Chicago: Society of American Archivists, 1984).
12. "Preservation Training Program," Grant proposal to the National Endowment for the Humanities from the Society of American Archivists, December 1990, 5.
13. "Archival Preservation Education Project," Grant proposal to the National Endowment for the Humanities from the Society of American Archivists, December 1989, [6].
14. Mary Lynn Ritzenthaler, *Preserving Archives and Manuscripts* (Chicago: Society of American Archivists, 1993).
15. Grant proposal, December 1990, 5.
16. Ritzenthaler, *Archives and Manuscripts: Conservation,* 7.
17. Howard P. Lowell, *Preservation Needs in State Archives* (Albany, N.Y.: National Association of Government Archives and Records Administrators, 1985).
18. Paul Conway, "Perspectives on Archival Resources: The 1985 Census of Archival Institutions," *American Archivist* 50 (Spring 1987): 174-91.
19. Grant proposal, December 1989, 4.

Access Services: The Human Factor

Ann Paietta

Network Programs Coordinator
The New York Academy of Medicine

INTRODUCTION

To state the painfully obvious, library materials are in jeopardy. Threatening libraries with the loss of their collections are:

- Materials that self-destruct because of their acidity
- Factors in the physical environment, such as reactant atmospheric pollutants and inappropriate or destructive storage methods
- Natural disasters, such as floods and hurricanes
- Human factors, such as careless handling and care by staff and readers, theft, and vandalism

Preservation manuals and library literature usually discuss the properties of library materials, environmental controls, and pollutants at greater length than the activities of the stack maintenance and circulation (access services) staff. The impact readers have on library materials is rarely mentioned. No one argues that control of the environment is critical for the preservation of library materials; however, careless or poorly trained access services staff and uninformed readers can undo preservation work and negate a clean, controlled library environment.

This essay discusses how to achieve good stack maintenance habits in access services staff and raise readers' consciousness about the proper handling of library materials. The life of library materials can be significantly extended through comprehensive staff training and reader awareness programs. Formal educational programs for both staff and readers will ensure that careless handling is avoided and proper care is encouraged. These programs could be characterized as preventive maintenance, with a focus on deterring the deterioration of materials by adequately instructing staff and informing readers.

PLANNING FOR STAFF AND READER EDUCATION

The design and implementation of education programs requires that a number of decisions be made. One of the first is the selection of knowledgeable staff members to develop and ensure the continuation of the programs. When deciding who will design and implement training, examine the experiences and knowledge of the staff. Further, will the programs only need one person, or is a group effort necessary?

Instructing staff and educating readers can often be accomplished without increasing the library's current budget. Programs that can be instituted with existing personnel and resource allocations are easier to sell to the administration, and for educational and preservation programs to be truly effective the library administration must support them. Also, when the staff is broadly included in decision-making and implementing the new procedures, they are more likely to be supportive of program content.

Another issue to address in the planning process is how this training will be incorporated into an already existing preservation program, and the day-to-day operations and responsibilities of access services staff. Finally, any special situations with regard to handling or shelving materials—unique collections, building peculiarities, reader requirements, and so forth—should be taken into account during the planning process, since these may require specific staff training. For example, if folios or oversized materials are shelved in a special manner, or if the library has closed versus open stacks, this should be addressed when planning the training program. Realistic goals for training should also be established during the planning period.

THE STACK PRESERVATION MANUAL

An important part of implementing the staff program is the preparation of written documentation. The compilation of a stack preservation manual, tailored to the library's organization, should be developed. Because information changes continually, design the manual for a loose-leaf binder so that pages can be easily revised, removed, and added.

The manual might include information on how to shelve materials, retrieve an item from the shelf, photocopy bound volumes, shelf read, and care for books that are in poor condition. Disaster planning is another important component of this program; emergency information, such as step-by-step instructions to follow when disaster strikes, building maps, and important telephone numbers, should also be included. For example, the handbook might incorporate procedures to be followed if a staff member encounters water in a stack area. Emergency plan information should be reviewed with staff on a regular basis, or they may forget the procedures.

The manual might also include pertinent articles, as well as sections from or references to books on preservation that can be kept in the preservation department or perhaps in the staff's professional reading area. For example, the drawings of the anatomy of the book in Jane Greenfield's *Books, Their Care and Repair* can help staff become familiar with the physical parts of bound volumes, learning the location of their stress or weak spots.[1] Staff who understand the characteristics and functions of hinges and textblocks will be more likely to keep books upright on shelves and book trucks.

How will the manual be distributed? It must be available to access services staff at all times. Copies of the manual should be provided to each staff member; it should be thought of as an important source of staff support, especially when there are no supervisors available. Once the manual is completed, a comprehensive training program should be implemented.

TRAINING FOR LIBRARY STAFF

Access services positions (professional or supporting staff) are often entry-level, making in-house preservation training even more critical. Because of ignorance, lack of training, or the absence of proper supplies, staff may inadvertently follow practices damaging to the books, journals, manuscripts, and other library materials housed in stack areas. The training of access services staff and the education of readers are the keys to controlling the human factor's impact on library materials.

The training program should include a few maimed books—that is, books that have had the misfortune to be mishandled. The proper methods for removing books from the shelves and photocopying them can be reinforced by exhibiting books with torn spines or pages damaged by improper handling. A display of repaired pages where household tape was used instead of the appropriate repair material, showing the resulting yellow, brittle mess, can provide an eye-opening experience. Other examples of incorrectly repaired volumes, water-damaged materials, the results of high humidity, or environmental destruction can also be assembled and shown. An educational component about the history of papermaking and the ways in which paper may be damaged will strengthen the program. Historical information or recent scientific research can serve as interesting background reading; it compliments the staff's intelligence and takes the program beyond dull "do's and don'ts."

The training program should include a pre-test and a post-test, to engage staff in the learning process. Questions such as, "How fragile is too fragile, for materials to be photocopied?" or "What is the effect of food and drink on materials?" may be asked. By comparing the results of the two quizzes, an assessment can be made of what was learned and how effective the training was.

Human safety issues should also be incorporated into the training program. Explaining that stools or ladders (not the shelving itself) should be used to reach high shelves, and that care is needed when lifting materials or pushing heavy book trucks, is very important. The point should be made that step-stools or ladders are always readily available, so staff and readers do not have to perch precariously on tiptoe to jostle a book off a high shelf, putting both themselves and the materials at risk.

The training program should include a demonstration of the correct way to remove and replace books from the shelves, training staff not to pull books by tilting or tugging at the head caps, which causes the top and the bottom of the spine to tear. Instead, staff will be encouraged to push the volumes on either side back just enough to grasp the one desired in the middle of the spine and pull straight back. If a book will not slide back on a shelf with a gentle push, the shelf is too full; a packed shelf can crack spines and cause damage when someone tries to remove or replace a volume. Access services staff can also be trained in the proper way to handle books during the check-out process. When barcodes have been attached to a volume's inside cover (rather than its textblock) staff may be shown how to provide support for the cover board during stamping, so as not to break it.

Another point to emphasize in the training program is how to handle materials when photocopying them. The spine of a book should never be pressed down with the hand or the cover of the copier, to insure a good image. Staff will think twice about photocopying books that have brittle pages or binding problems (or permitting readers to do so) if, as part of the training program, they are shown the signs of brittleness:

- The pages are cracked along the spine.
- The paper is brown, or is turning brown around the edges.
- The edges of the pages are flaking off.
- Corners of pages are missing.
- Some pages are protruding from the book.
- Pages are worn from copying.

Suggest that, if a book is too brittle to photocopy safely, it should instead be microfilmed and a photocopy made from the film copy. Demonstrate binding problems the staff may encounter when photocopying:

- The volume is oversewn or overcast, that is, it is sewn along the inner edges of the pages rather than through the fold. Pages of these volumes often break along the sewing when one attempts to photocopy them.
- The volume is stapled together, rather than sewn.
- There are small inner margins. Forcing these volumes open to photocopy the text near the spine will break the pages.
- The volume is oversized. Very large volumes tend to be fragile and difficult to handle.

A useful rule of thumb is that, when staff have doubts about whether a volume should be photocopied, they should consult a supervisor. An explanation of the chain of command for staff to follow when questions about the condition of books arise helps speed the process and ensure that it is followed.

If the library has staff who are responsible for preservation, explain that they may arbitrate disagreements between readers and access services staff. For example, if an irate faculty member does not accept the circulation staff's decision denying photocopying, the problem can be turned over to the preservation unit. Here, staff are sufficiently knowledgeable to recognize and choose alternate options, that is, to know when an item should be filmed rather than photocopied. Preservation staff may also have access to gentler photocopying tools. Access services staff should be encouraged to keep in mind that no reader is paying enough (whether the currency be taxes, tuition, or something else) to harm any part of the collection.

When the training program is concluded, a checklist should be completed for each staff member. This will help assure that all questions have been addressed and provide a record of the training for later reference. Post-training, supervisors must be made aware of the importance of good stack maintenance; it is a good idea to give them the practices their staffs are now expected to follow. Even after the best training programs, the library may have one or two problem employees who continue to handle materials carelessly; they will require consistent supervision and reminders about how to treat the volumes in their care. Another way to ensure that staff continue to act on the training they have received is to use rewards as incentives, and to build a sense of pride. The rewards may take many forms—a certificate or citation, cash, a book, movie tickets, or even a cup of coffee and a donut.

AFTER THE INITIAL TRAINING PROGRAM

After the initial training program, ongoing opportunities to learn more about preservation and minor repairs should be available for access services staff. Continuing education can be achieved by encouraging attendance at workshops, conferences, or seminars. The library may decide to create a preservation awareness workshop, possibly in conjunction with other nearby institutions, using a slide or videotape format. A workshop of this type could also help train staff in other departments of the library.

There may be employees who find they enjoy preservation work; this could lead to establishing a program for making minor repairs as part of routine stack maintenance. One cautionary note: staff must learn the correct mending methods from experts and use approved supplies in their repairs. In some cases, repair of materials will require the skills of a professional conservator.

STACK MAINTENANCE

Having completed the access services training program, stack maintenance staff are now ready to incorporate preservation in their day-to-day activities. These employees can participate in the daily care and maintenance of the collections through shelf reading and cleaning materials; they can also be certain that book drops are kept securely locked, and emptied on a regular and frequent basis.

While shelf reading, staff should be equipped with binding string and scissors. In this way, books with damaged covers or loose pages can be tied the moment they are discovered, keeping all the parts together until the volume can be repaired or perhaps replaced. A supply of acid-free pamphlet envelopes and boxes should also be near at hand, so that old, crumbling, acidic envelopes and boxes can be replaced as the worker proceeds with shelf reading.

Extra bookends should be easily accessible for straightening and supporting library materials. Appropriate book supports are very important—sturdy ones hold volumes firmly upright. However, staff should be trained to evaluate the condition of each bookend carefully:

- Sharp edges can cut books and people. These may be filed down, or the offending support discarded. Tape is used to cover sharp edges only as a last resort: in time it will slip, exposing adhesive which harms the books that the support is designed to protect.
- Rusty metal will dirty and damage covers. Until the library can acquire new bookends, some steel wool and a can of enamel paint can improve the condition of existing supports.
- Short bookends can't hold up tall books. As a rule of thumb, a book support should be at least an inch taller than half the height of most of the books on the shelf.
- Slippery bookends will tend to slide away from heavy books. A thin sheet or strip of rubber or other non-skid material cemented to the bottom of the support will help prevent this.

When shelf reading, staff should also identify overcrowded areas in the stacks and report them immediately to their supervisors. Every effort should be made to shift materials whenever a section becomes filled, because tightly-packed stacks lead to damage as books are wrenched off shelves or forced back onto them. Periodic stack inspections can prevent or minimize damage through early detection.

Preservation surveys (their purpose is to find damaged books and do something about them) can also be instituted. As part of this effort, stack staff will check books for dirt, mold, and insect damage, and also examine their general condition. Occasionally, a valuable old book may turn up, which should be removed from the stacks. Books that need attention are flagged or pulled, so that the appropriate staff may collect them from the stacks.

Cleaning library materials significantly extends their lives by eliminating the dust and dirt that abrades pages and binding surfaces, attracts insects, and contributes to an environment that supports mold growth. Cleaning should be done on a regular basis, but good judgment is needed in deciding how and when to act. Since cleaning has the potential to damage books, staff should be taught careful handling techniques.

Vacuuming materials to remove dust is beneficial, but extreme care must be practiced when the books are being treated. Dust that settles mostly on the head of a book can be removed with the soft brush attachment of a vacuum cleaner, or with a dust cloth. Staff should be trained to hold the book firmly with its head angled downward, so that the dust is not forced between the pages. An annual cleaning program (conducted during a slow period of library use) could be instituted.

READER AWARENESS

It is much more difficult to educate readers in the proper handling of library materials than it is to train staff. Readers are not paid by the library and the library cannot require them to attend workshops or seminars. Some readers may actually resent the library's preservation instruction (which they may perceive as restrictive), so more creative means of education are required. One way to educate readers is through a public relations campaign. The program may include exhibits, bookmarks, handouts, signs, and a well-informed staff.

If the library has a policy of no food or beverages, it is important to educate readers about why eating and drinking are not allowed in the library. The consequences can be reinforced by visual reminders such as posters and exhibits. Exhibits underscore the adage that one picture is worth a thousand words. Try displaying exhibits of yellowing and ripped pages, garbage collected in the library stacks, damaged or maimed books, or even insect infestation. An exhibit about the effects of food and drink on library materials and associated potential insect problems will create an awareness of the problem, and concern for library materials. This display gives the reader the opportunity to observe firsthand why eating, drinking, and smoking are not allowed in the library. (The Rivera Library at the University of California/Davis displayed live, crawling insects, such as cockroaches, termites, carpet beetles, and firebrats, all of which snack on serials and munch on books. They also exhibited books damaged by insects and patrons.[2])

What consequences can we reasonably impose on readers? Some libraries fine readers who eat and drink in the stacks. Another punishment may be to require offenders to attend a library awareness workshop (this approach has it antecedents in traffic court). Perhaps more than the threat of penalties, careful upkeep of the stacks reminds readers to be careful with library materials. If an area is cluttered, they will only add to the mess: garbage in the stacks encourages readers to be messy. Conversely, when an area is clean and there are plenty of wastebaskets, garbage and clutter will not pile up. Signs encouraging readers' assistance in keeping order are also useful.

A library that allows, and even encourages, circulation must accept the fact that a certain amount of damage is inevitable. To most readers' way of thinking, library materials exist for their personal use. In public libraries, adult fiction and picture books are usually found to be in the poorest condition. These materials may be newer, but they are heavily used by the public and frequently returned through book drops. The bindings of many of today's books are considered to be of poor quality and do not last long.

Clearly stated policies for use and circulation may offer some deterrent to mishandling by readers. In addition, the library can encourage readers to care for books by providing plastic bags (perhaps bearing preservation slogans) during inclement weather, and including a handout or bookmark (perhaps stressing "do's and don'ts" for book handling) with volumes when they are charged out. This information might be included:

- Take care to prevent the book from coming into contact with dirty hands, foods, smoking materials, or sources of potential water damage.
- Never force open or "crack" a book.
- Support a book while it is in use.
- Do not place foreign objects, including paper clips, pencils, Post-it™ Notes, and bulky items, between the leaves of the textblock.
- Do not stack opened books one atop the other to hold places in texts; this damages and dirties leaves.
- Do not mark the text of books in any way.
- Never turn down page corners to mark places in the text.
- Use no rubber bands, staples, or pins in a book.
- Support the cover and pages of a book while the book is being photocopied.
- Do not force a book flat on the photocopy machine.
- Do not photocopy oversized, tightly bound, or brittle materials.

If a library is concerned with preservation, it may decide to consider restrictions on the use and circulation of certain materials. Circulation, especially of fragile materials, may be denied and their photocopying limited. All staff must be willing to speak up whenever they see abuse of library materials by readers. In many situations, readers may be unaware of the correct way to handle materials. Encourage staff to observe readers who are photocopying and let the readers know when they are doing something harmful to materials. Staff will find it easier after their training, which will strengthen their confidence levels.

Use signs to mark prominently the areas where readers are to place books to be reshelved. Tables or empty shelves should be available at regular intervals in the stacks. When a library has open stacks, there should be enough room to allow easy access to materials on the shelves.

CONCLUSION

Librarians must be prepared to deal with the human factor, before library materials are destroyed. A well-trained, preservation-conscious access services staff will perform good stack maintenance and keep the collections in serviceable condition. A great deal of time is required to design preservation training and reader awareness programs. However, a well-planned preservation training program for staff and readers is certainly worth the time and effort, because of the dividends in collection protection that it will yield. The library's administration may decide to tackle one program at a time. However, libraries should be evolving into partnerships with their readers. In terms of use, many more readers have contact with library materials than staff; thus, it is critical to address readers in any preservation program.

Preservation training benefits not only library materials, but the access services staff as well. With preservation training, these employees gain new skills, increase job satisfaction, and learn the value of teamwork. Thus the library creates a "win-win" situation. Also, the support and cooperation of all library staff should be cultivated and encouraged. While this will take time and cannot be accomplished overnight, for the programs to succeed, the full support of the staff is required.

SUGGESTIONS FOR ADDITIONAL READING

Morrow, Carolyn Clark. *The Preservation Challenge: A Guide to Conserving Library Materials*. White Plains, N.Y.: Knowledge Industry Publications, 1983.

Northeast Document Conservation Center. *Preservation of Library & Archival Materials: A Manual*. Andover, Mass.: Northeast Document Conservation Center, 1992.

Research Libraries Group. *RLG Preservation Manual*, 2d ed. Stanford, Calif.: Research Libraries Group, 1986.

NOTES

1. Jane Greenfield, *Books, Their Care and Repair* (New York: H.W. Wilson, 1983).
2. "News Fronts: When Books are Bugged," *American Libraries* 24 (April 1993): 291.

Disasters for Directors:
The Role of the Library or Archive Director in Disaster Preparedness and Recovery

Barbra Buckner Higginbotham

Chief Librarian and
Executive Director of Academic Information Technologies
Brooklyn College
The City University of New York

Miriam B. Kahn

Preservation Consultant
MBK Consulting

BACKGROUND

In 1992 the Brooklyn College Library (which has 1,000,000+ bound volumes and a staff of 60 FTEs) experienced two serious floods; after the second event, a major mold outbreak occurred and the director engaged the services of a preservation consultant to manage the recovery process. This paper is the product of lengthy discussions between these two women about the proper role of the director in emergency planning and disaster recovery. While its context is water-related emergencies in academic institutions, its counsel is broad enough to assist directors in any sort of library, regardless of the type of emergency. The paper will be especially useful in settings that do not have well-staffed preservation units; in these environments the entire library staff may well become involved in emergency planning and recovery.

THE LIBRARY DIRECTOR: FIGUREHEAD OR LEADER?

There are those library directors who believe that they can best demonstrate respect for the work of the library staff (and the staff themselves) by actually performing this work. They may, for example, spend some time each day shelving books or barcoding. In an emergency like a flood, these same directors might be seen shoulder to shoulder with other staff members, pulling wet books off shelves or interleaving them with paper toweling. In contrast, the authors see a very different role in emergency planning and recovery for the library's chief administrator, one of leadership, coordination, and public relations. And there will never be a time when the director's most basic role—obtaining for the library staff the resources they need to do their jobs—will be more important than in planning for and recovering from disasters.

Much has been written about disaster preparedness planning and recovery, but the part of the library director is often neglected. However, if the library is to execute an emergency planning and recovery process efficiently and cost-effectively, its director's role is a critical one. When disaster causes the orderly world of the library or archive to run to chaos, the director must lead the institutional and human struggle toward recovery and normalization. Even then, his or her job does not stop when the immediate emergency is under control: as this paper will show, recovery is a lengthy and complex process. How involved the director becomes in the actual rescue operation will depend upon the size of the institution (and, to some extent, on the size of the disaster): in the very small library, the director may be handling wet books alongside the rest of the staff. However, there are some jobs that *only* the director can accomplish, such as finding funds to cover unexpected costs and interacting with the college or university's administration or the media. This paper will discuss the aspects of disaster prevention, planning, response, and recovery that are the province of the library director.

BEFORE DISASTER STRIKES: GETTING READY

Little is sadder than the smugly self-satisfied director who feels certain that, because no emergency has yet occurred in his or her building, none ever will. In terms of disasters, a library or archive director is much better advised to be an ant than a grasshopper (although insect analogies may be inappropriate in papers about preservation), and to prepare well for a future that will almost certainly include one or more emergencies. Preplanning for disaster is essential to a smooth recovery, and these are some of the preparatory steps the director should take. Some of these tasks can and should be delegated, depending on the size of the library and its mission; however, the director is integral to the process that returns the library to "normal," and most of these responsibilities belong to her or him.

• *Establish the value of the collections in the mind of the college or university's administration*

It is probable that the library's collections represent one of the parent institution's most valuable tangible assets. Indeed, if one multiplies the number of volumes in the library by, say, $100 (probably a conservative figure, when the several costs associated with replacement—reordering, cataloging, processing—are added to the actual price of a new volume), it is easy to see that the collection may well out-value the building that shelters it. Thus, before disaster strikes, it is important that directors help college and university administrators (who may view the library more as a bottomless pit which no amount of funding will ever fill, than as a proud but vulnerable treasure) to see that even costly recovery plans must be considered well worth the money, when considered in the context of a multi-million dollar asset.

• Identify sources of funds for cleanup, recovery, and replacement of lost collections

Disasters are costly events; formal weddings and bar mitzvahs pale beside them. Despite the fact that recovering, drying, and reshelving the collections is much less expensive than replacing them, one must still identify resources for this work. Many publicly-funded institutions are "self-insured," a euphemism for "uninsured." However, if the parent organization has insurance, the director should meet with the institution's risk manager and insurance company to determine what the insurance covers, where the limitations lie, and how much money can be expended before the company arrives.

If the institution is uninsured or has a high deductible, the director should determine whether a "contingency fund" of some sort or "soft money" exists, and who has the authority to allocate this emergency funding. Determining the value and replacement costs of all assets, including books, furniture, equipment, and non-print collections, will help justify emergency funding and perhaps more thorough insurance coverage as well.

• Establish appropriate relationships and routines with other departments and divisions of the institution

It is important to predetermine the extent of assistance the library can expect from physical plant, maintenance, and security staff during a disaster. The director should explore this question with the heads of the other departments and ensure that appropriate emergency routines are established. Similarly, security, maintenance, and the physical plant staff should be included in emergency training sessions that are relevant to their roles.

During the planning process, the director should discuss with the organization's labor relations specialist the reassignment of jobs and work that emergencies often necessitate; this can save time and help eliminate concerns about "working out of title" when a disaster actually occurs. If these potential situations are discussed and clarified beforehand, the organization can avoid misunderstandings in the midst of an emergency.

The director should also discuss with the food services manager the possibility of using food freezers as temporary, safe, time-buying solutions, if unexpected decisions must be made or funds need to be raised before the actual recovery of materials can begin. In an academic setting, the disaster's timing can mean everything: during intercession or holiday periods, large amounts of cafeteria freezer space may be available. When school is in session, the library will probably have to look elsewhere.

• Develop a budget for the emergency planning process

The emergency planning process itself costs money and staff time. The director should allocate funds to design, test, and rewrite an emergency plan;

stock emergency supplies; and train library and other campus staff.

• *Encourage the staff to write and practice a disaster preparedness plan*

The director is well-placed to determine who is best suited to work on the planning team, which should consist of a mixture of professionals and paraprofessionals selected from various areas of the library. The participation of the security, physical plant, and maintenance staffs will also be helpful; it will give these units a sense of "ownership" in the library's emergency preparedness program. When considering team members, the director should value the ability to work within the bureaucracy and to accept various administrative constraints. The team will consider a variety of crises and outline procedures and policies for dealing with them. The director may provide guidance and feedback; he or she will also encourage the completion of each step of the plan.

• *Prepare a collections retention plan*

When survival of the library is uppermost in the director's mind, it is almost impossible to begin setting priorities for collection recovery. Part of the emergency planning team's responsibility should be to establish, in advance of an emergency, retention and discard priorities for each major collection, and floor plans indicating where these collections are; certainly collection development officers will help in this effort. The director may provide broad guidelines for these decisions and request justifications for discard and retention choices.

• *Determine to whom to delegate authority during a disaster*

The director need not be the leader of the emergency recovery team. In fact, with all the other responsibilities that he or she must perform, it is highly advisable to choose someone else for this important job. The director will have a sense of who on the staff is prepared and committed to be a member of the response team. Someone who has proven him or herself in another emergency situation, or a staff member who has actually participated in disaster recovery, may be a good choice. (Despite the fact that Brooklyn College had a well-documented emergency plan, it was the leadership provided by a librarian who had helped with flood recovery at another institution that seemed to serve us best.) In any case, reliability and strong leadership skills are essential qualities for members of the disaster response team.

For many reasons, appointing a pair of recovery team leaders is a good idea. There will be a great deal of work for only one person to accomplish. If there are two team leaders, their vacation and other schedules can be arranged so that one of them is generally present. The director should let the library staff know that the team leaders have been given full authority in case disaster strikes: in an emergency, they can reassign staff from any area of the library to recovery work. If a consultant is brought in, they will be his or her chief contacts. Not only do the team leaders assign work and supervise staff during response and recovery, they may also do other important jobs, such as taking appropriate photographs and calculating the costs of the disaster in several different categories (staff time, replacement of materials, salvage costs, and so forth).

• Identify and implement a series of relevant preventive measures

Disaster prevention is an important component of disaster response planning. Slighting preventative measures can increase the amount of damage and loss during disaster. Some decisions (such as installing costly sprinkler systems) will be encouraged by the director but made in conjunction with other campus administrators. The director should be equipped to argue for such improvements from a financial standpoint that emphasizes the cost of lost assets.

The director can work with the campus facilities manager to develop a plan for correcting building problems before they lead to disaster. The plan might include such things as repairing or replacing leaking windows and roofs, installing water detectors, regularly inspecting fire alarms and smoke detectors, and so forth. Similarly, the director and the head of campus security can design a plan for enhancing the safety of the collections. Some of the elements in such a document might be schedules for the regular recertification of fire extinguishers and conducting fire drills.

• Seek qualified external guidance and assistance

The director may invite police officers and fire fighters to tour the library building, familiarizing themselves with the disaster response plan and the library layout. Seeking the help of a consultant in writing the emergency plan or training staff in recovery procedures can also be a sound decision for libraries that lack resident preservation expertise; later, a qualified preservation professional who is already familiar with one's building, staff, and collections may prove invaluable when disaster strikes. There are also library and archival organizations, consortia, and associations that will provide preservation education, information, and training; the director may wish to contact them.

"WATER, WATER EVERYWHERE. . ."

When a disaster occurs, speed of response is crucial. If action is deferred, the associated costs and collection losses escalate. When disaster strikes and the library has a good emergency plan and a well-prepared staff, its director will take the following steps.

• *Alert the emergency response team*

When the director receives that dreaded call in the middle of the night, he or she should do whatever is necessary to get the disaster response team into the building as soon as the fire department or other authorities permit. Other staff should also be called, as well as campus security and facilities personnel. It is important that the director, having appointed the disaster team leaders, now trust their judgment to make the correct decisions. The emergency response plan, written and tested when life was calm and sane, should be treated as a reliable guide for all activities and procedures.

• *Inform the insurance company*

The director should inform the insurance company immediately, but begin response and clean up as soon as possible—it is neither necessary nor advisable to wait for an adjuster to arrive. Recovery team members can make photographs to document the disaster and all staff actions.

• *Evaluate the safety and security of the library facility*

The director must decide whether to close the library (or perhaps close only certain areas); this decision will likely be made in consultation with facilities, personnel, and security staff, as there may be issues of health and safety for the staff, readers, and the collections. Once these matters are resolved, the director will decide when (and to what degree) to reopen the building. If the disaster is great, the possibility of establishing temporary library services in some other location may present itself. It will be important for the director to keep the academic administration—the chief academic officer, the person in charge of student life—fully informed about the availability of the collections and other library services.

Health and safety issues aside, nine out of 10 directors will do everything possible to maintain as full a service program as possible, while recovery takes place in the background. However, there may be considerable value in closing the building during immediate disaster response activities. Closing to the public helps to assuage the staff's mixed loyalties between responding to the disaster and performing their regular duties, and thus allay some of the considerable stress the staff will be feeling. It also provides bodies to assist with recovery: if the library is taking a "business as usual" approach and half the staff is covering service points, there may not be enough workers to handle important tasks related to the emergency. And, behind-the-scenes employees (those in technical services, for example) may resent being pulled from their jobs to work with wet books, while their counterparts in information and access services perform their regular (and presumably neater and cleaner) duties. When the building is closed, even if only briefly, the campus quickly understands that the library is in serious difficulty. Any unexpected interruption of service underscores the integral nature of the library in the fabric of college or university life.

Except in the case of the worst disasters, the library building will probably reopen (if indeed it ever closed) long before recovery is complete. The director must then decide how to balance the delivery of service with continuing recovery efforts, probably in the context of a crowded, busy facility where there is no obvious space suitable for staging and drying wet materials. For example, if the library decides to dry on-site those materials that are only nominally wet, it may be necessary to commandeer reading tables and limit access to the area of the building where the drying activity will occur.

• *Assign a high priority to sensitive "human" issues*

During the disaster (and well into the recovery process) the emotional and physical stress on staff is extraordinary. Employees often have an established and almost personal interest in the collections; this means that feelings of guilt ("Could I have done something to prevent this?") or territoriality ("I'm busy working on 'my' collections—those science books are someone else's problem") are not uncommon. Some staff (bibliographers, for example, who have spent their careers developing particular collections) may push themselves to a state of exhaustion in an attempt to "fix" the disaster. Here, the director's role is very important. He or she can help to smooth such difficulties with active communication, patient understanding, and enforced work breaks where food and drink are provided in a warm place, preferably removed from the disaster area. (When major disasters occur, the Red Cross may provide useful services for the staff; the director should ask whether this organization is available to help.)

After the adrenaline begins to wear off, about 48 hours into any crisis, the director will find it more difficult to maintain staff morale and efforts. Now it becomes especially important to reassure staff that their work is appreciated and the results are worth the effort. High visibility for the director—walking through recovery areas several times a day and talking with staff who are working there—will serve the library well. Getting the president and the chief academic officer into the library to speak with staff and commend their efforts is also an important responsibility for the library director.

In a library that does not have a large and well-trained preservation staff, it is important for the director to keep reminding him or herself, "Disaster recovery is not in *anyone's* job description." Performing recovery activities may be a theoretically ennobling experience, but in reality this work is dirty, wet, and often requires much more physical exertion than the typical library worker's regular job: pulling heavy, sodden volumes off high shelves or swabbing down books covered with slimy purple mold is strenuous, disagreeable work. In fact, some staff may not be able to manage the stress associated with an emergency, or may not wish to participate in the physical work. Others will seem powerless to respond, to delegate, or to lead during a crisis. In some cases, beginning to participate in recovery work will reduce the stress, but in others this will be counterproductive. The director should discuss these issues with the disaster response team and ensure that tasks are assigned to suit each staff member's capabilities.

• *Enlist the help of the institution's health and safety officer*

The aftermath of a disaster can be quite intimidating for the library's staff: mold and strange smells are frightening, and environmental and work issues may arise. However, enlisting the support of the right professionals will be very helpful. The director can invite the institution's health and safety officer to meet with the entire library staff to air their fears. He or she can listen, sympathize, and explain the minimal dangers associated with the existing conditions. This presents a good opportunity for the director to let the staff know he or she is aware of these working difficulties and appreciative of their willingness to work.When health issues seem serious, the director should arrange to have air or mold tested, informing the staff of the results.

At Brooklyn, we requested help from both the Environmental Health and Safety Officer and the Biology Department; within a half-hour a professor armed with Petri dishes appeared and began taking mold samples. He was able to reassure staff immediately that the mold appeared to be the common household variety; within a few days, the cultures proved this to be so. He submitted a written analysis to the Environmental Health and Safety Officer, and this document was shared with library staff and union leaders.

• *Work with other units of the parent organization to get needed help*

The director should ask facilities to provide staff to help library employees with wet-vac-ing and other gross recovery tasks. At the same time, he or she must be certain that well-intentioned but uninformed people do not begin doing the wrong things—for example, repainting wet walls or replacing buckling floor tiles before the building has completely dried out.

• *Maintain frequent communication with staff and other key constituencies*

During a disaster, good communications are vital. The director will meet frequently with disaster response team leaders, both to keep her or himself informed and to lend encouragement. Recovery team leaders need to be kept well informed of the director's emergency-related actions and decisions. Regular meetings with the library's management team, listening to their concerns and conveying important information that they in turn can pass on to their staffs, are also important.

It is vital to get news of the disaster, the damage, and the library's specific needs into the press and to keep it there with articles and interviews. When a major disaster occurs, the parent organization's public information or com-

munications officer may well deal with the media. When the emergency occurs on a somewhat smaller scale and is confined to the library, this job can
fall to the director.

If the event is only of local or campus interest, he or she should meet with
the student press and keep them well-informed about what is happening. The
director will probably attempt to put a somewhat positive "spin" on the emergency, emphasizing the contributions of the staff and other campus units in
the recovery operation. Good press can be very helpful if volunteers are
needed to assist in recovery, and if the library subsequently begins a campaign to raise funds to replace collections.

•Enlist the help of external experts

One of the most critical matters for a director is knowing when to cede
the field to an outside expert—a consultant, perhaps—who is better
equipped to manage certain aspects of the recovery operation than the library's chief administrator. At Brooklyn College, we recovered nicely from
our first flood on our own, with no external assistance: staff salvaged nominally wet volumes on-site, some materials were withdrawn or replaced, and
many of the truly sodden were sent out for freeze-drying. However, when a
second and even more serious deluge occurred less than a year later (followed by a major outbreak of mold), the director found that she and her staff
were both discouraged and somewhat out of their depth, in terms of knowing how to respond to the microorganisms growing on significant numbers
of volumes: it seemed wise to bring in a preservation specialist to help the
disaster team leaders marshall and support the staff during this new crisis,
make treatment recommendations, and identify off-site facilities to assist in
the salvage effort. The availability of gift funds to support this work enabled
the director to act quickly, rather than working through the larger bureaucracy to bring in a consultant.

In fact, the consultant did all the things mentioned above, and more. Her
very presence reassured the staff that both the library and the college
administration cared about them and the trauma they were revisiting.
The consultant met and talked with academic, security, facilities, and health
and safety officials; she also wrote a series of reports that carried the weight
of an expert's opinion. These reports were helpful in effecting the recovery
of the library building and collections, as well as preventing a recurrence
of the flood.

A consultant can provide the extra assistance an already strapped staff
needs to identify outside organizations to dry, freeze, or disinfect materials;
inspect materials for adequacy of treatment when they are returned from a
commercial company; design staff and other education programs; and help
re-evaluate and redraft the library's emergency plan. This specialist should
have excellent communication skills and good contacts in the preservation

field, in the event he or she needs to arrange external recovery services. A certain "cheerleader" quality is by no means undesirable: by now, the staff is likely disheartened and in need of the leadership a knowledgeable and supportive person can provide.

The consultant's presence reassures the staff, provides focus, and generates solutions. He or she is clearly a person who respects library collections, yet does not have the same emotional ties to the materials that the library staff has. This factor can prove very beneficial: while less expensive than replacement, the cost of drying and disinfecting damaged volumes is still considerable. This means that some wrenching decisions about discarding certain materials will inevitably have to be made. In this situation, the consultant can be the calm voice of reason as the library staff debates its options.

"IT AIN'T OVER 'TIL IT'S OVER": RECOVERY AS A LENGTHY PROCESS

The director's job continues long after the disaster has passed; one could say that, when the immediate emergency subsides, the real work of the director begins.

• Initiate a fund-raising campaign

If the disaster has been a major one and the financial implications are large, the director may initiate a fund-raising effort as soon as the immediate response period is ended. For maximum effectiveness, the campaign should begin within six months of the disaster's occurrence.

• Develop appropriate documentation

Thoroughly documenting the disaster, from the very beginning when it was discovered, through the initial recovery process, and projecting the steps required for complete recovery, is critical. This report will also include the costs associated with recovery; it may be tailored to a particular audience—the academic administration; the faculty library committee—or written more generally, for use with a variety of constituencies. Such a document can help to prevent another disaster, or to effect needed improvements in the library facility. Suddenly, the library may go to the top of the list of campus renovation projects.

• Acknowledge the efforts of the staff

The director should write to the disaster team leaders and other library and college staff who were key in the recovery effort, recognizing their contributions. At Brooklyn College the director planned a "We Survived the Floods of '92" party for the library staff. The presence of the president and the provost at this event demonstrated their regard for the staff's hard work.

• **Establish new or temporary staffing patterns**

Some temporary job reassignments may be necessary following an emergency. The director may also consider authorizing additional working hours for some staff, or hiring temporary employees in order to get displaced materials reshelved, or new materials ordered, processed, and cataloged.

• **Obtain commitments for funds, repairs, and other needed resources**
  from the institution's administration

Purchasing materials to replace destroyed collections is just one cost center in disaster recovery. The charges of freezers, dryers, and mold removers; the costs associated with reordering and processing new materials; the staff time required to repatriate and reprocess treated books—all these costs are both real and substantial.

And, perhaps more than just the collections have been affected by the emergency: the building may require costly repairs. Furniture can be ruined and require replacement. Expensive computer equipment may have been destroyed. A major task for the director (and an extension of his or her most basic responsibility—obtaining the resources the staff need to do their jobs) will be securing the funds needed for complete recovery.

• **Communicate to the administration a set of reasonable expectations**
  for library staff

As discussed earlier in this paper, it is a mistake to discount the amount of unpleasant physical labor involved in dealing with an emergency: working in rancid water, pulling hundreds of wet books off shelves and loading them onto trucks or wrapping and boxing them, wet-vac-ing floors, handling reeking, fungi-infested books while wearing gloves and masks—none of these tasks is easy or pleasurable. Furthermore, this type work is in no one's job description, and an organization should count itself lucky when the staff rises to the occasion following an unfortunate event. An expectation on the part of the college or university administration that library staff will work long hours stoically and without complaint (or even with complaint), "out of title" and under the most unpleasant physical circumstances, is unrealistic and unfair. It is the responsibility of the library director to help the academic administration understand not only that the staff's efforts are worthy of remark, but that extra-library labor may be necessary when the emergency is very severe. Under some circumstances, kind words and party cakes may be insufficient palliatives.

• **Evaluate the library's response to the disaster and adjust the**
  emergency plan as appropriate

While recovery is in full swing, the director and the emergency response team will keep track of problems that deserve review when the crisis is over.

These issues, and the emergency plan itself, should be re-examined post-disaster, and the plan modified as needed.

• Put the building back together

Putting the building back together can be no small matter. Decisions about replacing furniture, equipment, and critical library systems may present themselves. Administrative offices (perhaps even the office of the director) and their functions are often overlooked in disaster response; nonetheless, at the same time he or she confronts collection and equipment damage, the director may also be facing disaster very close at hand. This was certainly the case at Brooklyn College, where the director's desk filled with water and collapsed, and key administrative documents were ruined.

CONCLUSION

Recovery is a lengthy process. Months, perhaps more than a year, may pass before a building completely dries out, or damaged collections are returned from outside treatment facilities and reprocessed. And, once a building has experienced an emergency, it is often left more vulnerable to certain predators, such as mold and fungi. (Anyone who lived through the 1950s knows that the Blob and the Mummy both returned; long after the flood waters have subsided the Giant Spore will also be lurking, waiting to attack, should temperature and humidity conspire to create an hospitable environment.) As the Girl Scouts enjoin, "Be prepared"—disasters are not necessarily "one to a customer."

Being prepared is the easiest way to survive a disaster. The director should trust the emergency response team and let its members manage the immediate work of recovery. At the same time, he or she should be visible and interested in the actions and needs of the library staff. It is the director who must maintain the momentum of disaster recovery by making key management decisions and working with library boards and academic administrations. Finally, it is important for the director to let peers—the directors of other libraries—know that he or she will be there for them, if disaster strikes: a director who has managed and recovered from an emergency can be a great deal of help when another institution is hit by a disaster.

ACKNOWLEDGEMENTS

While the role of the library director is certainly an important one, many other persons also play key parts in emergency planning and recovery. The authors acknowledge the extraordinary energy, resourcefulness, and commitment displayed by both the professional and supporting staff of the Brooklyn College Library during the recovery process associated with the floods of 1992; their work and thinking helped shape this paper. Particularly, we would like to recognize the work of Miriam Deutch and Sally Bowdoin, our Disaster Team Leaders, two young women who emerged from the winter waters of 1992 as heroines, as well as Bertha Bendelstein, Head of Acquisitions; Susan Vaughn, Associate Librarian for Collection Development; Jane Cramer, Government Publications Librarian; and Howard Spivak, Director for Library Systems and Academic Computing.

We also acknowledge the assistance provided by Steve Czirak, Assistant Vice-President for Facilities Management and Planning; Professor Carl Schuster, Biology Department; and Aldo Orlando, Environmental Health and Safety Officer. The flood of August 31, 1992, occurred on President Vernon E. Lattin's first day on the job at Brooklyn College. Nonetheless, he took the time to come to the Library, survey the damage, speak with staff, and generally encourage the recovery process with his presence and concern. We submit his example as a fine one for all academic administrators.

INDEX

AALL [*see* American Association of Law Libraries]

ABLE [*see* Automated Binding Library Exchange software]

AIC [*see* American Institute for Conservation of Historic and Artistic Works]

AIIM [*see* Association for Information and Image Management]

ALA [*see* American Library Association]

ALCTS [*see* Association for Library Collections and Technical Services]

AMC [*see* American Movie Classics]

ANSI [*see* American National Standards Institute]

ARL [*see* Association of Research Libraries]

ARTFL [*see* American and French Research on the Treasury of the French Language]

AVIAC [*see* Automation Vendors Information Advisory Committee]

Abell, Millicent, 39

Access to collections, 3, 16, 26-28, 44, 101-102, 105, 118-29, 207, 227, 236, 239, 242, 281-84, 310-13, 315, 319, 322, 324-27, 333, 335-36, 378, 391-99

Achenbach Foundation for the Graphic Arts (San Francisco), 163-67, 172, 174

Acid-free paper, 7, 13, 322-23, 343-45, 396

Acidic paper, 8, 17, 28, 30-31, 34, 59, 203, 210, 214, 217-18, 226, 294, 302, 317, 320, 322-23, 330, 340, 343-44, 347, 391, 394

Acquisitions activities and units, 16, 140, 184, 358

Action surveys, 202-206

Adhesive binding [*see also* double-fan adhesive binding], 318-20, 341

Advanced Optochemical Research, Inc., 65

Advanced Revelation software, 140

Agfa Company (Belgium), 290

Agricultural information resources, 119, 122-25

Air-handling systems, 32, 55-76

Air pollution, 30-31, 55-76, 80, 391

Air quality standards, 62, 66

Air sampling, 62-71

Akzo Chemicals, Inc., 79-99, 324

Albums [*see also* scrapbooks], 120, 167, 339-51

  contents, 341-42

  cost of preserving, 343

  definition, 339-40

  materials, 340-41

  storage, 350

Allen, Woody, 280

Alper, Diana, 384

Alpha 4 software, 214

America Online online service, 122

American and French Research on the Treasury of the French Language (ARTFL), 11

American Association of Law Libraries (AALL), 40

American Institute for Conservation of Historic and Artistic Works (AIC), 48, 158, 351

American Library Association (ALA), 48, 312, 316, 318, 320, 339

American Memory project, 119, 125-27

American Movie Classics (AMC) television network, 280

American National Standards Institute (ANSI), 62, 184

Amigos Bibliographic Council, 236

Andrew W. Mellon Foundation, 104, 134, 195, 331

Archives, 24-36, 77-99, 104, 107-108, 118-21, 128-29, 158, 160-61, 168-69, 172, 186, 194, 206-207, 235, 242-44, 248, 251-52, 262, 268, 280-85, 287-92, 302, 321, 329-37, 339, 370-72, 376-89

  preservation programs, 376-89

Archivists, 126, 342, 344

  education and training, 376-89

Armbruster Collection Data Base Project, 141

Art and architecture materials, 20, 119, 127-28, 136
Association for Information and Image Management (AIIM), 109
Association for Library Collections and Technical Services (ALCTS), 320, 323
Association of Recorded Sound Collections, 311
Association of Research Libraries (ARL), 20, 37-40, 47-51, 78, 186, 194, 197
    Committee on Preservation of Research Materials, 39
    Office of Management Services, 39, 194
    Preservation Planning Program, 194
Atkinson, Ross, 50, 207-208
Audio materials, 7, 13, 19, 28, 160-61, 244, 301-303, 310-11, 320, 329, 370, 385, 387
Authoring tools, 169, 171-74
Authority control [*see also* catalogs and cataloging], 101
Automated Binding Library Exchange software (ABLE), 136, 140, 183
Automating preservation management, 133-77, 180-86, 199-208, 214-15, 234-52, 254-66
Automation Vendors Information Advisory Committee (AVIAC) Working Group on the Communication of Binding Data Elements, 181-83
Awk (computer programming language), 162
Ayres, Marx, 66
Ayres & Ezer Associates (Los Angeles), 66

BASIC (computer programming language), 164
BSDP [*see* Bibliographic Service Development Program]
Baer, Norbert S., 63
Bandwidth, 116
Banks, Brenda, 384, 388
Banks, Paul N., 63, 299
Barcodes, 82, 148-49, 154, 163, 184, 394

Barker, James, 325-26
Barrow, William J., 30
Battelle Memorial Institute, 94
Battin, Patricia, 39, 50
Bay Area Preservation Planning Project [*see* Greater Bay Area Preservation Planning Project (California)]
Bendelstein, Bertha, 412
Bennett, Scott, 39, 94
Bibliographic control of preserved materials, 4, 6, 8-9, 14, 16-17, 45
Bibliographic Service Development Program (BSDP), 101
Billington, James, 125, 282
Binding [*see also* Automated Binding Library Exchange (ABLE) software; Automation Vendors Information Advisory Committee (AVIAC); double-fan adhesive binding; leather bookbindings; Library Binding Institute], 16, 134, 136, 139-40, 142, 146, 149, 151, 182, 195-99, 202-205, 212, 220, 356, 364, 366, 371, 394
    albums, 340-42, 347-48
    definition, 340
    music materials, 311-20, 327
    paperbacks, 197-98, 203, 213, 216, 218, 220-21
    periodicals, 197-98
    rebinding, 197-99, 203-205, 212-13, 216-23, 225-27, 240, 251, 263
    scrapbooks, 340-42, 344-46
Black-and-white films, 281, 285, 291
Blades, William, 56-57
Bogaty, Herman, 60
Book drops, 33, 220, 395, 398
Book jackets, 212, 218, 221, 317-18
Book supports, 396
Bookends [*see* book supports]
Bookstein, Abraham, 160
Boston Public Library, 311
Bostwick, Arthur, 315
Bowdoin, Sally, 412
Bowser, Eileen, 287
Boxes [*see* protective enclosures]
Brigham Young University, 62-71
Brittle books, 38, 158, 181, 184, 194, 199-200, 202-203, 210, 217-18, 224, 226, 263, 320-24, 394, 398
Brookline (Massachusetts) Public Library, 314

Brooklyn College Library, 400, 403, 407-409, 411-12
Brooklyn Public Library, 312, 314-15
Brown, James M. III, 279
Brown, John Carter, 127
Bruer, John Michael, 133-45
Brysson, Ralph J., 59
Buchanan, Sally, 159, 194
Burckel, Nicholas C., 388
Burke, John, 173-74
Burnard, Lou, 302-303
Byrne, Sherry, 39-40

C (computer programming language), 162
CALIPR software, 212, 236, 240-45, 247-48
CAUSE, 48
CD-ROMs [*see also* digitization; electronic information; reformatting], 11, 113-16, 120, 125-27, 299-301, 303, 326
CENTRO [*see* Central New York Library Resources Council]
CHIN [*see* Canadian Heritage Information Network]
CIC [*see* Committee on Institutional Cooperation]
CIN [*see* Conservation Information Network]
CLR [*see* Council on Library Resources]
CNI [*see* Coalition for Networked Information]
CoOL [*see* Conservation On-Line (CoOL) information service]
CPA [*see* Commission on Preservation and Access]
CRL [*see* Center for Research Libraries]
Cage, John, 336
California libraries, 236-37
Canada, 37-51
Canadian Heritage Information Network (CHIN), 184
Carrier, Willis, 57
Case Western Reserve University, 325-27
Cass, Glen R., 59-61
Cassettes [*see* audio materials]
Catalogs and cataloging [*see also* bibliographic control of preserved materi-

als], 7, 10, 14, 101, 105, 115, 126, 135, 137, 149, 157-58, 161-63, 167-68, 171, 183-84, 193, 207, 235-36, 238, 254, 311, 315, 321-22, 325, 332-36, 356, 358-59, 362, 364, 366, 368, 371
Catholic University, 124
Center for Research Libraries (CRL), 40, 48
Central New York Library Resources Council (CENTRO), 234-52
Central New York Preservation Needs Assessment Project (PNAP), 234-52
Centre de Recherches sur la Conservation des Documents Graphiques (Paris), 60
Chaplin, Charlie, 302
Chicago Historical Society, 33
Chicago preservation planning conference [*see* Preservation Planning Conference, Chicago, May 1992]
Chicago Public Library, 312
Child, Margaret, 40
Cibachrome, 109
Circulation, 135, 183-84, 206, 211, 213-14, 220-27, 311-13, 317, 319, 358, 391, 394-95, 397-98
Clarkson, Christopher, 351
Cleaning library materials, 134, 140, 395-97
Client-server system architecture, 184, 186
Climate controls [*see* environmental controls and monitoring]
Clipper software, 120
Clippings, 324, 329-30, 336, 341, 343-45
Coalition for Networked Information (CNI), 45, 47-48
Cobden-Sanderson, T. J., 57
Cockerell, Douglas, 57
Coleman, Sandra, 194
Collection condition surveys, 148-51, 163-64, 199-202, 207, 210-32, 237, 254-66, 387
Collection integrity, 8-9, 17
Collection management [*see also* housing library collections; stack maintenance], 150, 184, 356, 358-59, 362, 364, 367-68, 371, 378
Columbia University [*see also* Teachers College of Columbia University], 40,

102, 194, 322
School of Library Service, 40, 355,
    365, 370
Commission on Preservation and Access
    (CPA), 20, 38-40, 45-51,
    102, 105-106, 113, 115-16,
    378, 384
Committee for Film Preservation and
    Public Access, 283
Committee on Institutional Cooperation
    (CIC), 79, 93
Committee on Preservation of Historical
    Records, 62
Compact disks [*see* audio materials; CD-
    ROMs]
CompuServe online service, 122, 125
Computers [*see* automating preservation
    management; laptop computers; main-
    frame computers; microcomputers;
    minicomputers; specific computer
    programming languages and software
    packages]
Concord Free Public Library, 211, 213,
    215, 217-18, 220-21, 223-26, 228-32
Condition surveys [*see* collection condi-
    tion surveys]
Conference on Priorities for Historical
    Records of 1977, 379
Connecticut Micrographics, 107, 111
Conservation, 8, 16, 18, 19, 34, 38, 77,
    134, 140-44, 146, 151-52, 156-77,
    181, 195-96, 203-206, 221, 240, 249,
    252
    definition, 25, 339, 377-78
    documentation, 16, 157-58, 167-77,
        206-207, 255-56, 258-61, 264, 266
    techniques, 355-56, 364-66, 371
    treatment centers, 379
Conservation Information Network
    (CIN), 142
Conservation On-Line (CoOL) informa-
    tion service, 180
Conway, Paul, 377-78
Copyflow machines, 113
Copyright, 6, 12, 17-18, 116, 281-84,
    321, 323, 325, 334
Cornell University, 12, 40, 50, 102, 105-
    106, 115, 181, 195-208, 385
Council on Library Resources (CLR), 40,
    101-102, 116
Cramer, Jane, 412

Cuban materials, 5
Cultural Education Center (Albany, NY),
    268
Cunningham, Merce, 336
Cunningham Dance Foundation Archives,
    336
Curtis Botanical Magazine, 125
Czirak, Steve, 412

DEZ [*see* diethyl zinc]
Dance Anthology Project, 336-37
Dance Heritage Coalition, 335-36
Dance Librarian's Discussion Group, 336
Dance materials, 326, 329-37, 344-45
Daniel, Floréal, 60
dBase software, 120, 141-42, 161, 236,
    257-59, 261
Deacidification [*see also* mass deacidifi-
    cation], 34, 60-61
Dean, John F., 193-209
Delaware State Archives, 388
DePew, John N., 322-23
Deutch, Miriam, 412
Developing countries, 4, 20
Diethyl zinc (DEZ), 78-99, 324
Diffendal, Anne, 384
Digital signatures [*see* electronic infor-
    mation—integrity and accuracy]
Digitization, 3, 10-20, 44, 77-78, 102,
    105-106, 109, 113-21, 125-29, 134-
    37, 203, 311, 320, 324-27
    costs, 17-18, 106
Digix Corporation, 115
Dirt [*see* dust]
Disaster preparedness [*see* emergency
    planning and recovery]
Documentation [*see* conservation—
    documentation]
Double Helix software, 139
Double-fan adhesive binding, 198, 319-20
Dove, Jack, 318
Drawings and prints, 166-67, 171-72,
    206-207, 262, 329-30, 347-48
Drott, M. Carl, 200
Druzik, James, 55, 171
Duke University, 322, 325
Dust [*see also* particulate matter], 33, 58,
    61, 221, 396-97
Dust jackets [*see* book jackets]

EDUCOM, 48
Eastman School of Music, 318, 321, 323
Eating [*see* food and drink]
Eatough, Delbert J., 55-76
Edwards, C. J., 59
Electronic information [*see also* digitization; optical disks; specific projects and products], 3, 10-20, 293-304, 371, 378, 385, 387
  equipment for retrieval, 11-14, 17, 29, 301-303
  illustrative material, 12-15
  integrity and accuracy, 13-15, 17, 29, 169-70, 174-76, 298
  journals, 293-94, 297-301
  preserving electronic information resources, 10-15, 18, 28-29, 36, 44, 244, 293-304
  refreshing electronic information resources, 7, 13, 17, 19, 170, 302-303
  software retrieval programs, 11-14, 17, 29
  standards, 14
  storage, 14, 17-19
  transmittal, 13-14, 16-19
Electronic mail, 29, 162, 170, 176
Elke camera, 111
Emergency planning and recovery, 32-33, 181, 199, 201, 237, 240, 248, 251-52, 268-79, 387-88, 392, 400-412
  health and safety issues, 405-407
  planning, 400-404, 408, 410-11
  recovery, 404-411
Emley, A. L., 57
Encapsulation, 345-47
Enclosures [*see* protective enclosures]
Environmental controls and monitoring [*see also* air-handling systems; light; relative humidity; temperature], 7-8, 13, 17, 30-32, 77-78, 94, 134, 142, 181-82, 196, 199, 201, 238-40, 248, 252, 348-50, 371, 378, 387-88, 391
Ethernet, 138, 145
Evelyn, John, 56
EXCEL software, 139
Exhibits and exhibit cases, 56, 60, 167, 263, 266, 350, 388, 397

ExpoSure™, 112, 117
Exxon Education Foundation, 102, 104
Eyles, Allen, 284

FIAF [*see* International Federation of Film Archives]
FMC process, 85
Fabric, 59-60
Faraday, Michael, 57
Farr, George F., Jr., 39
Farrell, David, 40
Farrington, Charles, 314
Fashion Institute of Technology (New York City), 346-47
Federal agencies, 104, 118-29
Ferguson, Anthony, 40
Fenske, David, 326
FileMaker Pro software, 258, 260
Film [*see* microfilm and microfilming; motion picture film preservation]
Film Foundation, 280
Film Preservation Festival, 280-81
FILMLOG software, 180, 185
Fine Arts Museums of San Francisco, 163-64
Fire detection and suppression, 32-33, 201, 239-40, 248, 252, 263, 404-405
Fleischhauer, Carl, 130
Floods [*see* water damage]
Folders [*see* protective enclosures]
Folger Shakespeare Library, 58, 164-65
Folios, 392
Food and drink, 33, 220-21, 393, 397
Ford, John, 302
Forde, Walter, 284
Fore-edge shelving, 220, 249
Fortson, Judith, 384, 388
4th Dimension software, 174
FoxBase software, 137
Fractional sampling, 201
Framingham (Massachusetts) Public Library, 211, 213, 215-16, 218, 220-21, 223-26, 228-32
Frangakis, Evelyn, 376-90
Freezing wet materials [*see also* microfilm and microfilming—freezing microfilm], 402, 408, 410
Frieder, Richard, 77

Frost, Murray, 75
Full text [*see* electronic information]
Fumigation, 24, 134
Furbish, Kate, 347-48
Fusonie, Alan, 118-30
Fussler, Herman H., 160
Futas, Elizabeth, 367
Futernick, Robert, 163, 172

GCI [*see* Getty Conservation Institute]
Gardner, William, 296-97
Garlick, Karen, 384
Garrity, William, 39, 42
Gas light, 56-57
Gavitt, Sharon, 268-79
Gene Autry Museum (Los Angeles), 67
GEnie online service, 122
Georgia Department of Archives and
    History, 384, 388
Getty, J. Paul, Jr., 284
Getty Conservation Institute (GCI), 60,
    65
Gibbons, H. R., 61
Gitt, Robert, 287-89
Goldberg, Bessie, 312
Gottschalk camera, 111
Gould, Constance C., 294
Gracy, David B. II, 24-36, 388
Graham, Peter, 170
Graphic materials [*see* drawings and
    prints]
Gratek Congress camera, 111
Greater Bay Area Preservation Planning
    Project (California), 237-42
Greenfield, Jane, 392
Griffith, D.W., 287
Grosjean, Daniel, 60-61, 67-68

H&K [*see* Herrmann & Kraemer]
HVAC systems [*see* air-handling sys-
    tems]
Hackney, Stephen, 61
Haefliger, Kathleen, 310-28
Handling library materials, 33,
    391-99
Hanson, Martha, 234-53
Harris, Kenneth, 50

Harris, Robert, 289
Harry Ransom Humanities Research
    Center, The University of Texas at
    Austin, 40, 77-99
Hartford (Connecticut) Public Library,
    314
Harvard University, 40, 51, 79, 93-94,
    194, 202, 206, 321, 335
Haverhill (Massachusetts) Public Library,
    314
Hawking, Stephen, 299
Hayes, Robert M., 366
Hazen, Dan C., 3-23
Heating, ventilation, and cooling systems
    [*see* air-handling systems]
Helix Express software, 138, 142, 150
Hendriks, Klaus B., 269
Henry, Walter, 156-79
Herrmann & Kraemer (H&K) camera,
    110-16
Higginbotham, Barbra B., 368, 400-412
Hitchcock, Alfred, 284, 302
Holden, Maria, 384
Honea, Ted, 318-19, 323
Hooper, Louisa M., 314
Hoover Institution, 384, 388
Horacek, Juraj, 325
Housing library and archival collections
    [*see also* stack maintenance], 193,
    220, 223-26, 239, 242, 249, 350, 377-
    78, 391
Hudon, Paul, 351
Hudson, F. L., 59
Humidity [*see* relative humidity]
Hygrothermograph, 84
Hypermedia, 11, 297

IBM, 326
IKM camera, 111
ILL [*see* interlibrary loan]
Ilfochrome, 109
Image Concepts, 123
Image Permanence Institute, 114, 116
Indiana University, 326
Indianapolis Public Library, 316
Ink, 59
Insect damage and infestation, 30-34,
    263, 348, 396-97
Insurance, 402, 405

Intensive Cuban Collecting Group, 5
Interlibrary loan [*see also* resource sharing], 6, 8, 105, 151, 210-11
International Federation of Film Archives (FIAF), 285
International Museum of Photography at George Eastman House, 280
Internet, 14, 83, 127, 170, 176, 303, 325, 336
Intner, Sheila S., 355-75

Jackets [*see* book jackets]
Jacob's Pillow Dance Festival, 336
Japan, 4
Jeavons, Clyde, 284, 302
Jennings, Edward, 301
Jessup, Wendy, 76
Johns Hopkins University, 39-40, 79, 197-98
Jones, C. Lee, 101-117
Jurow, Susan, 39, 42

Kahn, Miriam B., 400-412
Kaplan, Hilary, 384
Katzenberg, Jeffrey, 280
Kellerman, L. Suzanne, 310-28
Kenney, Anne R., 384
Kesse, Erich J., 180-89
Kiesling, Kristi L. R., 77-100
Kimberly, A. E., 57
Klein, Henry, 269
Klinger, Jane, 385
Kodak Corporation, 106-107, 110, 114-17, 276, 285, 289-90, 321
Kodak MRD camera, 106-112, 117
Kodak Photo CD, 115-16, 122
Koepp, Donald W., 102
Kohler, Stuart A., 254-66
Kopp, Leslie Hansen, 329-38

Labels and labeling [*see* shelf preparation]
LabLog software, 173
Lamination, 30, 318
Lang, Fritz, 302

Langlois, Henri, 290
LaPlante, David, 279
Laptop computers, 141, 149-50, 161, 174, 203, 214-15, 261
Laser disks [*see* optical disks]
Latin America, 6
Lattin, Vernon E., 412
Lawton, Dorothy, 316-17
Leaf casting, 164-65
Leather bindings, 56-57, 59, 77, 205, 341, 348
Lehigh University, 102-103
Lemcoe, M. M., 310
Leonard, William R., 121, 130
Lesser, Brian, 269
Library Binding Institute, 197-98, 318-20
Library directors, 400-412
Library Journal, 311-12
Library of Congress, 40, 48, 51, 58, 78-79, 111, 119, 125-27, 133, 194, 280, 282-83, 287, 289, 291, 311, 321
Library school curricula, 355-73
  conservation techniques, 355-56, 364-66, 371
  foundations of librarianship, 355, 370
  internships, 355, 366-72
  library school/teaching library partnerships, 356, 359, 361-62, 366-70
  management of preservation programs, 355-56, 362, 365, 370-72
  preservation course work, 356-66, 370-72
  scientific content, 356, 364, 371
LifeForms software, 336
Light, 31, 59, 348-50
Lighting, 7
Likens, Peter, 102
Local area networks, 136, 138, 141-42, 145
Long, Margery S., 380
Long-playing records [*see* audio materials]
Los Angeles County Museum of Art, 171
Los Angeles Public Library, 315
Lowell, Howard, 388
Lubitsch, Ernst, 302
Ludwig, Kathy, 384
Lull, William P., 76
Lundberg, Constance K., 55-76
Lyman, Peter, 298

MAPS The MicrogrAphic Preservation Service, 101-117
MARC format [see USMARC format]
MOMA [see Museum of Modern Art]
MRD camera [see Kodak MRD camera]
Magnetic media [see audio materials; electronic information]
Mainframe computers, 136, 145
Manchester Central Library (England), 198
Manchester Polytechnic (England), 290
Manuscript collections [see archives]
Mass deacidification [see also deacidification; diethyl zinc (DEZ)], 3, 7-9, 16-20, 38, 77-99, 302, 320, 323-24, 327, 371, 379
    archival materials, 77-99
    costs, 8-9, 17, 19, 77, 81, 84, 92-94
    effects on:
        adhesives, 80, 85, 94
        appearance, 79-80, 88-92
        boards, 80
        book cloth, 6, 85
        cellophane, 91
        cellulose acetate sleeves, 86, 90-91
        coated papers, 80, 85
        colors, dyes, pigments, etc., 79-80, 89-90, 94
        film, 80
        foam, 80
        media, 79-80, 95
        paper, 79-81, 90, 94
        photographs, 77, 79, 86, 87, 92, 95
        plastics, 80, 90
        polyester sleeves, 80, 88-92
        printing inks, 80-81, 85, 90, 94
        tactile qualities of materials, 79
        thermal papers, 80, 86-87, 91
        writing inks, 79, 80-81, 90, 94
    inappropriate materials, 17-18, 20, 77, 80, 85-87
    long-term effects, 78, 94
    odors, 81, 84-85, 91
    packing for treatment, 81-82, 87-89, 92
    quality control, 89, 95-99

record keeping, 83
selection, 85-87, 91, 92
time requirements, 92-93
toxicity, 78, 94
tracking shipments, 82-83
transportation, 82-83, 89
Massachusetts Board of Library Commissioners, 210, 226
Massachusetts libraries, 210-32
Mats and matting, 166-67
Mazel, Charles, 164
McColvin, Lionel Roy, 316, 318
Medfield (Massachusetts) Public Library, 211, 213, 215-16, 218, 220-21, 223-26, 228-32
Medical information resources, 119-21
Meeker, David, 284
Megatronics, Inc., 136
Mekel scanner, 113, 115-16
Mellon Foundation [see Andrew W. Mellon Foundation]
Mending [see repair]
Merrill-Oldham, Jan, 50
Michaels, Jan, 293-307
Michigan State University, 79, 125
Microcomputers [see also preservation—software], 133, 135-40, 145-77, 236, 244, 254-66
Microfiche, 113, 116, 139, 268, 297
Microfilm and microfilming, 3-9, 12-13, 15-20, 26-27, 30, 34, 38, 60, 77, 101-117, 120, 126, 136, 139, 142, 144, 149-55, 158, 161-63, 182, 185, 203, 241, 244, 268-79, 320-24, 327, 339, 342-44, 346, 364, 366, 371, 379, 394
    boxes, 269-70
    cameras [see also specific cameras], 103-117
    centers for microfilming, 5-6, 101-117
    color microfilming, 3, 15-16, 109
    conversion to digital formats, 12, 15, 105-106, 113-17
    conversion to paper, 113
    costs, 8, 16-19, 103-104, 106
    diazo film, 268, 270, 274-75
    films [see also specific films], 107-109, 113, 116-17
    freezing microfilm, 268-79
    gray scale, 106, 114-15, 117
    illustrative material, 16
    laboratories, 101-117

life span, 114
masters, 3-5, 105, 151-52, 154, 322
music materials, 320-24, 327
pricing, 5-7
projects, 5
quality assurance, 104
queuing, 137, 139, 144
reading and printing equipment, 116,
  270, 272, 275, 279
resolution, 105-108, 110-13, 115-17
service copies, 113
silver film, 8, 13, 268, 270-72, 274-76
standards, 104-105, 107-110, 112-16,
  321
storage, 5, 13, 105, 279
supplies, 107
water damage, 268-79
MicrogrAphic Preservation Service [*see*
  MAPS The MicrogrAphic
  Preservation Service]
Microsoft Windows software, 256, 258,
  260-61
Mid-Atlantic Preservation Service [*see*
  MAPS The MicrogrAphic
  Preservation Service]
Mid-Atlantic States Cooperative
  Preservation Service [*see* MAPS
  The MicrogrAphic Preservation
  Service]
Miller, Catherine K., 318
Miller, Max, 284
Minicomputers, 145
Minolta scanner, 116
Minnesota Historical Society, 384
Minuteman Library Network (Massachu-
  setts), 210-32
Mold, 32, 263, 269-70, 272, 279, 344-45,
  348, 396, 400, 408, 410-11
Moore, Carole, 51
Morrow, Carolyn Clark, 40, 51
Mort, Sarah L., 364
Motion picture film preservation, 28, 62,
  120, 123, 126, 128, 244, 269, 280-92,
  302-303, 320-21, 329-30, 336-37, 385
cellulose diacetate stock, 330
costs, 280-81, 283
ethics, 287-89
nitrate stock, 281, 285-86, 289-91,
  302, 330
preservation versus restoration, 285-
  89

safety film, 285, 289-90
silent films, 286-87, 291, 302, 321
storage, 281, 285, 289-90
Mowery, Frank, 164
Multimedia, 46, 112-13, 176-77, 297, 381
Munoff, Gerald J., 37-51, 380
Museum of American History [*see*
  National Museum of American
  History]
Museum of Modern Art (MOMA), 280,
  283, 287
Museum conservation, 55-58, 60-61, 66,
  104, 118-19, 127-28, 158, 163-69,
  171-73, 184, 334, 339, 364
Music materials [*see also* audio materi-
  als; binding—music materials], 310-
  27, 330
Music Library Association, 316, 318, 320
Mutilation, 212-13, 217, 220-21, 223,
  398
Myers, Richard F., 118-30

NAGARA [*see* National Association of
  Government Archivists and Records
  Administrators]
NAL [*see* National Agricultural Library]
NARA [*see* National Archives and
  Records Administration]
NBS [*see* National Bureau of Standards]
NEA [*see* National Endowment for the
  Arts]
NEDCC [*see* Northeast Document
  Conservation Center]
NEH [*see* National Endowment for the
  Humanities]
NHPRC [*see* National Historical
  Publications and Records
  Commission]
NIH [*see* National Institutes of Health]
NIST [*see* National Institute for
  Standards and Technology]
NLM [*see* National Library of
  Medicine]
NTSC [*see* National Television System
  Committee]
NYPL [*see* New York Public Library]
National Agricultural Library (NAL),
  119, 122-25
National Archives and Records

Administration (NARA), 26, 48, 385, 388
National Association of Government Archivists and Records Administrators (NAGARA), 382
National Bureau of Standards (NBS), 57, 62
National Center for Biomedical Communications, 121
National Center for Film and Video Preservation at the American Film Institute, 280
National Conservation Advisory Council, 379
National Endowment for the Arts (NEA), 281-82, 331, 336
National Endowment for the Humanities (NEH), 38-39, 48, 78, 80, 376, 379-80, 382-86
    Division of Preservation and Access, 39
National Film Archive (United Kingdom), 284, 290, 302
National Film Preservation Act of 1992, 282
National Film Preservation Board, 282
National Film Registry, 282
National Fire Protection Association, 33
National Gallery of Art, 58, 119, 127-28
National Historical Publications and Records Commission (NHPRC), 48, 379
National Institute for Standards and Technology (NIST), 170
National Institutes of Health (NIH), 119-21
National Library of Australia, 180
National Library of Canada, 296
National Library of Germany, 112
National Library of Medicine (NLM), 40, 48, 119-21, 236
National Museum of American History, 122, 384
National Recovery Administration Act of 1933, 317
National Register of Microform Masters, 34
National Television System Committee (NTSC), 118
Nazaroff, William W., 61
Neavill, Gordon, 296, 301

Needs assessment [*see* preservation—needs assessment]
Nelson, Ted, 293
Neuwirth, Erich, 165
New York Public Library (NYPL), 39-40, 58, 102, 133-55, 194, 311-12, 316-18, 321-22, 335, 388
New York State Archives and Records Administration, 268, 271, 385
New York state libraries [*see also* specific libraries], 195, 234-52, 268-79
New York State Library, 102, 268
New York State Museum, 268
New York State Program for the Conservation and Preservation of Library Research Materials, 78, 195, 235, 252
New York State Seminar on Mass Deacidification, Albany, NY, October 1992, 78, 85
Newberry Library (Chicago), 58, 311
Newspapers [*see also* clippings], 20, 28, 324, 344
Nikon scanner, 121
Nisonger, Thomas E., 362
Non-print materials, 3, 7, 13
North American preservation program, 37-51
North Bennet Street School (Boston), 364
Northeast Document Conservation Center (NEDCC), 24, 38, 78, 351, 364
Northwestern University, 40, 51, 79, 322-24
Notebook computers [*see* laptop computers]

OCLC (Online Computer Library Center), 9, 20, 48, 103, 110, 116, 152, 236, 322, 368
OCR (Optical Character Recognition) [*see* digitization]
Oakland Museum, 172-73
Off-site storage [*see* housing library and archival collections]
Offline sampling, 161-63
Ogden, Barclay, 51, 237, 242, 251, 384
Ogden, Sherelyn, 339-52
Ohio State University, 40, 79

Online Computer Library Center [*see* OCLC]

Online Journal of Current Clinical Trials, 297

Optical character recognition (OCR) [*see* digitization]

Optical disks, 118-29, 283
   analog applications, 118-19, 122-26, 129
   digital applications, 118-22, 125-27, 129
   life span, 119
   resolution, 119, 122, 124
   software, 121, 126
   standards, 118, 129

Oral history, 329-30

Orlando, Aldo, 412

Orr, Gloria J., 323

Osborne Collection of Early Children's Books (Toronto), 296

Out-of-print materials, 6

Oversewing, 318-19

Oxford Text Archive, 302-303

PNAP [*see* Central New York Preservation Needs Assessment Project]

PageMaker software, 139

Paietta, Ann, 391-99

Pamphlets, 139, 141-42

Paper [*see also* acid-free paper; acidic paper; mass deacidification—coated papers; mass deacidification—paper; mass deacidification—thermal papers; microfilm and microfilming—conversion to paper; newspapers; papermaking; permanent paper; photocopies and photocopying; strengthening paper], 44, 56-57, 59-61, 199, 202, 311, 387, 393

Papermaking, 364, 366, 393

Paradox for Windows software, 258, 260-61

Parker, A., 59

Particulate matter [*see also* dust], 55-56, 58, 61-66, 69

Patrologia Latina database, 11

Paul Taylor Repertory Preservation Project, 337

Pearce, Karla, 294

Pearson, George, 284

Pennsylvania State Library, 102

Pennsylvania State University, 79

Perl (Practical Extraction and Reporting Language), 162-63

Perlin, Ruth R., 129

Permanence [*see also* permanent paper], 9, 11-13, 18-19, 312, 323

Permanent paper [*see also* paper], 7, 13, 28

Personal computers [*see* microcomputers]

Peterson, Trudy H., 388

Phase boxes [*see* protective enclosures]

Photocopies and photocopying, 6-7, 65-66, 69, 146, 151, 168, 203, 249, 262, 320, 322-24, 327, 339, 342, 344-45, 393-95, 398

Photographs, 7, 33, 62, 77, 114, 120-26, 128, 141, 168, 172, 207, 242, 244, 248, 262, 269, 324, 329-30, 336, 370, 380, 385, 387
   copying, 339, 342
   storage, 121

Pickett, A. G., 310

Plant materials, 346

Pollution [*see* air pollution]

Polyester film encapsulation [*see* encapsulation]

Posters, 120-21, 128, 329-30, 342, 397

Practical Extraction and Reporting Language [*see* Perl]

PreNAPP [*see* Preservation Needs Assessment Package]

Preservation [*see also* archives—preservation programs]
   administration [*see also* automating preservation management; library school curricula—management of preservation programs], 35, 38, 146-47, 149, 153-55, 193-208, 376-89
   automation [*see* automating preservation management]
   cooperation, 37-51, 234-35, 237, 246-47, 250-52
   costs and cost models, 44, 146-49, 156, 158, 160, 164, 166, 207, 235-36, 241, 245, 247-48, 343
   definition, 24-27, 339, 377-79
   documentation [*see* conservation—

documentation]
education, reader, 34-35, 45, 240,
    248-50, 334-36, 391-99
    program planning, 391-92
education, staff, 34-35, 45, 221, 226,
    237, 240, 248-49, 355-73, 376-89,
    391-99, 400-412
    program planning, 391-92
funding, 4-9, 16-17, 19-20, 38, 44-47,
    146-47, 186, 193, 206, 226-27,
    235-36, 329-30, 333-35, 387
future, 3-23
history, 310-18, 321, 362, 393
international issues, 4-5, 19-20, 44
needs assessment, 148, 195, 199, 201-
    202, 234-52, 254-66
public policy, 44-46
research, 45
selection, 8, 44-47, 236, 254, 343,
    387-88
software [*see also* authoring tools;
    specific software packages], 136-
    45, 146-77, 254-66, 303-304
standards [*see also* air quality standards;
    electronic information—standards;
    microfilm and microfilming—
    standards; optical disks—standards],
    45, 107-110, 112-16, 118, 129,
    376-77, 383
statistics [*see* surveys; specific soft-
    ware packages]
surveys [*see* surveys]
Preservation Management Information
System [*see* automating preservation
management]
Preservation microfilm and microfilming
[*see* microfilm and microfilming]
Preservation Needs Assessment
Package (PreNAPP), 180, 201-202,
212
Preservation Planning Conference,
Chicago, May 1992, 37-51
Preservation Program Development
Shared Consultancy (California),
237, 241
Preserve, Inc., 336-37
Prideaux, Sarah, 57
Princeton University, 102
Prints and drawings [*see* drawings and
prints]
Prodigy online service, 122

Project Gutenberg, 295
Project Open Book, 105-106, 113
Prolog (computer programming lan-
guage), 165
Protective enclosures [*see also* microfilm
and microfilming—boxes], 34, 78,
140, 142-43, 146, 149-52, 155, 166-
67, 203-205, 240, 249, 251, 263, 314,
342-44, 346-47, 350, 396
Public Archives Canada, 183
Public libraries, 210-32, 234, 242, 252,
311-18, 321-22, 334, 398
Purdue University, 79
Putnam, Herbert, 311

Q&A software, 258-60

RLG [*see* Research Libraries Group]
RLIN [*see* Research Libraries
Information Network]
Random sampling, 158-63, 201-202, 214,
234, 237-39, 241-42, 247, 264
Ransom Humanities Research Center
[*see* Harry Ransom Humanities
Research Center, The University of
Texas at Austin]
Rauschenberg, Robert, 336
Reader education for preservation [*see*
preservation—education, reader]
Reed-Scott, Jutta, 39-40
Reeves, Marc, 146-55
Reformatting, 4-20, 26-27, 34, 38, 77-78,
101-129, 134, 138-39, 146, 180, 203,
206, 226, 240, 249, 251, 311, 371,
387-88
costs, 17, 19, 106
documentation, 9
models, 34
Relative humidity, 30-32, 36, 78, 94, 239,
270, 285, 289-90, 348-49, 393
Repair, 16, 18-19, 25, 34, 134, 146, 151-
52, 196, 198-99, 203-205, 210, 212-
13, 215, 218, 220-27, 263, 356, 364,
366, 371, 393, 395
Reports [*see* conservation—documenta-
tion]
Research Libraries Group (RLG), 20, 40,

46-49, 104, 112, 116-17, 180, 196,
201-202, 294-95, 322
conspectus, 196
Research Libraries Information Network
(RLIN), 9, 151-54, 368
Resource sharing [*see also* interlibrary
loan], 3, 105, 225
Resources for preservation [*see* preserva-
tion—funding]
Restoration [*see* conservation]
Retrospective conversion, 9, 193
Richmond (Indiana) Public Library, 312
Riley, Mike, 112
Ritzenthaler, Mary Lynn, 380, 382, 385
Roberts, Donald, 324
Rodda, Richard, 325
Rosenberg Library (Galveston, TX) 343-
44, 346
Rosenthal, Joseph, 94
Roundtable on Mass Deacidification,
Andover, MA, September 1991, 78,
85
Royal Society of Arts (London),
56-57
Runkle, Martin, 39, 51
Russell, Ann, 24

SAA [*see* Society of American
Archivists]
SAS software, 159
SGML (Standard Generalized Markup
Language), 14, 126, 177
SOLINET (Southeastern Library
Network), 48, 384
SPSS-X software, 159
SSam (Stanford Sampler) software, 159
St. Louis Public Library, 315
Salmon, Lynn G., 61
Salvin, Victor, 59-60
Sample size, 200-202, 214, 224, 238, 242
Sampling [*see* fractional sampling;
offline sampling; random sampling;
shelf and object sampling; surveys;
systematic sampling]
San Francisco Performing Arts Library
and Museum, 335
Scanning, 3, 12-14, 18, 102, 105-106,
113-16, 119, 121, 126-27, 138, 163,
168, 261, 324-26

costs, 106
resolution, 106
Schellenberg, T. R., 377
Schrock, Nancy Carlson, 210-33
Schultz, Lois, 325
Schuster, Carl, 412
Scores [*see* music materials]
Scorsese, Martin, 280
Scrapbooks [*see also* albums], 92, 167,
262, 329-30, 339-51
contents, 341-42
cost of preserving, 343
definition, 339
materials, 340-41
storage, 350
Sed (computer programming language),
162
Shared Consultancy Project [*see*
Preservation Program Development
Shared Consultancy (California)]
Shaver, Cynthia L., 60
Sheet music [*see* music materials]
Shelf and object sampling, 159
Shelf preparation, 139-40, 149-55
Shelf reading, 392, 395-96
Shelving [*see* housing library collec-
tions; stack maintenance]
Shiva LanRover/4E, 139, 150
Sibley Music Library, 318, 321, 323
Sick building syndrome, 60
Side sewing, 319
Siegal, Marcia, 337
Silverman, Randy H., 55-76
Simmons College, 366, 368
Simmons College Seminar on
Recruiting, Educating, and Training
Cataloging Librarians of 1989, 366,
368
Simon Fraser University, 336
Sink, Robert, 388
Slide, Anthony, 280-92
Slides, 122-25, 128
*Slow Fires: On the Preservation of the
Human Record*, 102
Smith, Richard D., 59
Smithee, Jeannette, 234-53
Smithsonian Institution, 27, 119, 121-22
Smoke detectors [*see* fire detection and
suppression]
Smoking, 397-98
Society of American Archivists (SAA),

48, 376-89
Basic Archival Conservation Program,
380-82
Preservation Management Institute,
381
Preservation Management Training
Program, 381, 383-89
Society of Arts [*see* Royal Society of
Arts (London)]
Soft covers [*see* binding—paperbacks]
Software [*see* authoring tools; preserva-
tion—software; specific software
packages]
Solvents, 165-66
Somay, Errol, 146-55
Sonneck, Oscar T., 311
Sound recordings [*see* audio
materials]
Southeastern Library Network [*see*
SOLINET]
Sparks, Peter G., 61, 86, 93
Specification [*see* conservation—docu-
mentation]
Spedding, D. J., 59
Spielberg, Steven, 280
Spivak, Howard, 412
Stack maintenance, 33-34, 220, 223-26,
391-99
manuals, 392-93
training programs, 393-95
Staff education for preservation [*see*
preservation—education, staff]
Standard Generalized Markup Language
[*see* SGML]
Stanford Sampler [*see* SSam]
Stanford University, 33, 39-40, 51, 58,
156-77, 180, 194, 202, 212
Stati software, 159
Stavroudis, Chris, 171
Storage [*see* albums—storage; housing
library and archival collections; scrap-
books—storage]
Street, Robert, 51
Strengthening paper, 8, 20, 77
Stroud, James Grant, 77-100
Studer, William, 40, 94
Surveys, 148, 158-64, 199-207, 210-32,
234-52, 254-66, 380, 387-88, 396
form design, 261-64
Syracuse University, 103, 244
Systematic sampling, 201

TLG [*see* Thesaurus Linguae Graecae]
Tate Gallery (London), 61
Teachers College of Columbia University,
58
Teas, Jean, 165
TeasTime software, 165
Technical services [*see* acquisitions activ-
ities and units; authority control; cata-
logs and cataloging; circulation; col-
lection management]
Temperature, 31-32, 36, 94, 239, 270,
285, 290, 348-49
Texas State Archives, 31, 35
Thesaurus Linguae Graecae (TLG), 11
Third World countries [*see* developing
countries]
Thomson, Garry, 58
Time-stamping [*see* electronic informa-
tion—integrity and accuracy]
Tissuing, 344
Treatment records and reports [*see* con-
servation—documentation]
Turko, Karen, 85
Turner Broadcasting System, 283

UNIX, 162
U.S. Machine-Readable Cataloging [*see*
USMARC format]
USMARC (U.S. Machine-Readable
Cataloging) format, 125-26, 140, 151,
154, 171, 184-85
United States Department of Agriculture,
122
United States Forest Service, 122-23
United States National Bureau of
Standards [*see* National Bureau of
Standards]
University of California, Berkeley, 39-40,
51, 236-37, 322, 384
University of California, Davis, 397
University of California, Los Angeles,
Film and Television Archive, 280,
283, 287, 289
University of Chicago, 79
University of Chicago Library, 37, 39-
40, 79
University of Connecticut, 51
University of Delaware, 103
University of Florida, 125, 180

University of Illinois, 79
University of Indiana, 79
University of Iowa, 79
University of Maryland, 103,
 122-25
University of Michigan, 39-40, 79
University of Minnesota, 79
University of Nebraska, 127
University of Pittsburgh School of
 Library and Information Science,
 125
University of Tennessee, Knoxville,
 324-25
University of Texas at Austin, 39-40,
 77-99, 322, 355, 388
University of Toronto, 40, 51
University of Vienna (Austria), 165
University of Wisconsin, 79
Utah Department of Health, Bureau of
 Air Quality, 63-64

Vacuum cleaning, 397
Vaughn, Susan J., 412
Ventilation [*see* air-handling
 systems]
Video materials, 7, 28, 118-29, 244,
 283-84, 291, 295, 300, 329-30, 332-
 34, 336-37
Von Sternberg, Josef, 302
Von Stroheim, Erich, 302
Vorhaus, Bernard, 284

WLN [*see* Western Library Network]
WORM (Write Once, Read Many
 Times), 125
Wall, Larry, 162
Wallace, James, 121, 130
Wallace, Ruth, 316-17
Walt Disney Studios, 280, 283
Ward, Alan, 302
Ward, Christine, 376-90
Warner Brothers, 289
Washington University Libraries, 388
Water damage [*see also* freezing wet ma-
 terials; microfilm and microfilming—
 freezing microfilm], 32-33, 134, 221,
 248, 268-79, 344-45, 391-93, 398,

 400-412
Webster, Duane, 39
Weeding, 210-12, 215, 221, 223-26
Weintraub, Steven, 76
Welles, Orson, 289
Wellesley Free Library, 210-13, 215,
 217-18, 220-26, 228-32
Western Library Network (WLN), 115,
 368
Western Europe, 4
White, Herbert S., 364
Whitmore, Paul M., 58-60
Wide area networks, 145
Wiemers, Eugene, 51
Williams, Edwin L. II, 61
Williamson, Peter, 287
Word processing, 142
Write Once, Read Many Times [*see*
 WORM]

Xerox Corporation, 105-106, 113, 115

Yale University, 12, 39-40, 105-106,
 113, 199-200, 202, 212, 321

Zeronian, S. H., 59-60
Zeutschel camera, 111

Other Books of Interest

The Electronic Classroom: A Handbook for Education in the Electronic Environment
Edited by Erwin Boschmann ($42.50/240pp/ISBN 0-938734-89-X)

Document Delivery Services: Issues and Answers
By Eleanor Mitchell and Sheila Walters ($42.50/333pp/ISBN 1-57387-003-X)

Multimedia in Higher Education
By Helen Carlson and Dennis R. Falk ($42.50/176pp/ISBN 1-57387-002-1)

CD-ROM for Library Users: A Guide to Managing and Maintaining User Access
Paul Nicholls and Pat Ensor, Editors ($39.50/138 pp/ISBN 0-938734-95-4)

Electronic Image Communications: A Guide to Networking Image Files
By Richard J. Nees ($39.50/95pp/ISBN 0-938734-87-3)

Navigating the Networks
Deborah Lines Anderson, Thomas J. Galvin, & Mark D. Giguere, Editors ($29.95/255pp/ISBN 0-938734-85-7)

Challenges in Indexing Electronic Text and Images
Raya Fidel, Trudi Bellardo Hahn, Edie Rasmussen, and Philip Smith, Editors ($39.50/316pp/ISBN 0-938734-76-8)

ASIS Thesaurus of Information Science and Librarianship
By Jessica L. Milstead ($34.95/150pp/ISBN 0-938734-80-6)

Cataloging Heresy: Challenging the Standard Bibliographic Product
Edited by Bella Hass Weinberg ($35.00/270pp/ISBN 0-938734-60-1)

High-Performance Medical Libraries
Edited by Naomi Broering ($39.50/230pp/ISBN 0-88736-878-6)

Essential Guide to the Library IBM PC: Volume 13
By Marshall Breeding ($34.95/200pp/ISBN 0-88736-188-9)

Government CD-ROMs: A Practical Guide to Searching Electronic Documents Databases
Edited by John Maxymuk ($47.50/350pp/ISBN 0-88736-887-5)

Automated Library Systems: A Librarian's Guide and Teaching Manual
By Beverly K. Duval and Linda Main ($40.00/288pp/ISBN 0-88736-873-5)

Library Technology Consortia: Case Studies in Design and Cooperation
Edited by Jerry Kuntz ($42.50/165pp/ISBN 0-88736-886-7)

The Virtual Library: Visions and Realities
Edited by Laverna Saunders ($37.50/180pp/ISBN 0-88736-860-3)

Electronic Journal Literature: Implications for Scholars
By Jan Olsen ($25.00/100pp/ISBN 0-88736-925-1)

Small Project Automation for Libraries and Information Centers
By Jane Mandelbaum ($35.00/350pp/ISBN 0-88736-731-3)

Key Guide to Electronic Resources: Health Sciences
Edited by Lee Hancock ($39.50/494pp/ISBN 1-57387-001-3)

Key Guide to Electronic Resources: Agriculture
Edited by Wilfred Drew ($39.50/124pp/ISBN 1-57387-000-5)

CD-ROM Book Index
Edited by Ann Niles ($39.50/207pp/ISBN 0-938734-98-9)

CD-ROM Finder, 6th Edition 1995
Kathleen Hogan and James Shelton, Editors ($69.50/520pp/ISBN 0-938734-86-5)

Proceedings of the 16th National Online Meeting, May 2-4, 1995
($55.00/448pp/ISBN 1-57387-004-8)

Annual Review of Information Science and Technology, Volume 29
Edited by Martha Williams ($95.00/455pp/ISBN 0-938734-91-1)

To order directly from the publisher, include $3.95 postage and handling for the first book ordered and $3.25 for each additional book. Catalogs also available upon request.

Information Today, Inc., 143 Old Marlton Pike, Medford, NJ 08055, (609) 654-6266